THE PRIVATISATION OF EUROPEAN TELECOMMUNICATIONS

The Privatisation of European Telecommunications

Edited by

KJELL A. ELIASSEN
Norwegian
School of Management – BI, Norway
and
JOHAN FROM
Norwegian School of Management – BI, Norway

ASHGATE

Published by
Ashgate Publishing Limited
Gower House
Croft Road
Aldershot
Hampshire GU11 3HR
England

Ashgate Publishing Company
Suite 420
101 Cherry Street
Burlington, VT 05401-4405
USA

Ashgate website: http://www.ashgate.com

British Library Cataloguing in Publication Data
The privatisation of European telecommunications
1. Telecommunication policy - Europe 2. Telecommunication - Government ownership - Europe 3. Telecommunication - Deregulation - Europe 4. Privatization - Europe
I. Eliassen, Kjell A. II. From, Johan
384'.041

Library of Congress Cataloging-in-Publication Data
The privatisation of European telecommunications / [edited] by Kjell A. Eliassen and Johan From.
p. cm.
Includes bibliographical references and index.
ISBN: 978-0-7546-4260-2
1. Telecommunication--Government ownership--Europe. 2. Telecommunication--Deregulation--Europe. 3. Privatization--Europe. I. From, Johan. II. Eliassen, Kjell A.

HE8085.P75 2007
384'.04--dc22

2007001510

ISBN: 978-0-7546-4260-2

Printed and bound in Great Britain by TJ International Ltd, Padstow, Cornwall.

Contents

List of Figures and Tables

Figures

Tables

Contributors

Catherine B. Arnesen is Associate Professor of Political Economy at the Department of Public Governance, the Norwegian School of Management BI. She holds a Doctoral Degree from the NSM, and works on issues in competition, regulation and EU politics

Patrizia Cincera is PhD student at the VUB's Centre for Studies on Media, Information and Telecommunication (SMIT). Her research focus is on European media regulation and the regulatory activities of the European Union competition policy pertaining to the audiovisual sector and the related multimedia services.

Simon Delaere works in the VUB's Centre for Studies on Media, Information and Telecommunication (SMIT). He has a MA in Communications Policy. His research focus is on policy issues surrounding media and ICT in general and on policies for innovation and competition in the audiovisual sector in particular.

Kjell A. Eliassen is a Professor of Public Management and director of the Centre for European and Asian Studies at the Department of Public Governance, the Norwegian School of Management BI in Oslo and at the IEE at the Free University in Brussles. He has published several books and articles on EU institutions and decision-making, European affairs, telecommunications and public management. His books include: *European Telecom Liberalisation* (1999), and a new edition of *Making Policy in the European Union* (2001).

Johan From is Professor in Public Politics at the Department of Public Governance, at the Norwegian School of Management BI. He holds a doctoral degree from the University of Sussex, Sussex European Institute. His main research has been on European Union politics and public sector reorganisation, modernisation and management. He has published several books and articles on these subjects. His latest book is *Europe's Nascent State? Public Policy in the European Union* (2006).

Birgitte Grøgaard is Assistant Professor at the Department of Strategy, the Norwegian School of Management BI. She holds a Doctoral Degree from the NSM. Her research is mainly focused on strategy issues for multinationals, with particular interest in the internal alignment between the firm strategy and subsidiary roles.

Arnulf Heuermann has a PhD in Economics and is Head of Competence Centre Strategy and Management, with DETECON, Germany. DETECON is a consulting company operating worldwide in telecommunications and related information technology. Dr Heuermann was involved in several studies preparing the deregulation of the German Posts- and Telecommunications sector and has been involved in Telecom-consultancy projects in 38 countries.

Lars C. Kolberg holds a degree in Political Science from the University of Oslo. He is currently writing a PhD thesis on the modernisation of public sector organisations at the Department of Public Governance, Norwegian School of Management. His main research interests include public sector modernisation and organisational change.

Günter Knieps is Professor of Economics and Director of the Institute of Transportation Science and Regional Policy at the University of Freiburg (Germany). He has numerous publications on network economics, (de-)regulation, competition policy, industrial economics; sector studies on network industries.

Stine Ludvigsen is a PhD student at the Norwegian School of Management BI at the Department of Public Governance. She has a Masters degree in Business and Economics from BI and a Masters degree in Political Science from the University of Oslo. Her main research interests include public sector governance and transformation, especially state ownership, corporate governance, and organisational change.

Marit Sjovaag Marino holds a PhD from the London School of Economics. She works on EU politics, regulatory issues and state traditions, and is currently also devoting her time to the development of a new generation of researchers.

Jürgen Müller is Professor at the Berlin School of Economics (FHW) Germany, a business school with a long tradition in interdisciplinary management training, where he holds a chair in Economics. He has a PhD from Stanford University. He is author of a number of books on telecommunications and is currently working in the area of industrial economics and competition policy.

Caroline Pauwels is Professor and Head of the Department of Communication Sciences at the Free University of Brussels, as well as director of IBBT/SMIT. Her main domain of competence is in the field of European audiovisual policy-making, entertainment economy, and convergence and concentration issues in media industries. In 2006 she became Commissioner of the Flemish Regulator for Media.

Nick Sitter is Professor of Political Economy in the Department of Public Governance at the Norwegian School of Management BI, where he works on

European Union politics and public policy. He holds a PhD from the Department of Government at the London School of Economics and Political Science, and has taught at British, Hungarian, Italian and American universities.

John Vanhoucke is the Manager for all the streaming activities within the Telindus branch of Belgacom. He has a Masters degree in criminology from the University of Ghent, Belgium. He started to work in a start up streaming company and successfully integrated this company into Belgacom.

Preface

This book is about the transformation of European telecommunications companies following the deregulation and liberalisation of the telecommunications market in Europe. It follows the routes of the incumbents from being public monopolies to market driven organisations. During this process a new public sector of corporatised state owned companies evolved and today most of these companies are on their way to becoming fully or at least partly privatised. How does this happen in terms of transformational processes driven by and dependent on the type of ownership, market, management, internationalisation etc? In this book, we analyse how such transformation is accomplished. However, we do not pretend to offer a detached account of the transformation process in each case. The aim of the book is neither to advance a theory nor to construct a model, but rather to give some comparative and comprehensive accounts of different aspects of the transformation process. One argument often put forward is that the transformation of public sector organisations is largely a myth. Our case, the telecommunications sector, is special in this regard but it is still reasonable to argue that our account of the process could equally apply to other public sector institutions. In that sense it is endemic.

Our main concern in this book is to bring to the fore a perspective on public sector change that has not to date been the focus of much scholarly attention. Accordingly we offer particular thanks to those colleagues in many other countries, and those within our own Department of Public Governance at the Norwegian School of Management, with whom we have been working, for their contribution to this volume. In particular we would like to express our thanks to Lars C. Kolberg for his support with some of the more difficult technical tasks in producing a volume of this kind. We would also like to thank the Norwegian telecommunications company Telenor for the generous grant that has funded the research project of which this book is part. Learning about the transformation processes in this company from extensive interviews with senior Telenor managers and civil servants inspired us very much to adopt the approach taken in this volume. We are grateful for their cooperation and for the extensive knowledge and experience they so willingly shared with us. Ideas and opinions expressed in this volume, however, are those of the authors and do not represent the views of Telenor.

We also acknowledge the essential part played by Dr Verona Christmas-Best who so well managed the process from conception to publication. Without her help, inspiration and continuous encouragement, this book project would have been difficult to finish.

Kjell A. Eliassen and Johan From
Oslo, October 2006

Chapter 1

Introduction: Company Transformation – Corporatisation, Privatisation and Company Behaviour

Kjell A. Eliassen and Johan From

This chapter introduces the main topic of the book: the transformation of Western European telecommunications companies from state agencies to listed companies over a period of 15 years from the late 1980s on. The term transformation is utilised because the changes happening are comprehensive and far-reaching, far from being merely cosmetic changes in order to conform to standards of good organisation. At company level we see changes in organisational structure and company behaviour. Traditional centralised bureaucratic organisations are abandoned for more flexible and business-like structures (Pehrsson, 1996; Curwen, 1997; Turner, 1997; Monsen, 2004; Garnaut et al., 2005; Tossavainen, 2005). National public services strategies of securing universal affordable fixed-line services are supplemented with expansion into new areas both technologically and internationally. Ownership, regulation and competition policy give an important framework for these changes. A complicating matter is that the framework itself changes over time. Government ownership is established, professionalised and eventually diluted in the period covered. Further, old regulation is replaced with new regulation, proving once again that deregulation implies re-regulation. Finally, the significance of competition policy is eventually increasing. Albeit not an exhaustive list, these variables constitute a major part of the environment for the transformation processes. What makes them especially significant is their direct impact on how the transformation processes occur. Modelling the transformation processes in agency logic, accentuates the importance of the various roles of government; interests and strategies on company level; and the significance of the state-company relations.

In the present volume the focus is more on the changes in the telecommunications companies than on the regulatory framework of these companies, an area attracted much focus over the last years (Majone, 1990; Melody, 1997; Pelkmans and Young, 1998; Eliassen and Sjøvaag, 1999; Eliassen and Marino, 2001; Thatcher, 2004a). Identifying the role and strength of the driving forces behind these changes will be particularly emphasised. Hence, issues like the role of the owners and various shifts in ownership, the company organisational structure, and the strategies employed in the different phases of the corporatisation and privatisation process will be addressed. These issues are important not only in the telecommuniations industry but for a more general understanding of state ownership and possible consequences of institutional changes in the public sector. Similar developments of corporatisation and privatisation have taken place in sectors like railway, electricity, postal services and others. Thus, the aim is that this volume could shed some light also on the challenges and possible effects of transformation of ownership and operational rules and regulation in other parts of public services.

Most studies of telecommunications and other public sector privatisation processes have focused on regulatory issues and the British case of direct transformation from a state agency to a private company (Moon et al., 1986; Hills, 1986; Harper, 1997; Thatcher, 1999b). This volume focus more on company transformation in terms of all the different gradual steps most telecommunications companies in Europe have gone through from state agencies inside the state budget through budget independence, establishment of private subsidiaries, semi-corporate companies, fully state owned limited companies and eventually ordinary listed companies.

The Incumbents in a Competitive Framework

The main ambition set out in this book is to present a comprehensive and comparative perspective of the transition from being a state telecommunications agency to become a listed company. Most of the former telecommunications companies went through this process over a period of eight years in the end of the 1990s/beginning of the 2000s. Despite numerous studies of telecommunication liberalisation in Europe and the functioning of the European telecommunication market, few studies have been published with an explicit focus on the transformation, or institutional adaptation of the former incumbents through processes of corporatisation and privatisation. One exemption is Monsen (2004), which focuses on the effects of regulation on ownership changes and the incumbent telecommunications companies' structure and strategy.

The company level focus on transformation is valuable in giving us insight into the challenges and obstacles faced by governments attempting to modernise and reform public service delivery. For the last 25 years the public sector has increasingly come under pressure for not being cost effective, responsive and transparent. This is accentuated for a number of different reasons. Among these are a general ideological shift in the late 1970s, as indicated by Thatcher and Reagan taking offices; the need for more flexibility for quicker adaptation to technological and economic change; a request for higher efficiency/productivity for reducing strains on state budgets; and a call for clearer roles in order to sort out issues of political accountability (Dunleavy and O'Leary, 1987; Hills, 1986;

Lane, 1997; Aberbach and Christensen, 2003). The desire has been to make the service production more productive and efficient, i.e. to obtain a public sector that 'works better and costs less' (Gore, 1993) or getting more, better and cheaper services.

According to public choice theorists, monopoly production in a hierarchical bureaucratic structure creates 'agency costs'. The true costs of production are not known to the politicians and the bureaucrats can therefore engage in non-optimal strategies, pursuing self-interest instead of public interest. The solution to these agency problems is therefore to expose public services to the market. The establishment of smaller more transparent units in a competitive environment is a remedy for information problems (uncovering the real costs of production) and it aligns the interests of the bureaucrats and the politicians. This kind of reasoning is underpinning what has come to be known as the 'New Public Management' reforms in the public sector (Hood, 1991), albeit not always in a coherent way (Barzelay, 2002). What is interesting however, is the creation of new types of agency problems. The corporatisation of public service production introduces a separation of ownership and control. The traditional hierarchical organisation gives the possibility of using instructions on every aspect of the production. Separating ownership and control, as is the case in most modern corporations, means that discretion is delegated from the owners (government and/or private) to the management. Given incomplete contracts and imperfect competition, issues of 'corporate governance' arise. Interestingly, the potential managerial strategies incurring agency costs in these kinds of corporations pointed to by management scholars (e.g. Gedajlovic and Saphiro, 1998) are strikingly similar to the model of 'budget maximizing' (Niskanen, 1971) and 'bureau shaping' (Dunleavy, 1991) within the public sector. Owners face the challenges of selecting and monitoring the management. Ownership issues therefore stand out as a significant aspect of the transformation process.

We need to rethink it seems, some of the basic theories of privatisation and company transformation on the bases of the European telecommunications experience in the last decades. Ownership has largely been neglected in writings on the development of the new regulatory frameworks and the liberalisation process in European (and other) countries. What have been the mechanisms of change from state monopolies to private companies, and how should the efforts of the European Union and national regulatory agencies in this process be assessed? Political science publications have to a large extent excluded analysis of the newly privatised companies, their role in the various national liberalisation processes both before and after privatisation, and the interplay between the national political and company levels. Also in business and strategy studies there are few examples of this kind of studies (but see Monsen, 2004). This volume seeks to rectify such shortcomings with regard to political science and social science literature more in general.

Accordingly, this volume is organised thematically as shown in Figure 1.1:

1) Characteristics of transformation: What are the effect and the interplay of ownership, regulation and competition policy on the transformation process?
2) Examples of transformation: How are the processes of transformation conducted within various telecommunications companies? What are the challenges and how are they dealt with within the process?
3) Aspects of transformation: What are the main aspects of the transformation processes regarding company change, business strategy and internationalisation?

Studies of Telecommunication Change Processes

The focus on company transformation does not mean that we ignore the importance of external drivers for these processes, nor are we oblivious to their effects. This section will therefore introduce short overviews of what we consider the most salient drivers and effects, as shown in Figure 1.1. One should remember, however, that this book is mainly about peeking into the 'black box' of company transformation, and that the purpose of the following section is to set the discussion in context within the wider social science debate.

A. Drivers for Change

- *Ideology – at both the national and the EU level*

The American New Right gained popularity throughout the 1970s, resulting in the election of Ronald Reagan as president in 1981. One of the main themes of this movement was to reduce peoples' reliance upon government. The ideas had proponents also on the European side of the Atlantic, where Margaret Thatcher won the 1979 general election. The New Right wanted to reduce the scope of the state, much in line with writings from the so-called 'Chicago School of Economics', whose major tenet was that markets are more efficient than government, and therefore a superior form of management for public services as well as private business (Friedman, 1962). This line of thinking advocated deregulation, privatisation, and competition among service providers (Stigler, 1975; Demsetz, 1968; Posner, 1992). Governmental monopolies were seen as inherently inefficient, and privatisation and competition would provide efficiency gains as well as decreased pressure on state budgets.

In the UK, these ideas were central to the Conservative government's agenda after 1979 (Harper, 1997; Thatcher, 1999b). The poor condition of state finances rendered privatisation policies attractive; moreover, there was a separate political pressure to curb the power of the trade unions, which had caused much disturbance and social unrest in the 1970s. Margaret Thatcher therefore had strong political backing for her agenda when taking office.

At the EU level, the process of deregulation of the telecommunications sector started in the first half of the 1980s (Dyson and Humphreys, 1986; Eliassen, Mason and Sjøvaag, 1999), and served a double purpose. Firstly, it was regarded an arrowhead to the development of the Single European Market, which the Commission in the mid-1980s vowed should be completed by 1992 (Nugent, 1991). Telecommunications were important both because of its characteristic as infrastructure, and also because the 'new technologies' were seen as paramount to bringing new economic impetus to a politically and economically depressed Europe.

Furthermore, the telecommunications sector provided an important test of the Commission's regulatory powers. Whereas previously policy-making in the European Communities had been based on the original Treaties, telecommunications broke with this tradition, being among the states' 'special rights' that had explicitly been excluded from Community competencies. Some of the early legislative steps were taken as Commission Directives under the aegis of the then Article 90 (renamed Art 86 after the Treaty of Amsterdam), which reinforces the EU's rules on competition and permits the Commission to address directives or decisions to Member States in order to ensure compliance (Kamall, 1996: 89). The directive was contested in the European Court of Justice by France, but the Court ruled in 1991 that 'the Commission's supervisory function (...) also provide[d] it with the competence to specify the relevant obligations of the Member States under the Treaty including the specification and limitation of exclusive rights' (Scherer, 1995: 5). The path was thus largely cleared for an ambitious Commission wanting to expand its competencies.

• *Politics*

The European Union and its policy-making has been an important driving force in the process of liberalisation in Europe. The role of the European Commission is widely acknowledged as pivotal to the process of liberalisation both in Europe and also in the global arena (Sandholtz, 1992; Cincera, 1999; Kramer, 1992; Antonelli, 1997; Grupp and Schnöring, 1992; Schmidt, 1991). However, the great and rapidly growing importance of telecommunications and the ICT industry for the national economies means that national politics has played a central role in the transformation process over the last three decades. There is compelling evidence that the process of regulatory reform at the national level was already well under way in several EU member states, if not through actual new legislation, at least in the form of changing ideas among policy-making elites, ready to be applied to regulatory reform once the European Commission and the Council of Ministers started legislating (Marino, 2005; Werle, 1990; Witte, 1988a; 1988b; 1992; Stoffaës, 1995; Chevallier, 1989; 1996; Goldstein, 2000; Schmidt, 2001; 2002).

Even though EU legislation is the same for all affected countries, the actual implementation into national law has been left to each government, and leeway has been left within which political choices have had to be made. For example, EU legislation does not specify any organisational model for regulation of the sector; it only stipulates that the regulator must be independent from the service provider (Eyre and Sitter, 1999). This has in most countries been met by an independent regulatory authority, but detailed guidelines have been issued by national legislators, making of the national political arena an important battlefield for diverging interests, but also giving Member States the possibility to accommodate EU directives within their own political traditions (see Marino, 2005; Thatcher, 2004b).

• *The role of technology – digitalisation*

Technology has had a major impact on the development of the regulatory regimes in telecommunications for two separate reasons. Firstly, new technologies make existing regulation redundant in that it is often rapidly not covering the actual technical possibilities. For example, national voice telephony monopolies became practically impossible to maintain when satellite communications provided opportunities for call-back solutions from countries not covered by the national telephone service monopoly (Hills, 1986). More generally, the convergence between telephone services (fixed-line or mobile) and data services blurred the distinction between two previously separate areas of regulation, necessitating some form of regulatory change (Clements, 1998; Blackman, 1998).

Secondly, the ICT industry has important ramifications for both the economy and the political system. Telecommunications have traditionally been seen as closely related to national security, both for political and economic reasons (Rosanvallon, 1986; Marino, 2005; Holcombe, 1911). Ensuring safe transmission of communications is crucial for any state administration, but more important for the late twentieth and the twenty-first centuries, a healthy telecommunications sector is paramount to infrastructure and economic growth. It can play the role of 'locomotive' for the economy, through off-spins to smaller technological firms and through providing central infrastructure (OECD, 1997; Kiessling and Blondeel, 1999). Telecommunication policies can be seen within an economic context, where the focus will be on the services' role as infrastructure for the economy in general, or on the economics internal to the sector (Wenders, 1987; Cave, Sumit, Majumdar, and Vogelsang, 2002; Gruber, 2005). In the political system, technological possibilities open up for new channels of influence and participation as well as provision of public services (Mansell and Steinmueller, 2000; Mansell and Tang, 1996). Therefore, it became doubly important for governments to rapidly create a free market for telecommunications (and later ICT) services in Europe.

• *Globalisation*

Globalisation of trade and industry in general goes hand in hand with globalisation in telecommunications. Global firms demand global telecommunications services, and telecoms enterprises themselves become global players. The operators demand (ideally) similar regulations of all markets, and the WTO has provided a general framework for free trade in telecommunications services through the Uruguay round. Regional organisations (e.g., EU, ASEAN, NAFTA) also provide a supra-national arena in which enterprises and member states can negotiate and co-ordinate development of national regulatory systems. Globalisation therefore adds another factor to telecommunication organisations' environment; namely regional and global regulations.

The concept of 'one-stop-shop', where telecommunications services are delivered by one operator to multinational organisations regardless of national frontiers, has been a tantalising goal for telecommunications operators. In order to reach this goal, the operators needed to be present in all markets, and the 1990s saw a frenzy of global alliance building and mergers and acquisitions (Curwen, 1999; Amesse et al., 2004; Shearer, 2004). Such formation of new extended organisations entailed serious issues of corporate governance. Now, organisations that for decades, often more than a century, remained national monopolies are expected to integrate with new cultures and traditions, as well as meeting new business challenges under reformed regulatory systems in competition with other players. The process of adaptation and change is necessarily compelx, mostly difficult, and as yet, rarely studied (but see Monsen, 2004; Chin, Brown and Hu, 2004).

Ideology, politics, technology and globalisation are all drivers for change in telecommunications firms' environment. At the other end of the reform process are the effects of liberalisation and privatisation of public services. We have identified four effects as particularly salient in literature.

- *Efficiency*

One of the pronounced goals for reform was to increase efficiency and productivity in service delivery. Being monopolies and thus inherently inefficient, so the argument goes, exposure to competition should increase efficiency and productivity of the corporations. Much research has been devoted to analyse whether this tenet holds true.

The studies of efficiency change are subject to several problems but have produced some interesting results. The problems are both qualitative and quantitative. First, it is difficult to establish and demonstrate any direct causal link between liberalisation, privatisation, and efficiency gain. There is empirical evidence that privately owned firms are more efficient and productive than state-owned enterprises (Ehrlich et al., 1994; Majundar, 1996), but there are generally very specific reasons why some firms are government owned and others are privately owned (Megginson and Netter, 2001), and these reasons complicates any comparison of efficiency between private and state-owned firms.

Second, measuring efficiency is difficult (Stiglitz, 1998), and though this problem is more accentuated in other types of public services such as healthcare and education, it is possible to question what is the real output of telecommunications services (Stone, 2002; Worthington and Dollery, 2000), for example, whether there is a 'public good' aspect, such as access to information, that is less well catered for under the new regulatory regimes.

Third, the quality of data used in empirical comparative studies is often poor (Florio, 2001). They can be dated, or not complete, or both, or, because state-owned enterprises normally have other goals than purely profit-maximising, it can be difficult to interpret any difference in cost or other data (Megginson and Netter, 2001; Ehrlich et al., 1994). In the specific case of telecommunications a long-standing problem, not only for researchers but also for public officials wanting to compare its own national telecommunications operator's performance with those of other countries, is that exact costs for different elements of the service are simply not known, because of the budget and accounting structure of the public services (Marino, 2005; see also Bourniquel, 1949; Emery, 1966).

Despite these difficulties, some studies of efficiency in privatised enterprises have yielded empirical evidence of efficiency gain after privatisation (Ehrlich et al., 1994; Frydman et al., 1999), However, literature also indicates that institutional conditions (formal institutional framework as well as traditions and culture within such formal institutions) are pivotal to the success or failure of reform (James, 2006; Lane, 2001; Nemec, Merickova and Vitek, 2005; Doolin, 2003). Moreover, there is also evidence that privatisation is not the only possible source of efficiency increase in the public sector (Lyroudi et al., 2006; Andersen and Blegvad, 2006). Indeed, in some cases, globalisation and the increased competition to which state-owned enterprises become exposed, result in increased efficiency despite no change in ownership structure (Shirley and Walsh, 2000; see also Kole and Mulherin, 1997; Yarrow, 1986; Vickers and Yarrow, 1991).

- *Innovation*

Technological innovation is central to economic growth, and the telecommunications sector traditionally sees a large proportion of technological innovation. In most countries that have had a state monopoly on telephone service provision there have, at some point in time, been complaints about the state's lack of ability or willingness to fund research and development, thereby hampering important innovation (Marino, 2005). In the 1970s and the 1980s Europe, liberalisation was seen as an alternative means to foster innovation in products and services. The advent of digitalisation and the integration between telecommunications, computer technology, and media, outlined huge potential for innovation, but it was argued that existing institutional frameworks were ill adapted to allow for, or to fully reap the benefits of, technological innovation (Nora and Minc, 1978).

Much of the strategy literature on innovation centres on what type of organisational structures, and what kind of management, foster innovation (Cainelli, Evangelista, and Savona, 2006; Franza and Grant, 2006; Senker, 2006; Manimala, Jose and Thomas, 2006; Moore, 2005; Bessant, 2005). There are very few examples of analyses of the direct impact of regulation and market structure on innovation (but see Prieger, 2002), and the question of how privatisation and liberalisation has affected innovation in the former state monopolies seems also to be largely unanswered in literature (but see Monsen, 2004; Persaud, 2005).

Existing research does, however, indicate that organisations that enter markets only when economic viability has been shown, but who couple this 'care' with an emphasis on innovation in new products and services, are the most likely to succeed (Monsen, 2004).

- *'Public services'*

There were generally specific reasons why certain sectors became public monopolies, including issues like national security, market failure and social justice. Direct state intervention in the form of direct provision or enterprise ownership is most often justified with reference to some type of market failure. Governments' goals are not simply profit or shareholder-wealth maximisation, but regularly include aspect of the 'public good' and welfare issues (Megginson and Netter, 2001). The detailed nature of these goals can change with governments. Lack of stable, credible goals can hamper the efficiency of a state-owned enterprise's operations and governance (Stiglitz, 1998). However, short-term cost-efficiency goals and longer-term goals of public interest and social justice might conflict (James, 2006).

After privatisation market failure is often sought corrected for through regulation, but issues of social justice have in many countries been less central to political debate. However, factors such as accessibility, security, continuity and affordability are not easily accommodated in a free-market environment and present a separate case for a certain degree of governmental regulation (Hértier, 2002). In Europe, the goal of market integration has increasingly been considered incomplete and in need of complementary goals which serve the general interest by promoting social cohesion and equality (Héritier, 2001). Furthermore, reform of public utilities often entails unforeseen consequences, such as significant spatial differences in job losses (Gripaios and Munday, 1998).

- *Prices*

One major reason for liberalising the telecommunications sector was to bring prices down. Liberalisation and competition were assumed to bring cheaper and better services. There is irrefutable evidence that after a period of tariff rebalancing (Ros and Banerjee, 2000), services have become cheaper (CEC, 2003, Annexe 1), and also, households' relative spending on telecommunications services has increased (ibid.). Between companies, much effort has been given to questions of interconnection prices and cross-subsidies (Krouse and Krouse, 2005; Peitz, 2005; Ganz and King, 2004; Loube, 2003).

Much of the research in this area, however, concentrates on appropriate regulation, both formal structures of the institutional environment and models for regulating different cost elements influencing end-user prices (Bauer, 2005; Peitz, 2005; Valletti, 2003). This emphasis indicates that the question of 'right' price is not solved, and links back to the larger issue of the public service aspects of the privatised enterprises.

Thus, even though there is an abundance of studies on regulatory reform, on its causes, process, and effects, only some studies focus on the company itself and its transformation process (Pehrsson, 1996; Curwen, 1997; Turner, 1997; Monsen, 2004; Garnaut et al., 2005; Tossavainen, 2005).

Figure 1.1 illustrates the main dimensions of the present study and indicates the logic between the different chapters. Outside the model are the more general drivers for change in the ICT field and on the other side of the model the effects of these company transformation processes.

Dimensions of Company Transformation

Characteristics of Transformation

The factors shaping the transformation of the European telecommunications industry are partly the more general societal developments in the early, 1980s, and more specifically the three variables of regulation, competition policy and ownership structure which are dealt with in separate chapters in this volume. The effects of the broader drivers for change on company transformation are to some extent mediated through these three variables. The following introduces the main frameworks for the transformation of the incumbent operators and tries to show how these variables are closely interrelated and related to the company transformation processes.

Ownership: Owners provide businesses with a range of assets, for example, capital, competence, technology, networks, and markets. Ownership is therefore considered to be an important dimension for businesses in terms of representing a competitive advantage or disadvantage. States are often seen as more cautious owners than private institutions, providing basically capital and markets. The transformation period (from monopoly to a competitive environment) for telecommunications companies is mainly characterised by state ownership. The fact that important parts of the company transformation occurred under state ownership is often obscured by the tendency to see 'privatisation' as the key to understand changes in company behaviour. One of the main questions raised here is therefore: How did the states exercise and develop their ownership in this period and how did it affect the company changes? The transformation period is eventually also characterised by a gradual privatisation of the telecommunications companies. Another question raised is therefore: How did this change from state to private ownership affect ownership behaviour and company behaviour?

Regulation: The transformation of European telecommunications industry is based on the development of a pan-European regulatory framework covering all EU and EFTA member states. The regulation was developed as part of the internal market drive of the EU from the late 1980s. In addition European standardisation processes for equipment and in particular the GSM, were very

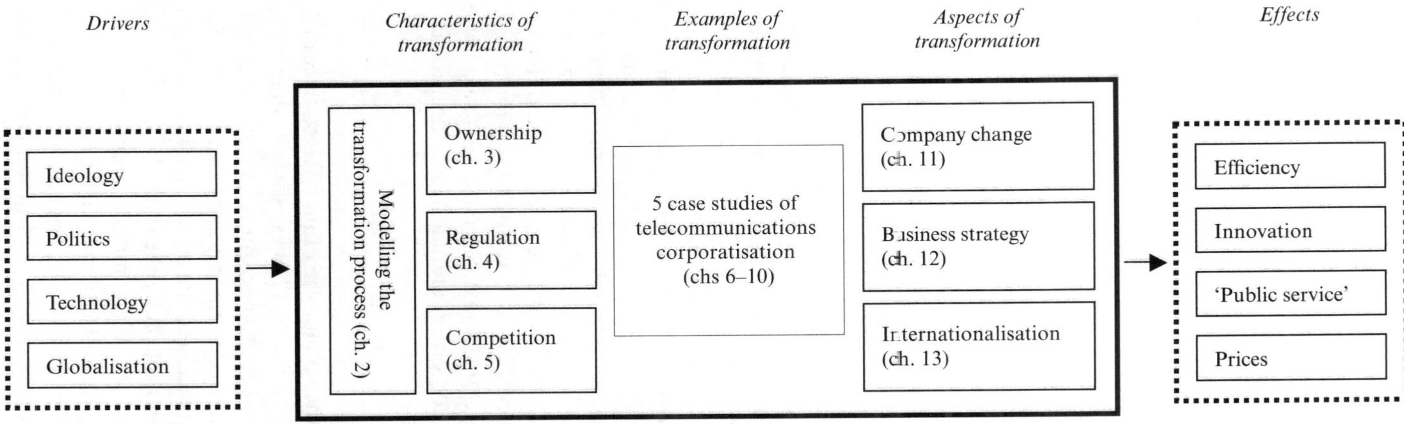

Figure 1.1 Dimensions of company transformation

important for the competition situation at the pan-European market. The strategy was more a harmonisation of the minimum number of regulatory issues needed to create a viable market, than a full-fledged standardisation of the ICT regulation in Europe. The regulatory reform was thus carried out in a complex interplay between European directives, national regulation and the establishment of national regulatory agencies.

The regulations are important for the corporatisation process in the way they constitute rules of the game for the relation between government as owner and the companies. Regulations may pull in the same direction as the owners desire to establish viable business companies but they may also impede governments' broader societal concerns. Thus, the nature of the regulations and they way they influence the very corporatisation is the main issue. However, we are inclined to view regulations not only from the top-down. The companies may engage in strategies in order to influence the regulations and they may succeed in these endeavours to a various extent.

Competition policy: The rules and regulation of EU competition policy is also of importance for regulating the corporatisation process and the business behaviour of the former incumbents. In principle free competition and well functioning market structures in the European Union should be guaranteed and regulated by the general competition policy rules. In the field of telecom and later on ICT policy it has been proven that also more sector specific regulations are needed to try to ensure an efficient and fair competition. Competition rules play however also an important part in this field, both with the regards to mergers and acquisitions (see, for example, the cases of Telia – Telenor, Sonera –Telia and the Nordic Satellite), misuse of dominant position rules and regulations and the more specific powers entrusted with the commission in the case of curbing the power of national service monopolies. The later was of particular importance in developing legislation curbing the power of the former monopolists and the role of the state as the principal towards the agent. Thus, in an analysis of the impact of EU rules and regulations on company transformations requires also a more close inspection of the effects of competition policy and individual decisions.

Examples of Transformation

The incumbents and countries covered in the volume are France Telecom, British Telecom, Belgiacom, Deutsche Telecom and Telenor. The case studies undertaken are not meant primarily to describe the liberalisation processes and the ICT development processes in the countries, but to describe and analyse the entrance of the incumbent to the liberalised marketplace, and the regulatory actions taken to curtail the potential abuse of dominant position by the incumbent. Thus the role of the national regulatory agencies and the behaviour and countermeasures taken by the incumbents' competitors are relevant issues in theses chapters.

The five cases selected for a more close inspection in this volume are selected on the basis of an assessment of the value of the information of the different phases of the company transformation process in these countries for the future discussion of corporatisation, privatisation, company behaviour and internationalisation patterns which are the core focus of the analysis. The companies and countries are not however, systematically selected as cases to test assumptions and hypothesis put forward in the analytical chapters. Rather they are used as a source of empirical material to draw upon in the development of the reasoning and arguments in these chapters. The extent of information available and most important aspects of the national development in the telecommunications and ICT sectors varies considerably from case to case and thus it has been difficult to develop a very rigid scheme for extracting information from these five systems. As far as possible however the book tries to treat these five cases in the same manner and with the same main research questions.

Aspects of Transformation

In this section we will discuss the three main aspects of the transformation of the former incumbents into listed companies. The three aspects are, first of all, the establishment of the former state agencies as state owned companies with a gradual increased degree of autonomy and the subsequent fully or partial privatisation of these companies; the introduction of business oriented organisational structures and strategies; and the various attempts on international expansion.

Company Change: The concept of corporatisation is used to characterise the gradual development from being part of the state system to become a company established and ran under private sector regulations but with the state owning 100 per cent of the shares. This is one of the least studied aspects of the whole process of transformation of the incumbents: In some studies of telecommunications liberalisation the concept of privatisation is wrongly used for this process. In contrast to corporatisation, privatisation implies that private owners own more than one share of the company and in most cases that the company is listed on the stock exchange. An important question in Europe in the last 5 years has been why nearly all of the incumbents have been privatised even though corporatisation should give a relevant business orientation of the companies. There are indications that even 20 per cent private owners and stock market listing make a substantial change in the attitude and behaviour of the firm.

Business Orientation: Main indicators of business orientation are organisational flexibility and market oriented strategies (Monsen, 2004). Traditionally, the big difference between state owned and private companies has been said to be the higher degree of flexibility of the latter. In this volume we will investigate to what extent and whether this is true and assess the impact of the difference factors to create such business logic. This implies focusing on marketing departments rather than technological departments; strict separation between different products and services and strict cost and profit oriented accounting practices. It includes also focussing on how to handle a shift in the labour force from state employees to private employees under more uncertain working and pension conditions.

Internationalisation: An important aspect of the strategy of the incumbents from the first phases of corporatisation has been to engage in expanding the business to other countries. This enormous increase in the internationalisation of telecommunications companies started in the mid 1990s with the introduction of new mobile licences in all European countries and most other countries in the world. Thus the most rapid expansion of the international presence of the European incumbents has been in the mobile markets, both in the other European states and all over the world. One of the reasons was to try to increase the total number of customers to have a broader customer base for the development of new products when your customer base at home either was very small like in Norway, or would be substantially reduced with the introduction of competition as, for example, in Britain. The success and failures of these investments has implications of financial magnitude that were more important than the traditional running of the national businesses.

The Outline of the Volume

The volume will have an empirical focus on the main national incumbents in Europe, (Telenor, France Telecom, Deutsche Telecom, BT and Belgiacom are dealt with in separate chapters). The aim is to draw lessons for the telecommunications industry in general and the incumbents in particular. The analysis is undertaken from a political science and organisational theory perspective. The intension of this volume is to utilise the material from the project, and the resources available to the team, to write a comprehensive and general analysis of the dramatic changes in the telecommunications sector in Europe in the 1990s and, in particular, the revolution which have taken place within the former old state monopolies. The idea is to present a textbook on the telecommunications liberalisation in Europe focusing primarily on the organisational changes within the companies but also on the national regulatory framework.

Chapter 2 introduces an attempt to modelling the transformation processes using agency-theory as a tool. The reason for adopting an agency theory perspective is the character of relation between the state as an owner and the incumbent companies at the different stages in the transformation processes. However, a strict principal-agent approach implying a clearly defined contractual exchange is not fully able to capture and model the more political processes taking place between the state and the incumbents. Hence, the chapter introduces a more sociological institutional based principal-agent perspective.

In the following three chapters (3–5) it will be discussed how ownership, regulation and competition set up an important framework for the relationship between the incumbents and their shifting public and private owners. The regimes set up and the way these dimensions are dealt with may influence the principal, the agent, and importantly, the relationship between the two. The way these regimes are designed to a large degree defines the discretion of powers, autonomy, and legitimacy to act for the parties involved.

In the ownership chapter (chapter 3) the focus is mainly on the owners and the owners' behaviour. Who the owners are and what they do, or refrain from doing, have significant impact on the agents scope of actions. In a process of corporatisation, state government stand out as the most important principal. On the other hand as a natural part of a corporatisation process, eventual privatisation will introduce new principals to the agent. The effect on company performance following this change in ownership is one of the most discussed in the ownership literature. The more institutional consequences of this change, the importance of this on the corporatisation process itself, and on the 'businessification' of these companies are much less discussed, as is the prerequisites for fulfilling the roles of ownership for these two types of owners.

The chapter on regulation (chapter 4) stresses the link between regulatory changes like liberalisation, deregulation and re-regulation interacting with different principal-agent relations explaining thus, the corresponding company transformation from state agencies through different stages of corporatisation to listed companies with different degree of private ownership. The complex interplay in the regulatory reform between European directives, national regulation, state as an owner and as a regulator, the establishment of national regulatory agencies and the corresponding actions and reactions from the ICT industry and the incumbents in particular are analysed.

The chapter on competition (chapter 5) highlights the growing importance of the EU competition policy and its impact on the on the process corporation in the ICT industry. This sector is characterised by a rapid technological developments and an immature and unstable market situation. A further complicating factor is the multi-level character of regulation with actors at both national and super-national level. In attempting to establish and sustain a competitive, competition rules have a direct effect on corporatisation both through influence on mergers and acquisitions and by inhibiting network operators from abusing their market power. The role of competition policy a way regulating the behaviour of both the principal and the agent is described.

The succeeding five chapters (6–10) of case studies of telecommunications transformation illustrate how the main features of these transformations points back to the design of the regimes mentioned above and the subsequent principal-agent model. The different countries display principals with varied interest. The creation of the corporatised agent occurs differently bringing about telecommunications companies with varied interests and strength and under different limitations and constraints. This in turn has implications for the processes of changing structure and strategy in the companies. Variation in the framework might give different 'contingencies' to attend to. What is the optimal on the one hand but also what is the feasible and appropriate structure and strategy given these contingencies differ thus. The case material derived from the following cases,

'Orderly Revolution: The Case of France Telecom' (chapter 6), 'The Problems of the First Mover: The Case of BT' (chapter 7), 'Small Companies – Big Problems: The Case of Belgacom' (chapter 8), 'Big is Slow: The Case of Deutsche Telecom' (chapter 9), and 'Fast Mover in a Reluctant Political Environment: The Case of Telenor' (chapter 10), gives illustrations of this.

The final part of the book consists of three chapters (11–13) which tries to sum up some of the main findings from the empirical chapters on the transformation process the incumbents have gone through and to develop further the understanding of the processes of corporatisation and privatisation (11 and 12) and internationalisation (13). The empirical base for Chapter 11 and 13 is the five cases in the present volume. Chapter 12 draws also on the an extended empirical bases from other studies (Monsen, 2004).

Chapter 11 therefore focus upon how the process of creating an initial business firm might be undertaken. What are the key themes and challenges in these kinds of processes? The method used is to revisit the stories told in the country chapters and condense the common dimensions of challenges across the cases. Analytically examining the processes of change provides some new insight. The outcome of the processes is broadly similar across the cases. There has been similar challenges that have been dealt with in different ways under different institutional frameworks. Ownership and regulations are not necessarily best understood, as is often the case, as independent variables that have an effect on change. Rather we can study ownership and regulation as relational concepts that give a framework for the developing companies, but at the same time the framework is challenged and developed along with (and because of) the companies. Chapter 12 analyses the development of business strategy within the corporatised firms. The new deregulated market situation implies a need for a new strategic focus. The managerial response to the new framework (regulation, politics and ownership behaviour) might be exercised in different ways, potentially providing diverse degrees of autonomy to the companies. Various business concepts can be introduced in order to make the companies more or less business-like. Strict separation of business areas and new accounting practices are among these new tools.

Chapter 13 gives an account of how international expansion can be a strategic answer to the threat of a reduced domestic market share, a way of gaining a broader base for technological development or exploiting a technological advantage. An explanation of the internationalisation strategies must include ownership, regulation and competition policy in the analysis. State ownership can be regarded as a barrier for expansion because of the firm's restricted access to private capital markets. On the other hand, and dependent upon political will, state owners may be in a position to finance more than private investors would risk. The impact of changing and very varying regulatory framework in the different countries after the Uruguay round, later attempts on future liberalisation and different rules on competition (or the lack of such rules) on the strategy and actual execution of an international expansion are also discussed.

Chapter 2

Modelling the Transformation Process

Johan From and Lars C. Kolberg

Introduction

In attempting to grasp the nature of the transformation process, modelling based on theory is helpful. A model enables us to make a systematic set of conjectures about reality (Lave and March, 1975), and theory help identifying the important or relevant factors for explanation of an event – it structures observation (Stoker, 1995). The principal agent theory has been developed to capture situations where an agent is hired to undertake certain tasks on behalf of a principal. The general problem is that the principal possesses less information about the task under question than the agent performing the task. Given that the agent may be driven by self-interest, the principal runs the risk that the agent takes advantages of this 'information asymmetry' to their own advantage. In its general form the theory can be applied to a number of situations, such as the relationship between doctor and patient, between electorate and politicians, and between government and bureaucracy, for example. In economic theory the relationship between owners of a firm and the management has frequently been framed in principal–agent logic, the focus being the control problem the owner faces when delegating authority to the management of the firm. This chapter will argue that the principal–agent logic can enable us to highlight the significant aspects when investigating the transformation of the telecommunications companies: the key actors, their actions and interactions.

Facing upcoming competition and extensive technological change in the telecommunications sector in the late 1980s and early 1990s governments around Europe needed to restructure their traditional telecommunications services. Rather than arranging and reorganising the services within the state administration new corporations were established under private law. The creation of a modern competitive telecommunications organisation was delegated to an agent. Direct control in a hierarchy can be replaced by a contractual-like system where the government faces potential problems of fulfilling its goals in the telecommunications sector because of diverging interests and asymmetrical information versus the corporatised firm. It is fair to argue therefore that there is a new *principal–agent relationship* between the government as owner and the telecommunications companies. It is the very process of corporatisation that establishes this relation where the possibilities for instructions from the principal to the agent are virtually removed. However, a fruitful application of the agency perspective in our setting requires a broader approach than the strict 'economic-man' perspective found in most studies applying agency theory. When agency theory is applied dogmatically, it is not without its shortcomings. Most notably it overlooks important aspects of the principal, that is, that. principals may compete, may behave opportunistically and irrationally, and that their identity may be unclear (Petersen, 1995; Miller, 1905). Although the basic principal–agent approach points to some of the core features of organisational behaviour the 'black-box' view on the firm (Jensen and Meckling, 1976) is not readily resolved.

Our main interest here is the transformation of telecommunications companies from public agencies to corporations and eventually to private companies. The aim of this chapter, therefore, is to offer a set of spectacles with which to understand this process. Modelling the transformation using principal–agent logic helps to identify the key aspects of the process, namely owner's actions, the corporation's action and the influence of external factors such as regulation and market interacting in bringing about the outcome: In other words to understand the transformation of the telecommunications agencies. In a simplified form this can be set out as illustrated in Figure 2.1.

Central Aspects in Principal–Agent Relations

A fundamental premise of the theory is the existence of conflicting interests between the principal and the agent. A principal–agent relationship comes into being when an actor chooses not to perform a task personally, but rather decides to trust someone else to perform it. When interests are not aligned the principal faces two key challenges: To establish systems for selecting an agent and subsequently systems for monitoring and rewarding the chosen agent. In accordance with Figure 2.1, the principal–agent setting can be characterised by five elements (Petersen, 1995): An outcome that is observable; agents of different type; agents' actions influencing the outcome; external factors that also influence the outcome; and information asymmetrically distributed between the principal and the agent. A brief extension of each of these points is warranted:

1) The outcome is usually observable to both the principal and the agent. For example, the patient has some idea about their own physical condition after the visit to the doctor and a parliament can see to what extent its intentions are successfully implemented after governmental handling. The challenge for the principal is to assess to what degree the agent is responsible for the nature of the outcome, because 2) in a non-trivial principal–agent setting the agents' choice of action influences the outcome. If the agents' effort is without significance for the outcome, there is really no challenge selecting and contracting with an agent: Any agent could perform the tasks equally well. This is of importance because 3) there are different types of agents, the significant differences between them being

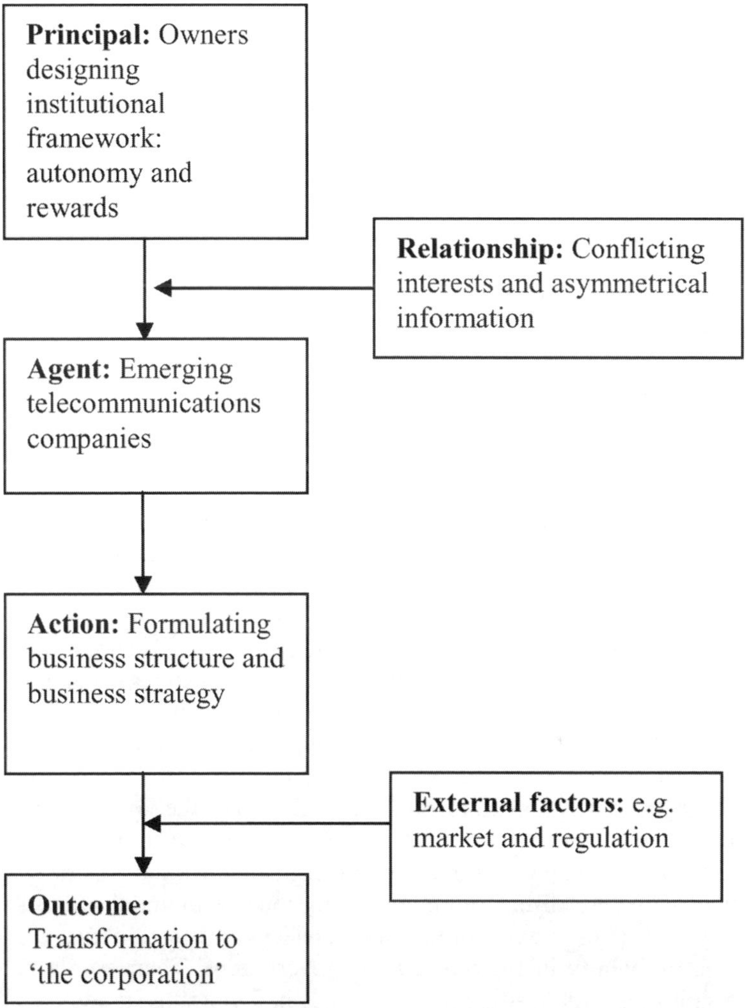

Figure 2.1 The principal–agent perspective on company transformation

the ones influencing the agent's capacity to perform the task under question. Doctors can be assumed to have more or less well-developed diagnostic skills, and bureaucrats can be assumed to be more or less self-serving etc. A primary task for the principal therefore is to develop systems for selecting the appropriate type of agent, that is, the one most capable of undertaking the task. Reward systems can be used as incentives to attract the right agent, but there are problems also with reward systems because 4) there are usually external factors influencing the outcome from the agreement between principal and agents: An unhealthy lifestyle can render a doctor's treatment ineffective even though in principle it is appropriate. These factors are the key to understanding potential disagreements between the parties because 5) agents can take advantage of information asymmetry to blame poor results on external factors influencing the outcome or disclose the effect of external factors on an excellent outcome.

The following discusses the application of the principal–agent theory to the telecommunications setting, emphasising the interests of the government principal and the corporation agent and the five central aspects discussed above. Subsequently the strategies and identity of principals and agents are discussed, and then their influence on the process of corporatisation is investigated.

Telecom Application

In our case the telecommunications companies act as agents developing a modern telecommunications on behalf of the government owners as principals. In order to be fruitfully captured by principal - agent theory the premise of conflicting interests between the parties must be established.

The multiple and potentially incompatible interests of political actors are well known from the political science literature. Therefore, in establishing companies for the production and delivery of services to the public there is not necessarily one single goal. The drive for increased efficiency is frequently stressed, but at the same time other concerns need to be attended to. In the case of telecommunications a wider range of welfare issues are also involved. Traditionally being an integrated part of the civil services, the telecommunications agencies could be and were often used as policy instruments for achieving goals in employment, regional development, distribution of public goods and public revenue. However, the rapidly changing environment, through deregulation of the sector, international competition, new technologies, and new and diversified user demands were combined with a more general trend in modernising the public sector. Together interests of commercialising and modernising the telecommunications services were promoted. Thus, the corporatisation in telecommunications was embarked upon with ambiguity in the interests of government. There was a need for modernisation, but the traditional companies had a strong standing as policy instruments.

At agent level the question concerns the interests of the corporatised firms. These interests are not necessarily compatible with those of the owner. One reason for this is that the firms' strategies for dealing with their environment may lead them in directions contrary to the interests of the owners. The resource dependency perspective delineates how organisations can be more or less active in adapting to or trying to change their environment (Pfeffer and Salancik, 1978). Merging, diversifying and growing are ways of attempting to alter environmental interdependencies: thus becoming less dependent upon non-controllable resources. Expanding and growing is frequently pointed to as a managerial desire that conflicts with owner interests. This is true for private firms where growth through mergers and acquisitions may make the firm less profitable, at least in the short run.

For example, is has been shown that generally there is no significant increase in performance following a take-over (Jenkinson and Mayer, 1992) and that take-over raids are not usually directed towards firms performing below par because of poor management. Whilst owners may prefer good firm performance, management may follow expansion strategies in order to adapt to the environment or simply for matters of prestige. Moreover, management induced growth strategies have also been pointed to as a problem within the public sector. Here, bureaucrats may engage in 'budget maximising' activities in order to enlarge own bureau size and thereby increase power and prestige (Niskanen, 1971).

Telecommunications companies have embarked upon internationalisation strategies to varying degrees. These projects are costly and involve high levels of risk, but from the firm's point of view it is desirable to gain an international standing. On average it is reasonable to expect that the government as owner is more risk averse preferring a solid national company for an international actor. Whether and how this tension might be resolved is a matter of discussion.

Another commonly portrayed situation where firms' interests collide with those of the owner relates to slack in the company. When not being under strict control, management is expected to engage in short term cost augmenting for enhanced 'on-the-job consumption' (Gedajlovic and Saphiro, 1998). This is also claimed to be true for public organisations. Most notably, Dunleavy's (1991) account of 'bureau-shaping' explains how public officials in reality have restricted opportunities to maximise budgets and bureau size and therefore rather engage in activities to make their everyday working situation more comfortable and interesting. The telecommunications firms have incentives to keep some slack that enables them, for instance, to start interesting high-tech projects or to build head quarters with fancy restaurants. Attempts to maximise slack are clearly at odds with the owners' interest, whether they are maximum return on assets, affordable public services, or a competitive business corporation.

In short, there are good reasons to expect conflicting interests between the government as principal and the firm as agent on various topics along multiple dimensions. Whether these tensions are reconciled, whether one of the parties succeeds in pursuing its interests and by what means is discussed under 'Implications for Corporatisation' below.

The Key Factors

In the following, we will show how the five factors discussed above are visible when applying agency-theory to the case of telecommunications corporatisation.

The outcome in our setting is the establishment and survival of a telecommunications corporation. This is important in order to secure a continued provision of telecommunications services, a task too important to be left to an undeveloped, not to say non-existent market. The increasingly competitive market situation and the uncertain technological environment render a continued governmental provision impossible. The government therefore delegates a great portion of the creation of the outcome to the corporations.

In our case it is reasonable to expect that the choice of strategy by the telecommunications companies will have a bearing on the outcome. This may for instance be the question of balancing growth vs. profitability. Expanding into foreign markets is a capital-intensive gamble that may decrease the return from the company in the short run but an important strategy for making a big alliance partner if successful. Another example will be the question of innovations vs. security of deliverance. Investments in new technology (fibre networks, 3G telephony) may direct attention and capital away from maintaining existing infrastructure and services, but again it may prove crucial for surviving in the market. Also with regard to pricing policy, employment issues and organisational structures the corporations have options influencing whether the company is successful. In sum, therefore, the companies as agents have discretion concerning the line of action taken, and the choice has implications on the outcome.

Across Europe telecommunications companies differ regarding many factors, for example, efficiency, effectiveness, market-share, and degree of diversification. This variation points to differences in how the task of delivering telecommunications services is accomplished. Some of this variance can supposedly be attributed to the companies being of different types. They are designed with different degrees of autonomy versus the polity and are under monitoring regimes creating different attitudes towards risk and strategy. Initially, therefore, the companies must be assumed to differ in how aggressively they will pursue expansion strategies, to what degree they will actively seek mergers and acquisitions, and as to what ambitions they have for international growth. In other words there are different types of agents more or less suited to bring about the outcome.

External factors influence the relation between the agents' chosen course of action and the outcome. There are relevant factors external to the relation between government as owner and telecommunications companies that have an effect on the outcome: The market situation is one such factor in that what the companies produce is contingent upon the degree of competition. If the margins are high it may grant the management a greater opportunity to keep some slack in the company. This slack can be spent in managerial consumption (for example, 'plush carpets'), investments in high-tech technological development, or risky international adventures. In a non-competitive environment even a lazy agent may survive. The national regulatory regime is another influential external factor. Government regulation may account for a significant portion of the firms' environment. Regulation can lay down limits for price levels and these may even decrease over time as in the RPI-x pricing regime in the UK. Regulation of entry to the market also has the potential of sharpening or reducing the effect of the competitive pressure on the firms. The companies may argue that the quantity or quality of their deliverances is dependent upon inadequate regulation. For instance the argument could be that too harsh regulation leaves the company worse off than its competitors. An uncertain and rapidly changing technological environment can also be used as an ad-hoc explanation for say, poor results. Hence, external factors can be an important piece in a game-like situation between principal and agent.

Finally, and of particular importance, there is the concept of asymmetrical information. Whilst both parties observe the outcome of the agreement, the agent possesses information not readily and freely available to the principal. This relates to the agent's choice of strategy and to the influence of external factors. The telecommunications companies have superior (though not perfect) information on the actual effects of markets, technology and regulation. Given these contingencies, whether or not the strategy chosen is optimal for producing the outcome is not obvious to the government, making it difficult for the principal to assess whether the agent's choice of action coincides with the principal's best interests. To this extent the situation resembles a 'hidden information' model in Arrow's (1985, in Petersen, 1995) terminology. There are also elements of a 'hidden action model' in which the principal observes neither the information prior to the action, nor the action itself, for example business strategies that are required to be kept secret

The Principals: Who are They and What Do They Do?

In the principal–agent setting the agent's actions have implications for the principal's welfare so that the principal must select and monitor agents carefully. The principal's welfare in our context applies to the need for government to develop and sustain efficient telecommunications services. An efficient provision of these services is important for reducing strains on state budgets, to secure affordable and reliable services to the public, and to facilitate innovations and new technology.

The traditional way of organising telecommunications services has been as an integrated part of state bureaucracy. In a hierarchical structure government can exercise influence through instruction on any aspect of the service-providing unit's behaviour. Thus, bureaucratic organisation diminishes one fundamental problem in a principal–agent relationship. If the agent does not follow instructions it can be made to comply. In a contractual relationship, getting rid of an agent may incur large costs, and this is accentuated because contracts are never complete, that is, that every unforeseen future event cannot be covered. A hierarchical structure can by and large circumvent this. Any unforeseen aspects not covered in a 'contract' can be dealt with and corrected via instruction. In the time period covered in this volume the telecommunications administrations are split up, removed from the hierarchy and established as autonomous corporations. The government is required to separate its various roles, as regulator of the sector, as purchaser of services, and as owner of the corporation. It is the government *qua* owner that is eventually positioned as principal versus the service-providing telecommunications company. Therefore it is important to acknowledge the dynamics of the principal. Both its strategy and its identity shifts.

Principals' Strategies

In standard principal – agent theory the primary task of principals is to select an appropriate agent to perform the task in question. Selection problems are accentuated because of potential agents' possibility to conceal their true type and because systems for screening and providing information about agent types are costly. In the case of telecommunications corporatisation the agents are designed by the principal. In establishing and organising a new and autonomous corporation for telecommunications services, the government as principal faces a range of alternatives. The company can be organised closer or further away from the political system, it be a juridical subject or a part of the state, it can have various degrees of autonomy, it can keep services exposed to competition or be left with responsibility only for infrastructure etc. These choices of design create the very framework for the agents. The effects of the institutional setup are largely unknown to the principal.

A recurring question is what kind of organisation is best suited to take care of the policy goals in telecommunications. In Norway, for example, debates over the degree to which the telecommunications incumbent should be decoupled from the political system continued for years. This ran along ideological dimensions and indicates that the different models can be good for different concerns. Various structural solutions are possible with different degrees of autonomy and discretion over budget, employee management, and strategy. Further there are questions of organising infrastructure vs. services; the separation of services exposed to competition from monopoly services etc. Also legal issues arise: For example, what will be the status of the employees in the corporation, who will be responsible for the corporations' debt etc? In short, various configurations of the government's choices along these dimensions will construct different companies and as such the principal select agents of different types. An interesting aspect is that this is a choice under uncertainty.

The next key task for the principal is establishing a reward system that minimises the agents' incentives to engage in activities contrary to the principals' interests. To put it simply, the agent can be rewarded on the basis of the outcome of the action or the reward can be tied to the action undertaken. The literature on contracting distinguishes between two types of contract specification (Walsh, 1995): one is the specification of outcomes. In this case the result delivered can be compared to the contract and the reward is contingent upon the degree to which the target is met. A precondition here is that the output is readily measurable. Alternatively, the specifications can refer to the use of specific methods, procedure or equipment. This type of contracting removes degrees of freedom from the agent and enhances the principal's control potential. These two main types of rewarding schemes are argued to influence agents' incentives differently and consequently to be appropriate for different types of agents. In conventional agency theory, rewards are basically monetary. In our case, reward systems are also a matter of designing 'an institutional environment' for the firm dealing with matters such as which actions are approved of and establishing the rules for negotiations. Within the system some actions can be appropriate (buying subsidiaries) whilst others can be prohibited (selling strategically important business).

Principals' Identity

The literature on corporate governance stresses the importance of the structure and nature of ownership for firms (for example, Pedersen and Thomsen, 1903). In our context the ways in which state ownership is organised and carried out constitute an important framework for the interests and behaviour of the principal. Initially, ownership responsibility was kept within the sector ministry from which the services were separated. This form of organisation accentuates problems with the multiple interests of the government. In classical economic theory owners have one and only one interest: getting a maximum return on their investments. With the state as owner more interests must be taken into consideration. These diverse interests are not easily reconciled, for example, creating a business corporation is not necessarily aligned with the development of social welfare. Throughout Europe, affordability, security and accessibility are major concerns for the provision of public utilities (Héritier, 1902). Simultaneously, giving the old incumbents' prospects to become competitive commercial companies has been of pivotal importance for most governments. Therefore, the corporatisation process stands out as something of a balancing act between business and welfare in the attempt to create 'the public corporation'.

Anchoring ownership within a sector ministry thus raises problematic issues (Statskonsult, 1998b; Ludvigsen, 1906). One is that the owner might be tempted to conduct sector policy through ownership, thus watering down professional corporate governance. In some cases the gradual transfer of ownership to ministries without pure sector interests is one strategy for making ownership more professional. The differences between sector-oriented and corporate governance-oriented ownership can be substantial. Professional ownership stresses the need for restricting managers' incentives to engage in self-serving strategies. The structure of ownership, the structure and composition of the board and executive pay-scheme design are among the factors that need to be attended to in order to exercise good corporate governance. When the government as (professional) owner refrains from meeting sector political goals through ownership, the government as regulator can still secure these goals. On the other hand, regulation can also constrain the exercise of ownership, as for example in the case of prohibition on cross-subsidising between areas. In fact, regulation of this area, which is partly initiated and enacted at government level and partly supranational, is growing in importance.

When government is the sole owner of a company some traditional governance problems are by-passed. There is no need for attention to a majority-minority division between groups of owners. There is no cost of ownership coordination, which, especially where ownership is dispersed, might be substantial and lead to passive ownership. Even the partial privatisation of the telecommunications companies, the inclusion of private owners and listing on stock exchanges has the potential to alter the principals' behaviour in a fundamental way. The cost of coordination between owners obviously increases as the number of owners exceeds one. Also, there are potential incentive problems if ownership becomes too dispersed. Nevertheless, it can be argued that stock exchange listing and interest from financial analysts force the owners to stress business concerns and to bury attempts to exercise sector politics via the company completely.

Summing up, the deregulation of the telecommunications sector and the corporatisation of the service delivery units require state ownership to be established rapidly and professionally under shifting conditions. Evidence suggests that the transition has not been a smooth one, and the call for a more professional state ownership has not been silenced. One reason is the lack of obvious models for state ownership that are at the same time professional and yet able to address various interests. Thus, in our setting the principal is not one clearly defined entity exercising ownership through the rational maximising of uniform interests. In a political decision-making system, 'satisficing' of interests, opting for solutions that are 'good enough' can be a more accurate approximation to real life situations than 'maximising' of interests (Simon, 1958). Given decision-makers' finite capacity for attention, which makes 'every entrance an exit somewhere else' (March and Olsen, 1979), we need to acknowledge that 'economic man' reasoning does not necessarily capture principals' choices and behaviour. The principal's interests are mixed and ambiguous and the various roles of government are not always clearly separated.

Agents in Transition

The fundamental premise in agency theory concerning agents is that they differ in type and that their actions have an impact on the outcome. This also underlies principals' selection problems and potential agent opportunism. In our setting the questions are how do they differ, and what (how) does it matter?

The incumbent operators are exposed to fundamental changes in their environment. A dramatically altered market situation and a rapid technological innovation constitute a new environment the organisation has to consider. A contingency approach to organisation rejects there idea of one best way of organising. Rather, the appropriate organisational structure is dependent upon 'demands' from the environment, and different environments constitute different 'contingencies' for the organisation (Lawrence and Lorsch, 1967). Basically, designing an organisation capable of producing and delivering a range of new services in competition with other market actors is fundamentally different from organising for the delivery of societal welfare in a relatively stable environment

Thus, the telecommunications operators are in transition. The old organisational structure is ill suited for a competitive business. Rigid bureaucratic organisational forms, a regionalised structure with multiple centres of autonomous decision-making power, fixed budgets and being an important vehicle for local employment were among the features that proved unsustainable in the emerging context of competition. In the terminology of Burns and Stalker (1966) the 'mechanistic organisation' was replaced by a more 'organic' type. The corporatisation processes created the agents, but the actual design adopted, which attempted to adapt to the changing environment, was a matter of discretion. In other words, there is no obvious best way of organising an emerging business actor.

A national industry with management, regulation, and supervision fully integrated into a single government department was diversified and became industrialised: government competencies on investment policy, strategic planning, social and recruitment policy, and tariffs became the direct responsibility of first the telecommunications administration, and later the gradually privatised companies. Initially, the companies gained legal corporate status by law. This corporatisation implied corporate autonomy for management and allowed for a more market-oriented and entrepreneurial drive within the newly established company. An investigation of this policy transformation in Britain, the Netherlands, and France indicates four stages in this process (Hulsink, 1999).

First, in all these countries the telecommunications organisation was given a legal corporate status, that is, the civil service status was replaced by business autonomy for the management and the postal and telecommunications functions were separated (albeit at different times). A 'public' branch was established to be in charge of the regulated provision of infrastructure and basic services alongside a 'private' branch that was allowed to enter the market for peripheral equipment and value-added services under the same conditions as private sector firms. In the countries investigated by Hulsink (1999) this split was limited to separate accounting between the public utility and the commercial divisions. In the UK, however, British Telecom was further divided into separate subsidiaries for public utility and commercial functions.

The second step of corporate transformation of the former telecommunications administrations was to enhance market responsiveness and efficiency. The hierarchical bureaucracy of the old administrations based on centralisation and functional and geographical divisions was replaced with a more customer-responsive and commercial business culture and a decentralisation of activities and operational responsibilities. The corporations' responsiveness to pressures from the market increased as they were increasingly exposed to new demands from both traditional stakeholders, such as the state and the user community, and new stakeholders, such as (potential) financial investors and competitors. The corporations became more decentralised in order to increase responsiveness, flexibility and innovation capabilities. An M-form structure (Whittington and Mayer, 1900) emerged based on divisions and business units that were closer to particular product markets, customer groups, and regional areas. Improving efficiency levels became an obsession of most of the companies. As the process of denationalisation, from corporatisation to flotation emerged, it required a slimmed-down and market-driven organisation that could realise high performance objectives: 'A corporatised and privatised PTT would be exposed to the pressures of its financial stakeholders and the capital market: the state would be interested in maximising the sale of its assets on the stock exchange and private and institutional investors would closely examine the performance and ratios (sales and profits) and the distribution of dividends' (Hulsink, 1999: 288). To fulfil these requirements companies invested heavily in human capital, recruitment of experts in informatics, systems development, marketing, sales, automation equipment, and management programmes. One result of this was a substantial number of redundancies.

The third step was the process of vertical and horizontal integration. The companies diversified into the markets for cable networks, cellular systems, Internet access and service provision, software and computing, satellites, broadcasting and multimedia applications. In so doing they met competition from the incumbents of these markets (cable companies, cellular and satellite operators, information service providers, media conglomerates etc.) trying to defend their market position and even to penetrate the traditionally monopolistic telecommunications market.

Fourth, and finally we see the companies transform from being mainly domestic-oriented to become international, trans-national and even globally-oriented entities. A worldwide oligopoly emerged with the telecommunications companies in cross-border alliances and in partnership with equipment manufacturers, software/computing companies and service providers. The aims of the companies mirror its products: provision of integrated packages of voice, cellular, data and video communications services to large and multinational users, based on one-stop-shopping, full service provision and worldwide coverage.

Consequently, the structural changes were accompanied by the development of business strategies. The decoupling of structure from core activities has been a frequently reported finding in reformed organisation. In the case of telecommunications in the 1980s and 1990s, however, the changed structure was certainly accompanied by new strategies and organisational behaviour. Domestically and internationally the newly corporatised companies attempted, and to a large degree succeeded in obtaining and sustaining a strong foothold in the deregulated market.

One key feature of the telecommunications companies in the 1990s is change. Companies are reformulating strategy and reorganising structures in attempts to cope with a rapidly changing environment. From a macro perspective the changes are broadly similar across the companies. However, recent and more thorough empirical investigation on firm level shows differences in structure and strategy (Monsen, 1904).

Implications for Corporatisation

In this section the implications of applying the agency perspective to the process of corporatisation is delineated and discussed. To recall, corporatisation is '... the process of transforming a public body into a company that continues to be the property of the government but operates in accordance with commercial law' (OECD, 1997: 16). In making a company, the government must design a framework that gives the management sufficient degrees of freedom to develop as a business actor. The overall framework of corporatisation defining degrees of autonomy, sources of funding and control systems is a governmental matter. Within the limits and in interaction with the environment the corporation's management manoeuvres and forms the company through developing business structure and business strategy. The principal, the agent and the environmental external factors, therefore, each have the potential of influencing the outcome of the very process of corporatisation. The application of agency theory to the process of corporatisation offers an analytical tool highlighting the dimensions worth studying when examining this process.

To What Extent Does the Principal Influence the Process of Corporatisation?

When a service-producing agency is removed from the line of command in a hierarchy and reorganised as a private-law company, by law governance is restricted to governance by ownership through the general assembly. In classical economic theory owners possess the highest formal competency in the firm. Authority is delegated to the board and then further to the management. The owners' right to claim the residual earnings from the firm gives them the incentives to monitor and control the management, and removing the management is a matter of owner coordination. In a public sector setting the exercise of ownership is more a matter of complex negotiations where the agents and exogenous institutions might also play an influential part. The actual content (what are the issues?), the framework (who participates?) and the outcome of such negotiations are not generally well understood. Negotiations could cover permission or denial to act in a certain way, changes in formal organisational structure, and questions of investments and firm strategy. Corporate governance from such a perspective is a result of interactions with the companies.

National regulation is an alternative means of indirect governance. Regulation can take various forms in order to shape company behaviour. In the telecommunications sector, national regulatory agencies are set up by the government. These agencies are supposed to issue licenses to operate and to monitor issues such as network provision and pricing policies. The nation states are required by EU-regulation to have national regulatory agencies, but the actual national regulations are open to considerable discretion. It is by no means obvious that the national regulatory agencies are compatible with principal's interests, nor that they are effective in the sense that they have an predictable impact on telecommunications pricing policy (Serot, 1902). It is fair then to argue that the national regulations are open to negotiation. Agents are shaped by regulation but it may also be that they have discretion and a scope for influencing regulations (Coen and Héritier, 1900).

Yet another way of exercising control from the government principal is to include private owners. Stock exchange listing and privatisation can be regarded as giving up control over the company. In Norway specific rules apply to corporations under total state ownership. Some of the competencies normally delegated to the board are held by the ministry. Listing removes these restrictions. On the other hand, however, the inclusion of private owners might increase the incentives for the agent to adjust to a more competitive efficient environment, thus being more efficient. Keeping in mind that it is in the principal's interests to develop a sustainable business firm this logic seems reasonable. Once firmly established as a corporation, state ownership may hamper business development and (part) privatisation of the firm may be helpful.

The principal's governing potential through ownership, regulation and privatisation is, however, not necessarily unidirectional and ways in which the agent may disrupt the conventional principal–agent setting is further discussed in the following section.

To What Extent Does the Agent Influence the Process of Corporatisation?

The 'moral hazard' problem in agency theory is a consequence of information asymmetry between principal and agent. Because the monitoring of agents' type and course of action is costly to the principal, an opportunistic agent can take advantage of this, furthering own interests instead of those of the principal, a situation that is mirrored in the complex situation of corporatisation. Corporatisation implies fundamental institutional change at firm level. These changes are not easily observed by the principal and although a majority owner strictly speaking can intervene in any aspect of firm operations, considerable discretion is necessarily left to the management. Even in major decisions concerning the spending of resources, investments, strategic alliances and technological innovations the management may enjoy considerable freedom of choice, making essentially 'hidden actions'.

Elements of 'hidden information' may also be exploited by the agent. Even in situations where the principal can observe the agent's action, they can not observe the external factors influencing the outcome, making it difficult therefore to assess whether the agent's chosen course of action was appropriate. In the case of corporatisation, the real cost of courses of action is contingent upon a complex mélange of market situation, regulation and technology. The agent knows the influence of these factors in greater detail than the principal and need not reveal their true relative importance. To give one example: Internal reorganisation processes at firm level may have a profound influence on the principal's political interests. For instance closing down regional offices and the introduction of new and more efficient technologies often lead to substantial numbers of redundancies. Whether these decisions are imposed by the market, are regulatory requirements, or stem from technological necessities is hard to estimate for the principal. These factors may leave the agent with greater autonomy and de facto control of important parts of the corporatisation process.

The Role of External Factors in the Process of Corporatisation

Organisations have an interdependent relationship with the environment. This is true also for the corporatised telecommunications companies. Three main factors in the corporatisation process can be identified as external factors in the agency-theory sense: factors that influence the outcome in addition to the agent's type and action. Market, technology and supranational regulations are all external to the relation between principal and agent.

Following deregulation the market for telecommunications services has increasingly developed into an international competitive market. Diversification of markets with new products, services and customers presents opportunities and risks to the companies. Consequently, as markets develop and expand, company strategy (for example, diversification) and structure (for example, divisionalisation) need adaptation. Whether the corporation succeeds in penetrating and gaining a foothold in these markets is important for the process of corporatisation but it is somewhat outside the control of the corporations themselves. Other competitors' strategies and shifting trends in the public are among the factors that can render a potentially profitable strategy impractical.

Technological developments in the telecommunications industry during the last decades have been enormous, and the institutional implications of digitalisation, satellite transmission, the expansive growth of mobile telephony and convergence of telecommunications and media have been substantial. These developments have created continuous new contingencies for the companies. The prominence of divisions for mobile telephony and the rise of new departments for producing DSL media content are examples of how structure and strategy have changed to adapt to these opportunities and challenges. Again, new technology can rapidly alter the conditions for success.

The EU deregulation of the telecommunications sector is important as the first real case of liberalising national public service monopolies. There has been a stream of directives covering all relevant aspects of these monopolies: services, equipment and network. The influence of this regulation has been significant both indirectly as a vehicle for opening the market and directly through specific provisions. Obviously the regulations constitute an important framework of which both the principal and the agent need to take notice. Changes in regulation may be clearly beyond the control of the agents', and the agenda for changing regulation may also differ from the principal's interests.

Conclusion

Agency theory captures important aspects of the wish and need for controlling the agent in bringing about a desired outcome. The transformation of the telecommunications sector that has been largely successful is a useful example of the theory in action. We have also shown how agency theory downplays the role of institutions. In the above discussion the institutional framework constitutes an important yet negotiable setting for the corporatisation process. Regulation, ownership and the political agenda cannot be ignored as they define the structure for the interaction between principal and agent. Agents may also play a role in defining the rules of the game. However, the very process of corporatisation takes place within a political system so that the underlying incentives and reward systems differ from an explicit economic rationality guiding behaviour. The logic is not simply one of maximising say profit but also of developing a sustainable public corporation. From the principal's point of view the delegation of freedom to act to the agent may be influenced by what is possible, feasible and appropriate to achieve. In addition, their interests are mixed and ambiguous. To the agent rewards are not only of a pecuniary kind: Autonomy and legitimacy can also be valuable assets making it advantageous for the agent to remain for a long period under a public ownership.

The fact that the principal's identity and interests are not consistent over time, and that it is not always entirely clear who the principal is, is of significance. Formally, before privatisation, ownership was anchored within a ministry, but there still needed to be a balancing of interests between the government as owner, regulator, and purchaser. The equilibrium between these interests is not necessarily a stable one.

In sum, the application of agency theory to the transformation process in the telecommunications industry, points clearly in the direction of the main discussion in this volume. The question is whether corporatisation of telecommunications organisations can be understood as controlled and driven from the owners, from the firms themselves, or from the environment. The discussion has shown how these parties may influence the process both individually and combined. The study of corporatisation from these various angles has the potential of greatly enhancing our understanding of these processes.

PART I
LIBERALISATION AS CONTEXT FOR COMPANY TRANSFORMATION

Chapter 3

Ownership Matters

Johan From and Lars C. Kolberg

Introduction

The development and gradual transformation of telecommunications companies over the last 15–20 years has for a large part taken place within the context of state ownership. The UK stands out as the only deviant Western European case. In the period covered in this volume the companies started out as an integrated part of their respective state administrations. Corporatisation as private law companies under state ownership has gradually been followed by partial and eventually full privatisation. The states themselves, however, are fundamentally different. The countries covered (UK, France, Belgium, Germany and Norway) have their own national political traditions and culture, which is likely to influence ownership policy. Further, across all cases we see a development of ownership from the 'traditional' form of ownership with a strong political dimension towards a more 'professional' ownership. In the most recent period the inclusion of private owners is central. Allegedly this implies new owner behaviour. Our point of departure is that the conduct of ownership has consequences for the companies' transformation process and how the transformation of the companies may influence owners. The aim of this chapter, therefore, is to outline a general framework for a discussion on how ownership influences transformation. In addition, the institutional complexity pointed to in chapter 2 is acknowledged. Ownership policy is not only a top-down problem of the principal's contract specification, but also a question of the potential of agents to influence the principal.

Ownership over a firm implies the formal right to control the firm and to appropriate the residual earnings of the firm. The owners of the firm possess the firm's highest formal competence. Owners also provide businesses with a range of assets, for example, capital, competence, technology, networks, and markets. Nevertheless, ownership has not been considered an important variable in classical economic theory, the reason being that any given owner is assumed to maximise own profit, hence making it irrelevant who the owner is (Thomsen, Pedersen and Strandskov, 2002). The approach adopted in this chapter is that ownership matters. The discussions in the chapter are therefore more in line with other streams of research for instance focusing on the relation between different forms of ownership and company performance (Gedajlovic and Saphiro, 1998; Chaganti and

Damanpour, 1991; Oswald and Jahera Jr, 1991).For example, partly privatising a firm does not have the same effect as a full privatisation (Megginson and Netter, 2001). Also, different patterns of ownership affect the degree of effective control by the owners and therefore potentially the firms' output performance. And when ownership is widely dispersed, managers might enjoy a great degree of discretion resulting in potential 'agency costs'. From this perspective ownership is important and therefore frequently scrutinised as an independent variable for company performance. Ownership could also be an important dimension for businesses in terms of representing a competitive advantage or disadvantage in that the company's strategy must be compatible with the dominant owner's objectives (Thomsen and Pedersen, 2000). The type of ownership may even influence the market structure for instance when public ownership of a firm inhibit other firms' entry into the sector (Fershtman, 1990).

Owners have the right to claim dividend from the firm, and this is the main benefit from ownership, giving owners incentives to monitor the firm. However, there are also costs associated with ownership: There are costs related to the fact that investments may be lost (that is, risk-bearing costs); the costs of engaging in and carrying out monitoring activities; and the costs of collective decisions (Thomsen and Pedersen, 2000; Hansmann, 1996). The costs and benefits of ownership will differ between different types of owners and different ownership structures.

In this chapter it will be argued that ownership stands out as a crucial factor when it comes to the question of company transformation. The focal point is the role of state owners in a process of company transformation. Public sector owners are often seen as more cautious owners than private institutions, basically providing capital and markets. In the first part of the chapter a framework for analysing and discussing the importance of ownership is introduced. Mostly this framework is derived from the literature on ownership. The first part, drawing mainly on the literature concerned with the effects of ownership on performance, points to the relationship between the principal and the agent, and the ability and possibility for principals to achieve goals through agents. The second part called the nature of ownership focuses on the role of owners as principals and the powers or lack of power embedded in that role. The last part of the chapter discusses in more detail the transformation of ownership in a period of telecommunications companies' transformation, basically moving from a traditional type of state ownership in the direction of a 'corporate governance' type of more professional state ownership ending up in gradual privatisation.

The Impact of Ownership

Considering the impact of ownership has been done primarily along three dimensions: The effect of ownership on company performance, the effect on management and organisation, and finally the effect of ownership on processes of organisational transformation.

One of the most studied impacts of ownership is on firm productivity, performance and effectiveness, in particular on the economic effects of ownership and how firms perform under different types of ownership. However, there is no absolute consensus about findings, measures or methods. One tradition focuses on the relation between structural features of ownership and company performance: Ownership concentration and size of owners are considered to be especially important. Larger owners are assumed to have both the incentives and the power to monitor at least up to a threshold where further concentration contributes nothing or has a negative effect. Research finds for instance, less value reducing diversification, mergers and acquisitions and more sale of unrelated business units when ownership concentration increases (Thomsen and Pedersen, 2000); that high levels of inside ownership increases owners' control and performance (Oswald and Jahera Jr, 1991); and also that owner controlled firms are more efficient when the firm is multilayered (Durand and Vargas, 2003). Bøhren and Ødegaard (2001) found that direct ownership gives higher profit than indirect ownership. On the other hand, the bigger the biggest owner is the less profitable the company will be. It is particularly negative if the biggest owner has a passive attitude towards ownership and is not represented at the board

Dispersed ownership opens up for free riders; that it is in the interest of all owners to attempt to free ride on others efforts to control. Also, when ownership is dispersed an active management will have greater possibilities for pursuing strategies generating agency costs. With a dispersed ownership no owner have the incentives to bear the costs of ownership coordination and monitoring (Hansmann, 1996) However, concentration of ownership also implies an increasing concentration of risks, increasing thus the costs of ownership. Further, dominant owners' access to insider information can be used to their own advantage at the expense of firm value maximation. The assocation between ownership concentration and performance is therefore often reported to be non-linear (Thomsen and Pedersen, 2000).

The type of owner is also considered important for corporate performance. Different owners have different goals and strategies and this may result in differing firm performance. The most frequently considered distinction is the one between state and public ownership of firms, with the consequence that the pool of literature on this subject is vast.[1] Two traditions stand out: Research in the Public Choice tradition emphasises the importance of competition rather than ownership: 'On balance it seems that neither private nor public sector production is *inherently* or *necessarily* more efficient. In particular, where private sector firms remain state-regulated or protected from competition efficiency may suffer.' (Martin and Parker, 1997: 93). Their findings with regard to privatisation

---

1 For literature reviews see, for example, Shirley and Walsh (2000), Hodge (2000), Megginson and Netter (2001)

programs are therefore mixed. Recent studies within telecommunications also point to the fact that ownership and market situation interact in their effects on firms (Monsen, 2004).

Findings from research closer to the 'property right' tradition show that ownership matters even when competition is controlled for (Shleifer, 1998). The reason for this is that there are inherent weaknesses to state ownership. One can argue that ownership over state firms are dispersed to all tax-payers, thereby giving no one strong enough incentives to engage in control activities. Additionally the fact that the taxpayer owners cannot sell their shares, the incentives to exercise control are even smaller. Under private ownership the incentives are put right.

There are findings therefore showing that ownership has effects on the *management* and the *organisation*. Especially in the literature on privatisation one should look for attempts to provide the mechanisms that link ownership to performance. If ownership has an effect it should be possible to trace the intra-firm changes that contribute to performance developments. However, Martin and Parker (1997) argue that to date the change from state to private ownership has been advocated with surprisingly little exploration of the internal changes within the privatised companies. The literature in this field is thin. The main changes they found in the eight privatised firms studies were that goals became less blurred and more profit orientated, the bureaucratic and rule bound management became more entrepreneurial, the labour force and staffing practice became more flexible, and the organisational structure was becoming flatter. Political constraints on business development and localisation were largely removed.

Less ambiguous and more commercial goals give a clearer emphasis on profitability to be achieved by focusing on consumer needs. A private company on average will exercise greater flexibility in the organisation of work and its hiring and firing policy. This is related to a reduced role for trade unions with devolved bargaining. Organisational structures change in line with the 'structure follows strategy' doctrine. Firms in the market who adopt a diversified strategy (going into new businesses) follow up with a divisionalised structure (decentralisation of operation, centralisation of strategy/control). This is originally the American corporate model, but it is increasingly common in Europe, primarily due to the requirement to give separate responses to different markets (Stinchcombe, 1990). This implies a flattening of the organisational pyramid; devolved management: m-form instead of u-form structures and the introduction of profit centres. However other studies find no clear effect of types of ownership on corporate strategy (diversification) and structure (divisionlisation). It is not the case it seems that bank ownership and family ownership prohibits diversification. 'For strategy and structure, ownership does not matter' – that is, the firms are becoming more diversified and divisionalised anyway. With regard to the location of a business firm, privately owned firms gain greater flexibility. This facilitates expansion of the business into new areas of work and new geographical regions and acquisitions and joint ventures to support a new mission to become a global operator.

Martin and Parker also argue that it does not seem to be any simple template of internal change resulting from privatisation and that the degree of management change is less easy to summarise because of the difference in experience across the cases studied. The relationship between internal change and performance seems therefore unclear. This is also because of problems separating changes coming from change in ownership from the changes stemming from other sources, for example, technological change (1997: 202).

Throughout Europe state owned utilities have been criticised for poor performance. Partly as a consequence, their markets have been deregulated and the companies have largely been privatised. One question is whether this development is at odds with what has been regarded a societal responsibility to provide affordable utility services for all citizens. Recent reforms often labelled New Public Management have been argued to undermine public values (Fredrickson, 1996). A study of railway and telecommunications in UK, Germany and France indicates that technological development interacts with competitive pressures. The public service goals have to be secured by political interventions (Hértier, 2002).

The Nature of Ownership

The nature of ownership can be discussed by asking three short questions: Who owns; who rules; and who governs? The discussion under who owns concerns who the owners are and how we can categorise the owners acknowledging that the nature of owners makes a difference. One common distinction made here is the public-private one. The main focus under 'who rules?' is to what extent ownership policy is subject to national discretion, to what extent we see a more general professional standard (corporate governance) emerge influencing the performance of owners, and to point at the role, if any, of supranational bodies like the EU. 'Who governs' relates to the role that owners play, the exercise of ownership and whether and how this makes a difference. Relating this to the principal–agent relation set out in the previous chapter, it is not obvious that the main power base is on the side of the owner. The firm as an agent may exercise considerable influence both on the framework and on the principal.

Who Owns?

This question points to the fact that it is not irrelevant who the owner is. One of the most debated and analysed distinctions and one that is also relevant to the studies undertaken in this book, is the one between public and private owners. The basic idea here is that change in the principal makes a difference in principal–agent relations.

Owners are usually *patrons* to the company, that is, persons in a transactional relation to the firm either as suppliers (of goods or of capital) or purchasers of products (Hansmann, 1996). It is commonplace to view firms as the nexus of contracts (ref). The firm contracts with vendors, with workers, with financiers etc. Each transaction between the firm and its patrons occurs either under the logic of market contracting or by means of ownership. A firm owned by the suppliers of capital is referred to as investor owned, but it could also be regarded as a special type of a 'producer-cooperative' (Hansmann, 1996). In this case the producers are not delivering say, milk but capital. When transactions are undertaken with patrons owning the firm, control can be exercised via the firm's internal governance mechanisms. Ownership therefore, reduces the transaction costs. This points to the possibility of finding an optimal ownership structure, that is, the one that minimises transaction costs. In this case, the various costs of ownership must also be included. Ownership entails the costs of making collective decisions, the cost of monitoring, the cost of making poor decisions and the cost of bearing risks (Hansmann, 1996). These costs will obviously vary with the type of owner and the very structure of ownership.

The most frequently considered dimensions of ownership patterns are the identity of the owners and the structure of ownership. The former relates to how different groups of owners, may have different approaches to, for example, risk and strategy. A variety of owners may be identified: Listed companies can be owned by other listed companies, non-listed companies, funds, private persons, and national or foreign owners. For non-listed companies the list can be made even longer, for instance they can be owned by employees, companies owned by families, entrepreneurs, or a coalition of owners. The concentration of ownership is connected to the distribution of shares between owners. This has consequences for the owners' control incentives and potential. Mintzberg (1983) offers a typology of different features of owners and ownership. One distinction is between involvement and detachment. Owners who influence the decisions or actions of the firm are involved owners. The other distinction is between ownership concentration and dispersion. When ownership is concentrated the stocks are more closely held. The idea is that when owners are involved and ownership is concentrated, they should have more power in influencing the firm. The type of owner owning a company is assumed to have bearings on corporate strategy and therefore to have an impact on company performance (Thomsen and Pedersen, 2000).

The distribution of different types of owners varies across countries. (Pedersen and Thomsen, 1997). Family owned companies typically entail concentrated ownership and involved owners with an incentive to monitor management (Chaganti and Damanpour, 1991). One group of owners in contrast to family or individual owners is institutional ones. Examples of institutional owners are banks, insurance companies, mutual funds and pensions funds (Roe, 1994). Banks may be shareholders as well as debt holders (Li, 1994) as is often the case in Germany where banks frequently play a central role as owners. Forms of insider institutional ownership can be employee stock ownership and union funds.

Various forms of institutional ownership is growing in importance (Gillan and Starks, 2002; Bøhren and Ødegaard, 2001). Institutional owners place other demands on the company and have goals (lower debt to capital ratio, enhanced emphasis on financial performance) that diverge from other owners. Earlier it was assumed that institutional owners would not challenge management (Chaganti and Damanpour, 1991), that is, they are dispersed and detached in Mintzberg's typology. However institutional owners seem to be more active than we have thought. Institutional investors hold a higher number of shares per holding than individual investors. Such ownership of a sizeable block gives institutional investors a strategic position and is demonstrated to affect both corporate strategy and performance (Chaganti and Damanpour, 1991).

Public ownership can be regarded as a special type of institutional ownership. Across Europe and including USA, public ownership (public as largest owner, not necessarily complete public ownership) of listed companies is not very common. Only 3 per cent of 2,549 companies investigated by Thomsen, Pedersen and Strandskov (2002) are owned by the public as largest owner. However, the ownership concentration for this 3 per cent is 61 per cent as compared to 41 per cent across all cases. Ownership comes in many forms, not only on the private side but also for public ownership. While the diversification of ownership has for a long time been most visible on the private side, the diversification and sophistication of state ownership has increased substantially during the last decade. As was the case for many national industries after the War, the state no longer necessarily owns 100 per cent of these companies. Partial privatisation has resulted in minor to major state ownership for many industries, giving rise to different configurations of ownership. The way state ownership has been organised has also changed substantially: A range of new company structures has evolved. These structures can be described on a continuum from being close to the political/administrative system to having an arms-length distance to these institutions.

Who Rules?

In principle owners are supreme with regard to the company. They can hire and fire the management and they can choose to sell off the entire company if they so wish. Nevertheless, their power is not without its limitations and the rules of the game are not necessarily set by the principal. Rules that the principal has to adhere to may be set outside the competence of the principal and these rules may come in many forms: formal or informal, national or supranational, as regulations or 'hot couture'. Two such sets of institutions that will be discussed further throughout the book are competition rules and regulations. They clearly place formal constraints on the owners' behaviour and illustrate the point that rules can be established nationally or supranationally. They also show that national rules can be set up by national actors outside the control of the national principal. At the supranational level we see a more direct interest from the EU in the question of ownership. Even regarding this issue the EU seems to have ambitions of being a policy-making force. By introducing new legislation the EU aims at harmonising company law in member states and at making change in ownership smoother. This issue is particularly important as more than one-third of all companies within the EU will change owners within the next decade (Enterprise Europe, 2002). The fear is that malfunctions in the process will result in redundancies or close downs. To avoid this problem the EU has focused on how legislation, tax systems, and other factors in member states can ease changes in ownership.

Extensions and elaborations of formal rules, socially sanctioned norms of behaviour and internally enforced standards of behaviour count as informal constraints (North, 1990). The informal constraints can act as a 'logic of appropriateness', for example, Codes of conducts or conceptions of Good Governance. A set of limitation comprising both formal and informal rules is the conditions and framework for running companies, often referred to as Corporate Governance. Corporate Governance principles define the rules of the game to ensure that financiers to corporations get a return on their investments (Schleifer and Vishny, 1997). It can be defined broadly as 'the system by which companies are run' (Charkham, 1994), or more specifically as 'the institutions which determine the space of opportunity for the leadership' (Thomsen, Pedersen and Strandskov, 2002). Corporate governance principles reach from the polity level, with issues such as the level of legislative protection of minority shareholders, to informal rules recommending independent board members.

There are different systems of corporate governance. Parts of the systems are 'given' in national constitutions, legislation and culture; whereas in other areas it can be argued that the principal has a choice. The institutional context for corporate governance differs between nations but in general two different types of systems can be identified (Gedajlovic and Saphiro, 1998; Thomsen, Pedersen, and Strandskov, 2002; Jenkinson and Mayer, 1992): the UK and US model features relative passive shareholders, and 'one stringed' systems with boards not always independent of the management and no necessary employee representation on the boards, whereas the continental Europe model has more active (coalitions of) shareholders and a two-stringed system with independent boards usually with employee representation. Differences in corporate governance systems affect ownership behaviour, especially the potential to exercise control through the boards. The UK/US system restrain shareholder control but allow for greater degree of risk sharing (Jenkinson and Mayer, 1992). In these systems, therefore, we see a greater reliance on the takeover mechanism, ensuring in principal that bad performing firms are taken over by new owners replacing the management. Yet it is important to stress that this is a crude categorisation (Thomsen, Pedersen, and Strandskov, 2002). It is probably more useful to view these as ideal types that actual cases may resemble, rather than an absolute precise classification of models that can be chosen unambiguously.

The different institutional settings between nations have implications also for constraints of a more informal character. Examples of this can be differences in political and corporate culture – for example, that the Norwegian Social Democratic tradition results in a particular ownership structure for Norwegian listed companies (Bøhren and Ødegaard, 2001). The wide spread 'one share one vote' recommendation is another example. This is the convention in the UK and the US while Scandinavia and countries like Switzerland and Netherlands have high proportions of dual class shares (Jenkinson and Mayer, 1992). Yet, the recommendation has been added to the recent recommendations on good corporate governance in Norway. Still, there seems to be no unanimous research support behind this advice: 'It is unclear … whether dual-class shares act in the interest of or to the detriment of shareholders' (Jenkinson and Mayer, 1992: 5). It is tempting to regard such recommendations within the perspective of new institutional theory where emphasis is placed upon the construction, travelling and adoption of institutionalised ideas. These can be ideas about ideal ways of structuring organisations or of exercising ownership. Multinational consultancy firms' reports on corporate governance and the OECD are possible sources to these ideas. The independence of boards is another example. Despite the frequency of this recommendation there is no support in the literature that boards composed of outside, independent directors and with a separation of CEO and the Chair of the Board perform better (Daily, Dalton, and Cannella Jr, 2003).

Who Governs?

Ownership structure does not necessarily define ownership behaviour. The same owner may adopt different roles in different situations and different owners may adopt the same role in the same situation. Who owns therefore, does not necessarily define who governs. The relation between owners of the firm and the managers running the firm is regularly portrayed as an Agency Problem (Schleifer and Vishny, 1997; Jensen and Meckling, 1976). The problem arises when managers have incentives to pursue own interests at the expense of those of the owner.

The owners (shareholders) may wish to maximise the company's profit, while managers may prefer various self-interested strategies. With the separation of ownership and control, owners and managers have to contract. Given incomplete contracts, that is, that cannot cover every future unforeseen event, managers end up with discretion regarding decisions not foreseen in the contract: by this means they are allocated residual control rights (Schleifer and Vishny, 1997). Given managerial opportunism managerial discretion may lead to sub-optimal corporate performance – 'agency costs' (cf. chapter 2). The challenge of ownership in this perspective is to succeed in monitoring the behaviour of management, and owners' control problems are accentuated when ownership is dispersed. Therefore, the greater degree of stocks held by those with decision-making authority (inside ownership), the better the performance of the firm is likely to be. This is because inside owners are assumed to exercise tighter control over management. On the other hand, manager controlled firms are more likely to engage in activities that have the potential of shifting wealth from the owners to the managers (Oswald and Jahera Jr, 1991). Likewise, large owners are in a position to exercise control in that they possess both an incentive and the power to monitor effectively.

However, there is also a risk that owners which are too large might use the firm to generate private benefits.

Corporate governance mechanisms are often conceptualised as 'deterrents to managerial self-interest' (Daily, Dalton, and Cannella Jr, 2003). A simple way of putting it is that they are mechanisms which ensure that the suppliers of finance get a return on their investments (Schleifer and Vishny, 1997). Corporate control mechanisms can be divided between internal and external control (Gedajlovic and Saphiro, 1998). Internal constraints especially relate to the boards' control function exercised on behalf of the shareholders whereby the boards are given *decision control*, that is, the ratification and monitoring of decisions. Important characteristics of internal control mechanisms, therefore, are the composition and power of the boards and their relation to the owners. As an external control mechanism the market plays a significant role (Daily, Dalton, and Cannella Jr, 2003) especially in UK/US, in that, a least theoretically, it should see to that poorly performing firms are taken over. The stronger the competition, the less resources are available for managerial 'waste' (Bøhren and Ødegaard, 2001). The implication is that in a fully competitive market the managers' self-interest would be the same as the stockholders', namely to maximise the stockholders' value. However, research suggests that the market is not particularly good at identifying underperforming firms for take-over (Jenkinson and Mayer, 1992).

Owners attempting to control managerial behaviour face two groups of costs: the actual cost of conducting various forms of monitoring, and the agency costs given that the monitoring will never be fully effective (Hansmann, 1996). Monitoring costs include the cost of collecting information, the cost of communicating and the costs of bringing the decisions to bear on the management. A dispersed ownership structure therefore entails a standard collective action problem. A consequence of this is that large firms with many owners must have modest managerial opportunism costs or even higher costs under alternative ownership structures in order to balance the costs and the benefits of ownership.

The Transformation of State Ownership

Three main features of ownership can be identified in the transformation period of the telecommunications firms. They can be linked to the periods of 'the old state controlling old incumbents', a state adapting to 'modern management concepts to support modernisation of the incumbents', and a 'state providing openings for new owners in order to adapt to new market demands'. These categories must be understood as 'ideal-types'. As an analytical concept, ideal-types are not found in pure form, but empirical examples will resemble them to a greater or lesser degree so that, empirically, the categories can be seen as continuums. The analysis of the transformation processes, therefore, requires that we not only identify the role and impact of ownership in each of the transformation periods, but also that we understand the spill-over effect between them.

Table 3.1 Ideal-types of ownership in telecommunications

	Who owns? Owner identity and ownership structure	**Who rules? Ownership rules, norms and 'institutions'**	**Who governs? Ownership behaviour and amount of control**
State as traditional owner	*The state*	*Political values – 'stakeholder governance'*	*'Society'*
State as 'professional' owner	*The 'professional' state*	*Emerging 'shareholder governance'*	*General assembly i.e. head of ministry Regulations*
Shared ownership	*More or less dispersed ownership*	*Financial performance – 'shareholder governance'*	*General assembly, Boards of directors Competition policy?*

The State as Traditional Owner

In the telecommunications industry under traditional state ownership the government's ownership interests were typically anchored within a sector ministry. The question 'who owns?' seems easily answered. This was not necessarily the case for all major industries. It is vital to bear in mind that other industrial ownership structures were being used. Private ownership existed alongside state ownership in most countries but not as a joint ownership concept. Also, within telecommunications sector private companies played a role in early phases. However, although some private companies were operating as late as in the 1970s, the industry was effectively a state matter with the telecommunications administration integrated in the departmental structure.

Who rules, under traditional state ownership? Being the sole owner of a company the government faces few formal restrictions on possible actions towards the company and . The general assembly (the minister) is the only required link between the government and the company. This is far from the optimal point for a firm's performance as recommended in the corporate governance literature. This holds even if we turn the argument round and view state ownership as extremely dispersed, namely to all citizens. In practice, however, the singular ministry as an owner reduces the costs of ownership because of the absence of the need for owner coordination.

From an ownership point of view, in telecommunications the integrated model where services are being produced as a part of the administration resembles a model with an ownership concentration of 100 per cent. The pivotal point to stress here is that these are models where it is possible to take care of various political interests through instruction in the hierarchy or as general assembly. It is reasonable to use the label 'stakeholder governance', as national interests, employment and sector concerns may well enter the decision-making processes. For instance, state ownership was seen as a prerequisite for securing national control with key industrial companies. Giving the citizens equal access to services was a national concern too important to be left to the market. The ownership institutions – the norms, principles and procedures for ownership behaviour –are therefore infused with political values (Selznick, 1966 [1949]). This could be seen as analogue to dominant owner abuse: the company is used to pursue private goals (or rather public ones in the case of state owned corporations).

Attempts to develop an overall and viable ownership policy have been on the agenda of the state as owner for a long time. However, developing such a policy faced state owners with a substantial range of challenges and dilemmas: First, being both the one setting out the rules of the game and an owner, raised the question of how to separate the various roles as politicians, owners, and regulators? To each of these roles different tasks are legitimate and potentially important. Further, as there are many options it is difficult for a state owner to decide which objectives should be put in the same basket as state ownership. Should ownership of these industries mainly be used to secure the welfare state because the performance and development of these industries has an indisputable impact on the distribution of welfare to the citizens? These industries were also of vital importance in securing overall policy goals as keeping the unemployment as low as possible. Employment issues were therefore considered both legitimate and relevant considerations for the principal in designing and performing an ownership policy. It is also interesting to see that developing an overall ownership policy has represented a substantial challenge for states not only in modern times, but from the time long before deregulation and liberalisation of key industries. In many states a range of committees providing a huge number of reports have dealt with this problem, frequently resulting in no clear-cut policy. Being an owner has never lacked the component of ambiguity. This can be seen in terms of what the role or the main goals should be or in terms of which tasks to prioritise in order to achieve these goals.

Who governs then, under traditional state ownership? The questions relates to the actual ownership behaviour. Which parties are potential influential, and what amount of control do they possess (Christensen and Pallesen, 2001)? In economic theories of the firm the owners' right to claim earnings gives them an incentive to exercise control. In practice, however, the right to control is often restricted to electing board members and voting on fundamental issues. The boards thus assume a pivotal role in controlling the company. In state owned corporations in Norway boards have a more restricted role. Part of the competence that boards hold in private companies is kept by the general assembly (that is, the minister) and the parliament (Statskonsult, 1998a). For state owned companies the general assembly elects the board and is not constrained by the board's proposal to dividend. A special requirement in Norway is that no public servants sit on the boards. A consequence is presumably that the ownership becomes less active since the owner has no direct representation in the corporations' boards.

Even though the government owner is clearly dominant and potentially omnipotent, it would be misleading to see the actual conduct of ownership as isolated from the companies. Public sector decision-making has long since been characterised as a process of 'muddling through', indicating that processes of negotiations and mutual adjustments are more typical than top-down instructions. In Norway one main discussion has been the appropriate amount of autonomy granted to companies and the model has regularly been one of loose coupling between owner and company. Evidently, the companies have also known how to manoeuvre within and exploit this established framework (Byrkjeland and Langeland, 2000:31). One point to stress therefore is that even where the state is sole owner it is not necessarily the one exercising extensive control.

The Professionalisation of State Ownership

The 1990s witnessed a growing awareness of the importance of corporate governance principles for state owned companies. As discussed above, the literature on corporate governance stresses how active ownership promotes company performance by reducing managerial-induced agency costs. If the state is required by law to be a single owner, a change in ownership structure is not a candidate for strengthening incentives for ownership control. Still, under the heading 'who rules?' there is evidence that a shift in this situation is under way. Guidelines from the OECD and national spin-offs from these emphasise active and professional ownership policy. Predominantly ownership policy is supposed to take care of company concerns, and 'shareholder value' as opposed to 'stakeholder value' can be seen gradually emerging. Other political goals are largely no longer warranted. It is naturally to see the gradual switch of ownership anchoring outside sector ministries in this perspective. Company boards of directors take on greater importance in the discourse with company autonomy again being the issue, only this time in a slightly different wrapping. Decoupling from the political system is the crucial aspect and attempts to employ new methods for control are visible. Still, we do not see a totally coherent ownership policy. The approach in many cases is making policy on a case-to-case basis.

To the question of 'who governs?' the main point that needs to be stressed is the increasing importance of regulations. First, being effectively cut-off from fulfilling societal goals through the companies, government must rely on regulatory devices, and the obligation of universal service delivery to the largest telecommunications company is one such example. Further, as at this time the market is being opened up to competitors, regulations are required to secure equal access to the infrastructure, especially as in many places the fixed line network is still under the control of the previous monopoly producer. The 'Open Network Provision' thus serves a basis for a liberalised market (Eliassen, Monsen, and Sitter, 2003). When government employs regulatory agencies as agents, this exposes a further potential target for companies seeking to influence. The companies must be assumed to have interests in the way the regulatory regime is designed. Occurrences of 'regulatory capture', that is, that those who are regulated dominate the regulator, is a not uncommon finding in the literature. Still under professionalised ownership the telecommunications companies may be assumed to participate as governance actors.

Shared Ownership: The Consequences of Introducing Private Owners

From a slow start in the early 1990s, by the year 2000 all the incumbent telecommunications operators in Western Europe (except Luxembourg) were partly or fully privatised (Monsen, 2004: appendix V). Theoretically the move from 1 to >1 owner with as little as 1 share sold is fundamental. When multiple owners are introduced issues of investor protection and questions concerning dual-class shares take prominence. The cost of ownership increases, however, because owner coordination might become an issue.

Privatisation and possible stock exchange listing again changes 'who rules' in that shareholder value becomes the foremost concern: Private stockholders are supposed to have clearer incentives to engage in active controlling of the company. Further it will be expected to put a definite end to political values in the ownership policy. In Norway a manifestation of this is the removal of the special provisions for companies that are 100 per cent state owned. These provisions were potential political veto-points to the company decision-making processes. Also the composition and the role of the board may take on a different form and significance. What we see, therefore, is a framework for the company promoting even more business-orientation.

Who governs the company is again not clear-cut. At the outset this is obviously a question of ownership structure. In many but far from all cases the government proves reluctant to sell out. Control can be retained in the form of a substantial block or as a 'golden share'. Private owners may have interests that deviate from the government. Whether these interests influence company behaviour depends on factors such as block-holder size and coordination abilities. The political system still possesses powers and possibilities to control and correct company behaviour. Sector regulation is so far maintained and even more general regulation in the form of competition policy is a potential source of influence.

Ownership: All About Politics?

The question raised in this section is whether the point of departure adopted by a substantial part of the literature on ownership is too narrow to capture the nature and effect of ownership: how it is exercised and its effects on organisational behaviour. Portraying ownership in economic terms of designing effective institutions capable of controlling firms' management does not capture the ambiguity of the role and the effect of state ownership in different periods. The approach in this chapter, that is, focusing on 'who owns', 'who rules' and 'who governs', underlines the intricacy of ownership. This has been pointed out elsewhere: Whereas economic theory would suggest one ownership structure as being best for a given industry (Hansmann, 1996), experience shows that, 'there is more than one way of dealing with these economic problems. And the differences suggest that differing histories, cultures and paths of economic development better explain the differing structures than economic theory alone' (Roe, 1994). European ownership structures differ even when controlled for 'firm-size effects' and 'industry effect' (Pedersen and Thomsen, 1997). Hence, the institutional setting of ownership should be acknowledged. The subsequent discussion will touch upon three questions regarding 'professional state ownership', 'shareholder value', and the implementation of ownership.

The quest for a professional state ownership is regularly a quest for predictability, clarity and stability. The dividend policy has to be predictable, the framework and decision-making processes must be clear and transparent, and the objectives must be relatively stable across time. The nature of politics is, however, mostly about the opposite: adjust and define situations to changing political aims and ambitions, keep the back door open for changes in standpoints, and make compromise decisions under uncertainty. The distance between expectations of the public sector and its capacity to deliver is sometimes substantial. The politics of liberalisation and deregulation also divides political opinion. Although in many countries, this is not a clear-cut left-right dimension, it is a divide between those wanting to increase the speed of liberalisation and those wanting to slow it down or even reverse it. The question of the development, transformation and privatisation of the incumbent telecommunications operators is at the core of this discussion. Hence, differences in views on the pace and direction of telecommunications politics will be taken out on issues related to the development of the incumbents. How ownership is performed will reflect the political situation and the need for reaching compromises and negotiated solutions. In addition, politics has to adhere to certain rules of the game, be they related to issues of distribution across interest groups, cultural issues such as language groups, or gender issues. Accordingly, ownership is often more about politics than about anything else. Politicians need to take into consideration the preferences of the electorate and groups of stakeholders; employees, unions and customers and competitors.

The transformation of the incumbents attracts politics: What will be the legal status of the companies? Who should own it? How will the prices and the distribution of services be affected? What will be the role of the company within the national industrial policy? What consequences will it have for the employees, particularly for 'weak' groups such as women in peripheral areas? The examples should be sufficient to illustrate why politicians become involved. Accordingly it is fair to argue that lack of a professional ownership, argued to be a trademark of state ownership, has less to do with the ability or willingness of the state owner and more to do with the fact that it is different from private ownership. The fact that the owner is the state over a long period does not imply that ownership is similar and stable across cases and over time. This should be acknowledged. Inquiries into the various types of ownership demonstrate the significance of owner identity and ownership structure. However, state ownership tends to be treated as a homogenous category, for example, as a special type of institutional ownership.

Throughout the period covered, we observe a development in ownership. The principal's interests shift, initially from broader societal concerns towards establishing conditions for business-development, and further when privatisation happens, towards 'normal business' with shareholder value as the dominant principle. This gives an illustration of the ambiguity of the principal-agent logic as advocated in chapter 2. Principals can have more and conflicting interests and they can be diffuse and irrational. It is not necessarily the case that it is the principal that sets up ex ante specifications of the task that shall be undertaken. It seems plausible that in the process of corporatisation the principals' interests adapt to those of the agent to some extent. The development of the industry and the companies may require the principal to establish new institutions such as the establishment of private-law companies which can be seen as a 'credible commitment' (Miller, 2005) from the principal. The setting up of formal governance structures hinders politicians' aspirations to 'exploit' the company for political objectives. Hence, in addition to the well-established findings that ownership matters for firm performance, it has been argued that ownership also matters in the sense that it defines conditions under which the transformation of the telecommunications companies occurs. This becomes clear in the country studies in chapters 6–10.

Chapter 4

The Political and Regulatory Framework towards a European Information and Knowledge Society

Caroline Pauwels and Simon Delaere

Introduction[1]

This chapter discusses the changes in the overall political and regulatory framework towards the creation of a European Information and Knowledge society. Its focus is on the EU as a Principal political driving force behind the transformations the ICT sector went through from the 1980s onwards, encompassing both the audiovisual and telecommunications sector. It describes the EU Principal as a set of both competing and collaborating institutions (Council of Ministers, Directorates-General, Court of Justice, Parliament ...) with a complex and not always consistent policy outcome as a result. EU policy making in telecoms and audiovisual matters should be viewed in dialectics with, on the one hand, member-states reluctant towards EU interference in sectors they consider of major economic and cultural importance and, on the other hand, global political arenas such as the WTO pushing for more liberalisation in both the telecoms and audiovisual sectors. This EU policy is therefore stuck in the middle of a give and take game of multilevel governance, with its inherent conflicts of interest, unexpected coalitions and admitted adversaries. As Rifkin quite eloquently points out:

> The EU is the first transnational government in history whose regulatory powers supersede the territorial powers and the members that make it up. This fact alone marks a new chapter in the nature of governance. The EU's very legitimacy lies not in the control of territory or the ability to tax its citizens or mobilize policy or the military force to exact obedience but, rather, in a code of conduct, conditioned by universal human rights and operationalised through statutes, regulations, and directives and, most important, by a continuous process of engagement, discourse, and negotiation with multiple players operating at the local, regional, national, transnational, and global levels. (Rifkin, 2003: 29)

---

1 Some sections of this chapter are based on Eliassen, Monsen and Sitter 2003.

In this chapter we first provide an overview of the actors involved in policy-making at EU level, the rationale behind their actions and the means they have to implement an overall policy framework. Secondly, we will provide an overview of the different initiatives taken so far. In order to provide a coherent analysis, we will distinguish three complementary but often also conflicting periods. The first is qualified as the deregulatory period, with an emphasis on sector-specific liberalisation, standardisation and harmonisation initiatives (1985–1999). We identify the leitmotiv of this period to be 'as free as possible'. Subsequently, as the establishment of the single market and technological changes provoked increasing degrees of concentration and convergence in the media and telecommunications markets, a second, overlapping period commenced in which overall competition and antitrust policy became extensively used to complement and readjust the former sector specific liberalisation and harmonisation initiatives (1990–2000). The rationale during this period is qualified as 'as big as possible versus generic antitrust policy', indicating the two conflicting tendencies that mark this period. Subsequently, we describe a third period – 'as rational as possible' – crucial in this period is the introduction of a number of remedies to the inefficiencies of former regulatory approaches, which had become obvious in both telecoms and broadcasting, and which were responded to by attempts to decentralise policy to the level of the nation states, and to adjust overall competition policies and principles to sector specific conditions (1999–). The balancing of overall competition policy and sector-specific regulations on the one hand, and of overall EU and specific Member States' initiatives on the other, seems to be the outcome of this third period. Moreover, the initiatives taken in this period were framed within an overall trend towards digital convergence: from then onwards, the regulatory framework would no longer focus on telecommunications, ICT or media as separate worlds, but instead on the broad category of electronic communications. In other words, the broadening of the regulatory scope to that of electronic communications was combined with – and in a way, countered by – the horizontal introduction of a specific implementation of EU competition policy to this new sector: the new regulatory framework for electronic networks and services. Meanwhile, the Lisbon Summit in 2000 made the realisation of a European Knowledge society the new paradigm, as well as the driving force behind EU policy for both telecoms and audiovisual sectors. This is again highlighted in the recent EU Communication of June 2005, *i2010 – A European Information Society for Growth and Employment* (COM 2005).

In a final, third point we will raise some conclusions and insights stemming from the overall analysis. In summary, this chapter aims at providing an answer to Murdoch's political-economy questionnaire: 1) what happened, why then, why there and who made it happen; 2) what does it mean for all actors and factors involved; and 3) was it, in the end, a good or a bad thing?

From Rhetoric to Practice: EU Policy in the Making

The first report on the European Information society dates back to 1979 (Schneider and Werle, 1990); however it was not until the White Paper of 1985 that the creation of a common market for broadcasting and telecommunications was described as an urgent matter for the EU. The reasoning at that time was that the European dimension could offer these sectors new prospects for growth and competitiveness. In turn, these sectors could contribute to the realisation of a European dimension in other economic sectors, such as micro-electronics, consumer electronics, advertising etc. However, a lack of concerted action and national fragmentation was perceived to prevent this economic potential to be fully realised, leading to rhetoric concerning the 'cost of non-Europe' as calculated in different sectors by the Cecchini report (Cecchini, 1988).

European action was thus necessary, particularly in view of the economic and cultural threats increasingly posed by Japan and America in all software and hardware domains. If Europe was not to miss the boat as regards Information Society benefits, then concerted action was deemed to be absolutely necessary. This message was repeated in the Green Papers on TV (COM 1984) and on Telecommunications (COM 1987). It was expressed again in two important publications, which were supposed to put Europe on track for the Information Society – namely the 1993 White Paper on competitiveness, employment and growth (COM 1993) and the Bangemann report on the Information Society, published in 1994. In the meanwhile, the Single European Act and the Maastricht Treaty came into force, enlarging EU competences as well as facilitating EU decision making with the view of realising an internal market before 1993. Subsequently, the Lisbon summit of March 2000 labelled this whole process as eEurope, indicating a trend towards looking at the Information and Knowledge Society from a societal rather than a mere technological point of view (Pauwels and Burgelman, 2003). This message was reiterated just recently in the Communication on *i2010* (COM 2005).

When considering these documents as important political milestones, one should be aware that over the years discourse vacillated continuously between boom and doom scenarios, with a clear emphasis on the economic and cultural opportunities to be grasped. Significantly, The Lisbon Summit in 2000 made the realisation of a European knowledge society the new paradigm, as well as the driving force behind EU policy for both telecoms and audiovisual sectors. With eEurope, the discussion on what kind of Information Society Europe wants to develop was, to a significant degree, no longer exclusively technologically driven, as it had been at the beginning.

EU policy, which aimed at the realisation of an internal market in telecommunications and audiovisual networks and services, encompassed both negative integration, that is, the breaking down of existing national regulations that form an obstacle to European unification, and positive integration, that is, the creation of the EU's own community-wide regulations and policy. The latter meant that certain matters had to be withdrawn from the domain of autonomous national policy. This resulted in the adoption of a battery of Directives (secondary Community Law) that have liberalised, harmonised and standardised the production and distribution of both the hardware and software sectors. In addition, action was taken on stimulation programmes in the form of a community industrial and innovation policy that was intended to support, among other things, the production of broadcasting and telecommunications equipment, infrastructure and content. These are or often were prestigious industrial programs such as Race, the action plan relating to HDTV or even the more culturally inspired and – when compared to the previous two – largely underfinanced Media programme (Measures to Encourage the Development of an Audiovisual Industry in Europe) or e-Content programme. Moreover, at the crossroads of policy-making a very important role is attributed to overall competition policy trying to find a fragile equilibrium between economic and more societal objectives. By way of summary, an inventory of relevant EU initiatives aimed at both software and hardware, as well as production and distribution issues in the telecommunications and the audiovisual domain may be schematised as follows:

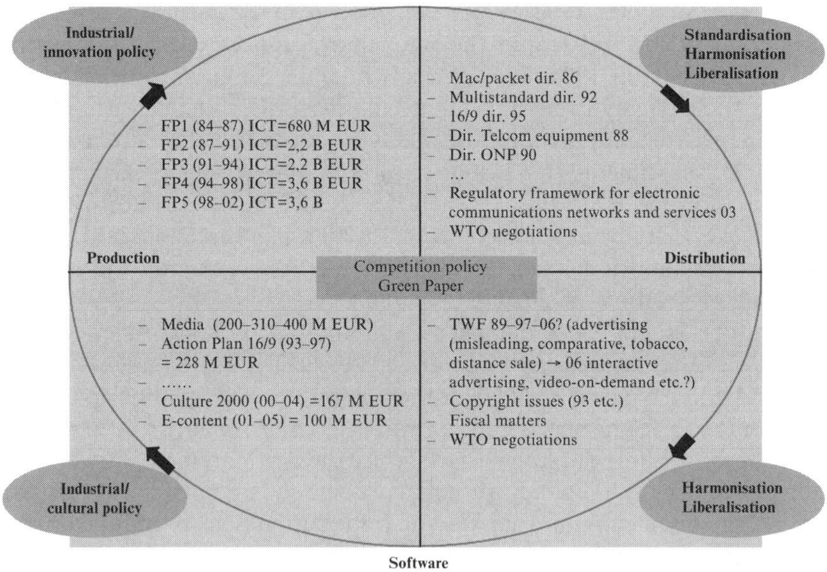

Figure 4.1 EU initiatives in telecommunications

The process of completing the Single European market and liberalising protected sectors such as telecoms or broadcasting has been anything but even or uniform, whether evaluated across the last two decades or comparing the relevant sectors.

In both cases it has involved a complex triangle of competing and, at some times, collaborating actors, that is, Commission, Court of Justice (ECJ) and the Member States, represented in the Council of Ministers (Figure 4.2):

- the *Court of Justice*, responsible for upholding EU law (implementation, compliance and interpretation). As a general rule, the EU institutions, and the ECJ in particular, apply the principle of 'free movement, no aid'. This ruling has a broad application, and exceptions are granted only restrictively by the ECJ. Furthermore, ECJ rulings are consistently framed within the overall aim of establishing an internal market. On several occasions, Court rulings have therefore been interpreted as 'communitarian fundamentalism' by Member States, individual actors etc. The 2005 Austrian Presidency, for example, raised criticism on the European Court of Justice (ECJ) for systematically expanding EU powers through its rulings (Beunderman, 2006). Indeed it needs to be said that, in the audiovisual as well as the telecommunications domain, ECJ rulings have very often smoothened the path for expanding EU activities in these areas. In broadcasting, the Sacchi ruling is a clear example of such a case; as for telecommunications, the ECJ intervened quite fundamentally in its ruling of March 1991.[2] In this case, France and other Member States (Italy, Spain, Belgium ...) had accused the Commission of making unlawful use of former art. 90 (now art. 86) for pushing ahead liberalisation in the telecoms sector.[3] The Member States argued that this was an infringement of their exclusive powers in the telecommunications domain and an unacceptable intermingling into the national monopolies of their telecommunications operators. The ECJ, however, followed the Commission's argumentation, thereby creating an important legal precedent. Later on (ruling of November 1992), the ECJ applied the same line of reasoning concerning the use of art. 90 for opening up the telecommunications services sector to competition. These different rulings confirm an analysis made by Homet: 'The West European judiciary does not participate routinely in the declaration or elaboration of national communications policy. They are not called upon, as are their American counterparts, to review on a regular basis the rules and decisions adapted by an independent regulatory agency. But when they do enter the area, it can be in a very important way' (Homet, 1979: 12–13).
- the *Commission*: with several amendments brought to the Treaties over the years (expansion of competencies, increased voting under qualified majority instead of unanimity ...), we have witnessed systematic attempts by the Commission to widen its powers. At the same time, however, reluctant Member States have just as consistently attempted to prevent the Commission from doing so. Also, the Commission's competencies are quite fragmented: EU policy making in both telecoms and broadcasting involves a wide range of

---

2 Judgment of 19/03/1991, France/Commission (Rec.1991,p. I–1223).

3 To be particular, the case concerned telecommunications equipment.

directorates-general as diverse as DG trade, DG Information Society and Media, DG consumer protection, DG education and culture, DG internal market and services, DG competition, DG research and others. All these DGs find their legitimacy in the treaties, although some can weigh more heavily on the decision making process than others. For example, whereas DG culture, due to a limited legal basis, has little leverage power, the opposite is true for DG competition. Contrary to some other policy domains, The Commission has indeed been given major competencies in the competition field, often against the will of the Member States. It is responsible for the implementation of the competition policy and can act on its own initiative or after a complaint by a private actor or a Member State. The Commission as such fulfils the role of executor, judge and even legislator, and can take decisions without interference by the European Parliament or the Council of Ministers.

- the *Member States*, through the Council of Ministers, have championed and attempted to derail liberalisation while opposing increased EU interference in domains they consider of strategic national importance, be it for economic, cultural, social, political or other reasons. Firstly, the Member States have been given a role in the Commission's legislative procedure through the system of *comitology*: as in other sectors, telecommunication policy is continuously monitored and adjusted by Member States (for example, through the Communications Committee, the Telecommunications Conformity Assessment and Market Surveillance Committee, the Radio Spectrum Committee and other groups such as the Radio Spectrum Policy Group and the European Regulators Group) before it is even converted to legislation. Secondly, to accommodate pressure from the Member States wishing to reserve some control over their own policies, the EU institutionalised the principle of subsidiarity with the Maastricht Treaty. This has resulted in the extensive use of directives as an EU legal instrument; a directive is, after all, binding in respect of the result but allows Member States to choose the means by which they achieve this result. This contrasts with a restricted use of Regulations, which need to be adopted in their entirety and leave no room for manoeuvre whatsoever. In this context, it is important to mention the existence of a much contested *Merger Regulation* in competition law, on which we shall elaborate below. Although an increased use of directives -apparent for example in the new regulatory framework for electronic networks and services, of which the core legislative body mainly consists of directives- was the only way to draw in reluctant states, it also leads to a situation in which the Member States regard Community legislation as a sort of *à la carte* system. This allows them to defend national interests both a priori, having the last word when introducing primary and secondary Community legislation, and a posteriori, when it comes to the often ambivalent and challengeable implementation and interpretation process. As a consequence, although economically unified, the internal market still is legally fragmented to an important degree.

Around this complex policy triangle, pressure comes from a large number of varying stakeholders and agents: the European Parliament, utilities and public services of general economic interest clamouring for protection, industry supporting liberalisation, civil society opposing it, and, in the end, WTO pushing for mere liberalisation:

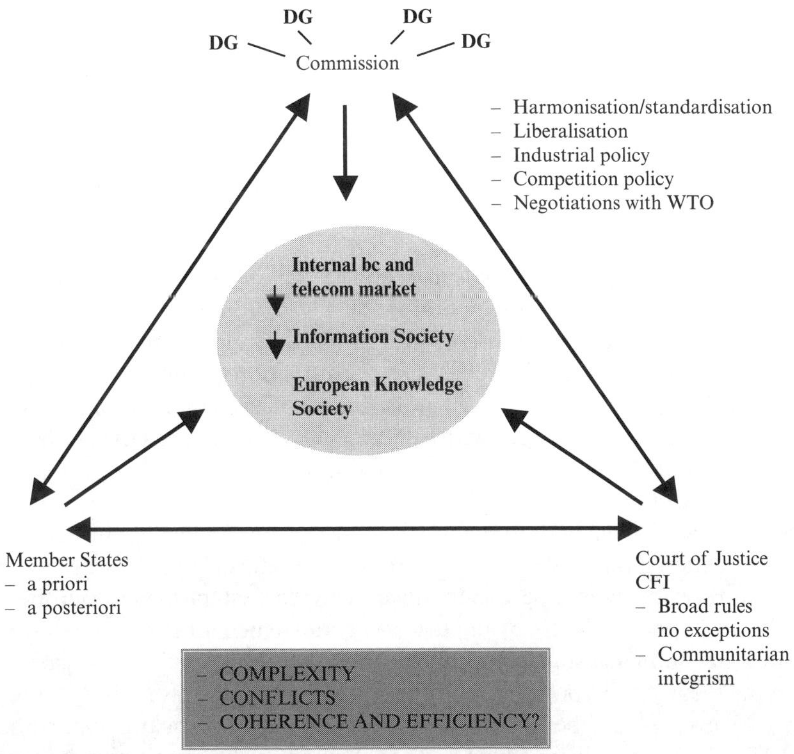

Figure 4.2 Stakeholders to the liberalisation process

It may come as no surprise that, in this complex decision-making process, the policy outcome is sometimes unexpected, often conflicting and seldom coherent or consistent. Moreover policy shifts may occur at all times, depending on the issues under scrutiny and the interests at stake. For what telecommunications is concerned, three periods, overlapping at some moments, and subsequent policy foci may be distinguished between the 1980s and 2005.

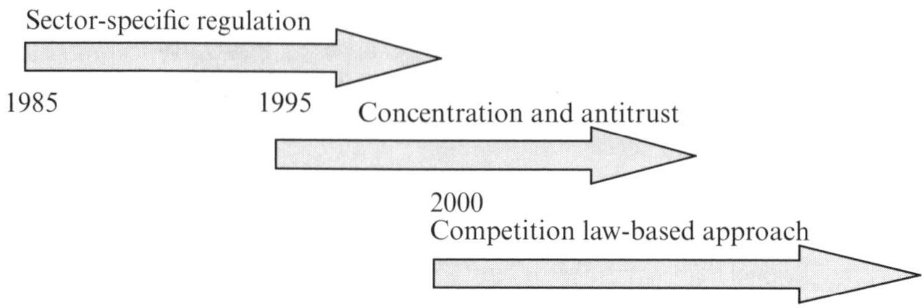

Figure 4.3 Developments in regulation

EU Policy-making in Telecoms and Broadcasting (1985–1999): *As Free as Possible*

The central characteristic of West European telecoms markets before liberalisation was the state-owned monopoly operator. This was broadly justified in terms of remedying market failures and constituting natural monopolies, though their history generally reflected the states' concerns to appropriate monopoly profits (dating back to pre-industrial postal monopolies). These single national vertically integrated monopolies, charged with fulfilling public policy objectives rather than pursuit of profit, provided formidable lobbyists against liberalisation. Inasmuch as technical equipment was supplied by a select group of privileged contractors, these added a third element to the protectionist cartel. Following the depression of the seventies, a rationale for the creation of an internal market where people, goods and services would be able to move freely, was established in Europe. The 1985 White Paper (COM 1986) and the 1987 endorsement of the Single European Act was the landmark starting points for this evolution, which would from then on be the focus of EU policies. As a specific, converging sector with great gains to be achieved from liberalisation and with equally significant opportunities for EU policy overspill in other sectors such as micro-electronics, consumer electronics, advertising etc., the telecommunications and audiovisual domain was a prime target for this move toward liberalisation starting from national monopolies (Pauwels and Burgelman, 2003). Furthermore, an 'electronic alliance' of large corporate users, multinational companies and IT equipment suppliers was increasing in importance and provided a central ally for the Commission (Davies, 1994). Come 1980, the Member States and the Commission thus found themselves under growing pressure to investigate avenues for liberalisation, from both domestic and multinational actors, despite the utilities' objections.

The initial focus on liberalisation of telecoms under Commissioner Davignon in 1979 almost coincided with Thatcher's call for telecoms liberalisation in UK opposition in 1978. By the mid-1980s this was affecting the balance of power in favour of privatisation and deregulation. Around the same time, the illustrious government-incited AT&T divestiture operation came to a close in the US, bringing an end to nearly a century of telecommunications monopoly and opening up competition in the long distance, manufacturing and R&D markets. In Europe, Davignon's calls for liberalisation were echoed by the Council of Ministers non-binding recommendation in 1984. By 1987, in the wake of the Single European Act, the Commission issued a Green Paper that would become the basis for all subsequent reform. It marked the point of departure for the liberalisation and for systematic EU legislation, deliberately starting with those parts of the value chain that caused the least controversy within the Member States. This way, a subsequent liberalisation of terminals, services and finally networks, would progressively be achieved with support from the Member State governments in principle, even if its specific directives would attract some opposition. The initial strategy was, however, not to use legislation to regulate the sector, but to progressively apply a competition and liberalisation policy, to encourage harmonisation of networks and equipment through the European standardisation institutions, to promote R&D cooperation through national and EU research programmes and to build networks of support for liberalisation (Héritier 1999). The Green Paper thus marked an important step in the Commission's drive to make Member States aware of the benefits of and need for gradual liberalisation, harmonisation and standardisation. It called for minimal changes to the status of the PTTs, which were separated from regulators but could remain as public bodies and retain their monopoly on basic telephone networks and infrastructure. This was in accordance with views of almost all the Member State policy review bodies, and demonstrated that the states were not yet ready to surrender the monopolistic position on basic services, nor be bounced into the kind of privatisation measures introduced in Britain and the USA. The Commission therefore sought to open the market to competition in all but 'reserved services' (effectively voice transmissions) (see Eliassen, Monsen and Sitter, 2003). Two directives were introduced, a first on terminal equipment in 1988 (88/301/EEC) and a second on value-added network services (90/388/EEC) in 1990. Both were issued unilaterally by the Commission under article 86[ex-90]. This was the first time this competition policy measure, which empowers the Commission to issue directives without the approval of the Council or Parliament, was used, and it would inevitably be controversial. During this period the principal opposition to the Commission's drive for liberalisation came from the more protectionist or interventionist Member States, led by France and Spain with Italy, Greece, and Belgium and, to a lesser extent, Germany (Schmidt, 1998). Another directive opened the market for terminal equipment, obliging the states to abolish all telecommunications operators' 'exclusive rights' regarding use and marketing of this equipment, to ensure that private suppliers could participate in the market and that users would have access to new public network termination points. Several states challenged the Commission's actions, resulting in a 30-month legal process that ended up in the Commission's favour. Yet from the mid-1990s the Member States would offer much more wholehearted support for liberalisation. In this context, the partial liberalisation could indeed evolve toward full opening of the markets (that is, including voice transmissions) with the Commission's 1993 Telecoms Review. This emphasised the EU context as the driver behind complete liberalisation and a requirement for a fully functioning competitive internal market. The new regime was laid down in the ONP Interconnection Directive (97/33/EC), passed in 1997. This replaced the concept of the monopoly network operator with the idea of many competing public network operators. The Commission emphasised the rights and duties of these operators, citing unfettered market and network access at transparent, equitable and non-discriminatory prices, and the obligation to guarantee universal service. The second crucial requirement for this new regime was the separation of market regulation and service provision, to ensure transparency. The 1997 ONP directive (97/51/EC) therefore demanded the establishment of a National Regulatory Authority (NRA) independent from industry and politics, which in most cases has resulted in an independent agency.

In the meanwhile, the Commission had also begun to shift its focus from 'old' telecommunications policies to broader questions of regulation of Information and Communication Technologies (ICT). Furthermore, the liberalisation of the audiovisual sector had come into effect with the adoption of the directive Television without Frontiers in October 1989, complemented with a battery of directives on copyright issues and sustained with industrial programs such as the Media program adopted in 1990. Furthermore programs such as RACE, EU95 (established in 1986) or the Action Plan 16/9 tried to clear the path towards ISDN and High Definition television and associated equipment and infrastructures in which HDTV applications (alongside the transport of data and voice) would play an important role. Also a Green Paper on satellite communications (COM 1990), designed to establish a more flexible regulatory system and foster the growth of these services, was issued in 1990, resulting in the related directive being adopted four years later (94/46/EC). A directive extending competition to alternative networks (including cable) followed in 1995 (95/51/EC). Instead of the initial idea of a single ISDN, the idea of competing networks, technologies and services gained ground all over Europe.

These evolutions offer a good example of the difficulties involved in separating regulation and operation of services in a sector with a multitude of actors. Regarding distribution of televised programmes, the regulatory authority lies with the nation states, whereas access to the means of satellite communications was organised through international organisations such as Eutelsat, Intelsat and Inmarsat. This 'institutional confusion' resembles the one found later with the convergence between IT services and telecommunications, where different providers, regulators and politicians which had been concentrating on their special segments (public broadcasting, newspapers, private one-to-one telecommunications) met in an attempt to form common policies. The shift in EU regulatory efforts from telecommunications policies to ICT policies brought many of the differences in the European regulatory regimes to the surface.

It must be noted that despite its long gestation period, the opening of telecommunications and audiovisual markets remained ambivalent. Many states sought derogations: some evoked cultural reasons for not opening up their audiovisual markets, whilst others were claiming that their industries were simply not ready to liberalise. Some of these derogations were granted: nevertheless, the most visible effect of liberalisation has been the proliferation of new actors in the markets. In the audiovisual sector, aside an explosion of commercial broadcasting channels, independent production houses also developed rather chaotically. In telecommunications, small firms have been given the chance to compete with the previously dominant operators, and many were taking the opportunity to undercut the larger operators and offer new and innovative services such as combined entertainment-internet-telephony applications. The mobile market in particular has seen an explosion in the number of companies bidding for licences and providing services. Moreover, operators tried expanding across borders, forming joint ventures and alliances abroad. Technological evolutions at the same time pushed for vertical and horizontal media and telecommunications integration, as well as ongoing digital convergence. This trend towards far reaching economic concentration and integration of the communications industry, as a consequence, led to a second, parallel phase in EU policy making, where overall EU competition policy came to supplement sector-specific liberalisation efforts and largely shaped the ICT related industries (Pauwels and Burgelman, 2003).

Conglomerates and Cartels: *As Big as Possible* (1990–2000) versus Generic Antitrust Policy

> The market is a jungle. It is nonsense to believe that the companies are going to stick to the rules on their own initiative (...) the more liberal the market, the more government control is necessary. (EU Commissioner for Competition Van Miert, quoted in De Morgen, 4 February 1998: 14)

Next to sector-specific policy-making specifically targeted at introducing competition in both telecoms and broadcasting, whether through the establishment of a legal framework or the set-up of tailored support programmes, general EU competition policy has had to intervene quite intensively since the late 1980s.

Alliances, mergers and take-overs indeed led to an increasing concentration of the audiovisual and telecommunications related sectors from the 1980s onwards, coupled with a transnationalisation of the sector. From the mid-1990s, the convergence between the telecommunications, media and information technology sectors amplified this evolution even more, which culminated in the birth of two spectacular media titans at the beginning of the twenty-first century (that is, AOL Time Warner and Vivendi Canal Plus, both formed in 2000). Even though some alliances tend to misfire, usually leading to a renewed focus on core activities, and the concentration boom seems to have passed its peak in the year 2000 due to economic recession and the dotcom bubble burst, there is no doubt that the integration of telecommunications, cable, film, programme packaging, and consumer electronics industries is here to stay (Mansell, 1993; Noam and Kramer, 1994; Noam, 1996). Furthermore, the fact that incumbents, be it the telecommunications incumbents or the national public service broadcasters, still hold dominant positions in their national markets, and therefore effectively undermine competition, increases the importance of antitrust policy.

EU competition policy has some particular characteristics. Firstly, it is used as a means to promote and protect market integration between the different Member States. Secondly, it is targeted at market distortions arising from the behaviour of private actors, but also of the Member States themselves. Thirdly, it has to be situated within the multi-level political system encompassing the EU institutions and the different Member States. Indeed, both the economy versus culture and the supranationality versus subsidiarity fields of tension are firmly part of the context in which EU competition policy is given shape. This is to say, EU competition regulation is a policy area where considerations related to trade and competition affect traditional national cultural priorities and measures in a way which goes far beyond cultural policy. The EU Commission has, contrary to some other policy domains, been given many competencies in this field, often against the will of the Member States: it is responsible for the implementation of the competition policy and can act on its own initiative or after a complaint by a private actor or a Member State. The Commission as such fulfils the role of executor, judge and even legislator, and can take decisions without interference by the European Parliament or the Council of Ministers. Next to the Commission, the European Court of Justice is an important actor as well, as a court of appeal for Commission decisions in these matters, and for prejudicial questions. As a result of the confrontation between different fields of tension, the interference of the EU through competition policy regulation has often been controversial. When considering the EU's competition and anti-trust policy-making, we have to take into account that it is wedged in between two conflicting tasks: establishing an internal open market and striving not to hinder the activities of large-scale groups on the one hand, and ensuring diversity, fair competition and pluralism on the other hand (Pauwels, 1995: 660ff). Sizeable corporations are essential for accomplishing internal market objectives and strengthening European competitiveness, but these holdings should be deterred from taking advantage of their increased market power to undermine competition, that is, their potential for anti-competitive behaviour towards both their competitors and suppliers and the abuse of dominant position vis-à-vis the users (Kiessling and Johnson, 1998: 157; Cini and McGowan, 1998).

In the Commission's actions regarding concentration trends and market distortions in the media sector, two levels of intervention can be discerned. The first one is the direct enforcement of competition rules as they are included in the EC Treaty, more specifically through articles 81 (restrictive practices policy – former art. 85) and 82 (monopoly policy/abuse of dominant position – former art. 86); Article 86 on services of general interest also has to be noted in this regard.

The second instrument is the general Merger Regulation, first established in 1989 and revised in 1997 and 2004. Since its inception, most convergence issues have been dealt with under this Merger Regulation, and a significant number of mergers involving converged services have been reported and sometimes forbidden.[4] However, it appears that the concentration activity in general has dwindled in recent years. While the number of notified cases –often significantly – increased until 2000, it has stabilised or even slightly decreased since.

Regarding the decisions that have been taken, a number of important criticisms have been voiced in the literature. Firstly, one can raise the question whether the negative decisions taken are not merely token decisions, 'superficial pinpricks' (Galbraith, 1975: 241). Secondly, the Commission is in general accused of being too lenient in its treatment of merger cases. Critics hereby refer to the overwhelming majority of cases that have been approved, and the very small number that have been prohibited (Cini and McGowan, 1998: 126).[5] Thirdly, efficiency in control presupposes a well-staffed department, but an increasing case load, an undermanned Task Force etc. make the regulation more into an instrument for economic efficiency and rationalisation than for the protection of fair competition (Cini and McGowan, 1998: 47). Lastly, the referral to national legislation, in accordance with the subsidiarity principle, has been evaluated negatively as well. Anything under the thresholds of the Merger Regulation, and possibly even above them (for example, in the case of legitimate interests such as media pluralism, art. 21), can be referred to national legislation,[6] but this presupposes that an adequate national legislation and regulation instrument effectively exists, that it is being implemented and that it is indeed meant to enhance and protect media pluralism. Decisions made at the national level often serve an economic rather than a cultural objective, and its agencies are sometimes operating with an inadequate legal framework and insufficient resources (Lensen, 1991: 16). Even when the national supervisory authorities have the means to operate efficiently, cooperation problems may arise between national and Community policy institutions. The transfer of control to the national level may have the effect

4 Of the 2,940 cases that have been notified to the Commission between 1990 and November 2005 on the basis of the Merger Regulation, about 70 decisions are related to the media sector and 200 to the telecommunications sector. More importantly, however, six of the 19 negative decisions made under this regulatory framework until now, directly affect the converged media and telecommunications sectors: MSG Media Service (1994), Nordic Satellite Distribution (1995), HMG (RTL/Veronica/Endemol (1995), Bertelsmann/Kirch/Première (1997), Deutsche Telekom/Betaresearch (1997), MCI Worldcom/Sprint (2000). The latest merger to be forbidden, Sony/BMG, only dates from july 2006. Other negative decisions such as Telefonica/Sogecable and Time Warner/EMI were avoided at the very last minute by the withdrawal of the alliance (Kiessling and Johnson, 1998).

5 Also see http://europa.eu.int/comm/competition/mergers/cases/stats.html.

6 According to article 22, the opposite is also possible: Member States can ask the Commission to evaluate mergers below the thresholds if, for example, national legislation is lacking. This was the case for RTL-Veronica.

of turning Member States into both judge and judged, a situation which obviously does not promote the effectiveness and consistency of competition policy. Insofar as competition and anti-trust policy is used as a means of taking care of national interests, the easy flow of information between the various levels (local, national, Community, global) is not always self-evident. The fact that the Commission has long been unsuccessful in its attempts to gain more control – among other things through lower intervention thresholds – shows that it does not have objective allies in the Member States. As a consequence, competition policies are, if not primarily, then certainly to a high degree, the result of political compromise. The political pressure exerted by Member States makes implementation of a truly independent supranational competition policy very difficult (Pauwels, 1995; Cini and McGowan, 1998: 133).

The recent adoption of a new Merger Regulation (applicable since 1 May 2004), has brought about both substantive and procedural changes meant to achieve more flexible and transparent procedures so as to respond to the 'legitimate concerns of businesses' (European Commission, 2003: 5). Whether this increased 'flexibility', for example, with regard to the assessment of commitment proposals, will translate into a weakening of the EU's stance and control vis-à-vis concentration, and whether it will therefore move towards a more economic-centred approach, remains to be seen.

The Aftermath of Convergence (2000 – Present): As Rational as Possible

Whereas the liberalisation of the pre-2000 period pushed actors to concentrate, mainly driven by boom and doom scenarios as well as by irrational diversification and internationalisation strategies, in order 'not to miss the boat', the post-2000 era can be qualified as the 'aftermath of convergence' in which actors searched, in a more rational way, for consolidation rather than concentration. In response EU policy, in its turn, sought to remedy inefficiencies that had been identified and heavily criticised in the meanwhile (Eliassen, Monsen and Sitter, 2003).

Compared to relatively similar utilities sectors such as gas and electricity, the Europeanisation and liberalisation in the telecoms sector had been a success story inasmuch as the market had been fully opened, indeed. Yet, this does not mean that a fully functioning single market had been established, even if a pan-European regime was starting to take shape and replace diverse traditional models. On the one hand, the sector was (and is) a highly technical one that is prone to change; on the other hand it was still dominated by strong incumbents, some of which still enjoyed close relations with governments. Despite formal market liberalisation, significant evidence of increased competition and considerable pressure for further liberalisation, there appeared to be several obstacles to the development of fully competitive markets.

One of the biggest obstacles was that the incumbents still retained considerable market power, generating pressure for further regulation. Therefore, although the markets had been opened, supplementary legislation was required to make the single market fully competitive. Some states remained also very closely aligned with 'their' operators even if the main elements of the government-regulator-incumbent trinity had been weakened. In addition, all Member States featured NRAs, but there was still a considerable national variation in their independence, power and resources. As regards the effective independence of telecoms regulators and competition authorities, the separation between regulation and politics now seemed adequate; however, several NRAs were facing limits in terms of lack of resources, power of enforcement and sanctions. Even though the pace of liberalisation was over, Europe's regulators still had difficulties with the specificities of EU directives. Furthermore, Europe's NRAs were struggling to keep up with the radical market change.

While the first lessons about liberalisation had been absorbed, few regulators were fully prepared for the next round. The Commission and independent regulatory bodies across the continent were all seeking ways to keep track of the new trends and, especially, to adapt to rapid changes in the marketplace. Even Europe's most advanced markets face considerable challenges: aside from the usual and ongoing disputes regarding interconnection and local-loop unbundling, complex new areas such as the field of broadband had to be tackled. These challenges, coupled to an uncertain future, meant that Europe's NRAs faced difficult decisions. Moreover, the EU regulatory regime featuring few detailed requirements concerning state structures meant great flexibility for government, NRAs and operators. This enabled national policy makers to tailor reforms to national circumstances, which resulted in degrees and forms of privatisation varying considerably. Likewise, differences in the structure of the new regulatory authorities, variations in number and methods of nomination and scrutiny of regulators (often to satisfy members of national parliaments) had the final consequence of still setting national markets apart from each other (Thatcher 1999c). These current and future challenges prompted a proposal for a new, competition based regulatory framework, facilitating the phasing out of sector specific regulation and implementing a transition towards a fully liberalised market (See Eliassen, Monsen and Sitter 2003).

This new EU regulatory framework, designed to strengthen competition in the electronic communications markets in the EU for the benefit of consumers and European economy came formally into force in July 2003, but is has taken some years to have it fully implemented in all member countries. The structure of the new regulatory package was driven by three main concerns: 1) the development of competition in local markets as well as across markets had been limited, inhibiting widespread take-up of new convergence services such as broadband internet; 2) the Commission's strategy should be not to use *hard legislation* to regulate the sector but rather to restrict itself to laying down a competition-based framework which can then be implemented and controlled by the NRAs; and 3) convergence between telecoms, information technology and the media were changing the relevant markets. The central aim of the new framework was therefore to drive forward the liberalisation of telecommunications markets by adapting regulation to the requirements of the Information Society and the digital revolution. This revolution, driven by convergence, implies that a service can be delivered across a range of platforms and received via different terminals, borrowing technologies from previously separate sectors such as audiovisual media and the internet. The reforms were therefore geared toward providing the best conditions for a dynamic and competitive industry across the ICT sector, that is, for all electronic communication services, in a rapidly changing technological environment where, at least supposedly, only fierce and fair competition will yield lower prices, better quality and innovative services. At the same time, the new framework should also ensure user rights and introduce privacy principles.

The new package had six regulatory aims: First to create a level playing field across EU by facilitating market entry through simplified rules. For example, licensed authorisations are limited to explicit cases such as the use of spectrum frequencies and numbering. In most other cases, these licenses are replaced by a general authorisation regime, which is the identical for all types of telecommunications services (including traditional fixed and mobile voice telephony, but also VoIP for example). Moreover, a harmonised application of measures is foreseen through strong coordination mechanisms at European level (for example, the so-called article 7 procedures, and the strict limitation of remedies in time and extent). Secondly it aimed at adapting regulation to increasing competition by limiting most of market power based regulation to dominant operators, as defined in EU Competition Law. Examples of obligations to SMP (Significant Market Power) operators could be: to give access to the 'last mile' of telecommunications markets (Local Loop Unbundling) as well as to associated facilities; to negotiate with access demanding parties in a non-discriminatory, timely, fair and reasonable way; transparency and account separation; price control and cost orientation.

The third element was to introduce flexible mechanisms in the legislation to allow it to evolve with future technology and market changes and to roll back regulation when markets become competitive. This happens both through access obligations pertaining to SMP operators in diverging networks such as fixed and mobile telecommunications, cable television, terrestrial broadcasting, satellite and generic IP based networks, as well as by stressing that all operators have both the right and the duty to negotiate interconnection, that is, the physical and logical linking together of competing networks so as to allow users from different networks to communicate with each other. The fourth objective was to promote interoperability of networks and services. Here the Directives recommend standards and specifications which could be made compulsory in case of insufficient interoperability, as well as by mandating (SCART, conditional access) and recommending (open API) certain standards with regard to digital interactive television.

The fifth element was to maintain universal service obligations in order to avoid exclusion from the Information Society and guarantee a minimum set of services available to the entire population. These obligations deal with the scope of universal service, the rights of users and measures for compensating providers of the service without distorting competition. At the same time, they open up the right for competing operators to be considered as a universal service provider. The sixth part was to ensure the protection of the right to privacy in an electronic environment, and regulate the processing of personal data, by introducing provisions to guarantee the security of public electronic communication networks, the confidentiality of data aggregated by means of these networks, and the secure processing of data as discussed in Eliassen, Monsen and Sitter (2003).

The three main themes of the package could be said to be simplification of the regulatory framework, a shift towards increasing use of horizontal, competition-based law to regulate the sector, and the re-balancing of regulatory power between the Commission and the National Regulatory Agencies. First, on the topic of simplification, the Commission has moved in the direction of less, but improved regulation. However, for a combination of reasons related to incumbent market power and incomplete legislation (see above), simplification also means new – and better – regulation. On the one hand, the new regulatory framework reduces the number of legal measures from 28 to eight. However, alongside a new consolidated and simplified Liberalisation Directive, the new regulatory framework consists of a Framework Directive (replacing the ONP Framework Directive) and four new, specific directives (authorisation, access and interconnection, universal service and privacy and electronic communications), as well as a decision on radio spectrum policy.

The regulatory package has been well received among experts in the field, community institutions and member states. Two aspects have however, been criticised (Cave and Larouche 2001). The first is an alleged lack of concern for internal market objectives on the part of the EU institutions, inasmuch as there is no internal market for electronic communications and the proposed framework does not make it much more likely that it will be achieved soon – although it can be argued that provisions have been laid out to perform market and SMP definitions on a cross-border level. Second, there is a clear distinction between the regulation of electronic services and content, which might be too strong given the actual and obvious links between the two. Cave and Larouche argue that the Community should not hide behind these conceptual distinctions to avoid presenting a coherent regulatory scheme that would advance the internal market in electronic communications. However, a new regulatory framework for electronic communications *including* horizontal content regulation seems as coherent from a market point of view as it is unrealistic from a political perspective, given the extreme sensitivity in Member States regarding content regulation and the notions of cultural identity and diversity so closely associated with it. The diverging principles of, for example, the TWF Directive need to be understood in this light. This notwithstanding, the fact that the rationale to separate content from infrastructure regulation seems to have put network and service regulation on a 'highway' towards flexibility and technological neutrality throughout the

European Union while at the same time 'parking' content regulation safely into the hands of national politics, will always to a certain extent remain a barrier to pan-European competition. Evidently, however, this is only true insofar as pan-European content is a marketable concept[7] (see Eliassen, Monsen and Sitter 2003).

The second dimension is that Commission envisaged a gradual shift from ONP to competition law. The new regulatory regime is intended to operate as a *sui generis* form of competition policy, and is therefore an important step towards normal competition governed by generic competition law. The end goal is a sector governed by competition law, and the Commission therefore proposes to move away from the rather arbitrary approach in the previous regulatory framework, towards a policy more consistent with competition law. However, competition law may still be applied in a pre-emptive *ex ante* form, should a market be considered non-competitive, besides the more traditional *ex post* fashion. In reality, the present EU regulation of telecommunications is therefore characterised by a duality of general competition rules running alongside sector-specific regulation. One the one hand, general competition law (Art. 81, 82 and 86 of the Treaty as well as the Merger Regulation) provides the flexibility to deal with new and unforeseen developments leading to market failures in telecommunications markets. On the other hand, a more sophisticated set of sector-specific regulation still exists, which is transitional in nature and aimed at solving temporary market failure, as well as reaching specifically defined social and political objectives such as tariff control and universal service objectives – which are not in the scope of Treaty provisions on competition. (Apostolos, 2006: 20–24) (see the next chapter for further discussions).

The implications of this are that the new regime is dependent on a definition of relevant markets, an identification of dominance and formulation of remedies. Within the uniform framework necessary for the internal market, but permitting flexibility and variable pace, the NRAs can define relevant markets, dominance and remedies. In line with the Commission's proposed model, 'relevant markets' will no longer be defined in directives (under the previous regime the relevant market was defined in the specific ONP directives on interconnection, voice telephony, leased lines). Instead, in execution of article 15 of the Framework Directive, the Commission has published a recommendation (2003/311/EC) on relevant product and service markets, defined along competition policy lines. This recommendation lists those markets – 18 in total – within the communications sector whose characteristics may justify the imposition of *ex ante* regulatory obligations. In addition, the Commission has published guidelines (2002/C 165/03) on market analysis and the calculation of dominance, or significant market

7 The relative failure and subsequent 're-localisation' of pan-European television channels such as Eurosport and MTV, and the ongoing adaptation of internet portals, search engines etc. to local markets are just two examples justifying a certain degree of scepticism with regard to pan-European content.

power (SMP). However, NRAs may depart from the decisions with respect to geographical market definitions if they believe this is appropriate in regard to their own circumstances (Eliassen, Monsen and Sitter, 2003).

Regarding their effect on the intrusiveness and effectiveness of regulation, market definitions could go both ways. A narrow, precise definition increases the prospect of firms falling into the SMP category, but it confines the scope of regulation to the product or service covered. A broad, more ambiguous, definition that does not distinguish between types of products or services reduces any firm's 'market share' by broadening the 'relevant market', but thereby permits the NRA to intervene across a wider sector when SMP is determined (Cave and Larouche, 2001). The risk is that this approach could lead to market fragmentation and legal uncertainty because the significant freedom of the NRAs to depart from the principles of competition law could result in divergence of regulatory decision-making across the EU (Nikolinakos, 2001), even though the Commission retains the right to withdraw measures taken by NRAs if it considers these to create a barrier to the single market or to be incompatible with Community Law (Art. 7 §4), and even though NRAs are obliged to take comments by other NRA's as well as the Commission into account when adopting measures (Art. 7, §5). In January 2006, at a point where 334 notifications had been received by the Commission and six cases had entered the second phase of analysis, a DG COMP official confirmed that considerable divergence existed between the different NRAs in their definition of markets – especially for what broadcasting transmission services are concerned (market 18).

Furthermore, dominance (or SMP) can be exercised by a single firm, or collectively, or leveraged into a vertically related market. This creates further uncertainty about the regulatory outcome. It is difficult for firms to forecast how widely NRAs or the bodies to which their decisions can be appealed will define dominance. Finally, with regard to remedies, the NRAs need to remedy when confronted with SMP – up until a forthcoming review of the regulatory framework SMP automatically implies remediation – but because of their flexibility application is highly unpredictable and can result in considerable differences among the Member States. This uncertainty is augmented by the fact that, contrary to market definitions and SMP assessments, the Commission holds no veto right over the regulatory remedies introduced by NRAs.

The third and final issue in the reform of European telecommunications policy is the extent to which regulation is re-balanced between the European Institutions and the Member States – or, between the European Commission and the NRAs. Although, in the spirit of the post-Maastricht subsidiarity rationale, the Commission decided to *devolve* the greater part of the implementation of its new framework regulation to the national agencies (market definition, assignment of SMP status to operators, remedies etc.), it keeps a firm grip on every stage of the process. Firstly, the NRAs need to communicate all measures they intend to take to all market parties, and provide ample time for comment. Secondly, measures need to be communicated to the European Commission as well as to other NRAs, which in their turn may pass comment on them; as has already been mentioned, the NRA then is required to 'take the utmost account' of these remarks. Thirdly, where measures define markets different from those outlined by the Commission, or wish to designate an operator as having Significant Market Power, the Commission reserves the right to review the measure and to withdraw it – using comitology procedures – if it is deemed to create a barrier to the single market or be inconsistent with Community Law. And fourthly, the guidelines to market and SMP definition as well as the repertory of possible measures to be taken against operators with SMP, has been explicitly and exhaustively defined by the Commission. As mentioned, the only true discretionary power for the NRA's – that is, a decision which cannot be vetoed by the Commission – is the regulatory remedy chosen once SMP has been designated.

Therefore, an apparently far-reaching decentralisation of competences is clearly accompanied by strong centralised control over the modalities of market analysis and possible remedies to apply. This, on the one hand, somewhat reduces the fears by competition policy analysts, as would the significant freedom of NRAs to deviate from Competition Law create fragmented regulations throughout Europe. On the other hand, however, to ensure a consistent application of the regulatory framework as well as other pieces of Community Law throughout a deluge of market definitions, SMP designations and remedies taken by a few dozen different NRA's coming from widely diverging political and economic settings, arguably is a tough task for the Commission, and demands considerable manpower and economic and political expertise from its side. The high workload of the Commission's Article 7 Task Force and the large amount of decisions taken – around 200 in mid January 2006 – are clear witnesses of this. Moreover, the decentralised approach demands a host of new competences in terms of market analysis from sometimes very small regulatory agencies –in many cases forcing them to hire new staff or outsource the analysis to consultants– provoking an unequal position vis-à-vis the larger and more experienced authorities and, hence, a possibly different pace and scope for reform in different Member States. In January 2006, as much as five Member States had not notified *any* market definitions whatsoever to the Commission, let alone started SMP designation or remediation, whereas other countries have completed their market definitions and have are steadily making progress in phases two and three of the regulatory process.[8]

These two factors, being the increased rather than decreased workload for the Commission as well as the considerable new tasks for unequally equipped NRA's with different agendas, make us wonder how simplified and unified the new framework will actually render telecommunications policy in the 25 Member States of the Union and whether, despite the clear intention of decentralisation, the

[8] As mentioning specific countries would quickly outdate this article, we instead refer to the Commission's website containing all the notifications and decisions per Member State: http://forum.europa.eu.int/Public/irc/infso/ecctf/library.

Commission has not transformed itself some kind of European 'super-regulator'. In this respect, the additional checks and balances provided by the competences of the Communications Committee (COCOM) in guiding the regulatory process within the Commission, the European Regulators Group (ERG) created by the Commission to interface with the NRAs, the somewhat broader Independent Regulators Group (IRG) and several other groups and committees providing feedback and/or control by national administrations and agencies (such as the Radio Spectrum Committee and the Radio Spectrum Policy Group) can be considered as positive, although they add many more layers of bureaucracy to an already complex system.

Five years after the Commission laid down its proposals for a new regulatory framework, SMP and dominance assessment remains a challenging exercise for both the Commission and the Member States. After periods of emphasis on liberalisation and consolidation, the thinking around concepts of competition and its two main concepts, dominance and abuse, has evolved to a less mechanical and more economic, rational approach; however, the intended simplification of regulation has in practice lead to a high workload on both the EU as a principal, and its agents in the different Member States, demanding considerable knowledge of national economic and political contexts from the former, and technical and analytical skills from the latter. Although the ultimate goal is to roll back sector specific regulation and revert to generic competition law, the very concept of SMP implies a permanent re-evaluation of markets and a subsequent adjustment of regulatory measures to changed conditions. Therefore, it is doubtful whether telecommunications regulation will ever be truly 'simplified'. Moreover, even though many tasks have been 'devolved' to the NRA's, the Commission remains a firm grip on the decision of its agents, and it is likely to continue to do so in coming years.

Conclusion

In this chapter, we have discussed the evolving role of the EU as a driving force behind the transformation of the telecommunications and ICT sectors. In doing this, three overlapping periods have been distinguished, in which different policy and regulatory frameworks outlined by the European Commission stepped into a dialectical process with other EU institutions such as European Parliament and ECJ having priorities of their own, with EU Member States reluctant towards EU intervention in sectors believed to be of ample economic and/or cultural importance, and with global forums such as the WTO pushing for more liberalisation.

In a first period, extending roughly from 1985 to 1999, there was a strong emphasis on sector-specific liberalisation of the telecommunications market, leading to the ONP framework in 1997 while slowly starting to take into account convergence issues and shifting the regulatory focus from sector-specific telecommunications regulation to more general and horizontal ICT policy; as we have seen, this 'complete' liberalisation of telecommunications as well as audiovisual markets has been ambivalent, with market opportunities being created (for example, for commercial broadcasters and independent producers in the media sector, or international cooperation and mobile market initiatives in the telecommunications sector) while many Member States requested – and received – derogations on the basis of cultural and/or economic arguments, allowing incumbent media and telecommunications firms to sustain their position. Subsequently, we have discussed a second period, partly parallel with the first period, roughly occurring during the 1990s, in which the creation of the single market as well as growing technological convergence provoked increasing degrees of concentration and convergence in telecoms and media markets. As a consequence, a large portion of EU policy intervention was aimed at monitoring and regulating the diverse alliances, mergers and take-overs proposed, and to try to maintain a sustainable single market through general competition and anti-trust policy. Critics of these policies argue, however, that these measures have largely been 'superficial pinpricks', that mergers have generally been treated too lenient by the European Commission (even though it has got very ample competences in the area of competition), and that the enforcement of regulation has been hampered by an understaffed Commission and, in many cases, by understaffed, unwilling and/or unprepared Member States which, in accordance with subsidiarity principles, are charged with the implementation of most EU policies. In a third and final period, the evolution towards corporate consolidation, full-blown technological and economic convergence and the according streamlining of policies at the start of the twenty-first century has been discussed. Here, the coming about and main objectives of the new regulatory framework for electronic networks and services has been outlined, which is deemed to pave the way for gradually phasing out sector-specific telecommunication policy and replacing it with horizontal policies based on competition principles.

It is important to emphasise once more that these three periods have not been mutually exclusive, but rather indicate major lines of approach that were gradually adopted while previous paradigms continued to exist side-by-side with them. In this sense, liberalisation measures have certainly not been replaced by general competition and anti-trust policies; neither have these Treaty-based policies, or the 'technology-neutral' new regulatory framework completely replaced the sector-specific regulation of the telecommunications (and audiovisual markets), still largely driven by social and cultural objectives voiced especially by the Member States. As has been said in this chapter, the present EU regulation of telecommunications is characterised by a strong duality of general competition rules running alongside sector-specific regulation.

In retrospect, evolutions in the political and regulatory framework for telecommunications in Europe seem to be logical and, in general, have had a positive effect on markets and policy-making alike – the cross-fertilisation between Commission, NRAs and NCAs being one example of the latter. Regulation itself has indeed become more simplified, and the broad approach taken to ex ante regulation has clearly made it more flexible with regard to technological and economic change. However, these evolutions are also a clear illustration of the fact that, despite the promise of simplification, a process of liberalisation in practice comes down to *re-regulation* rather than *deregulation*: firstly, in the case of telecommunications, the correct implementation of the new framework requires a complex new set of skills from both the Commission and the national regulators and has drastically increased their workload, which arguably has complicated rather than simplified their tasks. Secondly, the enduring absence of competition and presence of monopolies in many markets, which still hamper full unbundling and access, as well as the very concept of SMP which implies a permanent re-evaluation of markets and a subsequent adjustment of regulatory measures to changed conditions, will necessitate continuing vigilance from regulators in the future. Thirdly, it also remains to be seen whether the new regulatory framework will create a genuine European internal market for electronic communications, even though market analyses, SMP definitions and remedies might be laid out on a cross-border level. And finally, for firms the simplification brought about by re-regulation is also relative: the importance of market definitions (that is, whether these are interpreted narrowly and precisely or rather broadly and ambiguously by NRAs), and the significant freedom of the NRAs in drawing up these definitions as well as in defining dominance and imposing remedies, has not made it much simpler for operators to predict the regulatory outcome, and might create further legal uncertainty. Taking all this into account, one can wonder how simplified and unified the telecommunications policy in the EU25 actually is today, and whether the Commission, despite the clear intention of decentralisation, has not become an even more powerful European super-regulator, remaining a firm grip on the NRAs.

In spite of these evolutions, it remains doubtful whether the Member States, in the complex equilibrium of multi-level governance that constitutes telecommunications regulation today, have lost their obstructionist powers. On the contrary, politics will without any doubt continue to play their role and the Commission, besides needing sufficient technical knowledge and manpower, will have to take into account the various economic and political contexts in the different Member States when evaluating markets, SMP and remedies. In this sense, however the seemingly permanent oscillation of the power balance between the EU level and the Member States – which, following Maastricht subsidiarity, clearly swung towards the latter – may now have reverted back to a powerful Commission, the Nation State will remain a very important actor.

Chapter 5

EU Competition Policy and the Transition to a More Competitive Communications Industry

Patrizia Cincera and Nick Sitter

European Union competition policy has played a strong and direct role in the liberalisation of telecommunications markets in the European Union. The telecommunications sector was the first utilities sector in which the Commission used its formidable powers unilaterally to break up national monopolies, and this set the scene for the 'public turn' in EU competition policy (Gerber, 1998). By the end of the 1990s liberalisation was underway across the utilities sectors, from electricity and gas to transport and postal services. The first moves on the road to telecommunications liberalisation came in the late 1980s, and was driven by the confluence of three developments: the project to establish a Single European Market, privatisation and liberalisation in some Member States' telecommunications markets, and the strong position competition policy enjoyed in the EU (Levi-Faur, 1992). However, as the telecommunications industry has developed into the Information, Communications and Technology industry (ICT), or what we may simply call the communications industry, the challenges faced by competition policy have multiplied and become more complex. The present chapter explores the role played by competition policy in the development of an increasingly competitive communications industry in Europe.

European Union competition policy rests on the idea that a degree of regulation is required for markets to function. The core principles of most competition policy regimes in western liberal democracies (including the USA) is that regulatory regimes should prevent companies from abusing dominant positions in the market or colluding with other companies to fix prices or engage in other anti-competitive measures.[1] In the EU context, where there is a danger that states might distort competition by supporting their 'national champions', competition policy also includes provisions against state aid to industry. In the early 1990s, the most important tool as far as telecommunications liberalisation was concerned was the Treaty provisions that permit the Commission to break up

1 For comparative analyses, see Doern and Wilks, 1996.

national monopolies. This power does not depend on the consent of the Member States: the Commission can issue a directive that does not require approval by the Council of Ministers or the European Parliament. By the 2000s, however, with communications markets more or less liberalised across Europe, the most important tools were the more standard competition policy measures dealing with abuse of dominant positions, cartels and merger control. The new problems that have emerged as a consequence of privatisation, liberalisation and convergence between different communications markets are how to define market power and how to apply competition policy to a sector that is also subject to communications regulation, and particularly how to assess and deal with abuse of dominant positions in the market.

Competition Policy in the European Union: Economic Reasoning and Contested Concepts

EU competition policy differs somewhat from competition policy in most western liberal democracies because it was not merely designed with economic goals in mind (to correct market failures), but it was also designed specifically as a tool to help build the common market and to break down barriers to the free flow of goods and services between states. Although the organisation of the Directorate General for Competition drew on the French model, much of the original economic and legal influence drew on German and American models. McGowan and Wilks therefore argue that the Treaty of Rome's philosophy of free markets and cross-border competition found its home in competition policy, which was the EU's first supranational policy (McGowan and Wilks, 1995). Both its central principles, to promote competition and to break down national barriers, were compatible with neo-liberal economic thinking. While this did not sit well with a number of Member States in the 1960s and 1970s, the two decades from about 1980 saw a major change in the economic policies and philosophies of most Member States and competition policy began to operate in a more favourable political climate. However, by the early 1990s, the combination of the extension of competition policy to the long-protected utilities sectors and the spread of popular scepticism toward European integration gave rise to a new set of challenges. As in most liberal democracies, an important question became how to delineate the reach of competition policy and how to balance economic and non-economic considerations.

The first question is therefore the balance between economic and non-economic goals. Although most countries have seen an increasing influence of economic reasoning in the practices of their competition policy enforcers, in practice competition policy also takes account of a number of other considerations (Jenny, 2000: 20). This, in turn, raises questions about the legitimacy and accuracy of competition instruments as far as achieving economic efficiency in the marketplace is concerned. If the objective of competition policy is to promote economic efficiency as defined in micro-economic analysis, one might expect economic expertise to play the key role in competition policy. However, in practice most states include economic development and non-economic goals such as fairness or pluralism, and this in turn makes it more difficult both to carry out competition policy and to evaluate its achievements (Jenny, 2000: 23). It also leaves more room for political intervention. This becomes a particularly important challenge in fast-changing industries, such as the communications market, where a flexible ad hoc approach to policy making might be warranted because it is difficult to delineate the market and carry out classical economic assessment of competition.

A second important question for competition policy (particularly in the communications sector) follows from this shift to a focus on consumer welfare rather than actual competition. A number of economists argue that competition might not be the sole way to increase consumer welfare. Schumpeterian theory holds that the wellspring of innovation and technological change is found in giant corporations and in imperfect competition. Only large firms can gather enough financial strength to pursue intensive research and development. This argument is particularly pertinent to high technology industries, where successful operations often result in significant economic externalities. Imperfect competition need not be to the detriment of consumer welfare, inasmuch as R&D leads to new products and services. The R&D costs and investment required in the converging communications industries might therefore justify a high rate of mergers even if these mergers do not sit easily with current competition policy standards. This in turn raises questions as to whether competition is an appropriate means to seek economic efficiency in the communications sector (Laffont and Tirole, 2000: 2).

Third, over the last two decades a number of more specific criticisms have been made of EU competition policy that have some bearing on its application to the communications sector. This includes charges that the Commission's (economic) reasoning is insufficiently transparent and that competition policy has been politicised. Two questions that stretch the definition of abuse of dominant power have proven particularly important in the fast-changing technology-driven communications industry: the question of firms limiting access to 'essential facilities' and the notion of several firms exercising 'collective market dominance'.

As Whish notes, the Commission has been particularly active in promoting competition in the communications market by developing 'its practice under Article 82 [proceeding from the ECJ's judgment in *Commercial Solvents*] in such a way that a refusal to allow access to an essential facility could be found to be an abuse of a dominant position' (Wish, 2003: 669). This means, however, that the Commission faces a challenge in balancing the right of firms to own their facilities and to achieve legitimate return on investment on one hand, and competitors' access to essential facilities on the other. This is of course particularly problematic in network industries, not least in the communications sector.

The use of the 'essential facilities' doctrine in antitrust cases has raised concerns that EU competition policy has developed beyond its core task of securing competition. As Monti (2004) has pointed out the difficulties in striking the right balance between innovation and market access, which is reflected in the incoherence of EU case law:

> at times the case law goes too far and protects individual competitors and not the process of competition (…); while at times the law is too restrictive, showing a tendency to limit the scope of obligation only to cases where the holder seeks to extend the dominance into new markets. The reason for the unsettled state of the law is probably due to concerns that by imposing too extensive an obligation to share, innovation would be stifled. (Monti, 2004: 45)

In the *Oscar Bronner* judgment the European Court of Justice limited the extent to which this 'essential facilities' doctrine can be applied to exceptional cases, where a firm has a 'genuine stranglehold on the related market'. Moreover, the Court recalled that the objective of Article 82 is to safeguard competition and not to protect the position of competitors.[2]

The debates about the 'essential facilities' argument raised two questions that are particularly pertinent to the communications sector. The first is whether competition policy might be used as a tool to change market structures, and the second is whether it might turn out to protect competitors rather than competition itself. On the first point, Bavasso draws attention to the danger that markets might be defined in such a way that the 'relevant market' coincides with the 'essential facility', and that competition policy is used to change market structures (which is the task of the sector regulator, not competition authority) (Bavasso, 2002: 95). Similarly, Larouche warns that:

> [w]hen competition law deserts its well-established framework of analysis under Article 82 EC – by moving from market definition to market structuring, by replacing dominance with the vague notion of 'essentiality' and by abandoning the requirement of abusive behaviour – (…) then perhaps the proper realm of competition law, as a case-bound general regulatory framework, has been exceeded. (Larouche, 2000: 216)

On the second point, concerning protection of competitors rather than competition itself, Doherty warns that 'the formulation "likely to eliminate all competition on the part of the person requesting the service" suggests that there is an abuse if the refusal affects a single complainant, even if others are able to compete' (Doherty, 2001: 427).

---

2 The *Bronner* judgment sets the conditions which determine when a dominant firm's refusal to supply a rival amounts to an abuse of dominant position. The refusal to supply must be: 1) likely to eliminate all competition from an undertaking: 2) must be incapable of being objectively justified: and 3) the product or service sought must be indispensable for the competitors.

The question of whether several companies can exercise 'collective dominance' also represents a development that stretches the motion of abuse of dominant position somewhat beyond its earlier interpretations. The Commission has broadened the concept of collective dominance 'to ensure it encapsulates oligopolistic markets' (Richardson and Gordon, 2001: 416). In the *Gencor* judgment the concept of collective dominance is vaguely defined as 'the relationship of interdependence existing between the parties to a tight oligopoly within which (in particular in terms of market concentration, transparency and product homogeneity) those parties are in a position to anticipate one another's behaviour and therefore strongly encouraged to align their conduct in the market'. According to this rationale, a high degree of interdependence in the oligopolistic market suffices to determine collective dominance. However, critics argue that the Commission's concept of collective dominance 'is a legal concept that has no direct equivalent in economics' (Etter, 2000: 103). The Commission's concern is therefore 'no longer to prevent only mergers that create or strengthen market power for the merging parties themselves, but also mergers that lead to a market structure in which collusion between the merging parties and their competitors becomes more likely' (Niels, 2001: 168). The implications of this for the communications sector are discussed in the last section of this chapter.

Critics have pointed to the problem of gathering and assessing relevant evidence. Assessment as to whether a merger might lead to a situation that allows several firms to exercise market power collectively must be based on sound economic criteria and not simply on ill-defined concepts such as the oligopolist's interdependence. The problem, in Dethmers' words, is that 'the Commission made an attempt to stretch its control by enlarging the notion of collective dominance to 'non-collusive oligopolies', namely oligopolistic markets that enable a firm to derive profits from its unilateral behaviour without depending on the coordinated response of the other oligopolists' (Dethmers, 2005: 640).[3] This requires considerable market-specific economic expertise, and sound and transparent economic analysis. In the *Airtours* case the Court of First Instance found, for the first time, that the Commission's evidence was unconvincing. The CFI went on to clarify the concept of collective dominance by excluding non-

3 With regard to the extension of the Commission's interpretation of collective dominance, it is worth noting the Commission's decision in Airtours, where, as Whish notes, the Commission 'refers to the *individual* actions of the oligopolists, rather than to their likely tacit coordination. In other words, it appeared that the Commission was attempting to stretch the concept of collective dominance beyond its conventional scope – as a way of preventing parallel behaviour on the market – to capture a different type of problem, namely the ability of a firm within an oligopoly to derive benefits from its unilateral behaviour without being dependent on the coordinated response of the other oligopolists' (that is, 'non-collusive oligopolists'; Whish, 2003: 537).

collusive oligopolistic behaviour, as well as the relevant standard for a finding of collective dominance.[4]

Because the *Airtours* judgment brought collective dominance merger cases assessment in line with economic analysis, it may be of paramount importance for the coherent future application of competition policy. The CFI made a strong statement confirming that game theory is the underlying economic concept of collective dominance, and it emphasised the internal incentives and mechanisms of the affected market and the economic rationality of tacit cooperation and conditions for its lasting sustainability (Haupt, 2002: 443). One competition law professor argues that in this case, Community competition 'officials had preconceived a desired result and then shaped their interpretation of evidential data to achieve this end' (Scott, 2002: 12). At any rate, the *Airtours* judgment is of great significance in terms of the institutional balance between the Commission and the CFI, particularly as regards 'the strict standard of substantiation and evidence laid down by the CFI regarding the finding of [collective dominant] market position' (Haupt, 2002: 443).

This debate about the concept of collective dominance has proven particularly controversial in the communications sector. The increasing need for the Commission to demonstrate detailed economic analysis to prove collective dominance was reflected in its review and clearance of the joint venture between Bertelsmann and Sony (the *Sony BMG* case, which is discussed further below).[5] Independent music responded by complaining that the Commission had not applied the concept sufficiently strictly and in accordance with the flagship 'Lisbon Strategy' to make Europe the most competitive knowledge-based society in the world by 2010.[6] According to antitrust specialists, the major factor (which is not explicitly mentioned in the Commission's public statements) that influenced the Commission's decision to clear the *Sony BMG* case was that the

> European Court of First Instance has chastised the Commission on more than one occasion since 2000 for a failure to develop sufficient evidence to support collective dominance allegations. The decision not to oppose Sony BMG may signal the

---

[4] The latter is based on three cumulative conditions: transparency, possibility of retaliation and absence of competitive constraint.

[5] The *Sony BMG* merger initially raised concern because four internationally active majors companies share 80 per cent of the world market, with two majors alone – Universal and Sony BMG control of more than 50 per cent. However, the Commission had to conclude, taking into account a deficit in the transparency of the market, that the evidence found was not sufficient to demonstrate in a successful way that coordinated pricing behaviour existed in the past and that a reduction from five to four major recording companies would not yet create a collectively held dominant position in the national markets for recorded music in the future. Press release IP/04/959.

[6] IMPALA Press Realse, Brussels, 3 December 2004, document available at: http://www.impalasite.org/docum/04-press/press_0410_2.htm.

Commission's concern about its ability to meet the higher standard of proof now required to prove collective dominance.[7]

Competition Policy and Regulation in the Communications Sector in the European Union: from State Monopolies to New Industry-Specific Challenges

Although the early competition policy questions in the telecommunications sector primarily concerned the breaking up of national monopolies, the recent proliferation delivery mechanisms has attracted many new private economic players into the communications business and changed the Commission's competition policy concerns in the direction of the problems of abuse of dominant position discussed in the previous section. Market forces play an increasing role in determining the supply of media products and communications services, for example through pay-TV and other forms of transactions for communications services, and this has prompted a major shift in the involvement of the competition authorities in the communications industry, from driving liberalisation to regulating for competition. The old battles against protectionist Member States in the 1980s and 1990s have by and large been won, liberalisation is underway (even if it is far from complete) and, as in the case of any other type of business, competition policy now aims to ensure that the competitive process of the communications market functions properly.

In the 1980s and 1990s the main challenge was resistance from Member States that opposed telecoms liberalisation and protected national monopoly operators, and competition policy played a central role in breaking this deadlock (Eliassen and Sjøvaag, 1999). The central characteristic of European telecoms in the 1980s was the state-owned monopoly operators, and the Commission's initial strategy was mainly limited to encouraging harmonisation of networks and equipment through standardisation and R&D. However, as the project to establish a Single Market was agreed (even though it did not cover telecommunications) and some Member States began to take their first steps towards privatisation and liberalisation, the Commission moved toward more radical reform. Competition policy became its central tool in the effort to liberalise markets. In 1985 the Court of Justice confirmed that the telecommunications sector was not immune from EU competition law. The Commission began in 1988 by issuing a directive that opened the market for terminal equipment, and this was issued unilaterally under article 86 [then article 90]. This was the first time this competition policy measure, which empowers the Commission to issue directives without the approval of the Council or Parliament, was used. Inevitably, it proved controversial. The main opposition came from France and Spain, and to a lesser extent from Italy, Greece,

7 'Antitrust developments in the media and entertainment industries', Simpson Thacher & Bartlett LLP, New York (www.stblaw.com).

Belgium and Germany (Schmidt, 1998). The result was a 30-month legal process that ended in the Commission's favour. A directive that allowed for competition in value-added network services followed two years later, again based on the then article 90. The second Court judgment also went the Commission's way, but by this stage the then 12 Member States had already agreed in principle to liberalise telecommunications markets (Eliassen, Monsen and Sitter, 2003).

From the mid-1990s the Member States offered much more wholehearted support for liberalisation (in contrast to more controversial sectors, such as gas or electricity). This can be attributed partly to the impact of EU-driven telecoms reform on domestic markets and actors in key states like Germany, France and Italy, where proponents of liberalisation were able to employ EU regulations to their advantage in domestic policy games (Thatcher, 1999c; Bartle, 1999). It also reflected the fact that some states, such as Sweden, opted to liberalise their domestic telecoms market in anticipation of EU-level liberalisation, thus strengthening the balance in favour of liberalisation in the EU. The principal shift from partial, piecemeal liberalisation to full opening of telecommunications markets came with the Commissions Telecoms Review in 1993. This was followed four years later by a directive (this time under a procedure that required the Member States' and European parliament's assent) that replaced the old concept of monopoly operators with the idea of several competing operators, and opened the way for full competition even in voice telephony. The final legal barriers to competition were to be lifted on 1 January 1998, but progress was uneven across the Member States.

At the same time, during the 1990s, the Commission began to shift its focus from 'old' telecommunications policies to broader questions of regulation information and communication technologies (ICT). A directive on satellite communications in 1994, one coverning alternative networks, such as cable, in 1995, and a directive that removed the final restrictions on competition in mobile telephony markets (already partially liberalised) in 1996, indicated that communications markets were beginning to converge. This involved three main new issues or problems specific to the communications sector that came with the shift in competition policy concerns away from national monopolies toward abuse of dominant positions.

First, the cost structure of the communications industry makes economies of scale in content production an inherent characteristic of communications markets. As one report puts it,

> industries that are characterised by very low marginal costs relative to fixed costs are inconsistent with a simple textbook benchmark of perfect competition, irrespective of the actual effectiveness of the competitive process in these industries. Pricing media products at marginal cost is not a sustainable strategy because of the sunk costs of content production will not be recovered. Although firms may compete insofar as they act in line with incentives to innovate and make efficient trade-offs between price and

quality, such markets may not entail a large number of firms selling homogeneous goods at prices equal to marginal cost.[8]

The fact that media products are rarely directly supported by consumers makes economic analysis even more difficult, particularly because the concept of substitutable goods (and therefore the definition of the relevant market) is linked to consumer price.[9]

Second, digital convergence is bringing about a rapid transformation of the communications market. Since communications firms operate in several interrelated markets, the competition in each of these markets cannot be considered in isolation.[10] The expanding array of available delivery formats that digitalisation brings about merely exacerbated the problem.[11] Assessment of market power has therefore become more complicated in communication industries, as the attributes of products can change significantly and quickly. Major changes have 'taken place in terms of the size of the market, the identity and preferences of the market participants, and most crucially through innovation and the introduction of new products and services'.[12] The approach adopted for defining communications markets will cause the regulator to overestimate market power if markets are defined too narrowly and to underestimate market power if markets are defined too broadly. The choice of approach is therefore crucial.

Third, the application of competition policy to the communications market is highly distorted by the intervention of media-specific regulators and legislation. Clear demarcation of the goals (and limits) of interventions is complex, and the inevitable result has been overlaps between competition policy and sector-specific regulation in the communications sector. Community competition policy is faced with the need to balance vying interests: promoting innovation, preserving the economic welfare of communications firms, ensuring entry for newcomers, and protecting consumers. The objective of safeguarding competition in the communications market has to be weighted against the goal of preserving the economic welfare of communications firms, not least because digitalisation is

8 'Market Definition in the Media Sector – Economic Issues – Report by Europe Economics for the European Commission, DG Competition', p. 8, November 2002 (www.europe-economics.com).

9 Brenner, S. (1993) 'Competition Policy and Changing Broadcast Industry', p. 96, OECD report, Senior Associate of Charles River Associates: Washington.

10 'Market Definition in the Media Sector – Economic Issues – Report by Europe Economics for the European Commission, DG Competition', p. 9, November 2002 (www.europe-economics.com).

11 Directorate for Financial, Fiscal and Enterprise Affairs, Competition Committee, p. 29, OECD, DAFFE/COMP(2003)16, 'Media Mergers' (www.oecd.org).

12 'Market Definition in the Media Sector – Economic Issues – Report by Europe Economics for the European Commission, DG Competition', p. 10, November 2002 (www.europe-economics.com).

pressing communications firms to invest in costly distribution infrastructures and R&D standard settings.

Inevitably, therefore, the enforcement of competition policy involves trade-offs, and there is a risk that competition decisions may lead to incoherent or suboptimal outcomes with regard to the objective of economic efficiency in the communications marketplace. 'The failure to consider properly the *ex ante* implications of decisions that effectively dilute property rights is of paramount importance in the new economy industries, where innovation is the prime form of competition' (Ahlborn, Evans and Padilla, 2001: 164). In this context, the Commission's concerns about standards and market access for new entrants should be best handled by regulation rather than by competition policy (Monti, 2004: 28). The next section therefore turns to the Commission's efforts to monitor market power and promote competition in the communications sector today.

Promoting Competition in Liberalised Communications Market: Monitoring and Dealing with Dominant Market Power

The Commission's broad objective as far as the communications sector is concerned is to keep media and communications markets open and to stimulate their growth. The main challenge is how to identify and deal with firms that achieve a dominant position, that is, have sufficient market power to act independently of their competitors to restrict competition in the market without suffering serious consequences themselves. As one DG Competition official comments, 'this is a central concern where concentration of limited inputs, or foreclosure of such inputs from neighbouring markets, may lead to an elimination of competition'.[13] The Commission thus pays particular attention to the danger that the behaviour of firms in the sector can limit market access for new entrants and hamper the development of emerging communications markets.

The transition from monopoly markets to competition in the communications industry has raised several important concerns as far as market power is concerned, and many of these concerns are exacerbated by the fast-changing and technology-driven nature of the industry. The combination of liberalisation and digitalisation has sharpened the battle for market shares, and has encouraged communications and media companies to try to exploit commercial advantages across the supply-chain, from the upstream level of content programming down to the customer interface. This has prompted changes to ownership patterns of the communications industries, with an increase in both vertical and horizontal integration. This may result in a variety of forms of discrimination towards other competitors, ranging from, in Abbamonte and Rabassa's terms, 'outright

---

13 'Sector Inquiry New Media (3G)', speech by Philip Lowe, 27 May 2005, document retrieved from the DG for competition web site at: http://europa.eu.int/comm/competition/speeches/text/sp2005_007_en.pdf.

foreclosure (absolute refusal to deal or refusal to contract on reasonable terms) to higher prices or more subtle forms of discrimination resulting in tougher terms of access' (Abbamonte and Rabassa, 2001: 215).

At the EU level, these competition concerns are monitored by the Commission by way of its competition policy instruments: ex-post control on firms' dominant position (Article 82 EC) and ex-ante control on the development of the communications marketplace with regard to both mergers and acquisitions (EC Merger Regulation) and cooperative strategies (exemption provisions under Article 81(3) EC). As the general discussion on developments in competition policy (above) has shown, the Commission has sought to extend the concept of dominance to tackle complex forms of market power in the communications marketplace by both embodying the essential facility doctrine under the Article 82 instrument and by developing the concept of collective dominance within the EC merger regulation framework.

The Commission has identified five issues of particular importance in the communications market (each of which is discussed further below): 'gate-keeper' problems, 'source issues', 'path issues', 'leveraging' and 'network effects' (Mendes Pereira, 2002). The first arise when a company possesses a certain technology, know-how or technical standard (for example, a closed proprietary formatting technology for downloading and streaming music or films), a significant degree of control over the source of the different businesses at stake in the relevant markets (for example, the primary input at the top of the value chain of the product (for example, films, music) and where a company exerts a significant degree of control over the path to the customer (for example, distribution channel) (Mendes Pereira, 2002). These are problems of vertical integration (which may, of course, arise from a merger), because a company holding these advantages may exert undue pressure over competitors and jeopardise the process of competition in the communications industry. The last two, 'leveraging' and 'network' effects, concern problems that may arise if a company can leverage its power in one market to strengthen its position in a related market, or when firms control large shares of the markets become more attractive to consumers simply because of their large market share (for example control of content in the film or music sector).

Gate-keeper problems may occur when a company has exercised sufficient control of know-how and technology to impose its own product as the industry standard and force producers in related markets not to support competing standards. The AOL/TimeWarner merger, which the Commission opposed, is a case in point. In its negative opinion, the Commission explained that:

> [b]ecause of the breadth of Time Warner and Bertelsmann publishing rights, the popularity of their catalogue, AOL's know-how in the Internet field and its huge Internet community, the new entity would be in a position to impose its technology or formatting language as the industry standard.[14]

---

[14] AOL/TimeWarner, Case N°COMP/M. 1845, § 56.

The Commission feared that AOL/TimeWarner could force developers of music players not to support competing technologies, which meant that competing records companies wishing to distribute their music on-line would be required to format their music using the AOL/TimeWarner's technology. This merger would threaten competition in the music market because it would enable the new entity to control downloadable music and streaming over the Internet and raise competitors' costs through excessive license fees. The two parties have sought to mitigate these concerns by offering a package of commitments whose ultimate goal was to break the links between Bertelsmann and AOL: AOL and Bertelsmann have established a mechanism by which Bertelsmann will progressively exit from AOL Europe and the French joint venture AOL compuserve. Moreover, AOL/Time Warner will not take any action that would result in Bertelsmann music being available online exclusively through AOL or being formatted in a proprietary format that is playable exclusively on an AOL music player.[15]

Source issues can arise in cases where mergers lead to concentration of ownership of the content that gives a company a dominant position in a distribution market. The problem arose in the Vivendi/Canal+/Seagram merger, with regard to film and music. As Mendes Pereira observed, 'the merged entity would have the world's [sic] largest library of TV programming in the EEA. It would also be number one in recorded music combined with important position in terms of publishing rights in the EEA' (Mendes Pereira, 2002). The Commission found that the deal would have strengthened the new entity's dominant position in the pay-TV market:

> because of its vertical integration Canal+ will secure permanently the renewal of its contracts with Universal in France, Belgium, The Netherlands and the Nordic countries and will obtain the rights to Universal's films in Italy, preventing thus pay-TV rivals and new entrants from having access to these rights.[16]

The merger would also have increased Canal+/Universal's bargaining power vis-à-vis American studios. This would strengthen the company's position on the first-window premium films segment and further foreclose the pay-TV market where Canal+ is active. Consequently, the Commission considered that there were serious competition concerns because Canal+'s dominant position on the pay-TV market in France, Spain, Italy, Belgium and the Netherlands would be strengthened and Canal+ would become dominant in the Nordic countries.[17] In order to eliminate the competition concerns relating to 'source issue', the merging parties offered a package of commitments which included access for competitors to Universal's film production and co-production. They undertook not to grant to Canal+ 'first-window' rights covering more than 50 per cent of

---

15 Press release, IP/00/1145.

16 Vivendi/Canal+/Seagram Case N°COMP/M. 2050, § 43.

17 Vivendi/Canal+/Seagram Case N°COMP/M.2050, § 50.

Universal production and co-production. The Commission accepted that these undertakings significantly reduced the ability of Canal+ to influence other major US studios and eliminated the serious doubts as to the strengthening of Canal+'s dominant position.

The Vivendi/Canal+/Seagram merger also gave rise to concerns about *path issues*, that is, the danger that a merger can generate a dominant position in the market for dissemination. In this case, the merger prompted serious competition concerns about the creation of a dominant position on the emerging pan-European market for portals and on the emerging market for on-line music because of the addition of the Seagram's Universal music library to Vivendi's multi-access portal Vizzavi. Mendes Pereira also pointed to the clear 'path issue' with respect of Internet access via mobile phone handsets, which arose because of Vodaphone's significant market position in the market for mobile telephony in a number of European countries. Vodaphone already had a very significant customer basis and therefore a solid path to the future customers of the joint venture. Canal+ also held a similarly solid distribution channel for Internet access via TV set-top boxes through its customer basis for pay-TV services. The concern therefore arose with respect to both Vodafone and Canal+'s ability to transfer their customer basis from the mobile telephony and pay-TV markets to the Internet access markets by using the already existing distribution channels or paths (Mendes Pereira, 2002). In order to remove competition concerns relating to the 'path issue', Vivendi offered to give rival portals access to Universal's online music content for five years.[18]

Competition concerns about *leveraging* arise from the possibilities communications firms may have to use their market power in one market in a related market. Convergence in the communications sector has facilitated the migration of media products from one medium to another, and has prompted firms to extend their activities into several media products and communications service markets following the commercial strategy of economies of scale and scope. The Commission is especially concerned by transactions where the parties are able to leverage their economic strength in one market to gain competitive advantage in another. In Monti's words:

> [i]n complex network markets, one issue which has been of concern to the Commission in merger cases is the separation of complementary functions – the owners of content are not allowed to own the means of distribution of that content. The reasoning to justify this concern is either: (1) if a firm owns two segments of the market this raises barriers to entry for newcomers who would also have to own both segments; (2) one of the segments may be an essential facility, in which case the holder has an inherent interest in favouring its content and will discriminate against others. (Monti, 2004: 51–2)

---

18 Press Release, IP/00/1162.

The 'Vizzavi' joint venture (discussed above) raised concerns about the ability of the parties to leverage their market power in the market for mobile telephony into the market for mobile Internet access. The purpose of the Vizzavi portal was to create a horizontal, multi-access Internet portal and to provide customers with a range of web-based services across a variety of platforms (PCs, mobile phones, TV set-top boxes).[19] Other examples include the proposed Telia/Telenor merger. In the Commissions words, 'the market power of the parties will be reinforced by the benefits of the full vertical integration achieved by this merger at all levels of the TV distribution chain. Newco's [the new merged entity] benefit of the reinforced market power resulting from the vertical integration will be significantly increased in the future digital context'.[20] It added that

> Newco itself will have an incentive to leverage its privileged position at the infrastructures level into the downstream distribution levels. In particular, Newco will have the economic incentive to invest heavily in the acquisition of the most valuable content from content providers and broadcasters in order to irreversibly tilt in its favour the emerging multi-media markets in the Scandinavian countries.[21]

The fifth source of concern for the EU competition authority arises from *network effects*. As Shapiro explains:

> large networks offer more value to users than small networks, creating a virulent form of scale economies [... which in turn] generates positive feedback; the strong get stronger and the weak get weaker [... as] customers value a popular product (network) more than an unpopular one (Shapiro, 2000: 112).[22]

The advent of digitalisation has extended the form of media delivery to the interactive switched telecommunications network hitherto confined to voice telephony, and network externalities are therefore an increasingly important characteristic of communications markets. For example, in the Vivendi/Canal+/Seagram merger, third parties claimed that 'the merged entity will obtain the control of Universal Music libraries and will because of its large customer base be

---

[19] Mendes Pereira adds that the 'Vizzavi portal would combine a powerful new Internet access mechanism with paid-for content. Given the dominant position that the parties would acquire on the Internet access markets (...) the operation would allow the parties to leverage their market power in the markets for Internet access into the market for the acquisition of paid-for content for the Internet. (...) The leverage allowed for by the operation would naturally work in detriment of the parties' competitors in the markets for mobile telephony and pay-TV' (Mendes Pereira, 2002).

[20] Telia/Telenor Case N°COMP/M.1439, § 264.

[21] Telia/Telenor Case N°COMP/M.1439, § 265.

[22] Crucially, network effects linked to proprietary, non interoperable standards can give rise to powerful tipping effects and in addition can be an important lever for powerful barrier to entry in media markets.

able to launch the first comprehensive mobile online music service and thus obtain a first mover advantage'.[23] This kind of position easily triggers 'tipping effects' that confer long lasting dominance on the big firm, such as when a pay television station that attracts more subscribers can afford to pay more to buy a greater quantity of better quality programmes. The market then 'tips' in its favour, and gives it such a decisive lead over its competitors that the network effect begins.[24] The Vivendi/Canal+/Seagram transaction was also a source of concern for third parties because they feared that the 'merged entity will offer a large selection of content which will attract more users and which in turn will attract more content and users etc. Vivendi Universal will be the only company in a position to offer a comprehensive music site that can generate these networks effect'.[25]

The Commission is able, through it competition policy powers, to impose behavioural and structural remedies to eliminate or mitigate market power in the communications marketplace when mergers are deemed to generate negative vertical effects. For example, in the Telia/Telenor case the undertakings concerned the divestiture of the cable TV networks in Sweden and Norway (in order to remove the vertical effects of the bundling of satellite transponder services and retail TV distribution services) as well as the introduction of local loop unbundling (in order to reduce the competitive concerns identified for the various telecom services, and to enable new entrants to establish a unique customer relation with their clients).[26]

These cases show that EU competition policy plays a central role in the Commission's effort to promote liberalisation and competition in the communications industry, because it allows for flexible regulatory intervention in a sector characterised by fast-changing, non-mature technologies. The application of the EU competition rules on a case-by-case basis enables the Commission to monitor new and more complex forms of market power that are not foreseen by ex-ante regulation. In doing so, the Commission balances conflicting objectives: on the one hand the firms' interest in engaging in vertical integration, and on the other, the general interest in keeping markets open. These cases support the findings reported from other sectors: the Commission often negotiates the outcomes with the firms concerned, in the sense that the firms undertake specific measures in order to meet the Commission's criticisms (Cave and Crowther, 2004:

---

23 Vivendi/Canal+/Seagram Case N°COMP/M.2050, § 51.

24 Temple Lang explains that 'tipping effects' occur 'when a company obtains a market share which is substantially greater than its competitors, and when this is in itself causes it to attract more customers [...] Tipping effects are not the same as first mover advantages, although the effect is similar: the market does not necessarily 'tip' in favour of the first entrant into the market, but in favour of the first company to get such a decisive lead over its competitors that the network effect begins.' Temple Lang, J. 'Media, Multimedia and European Community antitrust law', document available at: http://europa.eu.int/comm/competition/speeches/text/sp1997_070_en.pdf.

25 Vivendi/Canal+/Seagram Case N°COMP/M.2050, § 51.

26 Telia/Telenor Case N°COMP/M.1439, § 386 and § 390.

27–8). As Mendes Periera argues, 'the main concern of the Commission [has been] to ensure *access*, access to the source, access to the path and access through the gate' (Mendes Pereira, 2002).

Conclusions – Negotiating Competition in EU Communications Markets

Competition policy has played and continues to play a central role in the liberalisation of EU communications markets. During the late 1980s and early 1990s this was primarily a matter of the Commission and the more liberally oriented states pushing for liberalisation and increased competition against the resistance of the more protectionist and interventionist governments. Although the Single Market programme was agreed, and most states accepted that telecommunications should eventually be liberalised, it was the Commission's use of its (competition policy) power to break up national monopolies that started the process. As telecommunications markets were liberalised, and the different information and communications technology markets began to converge into a broad communications market, the role of competition policy changed toward the more ordinary competition policy issues: vetting mergers, combating cartels and preventing abuses of dominant positions. Some of the central challenges that emerged in the late 1990s and early 2000s arose from the special nature of communications markets: their cost structures, the importance of technology and multiple (non-economic) regulatory goals. At the same time the relationship between the Commission and the Court changed, as a few rulings went against the Commission, and the Court emphasised the importance of solid and transparent economic analysis. Consequently the Commission has adopted a somewhat flexible case-by-case approach to the communications industry, which the fast-changing nature of the sector warrants. This kind of application of competition policy on a case-by-case basis enables the Commission to monitor new and complex forms of market power that were not foreseen in the ex-ante regulation. This approach has meant that the Commission can require substantial undertakings from firms, and thus help shape the market in a more competitive direction. It has thus been able to negotiate pro-competitive outcomes. Ultimately the legitimacy and effectiveness of competition policy rests both on rigorous economic analysis and on its acceptance by the central actors in the market. The objective of competition policy is to organise economic freedoms efficiently so that customers are protected against strong economic players. Economic activity is, therefore, part of the wider social ambit; it contributes to the promotion of the interests of society as a whole. Fundamentally, the power to determine what is expected in the communications sector – and hence, the power to establish a system of normative propositions – rests on the reciprocal relationship between the different societal forces accountable for the public interest.

PART II
THE TRANSFORMATION OF TELECOMMUNICATIONS COMPANIES: SOME CONTRASTING WEST-EUROPEAN EXAMPLES

Chapter 6

Orderly Revolution: The Case of France Telecom

Marit Sjovaag Marino

After a century of state monopoly in telephone service provision, the legislative and organisational framework in the telecommunications sector in France changed fundamentally in the 1990s. The national telecommunications service provider, France Telecom, changed status in 1990 from public administration to an autonomous corporation operating under private law. Legislation adopted in 1996 introduced full competition in the sector from 1998. Regulation was transferred from the ministry (the Direction générale des postes et télécommunications, DGPT) to an independent regulatory agency, the Autorité de régulation des télécommunications (ART), which began operating from 1 January 1997. At the same time, France Telecom became a limited company, and was listed on the stock exchanges in Paris and New York, the first 22 per cent of the capital being sold in October the same year. Until 31 December 2003 the state was constitutionally bound to hold more than 50 per cent of the shares. New legislation changed this, and the state sold shares and decreased its holdings in France Telecom to less than 50 per cent in September 2004.

It seems fair to say that France Telecom is now regarded as a 'modern', predominantly 'private' business enterprise, although its ties to the French State have only recently been formally severed. However, its history contains ample evidence that the divide between 'business models' and 'focus' for 'public' and 'private' enterprises are far from as clear-cut as literature occasionally will have us believe. For example, despite a degree of correlation between the type of ownership and the 'business-like character' of the telecommunications operator, the process of transformation to survive in an increasingly competitive environment had begun long before the introduction of private capital in 1997, and also before the first legislative changes in 1990.

After a short introduction where necessary contextual information is presented, this chapter will focus on the process of corporatisation, the privatisation process, the effect of these processes on France Telecom's 'business orientation', and finally, the role played by internationalisation.

Context and Conditions

Telecommunications policy in France was never high on the public agenda before the 1970s. After the nationalisation of the service in 1889, the policy area received only limited attention from Parliament (with the exception of a reform in 1923 which introduced a separate budget for PTT[1] services) and remained the domain of experts within the public bureaucracy. When economic planning dominated French economic policy-making in the post-Second World War years, telecommunications failed to be included among the 'basic sectors'[2] and was thus deprived of important investments. The result was technological backwardness and poor penetration rates that led to a general increase in public dissatisfaction with the telephone services.

An early sign of the unease with this state of affairs came in the late 1960s and early 1970s, when a consensus was formed among experts and high officials about the necessity of organisational reform and increased spending. PTT Minister Galley pronounced as early as in 1969 that 'it is difficult to envisage that one can continue to administer a large organisation whose functions are partly those of a bank, of a transport and distribution company, and an industrial producer, with the traditional public administration rules and norms' (Galley, quoted in Libois, 1983: 241). The telecommunications sector was subsequently included among the 'basic services' from 1974, and in the following decade important investments were made to upgrade the network (introducing automatic switching and subsequently digitalisation). In this period, telecommunications engineers dominated policy-making (Suleiman and Courty, 1997).

By 1985 the technical situation had improved. Penetration rates were increasing significantly, and digitalisation of the network was well under way. In 1990, the rate of digitalisation of the French telecommunications network reached 75 per cent (Libois, 1996: 173). Within the public service provider there was a clear perception that increased fragmentation of user demand and technological as well as international political developments had forced the organisation to improve its services. The convergence between telecommunications and information technology was also cause for concern, being perceived as threatening national independence and possibilities for control (Nora and Minc, 1978).

Among legislators, too, it became increasingly clear that a fundamental reform of the telecommunications sector was needed. However, proposals to give the

---

1 PTT stands for Post, Telephone and Telegraph, and this abbreviation was commonly used throughout the latter half of the twentieth century to connote the state administration responsible for these services (including, in many cases for a number of years, some banking services).

2 The 'basic sectors' were those targeted in the government's *Plans*, that is, detailed investment plans covering 4–7 years at a time, and forming the financial centrepiece of government industrial policy in the post-war period. Sectors not defined as 'basic' were largely neglected as far as investments were concerned.

public telephone service operator managerial and financial autonomy had been put forward by Parliament in 1974, and had been met with large-scale strikes in the autumn of the same year by civil servants fearful of loosing their status as *fonctionnaires*. This action illustrated the sensitivity surrounding the issue of employees' status, and effectively hindered political reform for the next decade (Thatcher, 1999).

In the mid-1980s, however, the European Union began to take an interest in the telecommunications sector. The Terminal Equipment Directive from 1988 was adopted by the European Commission rather than by the Council of Ministers. France (and other Member States) took the European Commission to court and challenged its powers, but the European Court of Justice upheld the directive and thus strengthened the Commission's position within the policy area. This action allowed French policy-makers to press ahead with domestic reform, using the EU as a 'scapegoat' that made reform 'inevitable' whilst preserving their own legitimacy vis-à-vis the French citizens (Marino, 2005). The first step in the reform process was to give France Telecom autonomy by transforming it into a public corporation.

Corporatisation

In the decade between 1975 and 1985 the French political establishment had not approached the issue of reform of the telecommunications sector because of fears of a repetition of the large social unrest in 1974, when reform had been proposed (Thatcher, 1999). When the issue was addressed in the late 1980s, the PTT Minister, Paul Quilès, established a consultative commission, the so-called Prévot commission, to investigate and clarify the challenges and possible options for the future of the *service public* of the post and telecommunication services. The establishment of such a commission, whose mandate comprised consultation with all interested parties including industry, new entrants into the telecommunications sector, users of telecommunications services, the incumbent operator, and the general public, was a novelty in French policy-making (Marino, 2005), and signified a rupture with the traditional style of policy-making where decisions were taken by a closed set of elite players and the general public had little or no access to the process.

The commission set out to define the missions of the *service public*, its role and place in the state and in the nation considering the impact of the establishment of the Single European Market, to pinpoint necessary regulation, and to identify ways of motivating employees, including the question of employees' future status, that had caused such instability in 1974 (Prevot, 1989:7). The report offered a synthesis of the interested parties' views, as well as recommendations concerning regulation, the social role of the PTT, and its obligations towards its employees. The Prévot commission's recommendations included (Prévot, 1989: 143–51):

- Separation of regulatory and operational functions, and the establishment of an independent regulator;
- Abolition of the budget annexe;
- Creation of two autonomous judicial persons – France Telecom and La Poste, the latter including the financial services, and each to have its own independent top management possessing 'real' powers (in, for example, budgetary matters, recruitment, and negotiations with the employees);
- Integration of the '*filiales*', that is, the numerous subsidiaries mostly state owned but operating under private law;
- Clear rules and tariffs for interconnection necessitated by non-discriminatory access by service providers.

The Prévot report devoted much attention to the concerns of the employees of France Telecom (Hubert Prévot himself was a former prominent trade unionist), and was favourably received. 'Within France Telecom, 'the *ingénieurs des télécommunications*' and senior management pressed hard for change, in order to allow France Télécom to adapt to a more competitive environment and obtain greater autonomy. The trade unions were divided: whilst Force Ouvrière and the CGT [Confédération générale du travail] were hostile, the CFDT [Confédération française démocratique du travail] was open to its conclusions' (Thatcher, 1999: 156).

Legal Framework

Two laws were instrumental in the corporatisation of France Telecom in 1990. The first, the Law on the Organisation of Posts and Telecommunications, passed by Parliament in 1990 with effect from January 1991, transformed the company into a public corporation with financial and operational autonomy separated from the postal services. Budgetary autonomy meant that France Telecom was no longer required to submit its budgets for government approval. In addition, from 1994, the corporation would be taxed as if it were a firm, rather than being subject to random demands for transfers to the state coffers. The law also established some general principles for the regulatory framework: territorial coverage, equality of users, and neutrality of services. The July law established that the *Direction de Service Public* (DSP) should participate in the definition of the main strategic choices of the public corporation, and defined the main economic and financial objectives the operators must reach (Huret, 1994).

The second law, the Law on the Regulation of Telecommunications (LRT) from December 1990, completed the process of corporatisation by dividing the provision of services into three areas; monopoly services; services subject to structured and controlled competition; and services fully open to competition. It also outlined the powers of the Minister, particularly in regulatory matters. A *Commission supérieure du service public des postes et télécommunications* (CSSP) was established to 'oversee the balanced evolution of the development of the telecommunications sector' (Art. L.32–2), through which Parliament re-gained some of the power it had lost when France Telecom's budget had been exempted from governmental approval in the law of July 1990. The *Conseil Supérieur de l'Audiovisuel* (CSA) saw its powers in telecommunications matters abolished and transferred to the Minister and the DRG (*Direction de la Réglementation Générale)* (Dandelot, 1993: 24). The DRG was given responsibility for defining the regulatory framework for the activities of France Telecom and other telecommunications service operators. Thus, by the beginning of the 1990s France's telecommunications regulator was not yet politically independent, in that it formed part of the PTT Ministry.

The existence of two regulatory bodies within the PTT Ministry, one regulating the market (the CSSP) and the other the incumbent (the DRG), was specific to France (Gensollen, 1991: 32). In 1994, the DSP and the DRG were merged to form the *Direction générale des Postes et Télécommunciations* (DGPT).[3] The lack of a regulator independent of government, which rendered long-term regulatory strategies more difficult, was the prime reason for the introduction of long-term contracts, the *contrat de plan,* between the incumbent service provider and government. This contract fixed tariffs as well as future activities, and constituted an important element of the French regulatory landscape in the early 1990s (Gensollen, 1991: 32). These contracts follow the tradition of governmental *Plans* from the post-Second World War period, and can thus be seen as an attempt to formalise (and make transparent) the principal–agent relationship between the government and its agent, France Telecom.

The LRT was inspired by the compromise at the European level whereby member states were able to maintain exclusive rights for infrastructures and voice telephony one the one hand, whilst on the other hand allowing controlled competition for other services. The law deliberately gave room for interpretation, which rendered it relatively flexible and hence adaptable to the developing international environment (Dandelot, 1993: 25).

Whilst it was clear that France Telecom's management accepted and even welcomed the development towards more competitive market conditions, particularly because of its own possibilities for expansion, the corporation also wanted to exploit its monopoly position for as long as possible. This latter point was true also for the political authorities, who were interested in a strong France Telecom for domestic political reasons as well as for the value of the company if it were eventually to be privatised (Roulet, 1988). Voice telephony was not to be opened up to competition until 1998, and for the most of the 1990s this segment remained by far the most income-generating part of the incumbents' activities (accounting for 92 per cent of revenues in 1996 – estimated to fall to 24 per cent in 2005).

---

3 The DGPT was responsible for implementing the government policies in the areas of posts and telecommunications, and for ensuring conditions for loyal and fair competition between the different economic actors.

The first public demands for a change in the regulatory system came in 1993 in the Dandelot report, which stated that

> the relations [of the state towards the enterprise] should be less as those of the 'tutor' (…) and more as those of a shareholder. However, it is preferable to dissociate the role of regulator from that of shareholder. If the administration in charge of the '*tutelle*' also holds the role as the shareholder, should one not consider developing towards an autonomous regulatory organism? (Dandelot, 1993: 57)

The idea of an autonomous regulatory organism was initially an anomaly in the French political landscape (although some scholars maintain that regulators in the Anglo-Saxon meaning of the word have a rather longer tradition in France, at least from when the Conseil Constitutionnel used the term to describe the CSA (*Conseil supérieur de l'audiovisuel*) established in 1983 (Autin, 1995)). However, another government report, from 1995, repeated the argument for an independent regulator, emphasising that the creation of a legitimate legal basis for regulation was a political task. Accounting separation (to determine the real costs of a service), and the separation of regulator and service provider (to ensure transparency and independence), were the central instruments in the new regime (Stoffaës 1995: 277–8). The regulator DRG (pre-1994)/DGPT (1994–1996) had sought a reputation for impartiality (Thatcher 1999: 216), making policy-documents publicly available and holding public hearings on central issues. This regulator therefore set a strong precedent for the new regulatory authority that was to follow: the Autorité de Régulation des Télécommunications (ART).

The ART was created on 1 January 1997. It consisted of five members appointed for a period of six years, three of which were appointed by governmental decree, one by the president of the Assemblée Nationale and one by the president of the Sénat. Observers were often questioning whether the ART would be truly independent from the French state administration or whether centuries of *dirigisme* and strong governmental intervention would prove too hard to break. However, the institution rapidly gained a reputation for impartiality and fairness. The first major test was the setting of interconnection charges, and analyses have indicated that none of the players was unduly discriminated against (Andresen and Sjøvaag, 1997). The ART subsequently built on and continued its tradition of transparency and accessibility. Following legislation from May 2005, the ART has become ARCEP (Autorité de régulation des communications électroniques et des postes/Electronic Communications and Postal Regulatory Authority), regulating not only the telecommunications but also the postal sector.

An assessment of the ART/ARCEP record is outside the scope of this chapter, focusing as it does, on the transformation of France Telecom. What is clear, however, is that the legal changes in 1990 did allow France Telecom to start developing its own corporate identity distinct from the former ministerial, bureaucratic culture, to prepare for increased competition, a process which became more marked with the advent of M. Michel Bon as CEO in 1995.

Organisational Changes

The perceived need for corporatisation and legal change was not a result of politics alone. French telecommunications services were in dire straits in the early 1970s, with low penetration rates, poor quality, and mounting public dismay. Political action accompanied by high investments from 1974 onwards led the DGT (the Direction Générale des Télécommunications – the bureaucratic office that was the forerunner of France Telecom) to implement a programme – the 'ΔLP' – to improve the situation,

The programme, which devolved much power to the engineers, did bring tangible results. The number of main telephone lines in France in 1975, which were 6 million, had increased to 22 million a decade later, and to 28 million by 1990 (Suleiman and Courty, 1997: 179). The ten-year period of intense network expansion led to a perceived need for new management systems to improve quality rather than quantity, and in 1985 a new programme was instigated, the 'SG85'. The public telephone service provider shifted its focus from the quantity of new telephone lines and instigated programmes to improve quality in different areas.[4] The programme was intended to improve inter-organisational communication, and opened the way for increased use of external consultants (Iazykoff, 1991), but it has been criticised for being just another example of a classic 'sedimentation' of 'new' and 'fashionable' management ideas on an environment of technocratic dominance in a mechanistic, bureaucratic structure (Amintas and Swarte, 1997).

The process was inspired by France Telecom's contemporary perception of the 'inevitable' development of competition in the global arena. France Telecom's Director General in 1988, Marcel Roulet, stated that 'France Telecom (…) will continue to adapt, and intends to take this opportunity to play a major role on the international telecom scene' (Roulet, 1988: 109). The conviction of the inevitable development of competition and the wish to become a 'mainstream' capitalist institution marked subsequent organisational development in France Telecom. For example, the budget, which had previously been characterised by 'envelopes' for general spending and investment plans, was replaced in 1993 by a 'project logic' that entailed a decentralisation of responsibilities from the central office to regional operational units. The aim of the 1993 and subsequent reorganisations was to reduce the number of hierarchical levels and to give responsibility to those 'on the ground'. France Telecom should also be transformed into a matrix organisation (Catelin and Chatelin, 2001).

Despite these efforts, France Telecom was still a 'top-heavy' organisation at the time of its corporatisation in 1990 (Iazykoff, 1991), and the process of indicative

4 The areas targeted for quality improvements and the corresponding programmes were: production (Qualité+); commerciality (Qualité Commerciale); financial management (Couples Objectifs/Moyens); and human resource management (Management Participatif) (Iazykoff 1991).

planning characterised the company until its re-organisation in 1996 (Amintas and Swarte, 1997: 56–8). Moreover, the 'capitalist' behaviour in certain cases did not imply that France Telecom stopped fighting for its domestic monopoly powers to reap the economic benefits thereof.

Privatisation

From the beginning of January 1991, France Telecom had been transformed into an '*exploitant public autonome*', [an autonomous public corporation] under the guise of giving the enterprise more managerial and financial flexibility in an increasingly competitive international environment, as well as reducing the Ministry's powers of direct intervention. The new regulatory instruments were a licence (*cahier des charges*) stating France Telecom's rights and obligations, and a *Contrat de Plan* running for four years. Regulatory functions were kept in the PTT Ministry, regulation of licences being the responsibility of the *Direction de la réglementation generale* (DRG), and the *service public* obligations being closely followed by the *Direction du service public*.

These two offices were merged into one single unit, the DGPT (*Direction Generale des Postes et Telecommunications*) from 1994. The DGPT was responsible for 'implementing the government policies in the areas of posts and telecommunications. (…) It ensure[d] conditions for loyal and fair competition between the different economic actors' (Texte official, 1993).

The new regime of 1990 had resulted in greater independence for the operator. 'There was a clearer separation between France Telecom and the political executive. The participation of elected politicians (…) continued, but in diminished form, over issues which were politically sensitive or required co-operation between France Telecom and the political executive, such as tariffs and internationalisation' (Thatcher, 1999: 215). The legislation did, however, maintain important state influence over telephone policy through licence conditions. The telephone service was to remain in the service of the public and in the general interest, and France Telecom was the state's means of implementation.

It proved difficult for the political authorities to stop using France Telecom as a tool for broader industrial policies. Until normal taxation rules were introduced in 1994, the company continued its direct contributions. In addition to direct transfers, politicians were seen to use France Telecom as a 'milk cow' by obliging it to invest in other enterprises, sometimes substantially above the market price. For example, in January 1993, the government obliged France Telecom to spend 1bn francs on shares in two insurance companies as a 'pure financial operation' into a sector where France Telecom had no immediate interest, thus using the telecommunications operator as a another source of funding for their industrial policies (Le Figaro, 1993b; Fabre, 1993; Le Monde, 1993).

After the introduction of normal taxation rules the state was further criticised for pocketing too much of France Telecom's profit. Tax and dividends for 1994 amounted to approximately 16bn Francs, that is, the same range as earlier direct contributions: 15bn Francs in 1992 and in 1993 (Le Coeur, 1995a).

Trade unions and political opponents condemned the government's behaviour, claiming that they '[distorted] the initiated reforms [which should give autonomy to a state-owned France Telecom] and [opened] the way to privatisation' (Le Figaro, 1993a). Whereas politicians' appetite for France Telecom-generated funds was perceived as a threat to the contemporary status of the operator, privatisation remained a sensitive issue. When, in Spring 1993, a government representative formally asked France Telecom's board to consider 'separating out its mobile activities', heavy protests followed from both top management and trade unions.

The government's representative, M. Couture, gave two main reasons for the government's demand; first, the increasingly aggressive competition in the mobile sector; and second, that mobile services in France lagged behind those in other industrialised countries (La Tribune Desfossés, 1993b). France Telecom's top management was more 'surprised' about the *form* of the message than shocked by its content; trade unions opposed any possible privatisation (La Tribune Desfossés, 1993a). The issue's sensitivity, combined with the presidential elections of 1995, resulted in legislative proposals being postponed until 1996.

Privatisation was, however, on the agenda from 1993 onwards, when Balladur's new Right-wing government was seen as comprising 'free-marketeers' and was assumed to work according to the (hidden) agenda of privatisation. The 'Dandelot report', a 'reflexion' on the future of the telecommunications sector in France and the possibilities of partial privatisation through divestiture of the mobile activities of France Telecom (Dandelot, 1993), recommended introducing private capital into France Telecom, subject to the state retaining more than 50 per cent ownership. Public ownership and state control were regarded as the best guarantee that short-term search for profit would not destroy longer-term policy goals. In addition to the political difficulties over selling a larger part of the company, constitutional constraints rendered selling more than 50 per cent impossible (Dandelot, 1993: 48).

The report argued that technological development and European legislation rendered competition, and therefore French legislative reform, inevitable. Greater financial flexibility and independence was perceived to be necessary if the public company was to survive in a global market, and international partnerships were seen as of paramount importance as cross-border service-provision increased. In order to engage in alliances and joint ventures, France Telecom needed its own capital. Moreover, foreign operators had expressed doubts as to whether it would be possible to maintain good business practice as long as France Telecom was completely owned by the state and controlled by the public administration. As a case in point, the American company MCI's search for an overseas partner culminated in it joining forces with British Telecom, particularly because of the French state's direct involvement in France Telecom, and because the enterprise was neither flexible enough nor possessed sufficient capital (Monnot, 1993a, 1993b; Quotidien de Paris, 1993; Nexon, 1993a).

The Dandelot report also called for clearer separation between the regulatory and operational functions, and envisaged a regulatory authority independent from the Ministry:

> The relations [of the state towards the enterprise] should be less as those of the 'tutor' (...) and more as those of a shareholder. However, it is preferable to dissociate the role of regulator from that of shareholder. If the administration in charge of the '*tutelle*' also holds the role as the shareholder, should one not consider developing towards an autonomous regulatory organism? (Dandelot 1993: 57)

Such views echoed recent legislation at the European level. EU legislation required a regulatory entity independent from the service provider(s), and although not compulsory, all member states, including France, opted for a model with a regulatory agency independent from the Ministry (Eyre and Sitter, 1999: 55–6).

The Dandelot report met positive reactions from the incumbent operator. France Telecom's president, Marcel Roulet, officially supported a change in status from public corporation to limited company, albeit with the state as majority shareholder, to ensure sufficient capital and flexibility to partake in international alliances and joint ventures (Monnot, 1993d). However, employees' status constituted a major obstacle to reform, and the PTT Ministry asked the top management of France Telecom to instigate a consultation process similar to the one conducted by Prévot in 1989 (Le Gales, 1993b). Here, the Minister had taken the initiative to conduct an 'open consultation' process with the employees, at the time a novel method for the French state to handle a reform. Throughout 1994 Marcel Roulet emphasised his wish for 'an internal campaign to construct a common project for the group and to open for a new social contract with the trade unions' (Le Coeur, 1994). The approach, which previously had entailed a peaceful process, failed to prevent the industrial action of October 1993 (Nexon, 1993b; Douroux, 1993), but was still a clear indication that consultation as procedure had gained ground in the French telephone policy-making environment, not only between central politicians and the general public but also within the state apparatus itself (Marino, 2005).

The major issue at stake for the employees was their status as *fonctionnaires*. The trade unions DGT-PTT and CFTC expressed their qualms and opposition to the proposed joint venture between France Telecom and Deutsche Telekom in terms of fears for job losses and ultimately privatisation, which they saw as an inevitable consequence of the alliance (Le Coeur, 1993). In November 1993, a solution was presented whereby the Conseil d'Etat ruled that:

> the law creating a private enterprise [*société anonyme*] could maintain state employed *fonctionnaires* in this enterprise and give the enterprise's president power to employ and manage these civil servants without breaking a constitutional rule or principle. (Conseil d'État, quoted in Devillechabrolle and Monnot 1993)

The employees would, however, need to perform a *service public*, implying that a law proposal would have to define the enterprise's missions, that more than 50 per cent of the ownership must remain with the state, and that license conditions would ensure the execution of the *service public* interests (Devillechabrolle and Monnot, 1993). The issue remained politically sensitive and the *Contrat de Plan*, the agreement between France Telecom and the relevant ministries for 1995-1998, made no reference to the future status of the enterprise, but obliged it to 'keep the growth of personnel costs lower than its value added' (Le Coeur, 1995b; Les Echos, 1995).

Despite the temporary closure of the subject, it remained clear that a change in employees' status was forthcoming, mainly due to the impossibility of a corporation without its proper capital to form alliances with other, notably foreign, companies (lack of proper capital had hampered a possible deal with MCI in 1993). The ruling by the Conseil d'Etat inevitably opened the question of how long employees would remain *fonctionnaires*, since one could envisage *service public* obligations being removed from France Telecom's remit (Boiteau, 1996). The ruling therefore provided a means of delaying the transfer of all employees to the private sector, as well as signalling the state's willingness to take on responsibilities for pensions and provide early retirement schemes (Boiteau, 1996: 383). However, the issue of employees' status remained largely untouched in French debate until 1995, when a new project for changing the status of the corporation was undertaken (Delion and Durupty, 1995: 180). The PTT Minister emphasised the inevitable forthcoming competition and the need for clear rules (M. Fillon, Minister for technologies and information, quoted in Monnot, 1995) and 'the government considered that a change in status of [France Telecom] is necessary' (Le Gales and Saint-Victor, 1995).

The privatisation plans had supporters abroad. Günter Rexrodt, the German Minister of Economics, demanded 'substantial' privatisation of France Telecom as precondition for any joint venture with Deutsche Telekom (Petit, 1993a; Monnot, 1993c), on the grounds that, '[o]ut of respect for competition it is not possible to join two state monopolies' (Günter Rexrodt, quoted in Monnot, 1993c). The domestic conflict regarding the employees' status, however, persuaded the French PTT Minister to temporarily renounce his privatisation plans: 'France Telecom's objective is not to be privatised, but to be a public enterprise, independent from the state' (radio interview with M. Longuet, Europe 1, 29 October 1993).

Michel Bon's advent as CEO of France Telecom marked the beginning of a new era in the corporation's history. Marcel Roulet, M. Bon's predecessor, was an 'Enarque, that is, he was educated at the elite school ENA (Ecole Nationale d'Administration), established in the 1940s, which continues to educate the majority of the higher civil servants in France. He had therefore been an integral part of the traditional bureaucratic elite in Paris. Michel Bon, in contrast, was a businessman. His track record included turning around the large consumer goods group Carrefour, experience that was viewed favourable for the task of the inevitable cultural transformation of France Telecom into a modern European business organisation. His nomination, therefore, should be seen as a clear sign from the political authorities (at the time the Right-wing government of Alain Juppé) that they wanted to initiate real transformation.

The Septennat 1995–2002

Michel Bon's period as CEO of France Telecom lasted for seven years, from 1995 until 2002. The first five of his years in tenure were conducted in favourable economic conditions, whereas his demise in 2002 was spurred on by events, amongst other factors, following on from the disastrous economic development in the telecommunications sector in general.

M. Bon was instated by PTT Minister Fillon, in Juppé's conservative government (which remained in power until 1997). His nomination followed the two-day presidency of M. François Henrot, a former DGT manager responsible for international activities (subsequently for sales and marketing) of the DGT (European Corporate Governance Institute: http://www.ecgi.org). The reason for the short span of his presidency was rumoured as being that he had made privatisation of France Telecom a precondition for him taking up the post, a condition which PTT Minister Fillon was unable to defend in public (personal interview).

Although not expressed in public, the new man at the top of France Telecom after 1995 was no stranger to private capital. Viewing himself as a 'grocer' rather than a civil servant, bureaucrat or administrator, Michel Bon's presidency was guided by three overarching principles. First, he was the first top manager to set out the importance and power of the *client* rather than of technology. Second, he saw that competition was *international* rather than only operating within the domestic market. Third, he realised the potential of the *new technologies* (mobile and the Internet). These three principles can be seen to have influenced France Telecom's strategies for the whole of his tenure and to continue to be central to strategies in the new millennium. The client focus resulted in organisational changes that emphasised a flatter management structure and increased the decision-making powers of lower-level managers. The focus on new technologies and internationalisation led to France Telecom attempting to build 'seamless' mobile and broadband networks, organisationally through Orange for mobile services, Wannadoo for Internet services, and Equant providing global services for the business segment.

M. Bon was company CEO through the first part of France Telecom's privatisation. The first public offering took place in October 1997, when the state sold 22 per cent of its shares. The state was constitutionally bound to retain more than 50 per cent of its shares until 31 December 2003, when legislation was passed to allow for a lower degree of ownership. In September 2004 the French state sold another '10.85 per cent of the operator's shares in an accelerated placement to institutional investors. Following the transaction and an offer reserved to employees, the French State held, directly and indirectly, 41.08 per cent of the company's shares on January 31st 2005. The Government noted that it intended to remain a significant shareholder in France Telecom for the medium term' (France Telecom Annual Report, 2004). France Telecom continued to fulfil its role as universal service provider within the framework of new regulations based on European directives. The status of civil servants employees was also unchanged, conforming to the French law of 31 December 2003.

After his departure Michel Bon was credited for having turned France Telecom from 'a sleepy monopolist into one of its industry's most aggressive competitors' (*The Economist*, March 2002).

Internationalisation

The development of the market for telecommunications services throughout the 1980s pointed to increased global competition and to increasingly sophisticated and demanding customers. In order not to lose out in this international competition, it was realised that the French telecommunications operator had to be active and also provide services outside France's borders. France Telecom has a tradition of international activity, particularly through its state-owned subsidiaries operating under private law (Vedel, 1991), but as we have seen, it was a problem to be taken seriously as an independent business partner as long as the company was seen as part and parcel of the French state. However, throughout the 1980s, France Telecom itself increased its international activity, targeting global customers with seamless solutions and offering 'one-stop shopping'. 'France Telecom International' was

> announced in Geneva at Telecom '87 (...) to confirm [France Telecom's] presence in all telecommunications fields on the international scene (...) [a move that showed] the organization's commitment to a stronger marketing orientation, efficient service provision, greater responsiveness to customer needs and increased attention to the international sector. (Roulet, 1988:113)

Global One

Until 1991, France Telecom's international strategy remained 'prudent', mainly relying on a cooperation with Deutsche Telekom, where every potential acquisition would have to be discussed in order to ensure partition of risks and responsibilities (Douste-Blazy, 2003). However, its engagement with Deutsche Telekom and American Sprint to set up Global One in the first half of the 1990s remained the most visible sign that the enterprise was becoming more aggressive on the international scene. Indeed, the venture has been claimed to have advanced the liberalisation process in France, because of the opposition from both the US Justice Department and the European Commission to the maintenance of the national monopolies in telecommunications services in France and Germany if these national operators were to join forces, thereby creating a major global player.

The US Justice Department approved the venture in 1996, but conditions attached ensured that before 1 January 1998, Global One was forbidden to own, control or provide certain services until competitors had the opportunity to provide similar services in France and Germany (Curwen, 1999a: 147). The European Competition Commissioner Karel van Miert 'made a preliminary ruling [in October 1995] that Atlas [the company jointly owned by France Telecom and Deutsche Telekom] would be allowed to proceed provided, *inter alia*, alternative utility networks had been opened to competitors in France and Germany by 1 July 1996 (Curwen, 1999a: 148).

All participants invested both money and other resources in Global One. However, the alliance took a serious blow in April 1999, when Deutsche Telekom entered merger talks with Telecom Italia without consulting or informing France Telecom (see *The Economist*, 1999; Douste-Blazy, 2003), who claimed DT's actions were a breach of contract. Later, in October the same year, Sprint was bought by MCI WorldCom, thereby consigning the joint venture Global One to history, and leaving France Telecom without any clear strategy for internationalisation at a time when the company's domestic market share was threatened. France Telecom henceforth engaged in a 'shopping frenzy' to gain access to foreign markets, particularly in Germany and the UK. In the UK, they bought 25 per cent of NTL in July 1999, in order to gain access to the most important alternative network to BT, to an important customer base, and potentially to a UMTS licence. The fact that they bought a minority share has been portrayed as a rational decision for a group with limited experience of controlling foreign subsidiaries.

However, also in the autumn of 1999, UK's Vodafone launched its attack on German Mannesmann. The Vodafone-Mannesmann merger was possible only if Vodafone sold off its mobile operator Orange in the UK, and if France Telecom was interested in buying. Surprisingly, France Telecom did not immediately sell its shares in NTL, but rather continued to invest in it, to the tune of $450 million in December 1999. Furthermore, it supported NTL in its acquisition of Swiss Cablecom in March 2000, despite its own acquisition of Orange, by then being identified as a strategic priority (Ministry of Finance, quoted in Douste-Blazy, 2003), and thus further increasing its own exposure to NTL to €1.85bn. France Telecom had therefore invested €8.122bn in a project which, once the buy-out of Orange was planned, lost close to all strategic interest, and in which the company held only a minority share. Political authorities as well as business commentators have subsequently expressed astonishment about the lack of competence within France Telecom's administration (Douste-Blazy, 2003).

In response to these criticisms, the CEO at the time, Michel Bon, said that 'France Telecom was at the time worth more than €200bn at the stock market. One does not view an investment of €4bn in the same manner as if the company is worth €10bn'.

France Telecom's somewhat confused approach to international expansion could also be seen in their activities in Germany, where they initially targeted E+, the third largest German mobile operator. In the autumn of 1999, the management negotiated buying 83 per cent of the company for €9.2bn. The deal, however, fell through because of Bell South, already a shareholder in E+, exercising its pre-emptive rights to buy together with Dutch KPN. The failed strategy meant France Telecom not only lost time and resources, but that the company was also punished by the financial markets' loss of confidence (Douste-Blazy, 2003).

The subsequent acquisition of Mobilcom, a smaller mobile operator but one which was also present in the fixed-line market and delivering Internet services, provides an interesting example of the potential conflict between the government as principals and the newly privatised utility company as their agent. France Telecom's CEO, M. Bon, was saying that the acquisition of Mobilcom had been presented to the Ministry of Finance as an alternative strategy in case the buy-out of E+ failed. His vice-president, M. Vinciguerra, however, gave the Ministry the impression that Mobilcom appeared as potential acquisition target only after the E+ deal had failed, and even then France Telecom was made aware of the company by the bank Lazard. A parliamentary report concluded that 'according to the evidence presented, the decision to invest a very important sum was never exposed to thorough investigation and reflection, even if it carried considerable risks' (Douste-Blazy, 2003). In March 2000, France Telecom paid €3.7bn for 28.5 per cent of Mobilcom, valuing the company at 80 times its EBITDA,[5] that is, €570 million above market price. The takeover was not conditional on Mobilcom obtaining a UMTS licence in Germany, one of the major strategic reasons for France Telecom's initial interest.

Global One was finally bought by France Telecom in January 2000 for $4.34bn (Renault, 2000). The company was further merged with Equant, bought by France Telecom in November 2000, and the resulting Equant/Global One was presented as 'a global leader in data transfer and IP services for businesses, offering the world's largest seamless network' (Jakubyszyn, 2000).

France Telecom acquired Orange in June 2000, as a result of Vodafone's takeover of Mannesmann. France Telecom's mobile activities in France, Itineris, were placed within the Orange framework, which was being led by the former head of Orange UK, Mr. Snook (*The Economist*, 1 June 2000). Orange was France Telecom's first acquisition after the dissolution of the Global One alliance and was therefore seen to confirm to the company's attempts at expanding beyond its secure domestic market (*The Economist*,1 June 2000).

These acquisitions and the concurrent significant drop in market prices for telecommunications shares left France Telecom with enormous debts, mounting to almost €70bn in 2002 (*The Economist*, 2002a). Management was in disarray

---

5 The financial markets had valued the company at 65 times its EBITDA prior to speculation about the takeover.

and M. Bon was ousted, to be replaced by Thierry Breton. M. Breton was, in contrast to M. Bon, seen to be of the 'traditional French capitalism school'.

> At the heart of traditional French capitalism was a belief that the state, embodied by France's top politicians, financiers and business leaders, should be the ultimate arbiter of important economic questions. The Messier [CEO of Vivendi Universal in the 1990s, another troubled utility, telecommunications, and media company at the time] and Bon fiascos have given renewed strength to supporters of that old model. First, this led to the brutal ejection of the discredited bosses. More subtly, it meant appointing replacements who can be expected not to cause the elite further embarrassment. (*The Economist*, 2002b)

Later Presidencies

Thierry Breton came to France Telecom in 2002 with a reputation for being able to turn around large corporations in dire financial straits, having saved both Bull and Thomson Multimedia. This mathematician/engineer was seen to be less 'aggressively capitalist' than his predecessor, and installed a plan called 'Ambition 2005' to redress the financial difficulties of the corporation. The France Telecom management team was reorganised at the end of 2002 by simplifying the organisational structure, and by giving greater accountability to senior managers. This reorganised team was responsible for the implementation of the 'Ambition 2005' plan, which consisted of:

- 'TOP'; a programme aimed at improving operational performance so as to provide €15bn to be used for debt reduction in the period 2003–2005;
- €15bn in additional equity;
- €15bn through restructuring of debts;
- A strategy focusing on customer satisfaction and integrated operational management.

The 'Ambition 2005' plan was complemented by a company reorganisation in the first half of 2003, reflecting its development and the structure of its operations according to the different activities and subsidiaries: The Orange segment, covering all wireless telephony activities in the world; The Wannadoo segment, including Internet access services, portals, e-Merchant solutions for businesses and directories; The Fixed line, Distribution, Networks, Large Customers and Operators segment (mainly fixed line services in France); The Equant segment, covering worldwide data transmission services; The TP Group services, covering activities in Poland; The Other International segment, comprising other fixed line activities outside France.

In 2004, another organisational change was implemented, to pursue a strategy to become an *integrated operator*. Three operating divisions were created to serve the three customer usage segments: Personal Communications Services (comprising the Orange segment), Home Communications Services (including Wannadoo), and Enterprise Communications Services (Annual Report 2004). The organisation of the company is thus based on usage of services, rather than technologies or geography.

February 2005 saw the coming of Didier Lombard as the President of France Telecom, when Thierry Breton left the enterprise to become Finance Minister. M Lombard announced in July 2005 the three year programme NExT (New Experience in Telecom services), aimed at 'enabling the Group to pursue its transformation as an integrated operator, supported by its renewed model to profitable growth, and to give customers access to a universe of services that are both high value and simple' (http://www.francetelecom.com/en/group/vision/strategy/next/). The emphasis is thus clearly on providing clients with an integrated service regardless of the technological platform over which these services are offered.

Conclusion

This chapter has shown that the process of liberalisation and privatisation of the telecommunications sector in France has been long and complex. Many actors were involved at different stages of the process, from the European Commission and the Council of Ministers through to the employees of France Telecom and even the 'ordinary citizens'. France Telecom has retained a central role throughout the process.

We can identify two central issues in the process of corporatisation and privatisation of France Telecom that have spurred the main foci of the debate: Firstly, the issue of investments, and secondly, the issue of competition.

Telecommunications is a high-*investment* industry. Technological research and development is expensive and with an uncertain rate of return. Lack of sufficient funds for investment in research and development has been an issue on the telecommunications policy agenda since the early 1900s, resulting at different times in various financing formulae, such as the *budget annexe* from 1923 and the establishment of several state owned subsidiaries operating under private law.

From the 1960s onwards the telecommunications engineers pushed for a larger degree of independence from the postal services, which they saw as hampering much-needed investments in the telecommunications sector because of the postal services' loss-making. The political and bureaucratic establishment, comprising the top management of the DGT, started to agree on the need for fundamental reform of the telecommunication sector from the early 1970s, but public opinion and opposition from the employees fearful of losing their status as *fonctionnaires* hampered reform throughout the 1970s and the larger part of the 1980s,

When corporatisation of the DGT – from 1988 France Telecom – appeared on the public political agenda in the 1980s, the need for substantial financial investments was one of the key arguments for those in favour of fundamental organisational change. The telecommunications engineers were, as we have seen, in favour of change, as was the top management of France Telecom. Also the government, who realised that not only would the state have problems providing sufficient funds, but also that their continued direct control hampered the company's attractiveness for international alliances and joint ventures, advocated corporatisation.

Parliament, however, was afraid of losing control of what was perceived as a provider of an important *service public*. The status of *service public* was traditionally one of the central arguments for the state's involvement in an economic sector (see Marino, 2005), and constituted a forceful *raison d'être* for the state. In the case of telecommunications, corporatisation was introduced with a host of safeguards to ensure continuity of the enterprise's *service public* status and its obligations, including the establishment of the *Direction des Services Publics*, the DSP. When in the late 1990s the enterprise was privatised, its *service public* characteristics were again particularly catered for. It was designated as responsible for universal service obligations, its employees were to remain civil servants because the enterprise was seen to perform a *service public*, and the state's ownership share could not go below the threshold of 50 per cent.

However, although the high investment needs had been pivotal in the corporatisation debate in the late 1980s, they were less so in the debate of 2003, and the law of 31 December 2003 opened the way for a level of state ownership below 50 per cent. Six years after the initial IPO, the issue of *service public* in direct connection with France Telecom and its importance to the general public was perceived as less prominent among policy-makers. Instead of being vested directly in the company France Telecom, the *service public* obligations (including universal service, fair and equal treatment of customers, and adaptability of service), were seen best taken care of through regulation, applicable to all market participants.

When political debate for legal reform started in the late 1980s, France Telecom's Director General, Marcel Roulet, saw increased *competition* in the sector as 'inevitable'. His views were in line with opinions among central European policy-makers at the time, and contributed significantly to preparing the ground for introduction of competition in France. However, both France Telecom's top management and government officials ensured that France Telecom was given maximal opportunity to benefit from its monopoly position in voice telephony. Moreover, throughout the period of competition in the French telecommunication sector, that is, from 1998, France Telecom has been named as responsible for universal service obligations, a status that undoubtedly entails a positive image, even if the direct pecuniary effects are difficult to pin down.

Although France Telecom itself, the government as owners, and Parliament as defenders of a strong *service public* were predominantly (at least publicly) against competition in the 1980s, they all embraced the idea prior to legislation in 1990. The French state's challenging of the European Commission regarding the latter's powers to issue decrees concerning public utilities that should be directly applicable in Member States, can be interpreted as an attempt to creating a 'scapegoat' and to persuade the public of the 'inevitability' of the development. In this case, Parliament, the government, and France Telecom had concurrent views. Even the employees, initially fiercely against privatisation, became less opposed to the development as the proportion of employees with civil servants status decreased. Moreover, their involvement in the early stages of the liberalisation debate through the Prévot report and its innovative measures for communicating with affected groups before the actual decision-taking in Parliament, contributed to the process seeing less social unrest than in the 1970s (although large-scale strikes took place in 1993).

One of the major developments *within* France Telecom over the period 1990-2004 was its immense turn-around from a state-hierarchical, bureaucratic structure and culture to 'modern', business-oriented enterprise. Although one will always find critics that point to the enterprise's heavy burden of bureaucratic culture there seems to be a general perception that France Telecom in the mid-2000s is behaving much like any large, multinational, capitalitst institution. The state ownership is reduced to just above 40 per cent, and is set to decrease further in the future. Internal reorganisations have been frequent, particularly after 1998, and these reorganisations have reflected developing views of the market in which the firm operates, as well as it role and best strategy. From being dominated by engineers and technological personnel in the 1980s, the development of the firm's strategies and management is now to a much larger extent influenced by economists and managers focusing on strategies and marketing. The development can therefore be seen to agree with the observation in chapter 12, that companies through change in ownership structure also go through a process of changing strategies and changing its views on the marketplace.

It is, however, important to note that this development did not start with privatisation. Changing management routines and internal reorganisations had also taken place before any broad public debate about telecommunications reform in France. The programme 'SG85', intended to increase management flexibility and focus on quality rather than quantity of network capacity, was criticised for being just another attempt at implementing 'new' management structures in an old administrative system, but nevertheless signified that ideas of private sector management methods were being absorbed in the organisation. The process has been a long one, and has indeed been strengthened if not primarily by intervention of the new owners, at least by the effects of new ownership structures and privatisation (such as the possibility to access financial markets, and thus being able to pursue a strategy for international expansion).

What did change with privatisation was France Telecom's possibilities to engage in international activities. Its first serious international venture, Global One together with Deutsche Telekom and Sprint, was approved by US and EU authorities on the condition that France opened up its domestic market to competition. MCI had dropped its engagements with France Telecom because of the French state's tight control. Once privatised, the legal strings on France

Telecom loosened and the company became more attractive as a partner. Moreover, France Telecom's many acquisitions in the 1990s can be interpreted as a sign that the enterprise wanted expansion over and above what it could achieve at home. Having had a monopoly of most telecommunications services in the French market, expansion could logically proceed through two means: geographical spread, or development of new services to expand the market in which it operated. Buying telecommunications operators in other countries allowed the company to continue doing what it perceived as its core competence, rather than venturing into new and uncertain business segments.

As the potential for geographical expansion has decreased, France Telecom has consolidated its activities and introduced a similar organisational model worldwide. During the 15 years from 1990 to 2004 it has also overcome its reluctance towards the Internet and has embraced new technologies as a means for providing the integrated, high-quality services for which the organisation should be known.

International engagements have therefore undoubtedly impacted on the organisation and mindset of France Telecom. Prior to corporatisation, France Telecom's international activities consisted mainly of state owned subsidiaries operating directly in other countries (for example, cable network operators in former French colonies), or through bilateral or multilateral research and development agreements. At the end of 2005, they had more than 145 million customers on five continents. In a competitive environment, all that is needed is to keep the customers happy.

Chapter 7

The Problems of the First Mover: The Case of British Telecom

Marit Sjovaag Marino

In 1984 British Telecom became the first major European incumbent telecommunications operator to be privatised and exposed to a new regulatory regime. The move took place more than a decade before similar policy developments in the rest of the EU countries, so that the British experience provided important lessons for policy-makers and regulators in all major European countries.

As a company, British Telecom itself underwent significant change, both organisationally and culturally, and this chapter attempts to trace the major developments within British Telecom after its privatisation in 1984. After a short historical overview the main part of the chapter is divided between BT's formal/external conditions and its internal development.

A Brief History

The first major reform of the British telecommunications sector in the post-Second World War era took place in 1969,[1] when the Post Office (PO) ceased to be part of the civil service and was transformed into a public corporation by the Post Office Act of 1969 (Harper, 1997: 13–21). The 1969 Act, however, did not give details concerning the PO's organisation; the PO 'was free to decide its internal structure and matters such as staffing and salaries' (Thatcher, 1999a: 95).

The Post Office's legal monopoly in network and service provision covered all forms of transmission of electric signals, with the exception of broadcasting by wireless telegraphy and cable television. In practice the PO was also monopolist regarding customer premises equipment (CPE), because it had to approve of equipment being connected to their network. The PO's finances were, however, linked to the general public expenditure, and thus to the general budget (Thatcher, 1999a: 98). This would prove an essential element in the Conservative government's

---

1 The Post Office Act of 1961 had changed the possibilities for the Post Office to borrow money in financial markets, but the organisation remained within the civil service.

arguments for transforming the Post Office into British Telecom after they came to power in 1979.

During the 1960s and the 1970s public discontent with the telecommunications services provision grew. Long waiting lists, sharp price rises, and the supply and export performance of the manufacturing sub-sector were all factors that contributed to the pressure for reform (Harper, 1997: chs 4–6). Large business users and computer companies claimed that the PO's monopoly of CPE 'resulted in inadequate supply of equipment such as modems and PABXs [private automated branch exchanges] and lengthy applications to approve non-standard equipment' (Thatcher, 1999a: 99). At the time of the Conservative Party's electoral victory in 1979, therefore, because of the public dissatisfaction with and general criticism of the telephone service, the PO was a natural target for reform. However, the extent of this reform and the impact it would have both nationally and internationally, could not have been envisaged at the time.

A New Telecommunications Landscape after 1981

Institutional Design of British Telecom

Before the Conservative party came to power in 1979 they did not have a strategy for radical institutional change of the telecommunications sector. However, within a short time span the sector underwent profound change. The intention to split the PO into two public corporations, the PO and British Telecommunications (BT), was announced in September 1979 (Thatcher, 1999a: 144), and the Secretary of State for Industry, Sir Keith Joseph, made a statement to Parliament about the general relaxation of the PO's monopoly in July 1980 (Harper, 1997: 138). Studies on the implications of allowing complete freedom to offer services to third parties over PO circuits were also commissioned (Harper, 1997: 138).

The British Telecommunications Act of 1981, setting up British Telecom as a corporation and separating it from the postal services after a century together, kept most of the institutional arrangements of the 1969 Act to BT, 'including the PO's monopoly over network operation, powers and duties to break even and provide services' (Thatcher, 1999a: 144; see also Florio, 2003: 201–3). Specifically, the Secretary of State in charge of telecommunications retained important powers regarding appointments of board members, overall strategies, borrowing, and capital spending (Section 15 of the Act).

The Secretary of State, however, also gained new powers through the Act, notably, the power to issue licences to supply services, and to set standards for equipment connected to BT's network. Moreover, BT could, if in agreement with the Secretary of State, also issue licenses to provide services, and the Secretary of State had the power to direct BT to do so. Section 16 of the Act allowed standards for equipment connected to BT's network to be set by the Secretary of State, and so the Secretary of State could end BT's effective monopoly over CPE by setting standards for it (Thatcher, 1999a: 144).

After 1981, privatisation of BT appeared on the political agenda, and the central piece of legislation was the Telecommunications Act of 1984. This Act represented radical institutional change, including the privatisation of BT, the ending of its statutory monopoly,[2] a new licensing regime, and the creation of a new, institutionally separate regulator for telecommunications.

Regulation of Competition

Pressure for competition in the telecommunications sector had been growing in the UK from the late 1960s, and by the late 1970s calls for competition in terminal equipment were frequent (Harper, 1997: 137). Carrier competition was also increasingly advocated, particularly because of the serious criticisms of the PO's service delivery in the City, who saw licensing of competitors as a potential solution to BT's poor performance. Therefore, in 1982, Mercury was granted a license, which established a duopoly, with the incumbent in a strong dominant position (Florio, 2003: 202).

The duopoly situation lasted until the licensing review in 1991. The fact that only one competitor to BT was licensed in 1984 was justified with reference to the possibility that open competition would result in the destruction of new entrants rather than of the entrenched former monopoly (Curwen, 1997: 129). Mercury concentrated upon the high-value-added parts of the network, such as major cities and the City of London, as well as on the long-distance and international segments.[3] Owing to this focus, Mercury could not gain a significant overall market share. In 1990, it had a share of 5–6 per cent of the British telephony market (Gerpott, 1998: 111), although in the international call market it was more successful (Börtsch, 2004: 600).

The 1981 British Telecommunications Act had transformed BT into a corporation separate from the Post Office, but the decision to privatise BT (announced by the Secretary of State in 1982) necessitated new regulations, which appeared as the 1984 Telecommunications Act. This Act established a new regulatory regime. In particular, a new regulator, the Director General of Telecommunications (DGT), was created. This was a government appointment although the DGT enjoyed a measure of independence. The DGT headed an office that became known as Oftel (the Office of Telecommunications), although powers were vested in the DGT as an individual and not in Oftel (Thatcher, 1999b: 94).

---

2 Up until 1981, BT had operated as a statutory monopoly, with some few exceptions, such as private closed networks.

3 By 1996, Mercury carried more than 50 per cent of outgoing traffic from the City of London (Kamall, 1996: 70).

Liberalisation was not the main aim of the 1984 reform of the British telecommunications sector, and this was reflected in the institutional design for the sector's regulation. Legislation laid down only broad guidelines for the Secretary of State and the DGT. Maintaining and promoting effective competition was only a secondary duty, albeit one that the DGT quickly came to see as central to the development of the regulatory regime. 'I strongly agree that competition is preferable to detailed regulation as means of promoting the interests of consumers and it is one of my key aims to promote the expansion of competition as far as it is worthwhile' (Carsberg, 1987: 237).

From the beginning the DGT and Oftel played a central role in the development of the regulatory framework in the UK. The initial regulatory framework lacked detail and left great discretion in the hands of the regulators, 'whose duties were otherwise very broadly defined' (Goldstein, 2000: 200). Being such an early mover in changing from a traditional bureaucratic, state-owned model of telecommunication provision to the independent regulation of a private enterprise, Oftel, 'had to build its own regulatory model more or less from scratch. Its method was to publish proposed regulations for comment and to modify the proposals where they could be demonstrated to be likely to cause unforeseen problems' (Curwen, 1997: 116).

The BT/Mercury duopoly lasted until the 'duopoly review' (Department of Trade and Industry, 1991) in 1991, when cable television companies were permitted to provide telecom services and other telecommunications carriers were able to enter the market. Oftel required incumbents to interconnect with competitors, and helped new entrants by waiving access deficit contributions to operators with small market shares, and by denying BT the opportunity to provide both television and telephone services. Thus, infrastructure competition was central to the regulator's strategy in the UK (Collins and Murroni, 1997: 475–6).

In 1991, 60 new licences were granted. The new licensing regime implied that any existing or future network would be licensed, with the exception of international networks. Also, the 1991 regime restated that BT was not allowed to enter the entertainment market. Despite these liberalising measures, and although the number of operators and service providers continued to increase,[4] BT did not see a drop in its number of domestic subscribers until 1995, and it continued to hold a dominant position in the market (Goldstein, 2000; Florio, 2003).

Oftel ceased to exist in 2003, when it was replaced by Ofcom, an independent regulator covering communications services (such as media and broadcasting in addition to telecommunications).

---

4 At the end of 1995, there were 1,159 licences in existence on the Oftel register (Curwen, 1997: 130).

Privatisation

Despite the new institutional structures introduced rapidly after their victory in the general election of 1979, the Conservatives' election manifesto had not mentioned privatisation. In July 1982, however, the Secretary of State at the Department of Industry, Patrick Jenkin, set out the government's intention to sell shares in BT and to create an independent regulatory body for telecommunications. The motives for privatisation were not so much to extend competition as a result of fiscal pressure, party political advantage, new ideas about competition and the role of the private sector, and the example of the United States (Thatcher, 1999b: 95; Hills, 1986).

In November 1984 more than 50 per cent of the ordinary shares were sold. The first placing was wholly a fixed-price public offering, with a small part of the stock reserved for employees (Florio, 2003: 202; Thatcher, 1999a: 148). British Telecom's flotation was the first of a series of privatisations of state-owned utilities throughout the 1980s and into the 1990s. The company's transfer into the private sector continued in December 1991 when the government sold around half its remaining holding of 47.6 per cent of shares reducing its stake to 21.8 per cent. Virtually all the government's remaining shares were subsequently sold in a third flotation in July 1993, raising £5 billion for the treasury and introducing 750,000 new shareholders to the company (BT, 2006a).

The tactic of underpricing shares to attract small investors, in line with the Thatcher government's strategy of 'popular capitalism', resulted in sales raising six times more money than any previous initial stock offering in the UK (£3.9bn) (Durant, Legge and Moussios, 1998: 123). Subsequent sales of government-held equity took place in December 1991 (reducing the state's ownership share to 25.8 per cent) and July 1993. The sale of BT shares reaped in excess of £17.5bn (Durant, Legge and Moussios 1998: 123). The government retained 0.5 per cent of ordinary shares (Goldstein, 2000: 200), but the 'golden share' (the government's right to veto unwanted takeovers despite only a minority holding of shares) was abandoned in 1997.

The nature of shareholders has changed since the first IPO in 1984. Whereas at the time of privatisation in 1984 there were 1.7 million shareholders, there was half that number in 1992. In 1994 the number peaked at 2.7million, before dropping again. However, in 1985, 98 per cent of the shareholders held too few shares for them to exert any direct influence on the company, and the list of main shareholders shows that BT is owned by financial institutions, each with a rather small share of capital (Florio, 2003: 227–9).

The British telecommunications sector has been said to provide a glittering example of how *not* to privatise a public sector enterprise, because it principally replaced a publicly owned monopoly with a privately owned one, relegating much of the state's control measures along the way. The view is a crude one, but it does highlight one major problem with the process, namely that increased efficiency in the sector is not only depending on the ownership structures, but also on the degree of (realistic threat of) competition. Although, as has been mentioned, the motives for the privatisation of BT were more complex than simply increasing competition, and that some of these goals (reducing fiscal pressure, gaining party political advantage), were at least partially reached, the fact that there were so few privatisation processes to learn from at the time made the event much more of an experiment.

Chapter 12 in this volume shows how the twin factors of privatisation and effective regulation work together to increase efficiency in the industry. In the case of the UK, the lack of other similar cases from which the regulators could learn, and the fact that there were only two licensed operators in the early years, rendered the 'information gap' between the regulators and the regulatee particularly important (Melody, 1997). However, in addition to the difficulties faced by the regulator, and their need to constantly develop and update policies, the BT itself was faced with similar challenges of having to adapt to a changing regulatory environment. This led to a series of organisational changes within the incumbent operator.

Organisational Developments in BT after 1981

Having looked at the changing landscape of telecommunications legislation, institutional design, and competition, we shall now turn to the changes within BT. The formal institutional framework was not the only thing that changed after the 1981 British Telecommunications Act. Significant changes took place within the organisation itself, but the most important was probably the increased visibility and emphasis on *the customer*. In the 1970s, BT, like its European counterparts, was a technology-driven organisation whose major decisions were taken by engineers and personnel who had had most of their – if not their entire – career within the PO. Diversifying customer demand (due to changing technological possibilities) and signs of increased competition both internationally and nationally necessitated changes in organisational behaviour and culture.

In 1981, the new BT chairman, Sir George Jefferson, transformed what since 1979 had been known as the Marketing Executive (ME), into BT Enterprises, 'with the flagship role of developing the new activities on which the future would rest' (Harper, 1997: 140). This reflected the view among BT top management that the future growth areas for telecommunications companies lay with new service industries rather than with manufacturing, and so BT Enterprises was established expressly to develop new products and services. BT's position was not exclusively bad at the time of corporatisation; service delivery was relatively good outside London, whereas both public network and private circuits within London were in need of improvement. However, customer relations remained problematic, not least because of a strong corporate culture of hierarchy and the interest of the unions in preserving separation of functions. The unions were fearful they would be the most affected by the 25 per cent cost savings that Sir George had publicly proclaimed to be the goal for his first three-year period, they were negative to losing their status as civil servants, and feared that a privatisation would negatively impact BT's residential service and its research and development efforts.

Mercury's appetite for engaging in the most profitable market segments, such as long-distance calls for business customers, implied that immediately after privatisation, BT concentrated on network modernisation for these networks. However, this came at the price of neglecting the other networks, especially the private client mass market, where quality deteriorated through massive cost-cutting (Börsch, 2004: 602). To address this weakness, BT invested massively in network modernisation in the 1980s, and in 1991 over 80 per cent of its network and almost 100 per cent of its long-distance network was digitalised (Gerpott, 1998, quoted in Börsch, 2004). The network modernisation made possible the offering of new services, especially value-added and data services for business clients.

After the creation of BT, the chairman chose *not* to institute a Management Board or any organisation-wide equivalent of the former Managing Director's Committee, a top-level institution that had been involved in a huge number of day-to-day operating decisions. Devoid of such an organ, headquarters staff had to take more individual responsibility and to find new ways to operate. 'The experience and the challenges it posed were an important element in the transition from the Civil Service environment to that of business' (Harper, 1997: 142). What is provided here is a tempering of the thesis that privatisation, rather than corporatisation, can be expected to lead to 'a movement away from rule-bound and centralised management to more local management accountability, profit centres and consumer awareness' (see Chapter 12, this volume). As this example shows, such developments can also happen within a publicly owned corporation, if the top management has the will and the powers to implement structures conducive to local accountability. However, one should remember that the process became more accentuated after BT's privatisation in the mid-1980s.

After privatisation in 1984, BT decentralised, took on a more divisional form, and created local profit centres (Börsch, 2004: 601–2). The new Telecommunications Act had to enable British Telecom to become more responsive to competition in the UK and to expand its operations globally. Commercial freedom granted to British Telecom allowed it to enter into new joint ventures and, if it so decided, to engage in the manufacture of its own apparatus. The reorganisation created problems of varying performance levels across the country, which, together with the increasing speed of technological development, network modernisation, and international ventures, resulted in another major organisational reform in 1991.

The 1991 reform, named 'Project Sovereign',[5] was intended to create a structure for BT's vision 'to become the most successful worldwide telecommunications

---

5 The name Sovereign was selected as it reflected the company's commitment to meeting customers' needs – 'The customer is King'. (www.btplc.com/Thegroup/BTsHistory/History.htm).

group' (Pospischil, 1993: 607). On 2 April 1991, the company unveiled a new trading name, BT, a new corporate identity and a new organisational structure. This reform saw the organisational focus shifted from a division based on geography to one based on customer categories (individuals, small businesses, and multi-national corporations). Another category comprised a set of products which, for business, legal, or regulatory reasons, were treated differently: Mobile communications, operator services, yellow pages, and visual and broadcast services. Whereas 'sales and marketing' had previously been integrated with production, 'Project Sovereign' divided sales and marketing on the one hand and production on the other hand. The new department 'Worldwide Networks' had no access to the market, but supplied 'Personal Communications' and 'Business Communications', who in turn served the market. However, the corporation largely retained a functional organisational design at this stage (Pospischil, 1993).

The re-orientation of BT's activities to 'put the customer first' meant introducing specific services both for business clients and individual households. In September 1991 BT announced the formation of a new subsidiary, Syncordia, which would provide multinational companies with tailor-made voice and data communications networks, Syncordia offered an international network with end-to-end solutions for their complex international communications systems. Traditionally, companies around the world had to negotiate with individual national telecommunications administrations for the provision of telecommunications services. By April 1993 the new company had won over $200 million of business. More specifically oriented towards private customers was 'BT Commitment', a complete set of service standards for customers, built on the success of the Customer Service Guarantee first launched in 1989. It specified target response times for orders and repairs, and connection rates and speed of connection. It also guaranteed compensation for missed targets, particularly if the customer suffered financial loss as a result. The 'BT Commitment' programme, which was part of BT's on-going process of continuous improvement, also promised easier and more flexible contact with BT (BT, 2006b).

Several changes in organisational structure followed (Lehrer and Darbishire, 2000: 91), partly because of internal requirements, and partly because of acquisition of new companies worldwide. In a study of a group of BT managers and their strategic behaviour, Grundy and Wensley (1999) found that 'managers expressed concerns that they lacked sufficient understanding of each other's mind-sets, or "mental maps"' (328). This problem was seen rooted in the wide range of strategic issues – and consequently the breadth of the strategic agenda – open to the managers. The strategic debate

> seemed to circle the issues slightly closer in analytical decisions but without really coming to firm decisions on the path forward. (…) An open and cohesive style of strategic behaviour may well be more conducive to reducing territorial barriers (…) organisational, cognitive or even emotional. (Grundy and Wensley, 1999: 328–9)

The period of organisational instability between the mid-1980s and the late 1990s suggests that BT faced serious organisational problems and even incompatibilities between different parts of the growing organisation, and that it experimented to obtain optimal adaptation to the new market requirements.

Internationalisation

The 1990s were characterised by international expansion, through joint ventures and alliance building, in a search for regional partners across the globe. Whereas international business had been a separate division in BT prior to 1991, the reform 'Project Sovereign' subsumed this dividing line under the higher-level segments of business and private customers (Pospischil, 1993: 620). The implication of this organisational move was that BT at least from the beginning of the 1990s saw itself as operating in a global market, where geographical location of the customers was less important than their requirements for specific types of products and services.

In the period prior to opening for full competition in Europe in 1998, it was increasingly assumed among European telecommunications operators that only a handful of firms would survive as independent companies, operating in the global arena. Thus, the general sentiment was that large scale, size, and vertical integration would help a firm to remain independent (Börsch, 2004). Moreover, the internationalisation of the most profitable customers – the business clients – implied that telecommunications companies had to build up an international presence and be capable of providing services across national borders, that is, to provide a 'one-stop shop'. Both these elements pushed the need for internationalisation right to the top of the agenda in BT in the 1990s.

BT had one significant advantage. Owing to the licensing of Mercury in 1982, it had more experience of being in an environment with a competitor than most of its European counterparts. Its early privatisation gave it a competitive edge also with respect to financial instruments. In the mid-1990s it was widely seen as competing for global leadership in its sector with AT&T. BT concentrated on the acquisition of smaller stakes in US firms in the areas of cellular telephony and value-added networks, and determined internationalisation started in the 1990s (Börsch, 2004: 603). Between 1993 and 1996 BT entered into co-operation agreements with more than twenty companies in order to offer services in liberalising markets, among them companies based in Sweden, the Netherlands, France, Italy, Germany, and Spain (Hulsink, 1999: 157).

BT has been characterised as adopting an 'aggressive and ambitious' strategy internationally (*The Economist*, 1998a). It has forged alliances with telecoms operators across Europe (it operated directly in 18 European countries in 2005), and operates directly in the Asia Pacific region, in the Americas, and in the Middle East and Africa. In 2005 it provided coverage in over 200 countries across five continents, it invested €450 million in 2003, and it offered one of Europe's most extensive IP-enabled networks and 'the world's leading MPLS network' (BT, 2006c).

However, the enterprise's strategies were also criticised for not being adapted to the new realities of the industry:

> Despite its forte for alliances, its expertise in running networks and its understanding of the counter-strategies of incumbents, it lacks the entrepreneurial agility, the speed of decision-making and the gung-ho investors to match the moves of companies like WorldCom, let alone a more recent phenomenon like Qwest. As telecoms becomes more like the computer industry with very rapid innovation and new services brought quickly to market, BT and its incumbent brethren are poorly placed to win the lion's share of new revenues from the boom in voice and data traffic. (*The Economist*, 1998a)

The origin of such criticisms was the attempted merger with MCI in 1998, thwarted by WorldCom's hostile last-minute takeover, leaving BT 'trying to put the pieces of its once-admired global strategy back together' (*The Economist*, 1998b). The merger process went back to the earlier part of the 1990s. In 1993 BT acquired 20 per cent of MCI, then the second largest carrier of long distance telecommunications services in the US, which gave it a competitive advantage in the market for international services for business clients. In 1994, BT and MCI launched Concert Communications Services, a $1 billion joint-venture company, which offered global services and communication for multinational corporations in particular (Börsch, 2004: 603). BT covered Europe and Asia, whereas MCI served the US. This alliance gave BT and MCI a global network for providing end-to-end connectivity for advanced business services. Concert was the first company to provide a single source, broad portfolio of global communications services for multinational customers. The joint venture was developed by BT and MCI into a leading supplier of global services to 3,000 multinational companies with more than $1.5 billion in revenue under contract by the end of 1996.

This strategic alliance progressed further with the announcement on November 3, 1996 that BT and MCI had entered into a merger agreement to create a global telecommunications company called Concert plc, to be incorporated in the UK with headquarters in both London and Washington DC. The merger proposals subsequently met with approval from the European Commission, the US Department of Justice and the US Federal Communications Commission.

Nevertheless, following US carrier WorldCom's rival bid for MCI on October 1, 1997, BT ultimately decided, in November, to sell its stake in MCI to WorldCom for $7 billion. WorldCom's offer, which was followed on October 15 by an unsuccessful counter bid from GTE, America's largest US based local telecommunications company, was made after BT and MCI had renegotiated the terms of the planned merger following a profits warning from MCI in July. The deal with WorldCom resulted in a profit of over $2 billion on BT's original investment in MCI, with an additional $465 million severance fee for the break up of the proposed merger.

In July 1998, BT reconfigured Concert with AT&T and announced the formation of a joint venture to serve multinational companies as well as the international calling needs of individuals and businesses (www.bt.com). Owing to its presence in the US and in Europe, Concert had a competitive advantage in the $500 billion market for international telephone services. The venture underwent a thorough regulatory approval process and, in November 1999, BT and AT&T formally launched the new company, called Concert, with financial closure in January 2000. Concert and BT's internationalisation generally served as a role model for other telecommunications companies, especially those wishing to find an American partner to provide a global network for business clients.

Following a downturn in the global telecommunications market, BT underwent a thorough review of its activities, and it was announced in October 2001 that BT and AT&T were to unwind Concert, returning its businesses, customer accounts and networks to the two parent companies (www.bt.com).

Further Restructuring – Post-2000

The turn of the century and its immediate aftermath were not happy times for the telecommunications sector. Virtually all companies were affected by poor financial performance and optimistic prospects for new technological advances were proven wrong. In addition to the financial problems, the first few years after 2000 were marked by regulatory difficulties particularly with local loop unbundling, and technological difficulties connected to the launch of the new generation (so-called 3G) mobile services, licences for which many large telecommunications operators had paid huge sums to obtain.

The financial difficulties in the late 1990s affected all companies in the telecommunications sector and BT felt the problems through mounting debts and failing strategies. BT restructured quickly and radically, concentrating on fixed-line business in the UK and in Continental Europe rather than striving to become a global carrier. Already in mid-2000 it undertook 'the biggest internal shake-up since privatization' (*The Economist*, 2000). Business lines were reorganised and subsequently based on the company's main activities rather than geography. Three businesses resulted: BT Wireless (combining British and international mobile business), BT Ignite (broadband), and BT Openworld (Internet service providers). The fixed-line business was separated into retail and wholesale. In addition, Yell, including the Yellow Pages brand, comprised the international directories and e-commerce business. However, the reorganisation was not sufficient to change the overall development of BT's falling share price and it saw its credit rating downgraded. BT then embarked on a far-reaching portfolio restructuring that completely reversed the general strategy it had hitherto employed (Börsch, 2004: 606). In order to reduce debt it sold off most of its minority holdings in foreign firms and dissolved the Concert alliance with AT&T.

In 2000, BT (through majority holdings or alliances) ran fixed-line services in eight European countries, mobile services in four European countries, and

Internet services in six European countries (Goldstein, 2000: 201–2). In May 2001, as part of a restructuring and debt reduction programme, BT announced the sale of Yell. In November that year, BT Wireless – BT's mobile business, re-branded as mmO2 – was sold off from BT: on 19 November 2001, mmO2 plc and the new BT Group plc shares commenced trading separately. By April 2002, having 'cut its debt, shelved its international pretensions and, by spinning off its mobile arm, isolated itself from the uncertainties surrounding 'third-generation' (3G) mobile networks, BT looks far healthier than its peers, France Telecom and Deutsche Telekom' (*The Economist*, 2002).

In spring 2002, under its new chief executive officer Mr. Verwaayen, BT decided 'to concentrate on access rather than services or content' (*The Economist* 2002). It 'embarked upon an ambitious, £10 billion ($17.5 billion) plan to replace its entire network – except for the bits of copper wire at the edges – with a new "21st-century" network based on internet technology' (*The Economist*, 2005). Three years later, however, in December 2005, the company elaborated on its plans for new video services and announced its first content deals, with the BBC, Paramount and Warner Music. BT's set-top boxes will plug into a broadband connection, and will also double as digital terrestrial receivers, so that receiving standard digital broadcasts will be free. Viewers will pay only to watch movies or 'catch-up TV' (a menu of the previous week's broadcasts), streamed on demand over the broadband link (*The Economist*, 2005).

During these three years the company also effectively struck a deal with the regulator Ofcom avoiding a splitting-up, a strategy originally proposed by Ofcom in 2004 (*The Economist*, 2004) as a possible solution to the problem of 'local loop unbundling' and the problem of the 'last mile' (see, for example, Sandbach, 2001; Cave, 2002). BT and Ofcom agreed to the establishment of 'openreach', a new multi-billion pound business responsible for the nationwide local BT network. Openreach will contain BT's field force of 25,000 engineers, operational from January 2006, ensuring all service providers have transparent and equal access to the local BT network. Whilst remaining an important part of BT, it has its own headquarters, distinct identity and around 30,000 staff. The staff come primarily from BT Wholesale and BT Retail. Openreach has its performance monitored by the newly created Equality of Access Board (EAB). This Board monitors the delivery of the undertakings given by BT to Ofcom and so also monitors the performance of BT Wholesale in certain areas (BT, 2006d).

The BT of 2005 was structured so that BT Group plc provided a holding company for the separately managed businesses that made up the group: BT Retail, BT Wholesale, BT Openworld and BT Global Services, each with the freedom to focus on its own markets and customers. In addition, BT Exact, BT's research and development organisation, supported all the businesses in the group. The rationale behind this structure was to combine the overall strength of the group with specialised knowledge about customers and markets in the individual business units. The BT Group re-focused its core activities on voice and data (fixed-line) customers primarily based in the UK and elsewhere in Europe. This market is characterised by fierce competition, but BT justifies the choice of core business on the basis of their technical and historical expertise (www.bt.com). After some two or three decades of experimenting, they were therefore deciding to focus on what they traditionally did best, namely to provide customers with fixed-line services.

Conclusion

British Telecom was the first European ex-bureaucratic telecommunications operator to be corporatised (not all European countries organised their telephone service provider as part of the state bureaucracy, but this was the dominant model on the continent). The PO was corporatised as early as 1969, and the process of corporatisation therefore remains outside the scope of this chapter. It is, however, clear that the PO of the 1970s retained many similarities with its counterparts on the continent, even though these latter remained within the state bureaucracy. A culture of strong hierarchical structures has been reported, likewise heavy influence of engineers in all levels of decision-making (Harper, 1997). Furthermore, their finances were linked to the general budget, putting severe strain on the corporation's possibilities for financial flexibility. As a result, the PO experienced the same sources of discontent in the 1970s and early 1980s as its European counterparts.

The British became the first in Europe not only to corporatise their telecommunications operator; they were also the first to privatise it.[6] The aim of this book is to shed light on the effect of the transformation process on company structure, business strategy, and internationalisation. Because of it being among the first telecommunications operators to be corporatised and then privatised, but also because of its sheer size and importance in the European telecommunications sector, the case of BT has been followed closely and experiences have been drawn for policy-making in other countries. Despite these factors, surprisingly little academic literature is focusing on the company and its role in the process of liberalisation and regulatory change that has taken place over then last three decades.

One notable exception to this is the *privatisation* of BT, which has attracted a certain attention from scholars and practitioners alike, both concerning various legal (for example, Moon, Richardson and Smart, 1986) and economic (for example, Puxty, 1997; Durant, Legge and Moussios, 1998; Cave, 1997; Collins and Murroni, 1997) aspects, but also regarding its impact on the corporate culture. In the 1990s, privatisation was hailed among advocates of public sector reform as increasing efficiency, effectiveness, and company performance, whilst

6 Again, some smaller countries had only private operators, and some countries had licensed private operators for certain regions or certain services, but a state-owned monopoly remained the dominant model.

lowering prices for the general public, thus bettering the overall use of resources (for example, Kiessling and Blondeel, 1999; Ikenberry, 1990; Vickers and Wright, 1989). Over the last decade, however, this hypothesis has been increasingly questioned (for example, Lane, 1997; Ikenberry, 1997).

It is difficult to muster hard conclusive evidence that a change in ownership *per se* significantly influences either of the above mentioned factors (but see Megginson and Netter, 2001). The history of British Telecom is a case in point, being the first major European telecommunications operator to be privatised in the 1980s. Florio (2003) concluded that although important factors such as prices and tariffs, costs and revenues, R&D investments, and profits, have changed between 1960 and 2000, 'it seem[ed] difficult to attribute substantial changes in operating profits, prices and costs to privatisation. Most of the changes [were] related either to new financial arrangements or to liberalisation and regulation' (p. 230). In a similar vein, Durant, Legge and Moussios (1998) found that 'gradual changes in ownership alone do not improve labor productivity or profitability' (p. 134).

Moreover, despite being exposed to gradually increasing competition over a period of 14 years, it was only after 1996, when BT's dominance became seriously threatened, that prices in Britain for international and long-distance calls plummeted (*The Economist*, 1998a). Its 'bureaucratic' culture, even 17 years after corporatisation, was still seen as BT's major problem, resulting in it being 'stifled by politics, committees and unclear objectives' (*The Economist*, 1998b).

The company did, however, show its capability to react quickly when, faced with sharply falling share prices, it sold off its mobile telephony activities because these underperformed (*The Economist*, 1998b). It seems clear that the ownership structure – there is no one major owner to be responsible to but rather a host of financial institutions each holding a relatively small part of the shares – contributed to management's power to impose radical change. Promoting the share price and reducing debts quickly was imperative because BT's dispersed ownership made it a tempting take-over target.

The BT of 2000 was therefore less inert than the BT of 1970. The change, however, cannot be attributed to privatisation alone. A host of factors contributed, not least the long process the company went through in the aftermath of the reforms of 1984/1991, with increasing (albeit slowly) individual responsibility among higher and middle managers, more power to different business units, organisational design according to function rather than to geography, and generally less hierarchical structures.

Internationalisation has left its mark also on British Telecom. In the 1990s BT partook in the great 'shopping frenzy' in an attempt to secure strongholds across the globe. Interestingly, in contrast to France Telecom, who organised its international activity according to three customer groups and strive to become an 'integrated company' worldwide, BT has shed loss-making activities in order to focus on its core competence, that is, providing fixed-line telecommunications services in the UK and Europe. From there, it has recently struck deals with content providers to expand its potential markets.

BT's path post-privatisation is unique in Europe not only because of its timing, but also because of the drawn-out character of the introduction of competition. And if there is one lesson to be learned from the BT experience, it must be that ownership is not the only, or even the most significant, determinant for behaviour. Rather, throughout the period from 1981 BT has reacted to events in its environment and has shown a capability to survive. It has, however, had to make significant organisational changes along the way, and will have to continue doing so in the future.

Chapter 8

Small Companies – Big Problems: The Case of Belgacom

John Vanhoucke

Introduction

This chapter provides an account of Belgacom's transformation from a state agency to a listed company from 1995 to 2003. We identify the gradual steps that Belgian telecommunications landscape has gone through to establish the partly privately owned Belgacom. With this Belgian case we identify the processes of transformation that have been conducted and the way in which the Belgian national telecom operator dealt with those challenges, for example, the liberalisation of the telecommunication market. We focus on two perspectives, first the traditional values and secondly the principal–agent relationships. In the case of traditional values four aspects that play a role in the process of change, each influencing the others, come to the fore. From an ideology-perspective changes occurred in national and supranational thoughts over this period of time and had subsequent effects for the Belgian national telecommunication operator. From a political perspective we see that telecommunications became increasingly politically important leading undoubtedly towards a degree of political influence in the establishment and aftermath of Belgacom. Over the years, technology had been changing at a fast rate, and subsequently those changes had their effect on society and forced the company to adapt to those changes in their daily operations. The waves of globalisation of telecommunication also had an undisputed effect in the different stages that Belgian telecommunications went through. These four parameters form the basis for identifying the extent to which the Belgian telecommunications and more specific Belgacom has changed as a company – in particular, how the company acquired a legal corporate status and changed their former telecommunications administrations towards a business responsive and efficient organisation. Further, we look at how Belgacom as a company started to diversify in an ever declining fixed line market and how they transformed and performed as a international oriented company. Over this period of time the company changed from an institution towards a partly privately owned company that ran under private sector regulations. Besides the traditional values for the process of change we model those changes by a principal agent logic that will help us in identifying the process, namely the owners' action, the corporation's action and the influence of external factors on the outcome.

From a Dysfunctional Institution to the Autonomous State Agency Belgacom

In the period 1986–1991 growing international political interest and regulation put pressure on Belgium to liberalise their telecommunications market, and demands were growing at home for the dysfunctional telecommunications state agency to become a functional and efficient entity. These two factors lead to the creation of the autonomous state agency Belgacom.

Internationalisation could be considered as a constant factor in the history of capitalism. This evolution was also noticeable in the telecommunication sector and in the 1980s we see that more and more international institutions showed their interest in telecommunications – so much so that the European Commission explicitly commissioned a department to oversee this matter, namely the Directorate General XIII, later to become the DG information society. This directorate was to focus on the telecommunications and information industry and on innovation. From a more global perspective, GATT (General Agreement on Tariffs and Trade) and the United States lobby were also driving towards a liberalisation of the European telecommunication sector.

The European Commission listened to the concerns of the industry and at the same time felt the pressure of the United States that already had liberalised their telecommunications market. The European Commission was actually convinced that liberalisation of the telecommunications market could provide an answer to their powerful American and Japanese competitors and therefore initiated regulation that would stimulate competition within the European market and moreover coupled it to a support programmes (Verhoest, Vercruysse and Punie, 1991).

To ensure the harmonisation of the European regulation in the member states a European Telecommunications Standardisations Institute (ETSI) was set up. If a terminal was approved in one member state it was automatically approved in the other member states without extra procedures.

For Belgium we saw two distinctive flows, namely liberalisation and increased state intervention of the RTT that were in correlation with the leading governmental parties. Before 1988 the liberal coalition partner of the government was thinking of completely privatising the RTT. The general idea behind this was that complete privatisation would put an end to the dysfunction of the institution and generate a supplementary income for the states' treasury. But these plans for privatisation were put aside as soon as the socialist Freddy Willockx and his socialist successor Marcel Colla became Minister of Post Telephony and Telegraphy (PTT). For the socialist party, privatisation was not a valid option and therefore the government created Autonomous State Agencies. With the law of 21 March 1991 the RTT became 'Belgacom', an autonomous state agency. With this law the Belgian government set in place a Master Agreement whereby the autonomous state agency is obliged to offer a number of specific services to the public. In return, the autonomous state agency could keep a monopoly on the basic infrastructure, on the reserved services and the telecommunication on the 'public domain' (Verhoest, Vercruysse and Punie, 1991).

Besides these services to the public Belgacom was free to do whatever was necessary to be competitive, for example, participate in other companies, create new entities etc. A third reform concerned the organisation and management, the responsibility of the company being put in the hands of a board of directors. A fourth but significant change was indeed the revision of the personnel statute (Verhoest, Vercruysse and Punie, 1991). In 1993 the unions agreed on a new personnel statute that allowed more flexibility, improved mobility, and for Belgacom to implement an evaluation system.

Stabilisation, enforcement and preparation of Belgacom for the liberalisation of the telecommunications market

Apart from internal changes the regulatory framework in Belgium was adapted to the European agenda in the early 1990s. Until the recent changes, telecommunications were governed under a series of ancient laws derived from the initial Telecommunication Law that had created the RTT (Régie des Télégraphes et Téléphones) in 1930. In March 1991, a new national law permitted reforming the RTT, resulting in Belgacom as a national dominant operator under autonomous public status. The strategic orientations of Belgacom were defined in an Agreement that covered the period from 1992 to 1997. At the same time the regulatory part of the RTT was split off, by creating the Belgian Institute for Postal services and Telecommunication (BIPT) in 1994. The BIPT had a triple focus:

- make sure that Belgium telecoms complied with the European Regulations;
- help the Minister with the negotiations of new Master Agreements;
- ensure that Belgacom complies with the new rules of competition; the BIPT has an advisory role for the Minister of Telecommunications.

At the end of 1993, the Belgian government declared its agreement to liberalise voice and network markets by 1 January 1998, in line with the EU recommendations. In 1994, two major points of the 1991 law were revised: the opening of the mobile phone market to competition and the partial privatisation of the national operator. In 1994 Belgacom also became a public limited company. In 1995, the competitive bidding concerning the first mobile telephony competitor was organised by Royal Decree of 7 March 1995. In so doing Belgian became one of the last European countries where the telecommunication sector was reformed (Verhoest, Vercruysse and Punie, 1991; http://www.eu-esis.org/Regulation/BEregQ8.htm).

With the establishment of Belgacom, an autonomous state agency, the Minister appointed Bessel Kok as CEO (the then acting chairman of Swift – Society for Worldwide Interbank Financial Telecommunications). With this action, that is, by choosing a commercial manager with no political track record, the government broke with its long track record of political nominations. Still Bessel Kok only received his mandate after he declined his right to propose his own executive management committee. As a consequence, the only two independent members in the executive committee were Bessel Kok and Georges Wanet (before Société Générale de Belgique). The rest of the executive management committee, (Lodewijk Eggermont, Baudouin Meunier, Tony Jossa, and Pierre Rernard) actually represented the four important political formations, namely the Flemish and Walloon Christian Democrats and their Socialist counterparts. The same political adherences appeared in the board of directors, who were directly appointed by the Minister responsible. It therefore comes as no surprise that the board of directors influenced the daily work of the company significantly in the first years. In a regular company the role of the Board of Directors would be one of control, making sure that the Master Agreement is executed. This was however not the case for Belgacom. For Belgacom, the Board received an extra responsibility for the operational planning of Belgacom. This strategic plan, which established the medium-term goals of the company, was drafted on a yearly basis by the Board of Directors. The increasing interference of the Board of Directors in the daily management of the company lead to a conflict between the board and Bessel Kok whereby the board blamed Bessel Kok for unlawful use of company finances in favour of some friends. Politicising and the typical regional differences came to the fore during the conflict. The press represented the conflict as a clash between Bessel Kok and the chairman of the Board of Directors, Benoit Remiche. One side of the press, the Flemish part, pointed at the far-reaching interference of the chairman in the daily business, whereas the Walloon press pointed at the unorthodox behaviour of the CEO in unlawfully commissioning friends with consultancy mandates. Again the same structural problem was revealed, that is, a politicised management structure. The outcome of this affair was the resignations of both Bessel Kok and the Board of Directors in 1995.

A new Board of Directors was appointed immediately, again according to the rules of the political proportionality. For the daily management John Goossens, head of Alcatel Bell Antwerp, was appointed as CEO, but remarkably the official appointment of John Goossens had to wait until the signature of a new Master Agreement between Belgacom and its industrial partners. This new agreement was in line with long known proportions: one-third for Atea and two-thirds for Bell, who where the leading companies in Belgium for the delivery of telecommunications infrastructure and means (Verhoest, 2000).

In the light of the liberalisation of the Belgian telecommunications market in 1998, Belgacom created its TURBO-plan in June 1995. This was based on five major priorities:

- earn customer loyalty;
- get combat-ready;
- innovate for growth;
- develop professional teams; and
- achieve world class efficiency (Belgacom Press Release, 23 October 1997).

Until that date, Belgacom was relatively protected by the government and was actually working in a non-competitive manner in a so-called liberalised telecommunication landscape. According to the government a solution needed to be found in order to enforce the market position of Belgacom and prepare it for competition (Verhoest, 2000).

Exploring privatisation, at least partly, seemed an option for the following reasons. First of all, the European liberalisation directive came into effect on 1 January 1998. By not privatising during this liberalisation process would have left Belgacom in an unfavourable position. Secondly, the Belgian telecommunications market (that is, Belgacom) needed a partner to help with the development of new network services and with the internationalisation of the telecommunications market. Finally, there was a need for the government to raise money in order to tackle some of the country's deficit.

To realise this, the Belgian government chose the 'consolidation' of Belgacom. The general idea was to look for a solid external partner to invest capital in Belgacom in return for shares. In first instance 25 per cent of the stakes would be privatised, but this was later altered to 49.9 per cent, which could be considered as an act of the government to maximise their gains. The government could have opted to sell their share to the public but this was not a valid option. The financial health of Belgacom proved problematic and selling its shares to the public would therefore probably have resulted in a lower income per share (Verhoest, , 2000).

In the same period (1994) the Flemish government decided to take the initiative in creating a new network operator. This initiative was of course partly motivated to enhance free competition but the main reason was the will of the regions to keep political control in this strategic sector, even though they realised that they were obliged to work together with another solid operator in order to build a new network (Verhoest, 2000). During this period Belgacom had over 26,300 employees, making it the third biggest employer in Belgium.

Looking at the turn-over and profits we can see a constant growth from 1991 with 96,294 million BEF to 1995 with 127,139 million BEF. The only exception was in 1992 due to a change of the valuation rules. We could say that appointing a commercial manager and launching the TURBO-plan had its positive effect on the Belgacom results.

On 6 and 7 May 1993 the members of the Board of Directors of Belgacom decided to invest in mobile telephony. For the investment in a mobile operator Belgacom needed the support of an experienced operator, who would provide them a with high quality mobile telephone services by 1 January 1994.

In their search for a strategic partnership Belgacom selected six operators that were interested in an alliance: Bell South, Cable & Wireless, France Telecom, Pacific Telesis, Southwestern Bell and US West. On 27 July 1993 Belgacom decided to work with Pacific Telesis International (Pactel), who best met the imposed criteria. As of 1 January 1994, Belgacom launched the Proximus mobile phone network covering 80 per cent of the country. The installations of numerous base stations enabled the use of 2-watt mobile phones on all the major road arteries, as well as in all larger towns and cities.

With the arrival of the GSM mobile telephones in Belgium, their forerunners – analogue mobile phones, Belgacom's old analogue mobile phone system MOB-1 and MOB-2 were withdrawn from the market. On 22 December 1994, Belgacom created Belgacom Mobile SA, whose shareholders were the Belgacom group (75 per cent) and its American partner AirTouch (25 per cent) (http://www.proximus.be, 2006).

If we look at the figures of the Belgian GSM market for this period of time we see a spectacular increase in subscribers, proving a successful introduction of mobile telephony in Belgium. In 1995 there were 189,000 customers and in 1996 this number has risen to 447,000 customers, representing a growth of 103 per cent (Armada – July 2004).

In this period Belgacom became a public limited company and invested into the mobile segment with the creation of Belgacom Mobile. In the face of the liberalised telecommunication market the real competition didn't come from abroad but was an initiative taken by the Flemish government to create a new network operator.

Privatisation, Competition, Diversification but No Real Internationalisation for Belgacom

The Belgian Government decided to sell 50 per cent minus one share of Belgacom. Selling more than 50 per cent was not possible under current Belgian law. The Cabinet was advised on the financial aspects of all privatisations by a committee called the Ugeux Commission (named after its chairman Georges Ugeux), as well as by the Morgan Stanley Bank.

During the course of privatisation the following potential partners expressed their interest: Ameritech Corp, Bell Atlantic Corp , GTE Corp, South Western Bell Corp, AT&T Corp, BT Plc, Koninklijke PTT Telecom Nederland, Swiss Telecom, France Telecom, Deutsche Telekom and STET. Subsequently, Ameritech formed a consortium including Tele Danmark and Singapore Telecom; KPN teamed with Swiss Telecom; and BT formed a consortium involving Bell Atlantic and Tele Danmark (before it joined the Ameritech team).

On 20 January 1995, the government announced its intention to establish a strategic partnership between Belgacom, the national telecommunications operator, and one or more qualified telecommunications operators. The selection process was led by both the European Commission and Belgacom with their respective advisers. On 30 June 1995, preliminary proposals were submitted by the following prospective strategic partners: Ameritech; Bell Atlantic (as leader of a consortium together with British Telecommunications); Dutch KPN (as leader of a consortium together with Swiss Telecom); and STET, the Italian operator. Only the first three candidates were approved as participants in the next stage of the process. On 16 October 1995, Bell Atlantic and British Telecommunications announced that they would not submit a final bid. On December 8, 1995, two final proposals for 50 per cent of the shares minus one share were submitted by the Ameritech-led consortium that included Tele Danmark and Singapore Telecom, and by KPN together with Swiss Telecom. The proposals covered both strategic and financial elements.

Upon unanimous recommendation from the Commission and Belgacom, the Government decided on 14 December 1995 to sell the shares to the Ameritech-led ADSB group for 73.3 billion BEF. The deal was closed in March 1996. Belgian financial institutions Credit Communal de Belgique, Kredietbank and Sofina subsequently joined the consortium as minority partners. In summary, the consortium gathered crucial players on the international telecommunications market, together with their strategic competences. Ameritech (Baby Bell) was at that moment one of the largest telecommunications companies in the world. Tele Danmark was a publicly-held company with a turnover of 100 billion BEF in 1995. The group was established in 1991 as a result of the merger of the Danish regional providers and the international telecommunications activities of the Danish government. Singapore Telecom was a telecommunications provider with over 40 subsidiaries providing a wide range of domestic, international and mobile telecommunications as well as postal services (Lane-Martin, personal communication, 1997).

In May 1998 Ameritech announced its intention to merge with SBC Communications. SBC and Ameritech officially merged on 8 October 1999 with SBC becoming the principal shareholder of ADSB consortium. In the summer of 2003 SBC notified Belgacom that it wanted to withdrawn its participation. Their initiative was soon followed by Tele Denmark and Singapore Telecom., meaning the unbundling of their consortium and the exit through the Initial Public Offering of Belgacom.

This partial privatisation had a significant effect for the Belgacom management. Over 80 expatriates had started to work for Belgacom, 50 from Ameritech, 20 from TeleDanmark and 10 from Singapore Telecom (De Tijd, 1998). At the same time the management committee was adjusted. John Goossens remained CEO of Belgacom and was accompanied by Ray Stewart (Ameritech) who took the position of CFO and Denis Johnson (Ameritech) who was in charge of the operational activities (De Standaard, 2005).

Due to the unexpected demise of John Goossens on 8 November 2002 (°1944) the management of Belgacom was put in the hands of Ray Stewart and Michel Dussenne, President of the Board of Directors (HRUpdate, 2002).

In February, 2003, the Belgian government appointed Didier Bellens as the new CEO of Belgacom. Previous to this appointment Didier Bellens was active as acting chairman of the RTL Group. His appointment as CEO came as something of a surprise because the government was then obliged to find a Dutch speaking chairman for the board due to the Belgian rules of language parity. The then chairman of the board, Michel Dussenne, was French speaking and therefore had to be replaced. At the same time, and remarkable considering previous developments, the appointment of Didier Bellens illustrates that the government had decided on the best candidate independently of language parity (De Standaard, 2003). In order to re-establish language parity the government appointed Jan Coene as chairman of the board of directors (De Standaard, 2003).

With Bellens, efficient management principles and a new organisational structure were introduced. Three weeks after his appointment, Didier Bellens announced a simplification of the Belgacom management structure. The Belgacom Group Council was reduced from 13 to a management committee of six. The Group Leadership Team disappeared from the scene and a new strategic committee consisting of seven persons came into place. The management of Belgacom was in the hands of Didier Bellens, Ray Stewart and Michel Vermaercke. Michel Vermaercke was previously the secretary general and played an important leading role for Belgacom in the aftermath of the unexpected demise of John Goossens. The other members of the management committee were Jean-Claude Vandenbosch (president of the wireline division), Philippe Vander Putten (CEO Proximus) and Bridgit Cosgrave (president Carrier Business division) (Datanews, 2003). The strategic committee today comprises the following members: Didier Bellens, Scott Alcott, Bridget Cosgrave, Astrid De Lathauwer, William Mosseray, Ray Stewart, and Michel Georgis (www.belgacom.be, 2006)

Due to some disputes with Picanol, Jan Coene who was acting chairman had to resign as chairman of the board of directors. He was immediately replaced by Theo Dilssen, the acting chairman of Real Software (De Standaard, 2004).

The partial privatisation and the appointment of a new CEO had also its effects on the employees. An ambitious plan 'PTS' (People, Teams, Skills) was elaborated to convert a number of Belgacom employees together with some major cut-backs. This program resulted in the cut back of 6,290 employees and the conversion of another 6,600 employees (De Tijd, 1998). This operation costs Belgacom €713 million (Persmededeling van CD&V, 24 November 2005). By June 2002, Belgacom employed 19,911 full time equivalents in 2001 this was 2,493 and in 1995 this was 26,300 (De Standaard, 2002).

In 2001 Belgacom launched BeST (Belgacom e-business Strategic Transformation), with the goal of enabling Belgacom to lead Belgium on the way in e-business. The BeST program resulted in another cut back operation of 4,157 people and had costs amounting to €773 million (Persmededeling van CD&V, 24 November 2005).

All these conversion and cut back operations proved satisfactory on a financial basis. In 1996 the Belgacom group posted a turnover of 138.7 billion BEF (€3.4 billion), that is, an increase of 9.1 per cent over the previous financial year. This growth in turnover was mainly due to the continuous growth in mobile telephony, the increase in national telephone service through ISDN (Integrated Services Digital Network), subscription fees, mobile telephone traffic, as well as an increase in international telephone business (Belgacom Annual Results 1996).

Belgacom results for 1998 again showed significant improvement: the Group's consolidated turnover reached 169.3 billion BEF (€4.2 billion). The increase in turnover was primarily attributed to Belgacom Mobile's significant growth in turnover (42 per cent) from 23.2 billion BEF (€575 million) in 1997 to 32.9 billion BEF (€816 million) in 1998, and to an increase in ISDN and value-added services. Results also reflected a change in accounting procedures for international agreements with other telecom operators (Belgacom Annual Results, 1998). In 1999 Belgacom results also showed things were developing favourably: consolidated turnover for the Group amounted to 185.8 billion BEF (€4.6 billion), an increase of 9.7 per cent. Taking into account other operating income, growth in revenue reached 10.3 per cent. The growth in turnover was primarily due to the significant increase (46 per cent) in Belgacom Mobile's turnover, the growth in ISDN (Integrated Services Digital Network), and to the revenues from interconnection and value-added services (Belgacom Annual Results, 1999).

In July 1995 Belgacom created a separated juridical entity for its pension funds. The complete amount of money that was set aside for paying the pensions of the statutory employees (46 billion BEF in 1995) was transferred to that fund (De Standaard, 2003). However, in January 2004 the European commission agreed to the transfer of the Belgacom pensions to the Belgian government (European Commission report, N567/2003, Brussels, 21 January 2004). In the same year Eurostat agreed to the use of income from the Belgacom-pension fund for government deficits, without which there would have been a deficit of 1.2 per cent in 2003 and of 0.9 per cent in 2004. This illustrates the grip of the Belgian state on Belgacom.

When looking at the results from 2000, the year the Euro was introduced, we see a stabilisation in turnover but an increase in profit. The turnover for the Belgacom Group came from the four business units (Wireline, Carrier/Wholesale, Mobile and Internet) set up when the new organisational structure was put in place in March 2001 under the BeST programme.

In 2001, the Belgacom Group had a turnover of €5,375 million, amounting to relative growth of 4.6 per cent as compared to €5,141 million in the 2000. The difference comes from a combination of the following factors. Firstly, sustained growth in mobile telephony activities, the commercial success broadband Internet access offer (ADSL – Asymmetric Digital Subscriber Line), the rise in interconnection and transit traffic and an upsurge in data communication. Secondly, implementation in October 2000, of lower rates for voice traffic, the reduction in leased-line rates in mid-2001, the decline in the number of analogue network lines (Public Switched Telephone Network – PSTN) and the increase in the number of ISDN (Integrated Services Digital Network) lines (Belgacom annual report 2001).

Having withstood the upheaval of the economy, and particularly the telecom sector, in 2002, Belgacom still finished the year with satisfactory results. The Group's consolidated turnover amounted to €5.220 billion, a slight decrease of 2.9 per cent compared to 2001 (€5.375 billion). Whilst its turnover tailed off slightly, it should be pointed out that this primarily reflected the successive sale of some of the Group's activities at the end of 2001 and in 2002 (Infonie, Belgacom France, Belgacom Security Group and Ben Nederland). Indeed, based on comparable figures (that is, without the change made to the scope of consolidation), turnover rose by 2.4 per cent (compared with 4.6 per cent in 2001), principally due to the growth in revenue from Belgacom Mobile, data communication (essentially ADSL) and, to a lesser extent, Wholesale & Carrier (interconnection and transit traffic). Also, despite a market that was close to saturation, Belgacom Mobile continued to post excellent results. The success of Belgacom ADSL (Asymmetric Digital Subscriber Line) was also confirmed in 2002: at 31 December 2002, there were 517,000 customers with an ultra-rapid Internet connection, that is, 290,000 more than in 2001, which greatly exceeded Belgacom forecasts (400,000) (Belgacom Press Release, 27 February 2003). But the most remarkable result for 2002 is that Belgacom became free of debts (De Standaard, 2002).

In the Belgacom Group results we saw that Proximus, Belgacom mobile participation, had a significant positive effect on the Belgacom results. During this period Proximus also underwent a number of changes. The initial Belgacom partner Air Touch merged with Vodafone on 30 June 1999 and created Vodafone AirTouch to become the biggest mobile operator in the world. In March 2001 Proximus bought one of the fourth generation licenses put up for auction by the Belgian government. In June 2001 Proximus launches the first services using the GPRS network. On 28 November 2002 Proximus was the first Belgian operator to launch MMS, Multimedia Messaging Service (http://www.proximus.be, 2006).

Concerning competition in the liberalised mobile communication market, it took until August, 1996, to create competition in the mobile sector with the arrival of Mobistar, a France Telecom subsidiary, and BASE as competitors for Belgacom Mobile. In 1996 a number of other shareholders came on board in the Mobistar capital: ABB, Cobepa, Gevaert, GIMV/SRIB, GIMB, Kredietbank, Mosane, SRIW. In September, 1998, Mobistar was listed on the Brussels stock-exchange. BASE, the old KPN Orange, had been totally in the hands of KPN Mobile since 1 February. This Dutch operator took the 50 per cent shares from France Telecom. In the contract of this share transfer it was stated that KPN could use the name Orange in Belgium until September 2002 (http://www.eu-esis.org, 2006).

With regard to the number of mobile telephone subscribers in Belgium, an enormous increase is seen during the period 1994 to 2000. Nevertheless, since 2001 the number of new subscribers has been slowing down, due to the mobile market saturation (Negende jaarverslag van het Raadgevend Comité voor de telecommunicatie 2002).

In the field of traditional telephony there has been a decline in the number of PSTN connections, but a rise in ISDN connections. Developments of PSTN-telephone connections during the period 1999–2002 show a decline of 14.3 per cent. When consolidated into the total number of telephone connections, however, the decline only amounts for 2.7 per cent.The reason for this is the increase of ISDN-connections and connections through the coax cable. By the end of 2002 a total of 5,120,370 fixed lines were in place, compared to 4,725,496 in 1996. Since January 1999 people have been able to make phone calls via cable that was only used previously for the TV signals. This impacted on the diversification of telephone subscribers. In 1999 there were 40,988 cable telephone subscribers, and in 2002 it already reached a total of 212,352 (Negende jaarverslag van het Raadgevend Comité voor de telecommunicatie, 2002). Taking a closer look at Telenet we see that in October 1994 the Flemish government decided to launch a second telecommunication network next to Belgacom network. In September 1996 the holding company Telenet Holding NV was established. The shareholders were MediaOne (25 per cent), the Gimv (20 per cent), intercommunales (35 per cent, private holdings owned by cities) and a financial consortium (20 per cent). In March 1997 Telenet was granted a license to operate their network in Flanders and to offer telecommunication services. In January 1998 Telenet signed an interconnectivity agreement with Belgacom, and in August of the following year the shareholder MediaOne was taken over by AT&T. However, in the same period AT&T was closing down its European activities, so its MediaOne shares were sold. In February 2001 Telenet sold its activities for 60 billion BEF to Callahan Associates. Callahan not only became the majority shareholder of Telenet, but it had also a 50 per cent stake in the Belgian cable network. In June 2001 Telenet losses had risen to 7 billion BEF despite a turn-over that had doubled. This resulted in the replacement of Chuck Carroll by Duco Sickinge as CEO. In January 2002 Telenet raised its tariffs for surfing the Internet by 13 per cent and telephone communication by 10 per cent. Nevertheless, the losses for Telenet came to a peak in 2002. The solution was provided by the shareholders (intercommunales) who gave an extra 170 million Euro of capital, resulting in them becoming the majority shareholders (De Standaard, 2002). On 11 October, Telenet did not do a very successful IPO (initial public offering) and did not fulfil its intent of resulting in a growth share (De Standaard, 2005).

The effects of Telenet in the telecommunication market were mainly in the field of the residential users for telephony and internet connections, and had no significant effect on the professional market. However this corresponds with the group's strategy. If we analyze the situation we could say that Belgacom suffered little from the competition and was able to keep their dominant position in the Belgian market.

If we look at the evolution of telephone prices with the introduction of this alternative operator we see that the pressure came mainly from the BIPT and the EU. A study performed in 2002, spanning the period between August 1997 (before the liberalisation) and August 2002, pointed out a significant decrease in the prices for both national and international telephone conversations. But comparing the tariffs with the other countries in the European Union, it can be seen that the local conversations in Belgium were one of the highest in the Union, that is, 35 per cent more expensive. And the prices for local conversations rose by 20 per cent between 1997 and 2002 while for the rest of the European Union they stayed more or less at the same level (Negende jaarverslag van het Raadgevend Comité voor de telecommunicatie 2002). The consumer organisation 'Test-Aankoop' compared the tariffs over six years of consumers switching from Belgacom to an alternative telecommunication provider. In 2005 there were 26 operators' active, offering 65 tariff rates differing as much as 76 per cent in price. An important factor was that consumers could only choose between Belgacom and Telenet for their telecommunications subscription (Test-Aankoop 485, 2005). In this context, it is hard to talk of a real competitive system it came as no surprise, therefore, that the EU Court of Justice blamed Belgium for not adapting the EU directive on telecoms liberalisation adequately. The EU deplored that the BIPT did not get enough power and related means from the Minister of Communications to act as a price regulator.

For Belgacom this period is also marked with the mixed success of the expansion and diversification of its business. Belgacom started its international aspirations in July, 1998, with the creation of Belgacom France, active in Lille, Paris and Lyon. Belgacom France aimed to offer all major corporate clients a one-stop shopping solution, with a 10 to 20 per cent discount in comparison with France Telecom tariffs (http://www.eu-esis.org, 2006). On 22 January, 1999, Belgacom SA and LDCOM Networks announced the integration of Belgacom France into the activities of LDCOM Networks. Under this transaction, the Belgian operator acquired a 10 per cent stake in LCDOM. The agreement became operational in mid-March 2002.

In 1999 Belgacom became active in the Euregio of Maastricht, Heerlen, Aachen, Hasselt and Liège with their 40 per cent participation in Tritone. The other shareholders were Accom, the telco subsidiary of the Aachen electricity company (25 per cent), the Maastricht and Heerlen public utility companies (12.5 per cent share each), and the Dutch development company Limburgse Industriebank Liof (10 per cent) (Belgacom Press Release, 22 January, 1999). In 2002 Belgacom had raised its participation into Tritone to 83.3 per cent and negotiated with KPN for the take-over of their 3,500 primarily Dutch customers (Blyaert, 2002). By 2003 Belgacom owned 100 per cent Tritone (Belgacom Annual Results 2003).

In 1999 Belgacom decided to invest together with Tele Danmark in the Dutch mobile operator Ben. In this same year Deutsche Telekom participated in Ben to form a strong consortium to acquire the UTMS licenses. Deutsche Telekom acquired 50 per cent minus 1 share and the remaining 35 per cent and 15 per cent were in the hands of Belgacom and Tele Danmark, respectively. From that moment onwards Belgacom reduced its shares in Ben, ending with 11 per cent in 2002, for which Belgacom eventually received €374 million. The off-loading of its shares in Ben from 35 per cent to 11 per cent to zero allowed Belgacom to bear the cost for the Best-program, which were estimated to be €600 million (De Standaard, 2002).

In conclusion we see that participating in other countries did not turn out to be so successful for Belgacom, and that its two participations performed below expectations. However selling its involvement in the Dutch mobile operator BEN helped Belgacom to fund their internal restructuring program.

In Belgium however, Belgacom Directory Services, establishment during the transition from RTT to Belgacom, was successful. This subsidiary was created to publish the Yellow Pages in direct competition with ITT Promedia monopoly. In June 1998 Belgacom decided in general agreement with ITT Promedia to stop their publication of yellow pages in return of 25 per cent of the ITT Promedia profits (De Standaard, 2005). On 1 February, 2005, Belgacom sold it shares to Promedia for a total of €284.9 million. The transaction was made in cash (Belgacom Press Release, 1 February 2005).

In 1997 Belgacom created Belgacom Security Holding (BSH). With Belgacom Alert Services, Belgacom provided tele-security systems in the Benelux. In order to be active in this market Belgacom bought the Belgian JW Electronics and the Dutch KERS International (http://cgi.belgacom.be/nl/about/operations/activities.htm). The Belgacom Security Holding employed 280 people. In April 2001 Belgacom sold their Belgacom Alert Services to Securitas. In 2002 Securis Direct International received a 72 per cent stake in Belgacom Alert Services. The activities of Securitas Benelux and France were integrated (De Standaard, 2001). In 2005 Securitas bought the remaining 28 per cent of Belgacom Alert Services for €50 million (De Standaard, 2005).

In 1995–96 Belgacom made a strategic shift and was convinced that multimedia would become a significant growth market in short term. Subsequently in 1996 Belgacom decided to start a new multimedia department called Multimedia and Information Highways Division. The division would focus on five operational sectors: Internet, Intranet, Enabling products, Content and Broadband. In February 1997 Belgacom created Belgacom Multimedia Venture Holding. This holding would participate in promising multimedia companies active in the Belgian Market that were complementary to Belgacom's core activities and its Multimedia and Infohighways division (De Tijd, 1998). The capital of BMV was 200 million BEF (~€5 million) and had been completely underwritten by Belgacom NV. The Belgacom Board of Directors had the intention of providing more money if necessary for interesting projects (De Tijd, 1998). In 1997 Belgacom took over the activities of the Internet provider Skynet, by raising their stakes from 25 per cent to 100 per cent (De Standaard, 2003). By the end of 1997 BMV was fully operational with a capital of 220 BEF million and four companies (Skynet, Interpac, Paratel and Event Network) that were consolidated out of the Belgacom Group into the BMV holding (De Tijd, 1997).

In 2000 Belgacom raised the capital of BMV with €25 million and expected to have 20 participations by the end of 2001 (De Tijd, 2000). In contrast with the decision to rise the BMV capital in 2000 Belgacom decided in 2001 to consolidate the BMV activities into the Belgacom Group. The reason given by Belgacom was the fact that BMV was already 100 per cent Belgacom and that the whole operation fits in the operation to simplify the group structure into a horizontal organisational structure. The internet related activities were subsumed in the Belgacom Internet Division. WIN was positioned under the corporate division and the 11 participations in start–ups were re-sorted under the Group Strategy and Business Development of Belgacom (De Tijd, 2001). In 2002 Belgacom participated in a number of joint ventures like Eduline. It participated in Certipost and Aditel, a 50/0 joint venture with the Belgian Post for the launch of e-id cards (Belgacom, 2004, annual result, p. 75).

Since the middle of 1999 the government was looking for a strategic partner for Belgacom. This partner would enable the government to reduce their stakes in the company. In 2001 the Belgian government changed the law allowing Belgacom to merge with another company (De Standaard, 2001) so that by the end of 2001 Belgacom and the Belgian government were talking with four interested partners KPN, Deutsh Telekom, Telecom Italia and Vivendi. Of particular importance in this story of merging was the summer of 1999 where Belgacom's then chairman, John Goossens, drafted a document stating the reasons for Belgacom to merge with KPN in the consolidating European telecommunications landscape. The Belgacom management had a definitive drive to merge with KPN, but, in the aftermath of the 'Sabena'-debacle, the Belgian government was very cautious and demanded numerous guarantees that a merger would result in a surplus value for Belgacom (De Standaard, 2001). In August, 2001, the fusion negotiations between Belgacom and KPN came to an end abruptly. The main reason was the downwards spiral of the KPN shares. As a consequence, in 2002 KPN announced that it was no longer interested in Belgacom (De Standaaard, 2002). The result was that Belgacom and the Belgian government had to look for a new strategic partner or opt for an Initial Public Offering (IPO) (De Standaard, 2001). The latter option was chosen and Belgacom was successfully launched on the Brussels stock exchange on 22 March 2004.

If we analyse the transition period 1997–2002 we see that Belgacom made significant investments in its own organisation, it appointed a CEO with an industrial rather than political track record, it launched two successful reconversion plans PST and BeST. In terms of intra-company performance Belgacom progressed towards excellence, but in terms of internationalisation Belgacom didn't perform as expected. Only in the Flemish speaking region of Belgium people can actually choose between two operators for telephone and Internet subscription. In the segment of mobile telephony competition is fiercer. In general we can say that internally Belgacom defines and expresses a clear vision, where the company should heading to. On international and participation level Belgacom didn't perform that well despite their international shareholders structure.

Conclusions

In conclusion we can say that Belgacom is a slow mover in adapting changes. It is difficult to say if the success of Belgacom today is the result of a specific business strategy or if it's the result of their slow decision making. From a corporatisation perspective we see that Belgacom was slow although successful in the establishment of a private law corporation, but we also see that this process requires a number of changes. Looking at the regulating aspect we see that the Belgian government created the BIPT in 1994 that would act as a watchdog for the compliance with the European regulations on telecommunications and advise the responsible Minister for telecommunications when needed. Nevertheless the means that the government gave to the BIPT were insufficient and the EU Court of Justice blamed Belgium for not adapting the EU directive on telecoms liberalisation adequately. The EU deplored that the BIPT did not get enough power and related means from the Minister of Communications to act as a price regulator.

Focusing on the dominant position we see that the political decision makers have helped the company by acting so slowly in the adaptation of the liberalised telecommunication market. By doing so they made sure that Belgacom was capable of gaining and maintaining their dominant position before competition was allowed. On the other hand the government made sure that Belgacom remained in Belgian hands and that the telecommunications served its common good. The government kept a firm hand on the decision making process within Belgacom as the principle shareholder but did so within a regulatory framework

The company underwent a number of restructurings in management structure and ways of governing a company. The part privatisation helped Belgacom to adapt itself to the new ways of governing a company. Business logic became more dominant resulting in the lay-off of 10,000 people. However the way Belgacom laid off this high number of employees didn't result in a social massacre but was elegantly done. Politics and unions have played an important role in this process. Becoming a partly private owned company resulted in a number of changes in order to increase the decision making and reactivity to market. Despite the dominant role of politics in the telecommunication landscape, people were chosen for the best leadership independent of the rules of language parity, for example, the appointment of Didier Bellens as CEO. From an organisational perspective and business responsiveness view we see that the Belgacom as organisation underwent a number of changes moving the company into new markets, for example, the creation of Proximus, the called Multimedia and Information Highways Division, creation of a venture capitalist fund BMV Belgacom continues to diversify to create an alternative for their declining fixed line market by creating added value services. In fact we can distinguish two new lines of business and focus the first on being the entry of the Belgian television market with a Belgacom TV offering and the second factor being the acquisition of Telindus, Belgian's leading network integrator with international allures. It remains to be seen if entering new markets such as digital television and system integration will be successful.

From an internationalisation perspective Belgacom had not been proven to be as successful as intended. There was the unsuccessful merge with KPN, but being unsuccessful in merging did not have any impact on the success of Belgacom as a leading telcommunications company in the European context. In their process of taking over another operator, three potential candidates came onto the scene, Cesky Telecom, Turk Telecom and Versatel but without result because Belgacom was only a modest bidder. Belgacom however remains with international aspirations and is looking further east in the hope to find potential candidates. On the other hand taking over Telindus enforced Belgacom's position in the integrator market and opened the way towards internationalisation as Telindus already operates in a number of countries.

In terms of profits Belgacom has proven to be as successful as could be and has reinforced Belgacoms' financial battle strength and its ability to scale the barriers towards competition. Being profitable and free of debts will of course help the company in their international aspirations and ability to merge or take-over other companies.

In a principal–agent context we see that Belgacom, with a long tradition of bureaucracy and hierarchical structure, managed to transform itself into a profitable and listed company. On the point of their legal corporate status we could say that the management has been given relative autonomy. The Board remains appointed by the Belgian government, but also has the extra responsibility for the operational strategic planning of Belgacom. This strategic plan is drafted on a yearly basis by the Board of Directors and established the medium-term goals of the company. In terms of changing a hierarchical bureaucracy into a customer-responsive business culture we see that the Belgacom management worked on this with two successful reconversion plans PST and BeST laying off 10,000 people and converting another 6,000. It established a corporate university in order to form and transform their current human potential, and by 2005, 92 per cent of the staff has attended at least one course organised by the university. Management structures have been simplified and slimmed-down by the different CEO's. This process will remain a big challenge for the company in keeping this process ongoing with the current and future take-overs and integration of new companies. On the other hand, however, integration could help in re-enforcing the current management and attract new potentials and new ways of governing.

Focusing on the upcoming years, in 2006 Belgacom defined its strategy in a long-term context. This revolves around three areas: operational excellence, maintaining market leadership around their core activities, and pursuit new development opportunities. This strategy can be summed up in four letters: BELG. B for 'Become Best in Class'. This means maintaining their Number One position on the Belgian market and ranking among the most efficient operators in Europe. E for 'Excel', meaning that they must make excellence a priority: in the way they manage costs, human resources, and technical know-how; in synergising activities within the Belgacom Group and in their customer interactions. L for 'Lead', meaning that Belgacom must continuously strive for a number one position, that is: maintain their leadership position in Belgium in the area of voice telephony, by launching new products and services; play a pivotal role in the triple-play market by promoting their network, ADSL and Belgacom TV; continue to build customer intimacy by offering a range of innovative products. G stands for 'Grow', which is a crucial priority. Belgacom must expand in the data and e-services markets; pursue international growth through their carrier subsidiary; extend their activities beyond Belgium, in both fixed-line and mobile telephony markets (Belgacom, Jaarverslag, 2005).

Chapter 9

Managing Complexity: The Case of Deutsche Telekom

Günter Knieps, Jürgen Müller and Arnulf Heuermann

Introduction

In this chapter we consider the evolution of the current industry structure in the telecommunications sector and the emergence of Deutsche Telekom from a domestic monopoly provider to an internationally positioned company. How has the institutional setting of the German deregulation and privatisation process and the subsequent regulatory structure influenced this development? This question aims to separate the external factors from operational considerations. Company structure and strategy will differ, given the contingencies and the different political coalitions that shape them. At the same time we attempt to show how the operational reform leading to the current company structure may have been influenced by a somewhat national regulatory orientation.

In the following section of the chapter we analyse the past role of the state in infrastructure provision up to the mid 1980s when the state monopoly and the role of the state as an operator were challenged by large users, and we examine whether this was to some extent due to external policy factors (such as the influence of the EU) and the imitation of policies employed in other countries that had engaged in early liberalisation, for instance the UK or the United States. The speed with which liberalisation was achieved was also influenced by other political factors, such as industrial policy considerations of the government and the strong political position of domestic equipment providers. We also have to examine the role of the labour unions, which feared losses of jobs and privileges as a consequence of increasing competitive pressures. Against this background, the emerging industry structure will be analysed. We look first at the 'corporatisation' of the German Ministry of Post and Telecommunications (DBP) into three separate companies in the form of joint stock holding companies (AG) and the commercialisation and internationalisation that followed, and then we examine the role of the other players that entered the industry and how the regulatory environment has influenced this development. The subsequent section looks at the results of this transformation process and the conclusions that can be drawn regarding the effect and interplay of ownership, regulation and competition policy. Here the particular focus is on the new Deutsche Telekom, in particular on how competition led to a more commercialised Deutsche Telekom and the internationalisation strategy in fixed and mobile services that followed this development. However, it has been suggested that major economic effects from liberalisation and privatisation policy do not result from better services of new market entrants but of productivity gains of the much larger incumbent. We will therefore elaborate the process of adoption of Deutsche Telekom to the new market structure, its organisational changes and strategies for growth and productivity increase.

The Historical Role of the German Ministry of Post and Telecommunications (DBP)

The Original Institutional Design

When analyzing the evolution of the current corporate structure in the German telecommunications industry, we must ask what the main characteristics of this transformation process are: What are the effect and the interplay of ownership, regulation and competition policy? One important element was the legal monopoly for post, telephony and telegraph services originating from the 1892 Law on Telegraphy, whereby the German Reich established the exclusive rights for telephony and telegraph services. This law and its follow up law, the so-called 'Fernmeldeanlagengesetz' (FAG) of 1928, dominated the institutional thinking up to the actual liberalisation process at the end of the 1980s. It formulated the framework for the provision of public services by the Ministry of Post and Telecommunications, and by the Defence Ministry for the military services. The Deutsche Bundespost (DBP) which exclusively provided the civilian services did so according to Article 87 of the Basic Constitutional Law of 1949, in the form of a federally-owned public administration.[1] A Board of Overseers, which was created under the same Law, exercised some control and had a supervisory function over the DBP. For example, it had to approve the annual budget, changes in tariffs and new service offerings.[2] Details of user guidelines, however, which were the legal rules for using the telecommunications system, were actually formulated by the Minister for Postal Affairs.

The DBP was the sole provider of the public switching and transmission systems. The network was also planned and installed by the DBP. It purchased the equipment from selected national equipment providers, maintained and extended it and had, therefore, an important monopsony power in the market

---

1 The precise details were laid down in the Postal Law of 1953 (PostVwG).

2 Its 25 members included a technical specialist for telecommunications and a specialist on budget and finance. The rest were political appointees, so that the control was more political and rather more one in name than in practice, thereby strongly relying on self-regulation by the DBP.

for telecommunications equipment.[3] In addition, the DBP also regulated the utilisation of the network, specifying who could use the network and to what extent. The utilisation of existing services for third parties was only possible under very restrictive criteria (for example only for wholly-owned subsidiaries).[4]

The evolution of the national telephone network was influenced by available investment funds and this of course depended to a large extent on the pricing policy chosen, in other words on the level and structure of tariffs. Traditional telecommunications pricing policy was characterised by two objectives: to cover costs and to contribute to the expansion of the network. The latter objective was supported by a pricing scheme in which long distance telecommunications users subsidised the access of local telecommunications users and thereby promoted the expansion of the network. This pricing policy was presumably in all groups' interests, since a growing network was not only good for the general public, but also for the equipment providers and employees of the DBP. Only the larger users with significant national and international traffic were feeling the financial burden of this policy and therefore pushed for institutional change when it became politically feasible.

This pricing policy continued, however, even after the completion of the network expansion in the 1960s and despite massive cost decreases in the long distance part of the telecommunications network. In fact, internal cross-subsidisation increased during these years.[5] As this pricing structure was protected by a monopoly of the dominant carrier and by legal entry barriers, it created a number of interest groups with (partially) opposing political goals. On the one hand, cheap local telephone access was seen as an infrastructure obligation that served the political goals, but at the same time required barriers to entry against the possibility of cream skimming, if entry in the profitable parts of the network were to be allowed. On the other hand, this continued monopoly protected the production factors like capital and labour from the competition of potential entrants. The nationally-oriented procurement policy allowed the seemingly 'costless' support of domestic suppliers of equipment and of medium-size firms ('Mittelstandspolitik') that would not have survived under a more globally competitive arrangement.

---

3 Technical conception, development and production were carried out by a number of selected domestic equipment suppliers in close cooperation with the DBP's office for technology, the Fernmeldetechnisches Zentralamt (FTZ).

4 For more details see Knieps, Müller and von Weizsäcker (1982).

5 For Germany it has been estimated that the mark-ups of prices over costs were about 300 per cent to 400 per cent for long distance calls within the country and to other European countries (Foreman-Peck and Müller, 1988, ch. 1.5).

The Interest Group Structure before Privatisation and Deregulation in Germany

Due to the rapidly growing importance of the telecommunications and Information and Communication Technologies (ICT) industry for the national economies, and the necessity of telecommunications for the basic functioning of the nation states, this area has been a key political issue in most countries. Even with the liberalisation introduced by the EU regulatory framework in the 1980s, the field was still open to various national political initiatives. Hence, the resulting national telecommunications policy cannot be understood without also looking into the political mechanisms operating in this sector.

In the old centralised structure of political decision making in post-war West Germany, all telecommunications issues were coordinated by only one authority, the Federal Minister of Post and Telecommunications and affiliated institutions. All interest groups[6] had to approach this single authority.[7] In such an institutional environment, the outcome of the decision making process is likely to be some compromise between the interests of all groups, no matter whether it is more strongly influenced by number voting, by money voting or by logrolling. We suspect, however, that the political process was dominated by a silent coalition between the DBP and its unions on the one hand and the small and peripheral users on the other hand. The DBP and its unions are interested in maintaining the monopoly, which in turn can be legitimised and supported democratically only by the subsidies it provides for the large majority of small and peripheral users at the expense of business users.[8]

As a consequence of the relatively strong influence of small and peripheral user interests in Germany a deregulation of the long distance telephone services could not be enforced politically for a long time. Indeed, the removal of legal

---

6 The political relevance of small and peripheral user interests can be illustrated by the example of the reform of local tariffs of 1978. The original purpose of this reform was to extend significantly the areas in which local tariffs applied, but at the same time to introduce time metering in a four minute pulse. Due to heavy resistance of local users an eight minute pulse had to be accepted politically which finally led to a strong improvement for local users.

7 The Minister was a member of the federal government nominated by the federal chancellor, who himself is elected directly by the parliament and indirectly by the voters. A comparative analysis of the situation in Germany and the United States can be found in Blankart and Knieps (1989).

8 The political relevance of small and peripheral user interests can be illustrated by the example of the reform of local tariffs of 1978. The original purpose of this reform was to extend significantly the areas in which local tariffs applied, but at the same time to introduce time metering in a four minute pulse. Due to heavy resistance of local users an eight minute pulse had to be accepted politically which finally led to a strong improvement for local users.

entry barriers in the telephone services requires giving up internal subsidisation.[9] Maintaining the telephone monopoly, however, also requires maintaining the physical network monopoly, since under network competition the telephone monopolist DBP could be easily bypassed. Thus the largest part of the telecommunications monopoly had to be maintained if internal subsidisation of small and peripheral users was to be preserved.

In summary, the main interest groups characterising the political scene in Germany before deregulation and commercialisation were:

1) The Deutsche Bundespost (DBP) and its unionised personnel as monopoly holders benefiting from monopoly rents and therefore favouring the maintenance of the status quo.
2) The domestic suppliers of the DBP benefiting from the actual monopoly regime by privileged supply and barriers to entry from outsiders (concept of 'der Hoflieferanten' or 'favoured suppliers').
3) Small users and users in peripheral locations required large installation and maintenance costs in the local network relative to the number of profitable long distance calls made. This group was benefiting from internal subsidisation enforced via legal entry barriers.
4) Business users requiring frequent long distance telecommunications services who are paying a large part of the internal subsidy for the other users. This group is obviously opposing the maintenance of the status quo.

The perspective expanded further as the options for liberalisation emerged. Concerning the 'favoured suppliers' (point 2 above), other domestic and foreign suppliers started to press for a reduction of the barriers to entry for this lucrative market, especially as some of them offered superior technology (for example, Nixdorf, IBM, Ericsson etc). Since they also needed access to the domestic market to prove the superiority of their products for export markets, industrial policy arguments started to emerge in support of their position.

In the distributive politics between the small numbers of intensive telephone users who were cross-subsidising large numbers of peripheral users, the former gained political status through support from industry associations and their direct lobbying efforts. This process was facilitated by the increasing importance of the ICT sector and the growing political attention devoted to it by policy-makers.

---

9 In order to make free entry into all parts of telecommunications politically acceptable it was necessary to break up the silent coalition between the telecommunications administration and the small users by setting up a universal service fund. The purpose of this fund is to keep the traditional subsidy of the small users stable, only changing the way it is financed from internal to external subsidisation. In order to make sure that the small users did not oppose deregulation it was important to guarantee the price-level of the traditionally internally subsidised services as upper boundary – 'social contract' pricing (Blankart and Knieps, 1989: 592–4).

Under the social–liberal coalition under Willy Brandt and Helmut Schmidt, the office of the Chancellor and the Ministry of Research and Technology (BMFT) started a coordinated assessment of the impact of the emerging ICT technology in a broader policy framework, thereby focussing increasing attention on the way this sector had been organised in the past.[10]

In this analysis, we also have to look at forces that relate to the international developments in this sector and specifically at the political initiative undertaken by the European Union. Under the strong influence of the EU Commission's 'Green Paper on the Development of the Common Market for Telecommunications Services and Equipment'[11] of June 1987, partial deregulation was introduced in member states. There were controversial debates on the costs and benefits of global entry deregulation. The obstacles to comprehensive entry deregulation did not, however, exclude the possibility of partial entry deregulation. Partial deregulation included free entry into terminal equipment supply and into value added network services (VANS) on the basis of the physical network provided by the network owner.

The 'Green Paper on the Liberalisation of Telecommunications Infrastructure and Cable Television Networks', issued by the Commission in October 1994,[12] again strongly influenced the process of liberalisation of European telecommunications. The 'Full Competition Directive'[13] of 13 March 1996 demanded that member countries permit free entry into all parts of telecommunications. The new telecommunications laws allowing overall market entry were enacted by the national parliaments during 1996, coming fully into effect on 1 January 1998.

The German Telecommunications Reform

Partial Deregulation at First

Partial liberalisation started already in 1981 with the liberalisation of the terminal equipment market and some value added services (VAS). Thus, the obstacles to global deregulation in Germany described above did not exclude the possibility of partial deregulation. A chronological overview of the deregulation process in Germany is given in Figure 9.1.

---

[10] Much of this concerns the investigations carried out by the Witte commission on the effects of ICT technology and not only on the telecommunications sector, but also on broadcasting and other user markets.

[11] KOM (87) 290 fin.

[12] KOM (94) 440 fin.

[13] Commission Directive 96/19/EC of 13 March 1996 amending Directive 90/388/EEC with regard to the implementation of full competition in the telecommunications markets, OJ L 74, 22. 3. 1996: 13 (the 'Full Competition Directive').

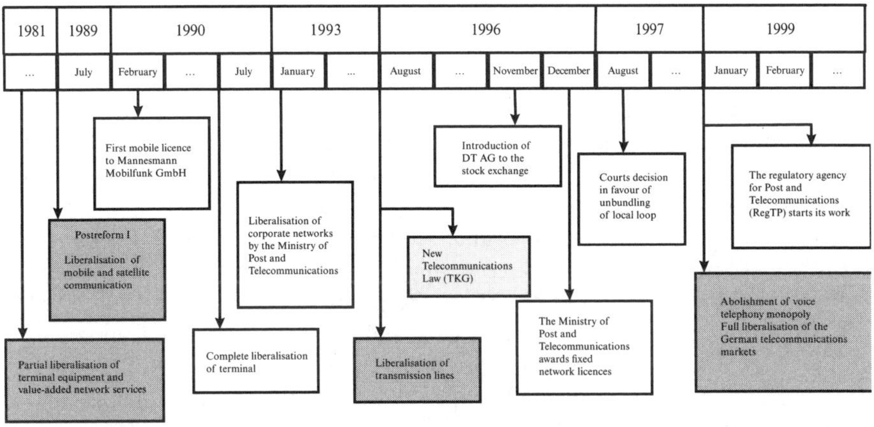

Figure 9.1 Steps in the deregulation process in Germany

Source: Späth (1999, ch. C117: 4) and own research (translation by the authors).

Partial deregulation is here meant to refer to the elimination of the monopoly provision for terminal equipment supply and value added network services (on the basis of the continued physical network monopoly by the DBP). There are two reasons why partial deregulation was politically feasible in Germany. First, the partial deregulation of the terminal equipment market[14] had proven successful in the US and parts of Asia and concerned only a small segment of the market, so giving in here did not challenge the fundamental network monopoly. The partial deregulation for value added services also concerned only a small, but politically very sensitive market. Further, relaxing some of the restrictions on network use was a useful measure to avoid large business users placing their data processing centres abroad and maintaining only smaller facilities nationally.[15] Second, because as a public monopoly the DBP had been relatively inefficient and unable to exploit the innovation potential within its telecommunications market, it had an interest in allowing partial deregulation and promoting VANS competition on its network. By maintaining the exclusive provision of network facilities, however, it could nevertheless provide a platform for innovative services whilst still having the option to skim part of the innovation rents generated by private entrepreneurs.

[14] The monopoly on the first telephoning for each household or business was still maintained for a time, until 1990.

[15] This danger was imminent because European countries are relatively small and therefore in a potentially competitive situation vis-à-vis each other.

Separating Regulation from Operation and Commercialising the Operator

The more substantial steps had to wait until 1 July 1989,[16] when the traditional Deutsche Bundespost (DBP) was separated from the Ministry of Post and Telecommunications and split into three independent enterprises: for postal services, telecommunications services and financial services (Postbank), which were then commercialised and later partly privatised.[17]

For the telecommunications branch, the publicly owned DBP Telekom was transformed into the joint stock company 'Deutsche Telekom AG' (DTAG) in 1995, so that its shares could be sold to the public. In November, 1996, DTAG sold common stock representing approximately 25 per cent of the company in a global stock offering that raised approximately DM 20 billion (US $13 billion), the largest equity offering ever in Europe.[18,19] Although the state still holds about 43 per cent of the shares of DTAG, privatisation can be considered to be a real one,[20] because a significant part of the shares are traded at the stock exchanges. Moreover, the government has no golden shares,[21] even though the Ministry of Finance is the largest shareholder and still a significant player in determining company strategy.

In the context of the postal reform the functions of the Ministry of Post and Telecommunications were partly transferred to the Ministry of Economics. Its sector-specific regulatory functions were transferred to a new regulatory authority for telecommunications and postal services (RegTP) that was to oversee the move from a monopoly to real competition. In particular, it supervises

[16] Gesetz zur Neustrukturierung des Post- und Fernmeldewesens und der Deutschen Bundespost (Poststrukturgesetz) vom 8. Juni 1989, Bundesgesetzblatt Teil I vom 14. Juni 1989, pp. 1026-1051. [Law on Restructuring the Postal and Telecommunications Services and the Federal Postal System] (PostStruktG), v. 8.6.1989 (BGB1. I. S. 2325) ('Post Reform II')].

[17] The legislation separated the three main activities of the Bundespost, telecommunications, postal services, and financial services, into distinct businesses, Gesetz zur Neustrukturierung des Post- und Fernmeldewesens (Postrefom I). In 1994, the second reform act made all three private stock corporations, Gesetz zur Neuordnung des Postwesens und der Telekommunikation (Postreform II) and contemplated their privatisation.

[18] The privatisation legislation restricted the government from further public stock sales until 2000 in order to give DT priority on public market access, see Gordon (1999a).

[19] The privatisation process slowed down after the end of the telecom bubble in 2001, but under pressure to meet the Maastricht budgetary criteria for economic and monetary union, the government subsequently decided to sell off a 25 per cent stake in DT to the state development loan agency, Kreditanstalt für Wiederaufbau.

[20] In contrast to a formal privatisation, where the state still remains the sole owner after the transition from a public enterprise to a firm under private law.

[21] Such golden shares called 'Kiwi Shares' were introduced, for example, during the privatisation process in New Zealand (for example, Ergas, 1996).

the interconnection of different telecommunications networks, shared use of technology locations (collocation), unbundling of subscriber lines ('last mile'), and number portability.

Mobile Licensees as First Real Competitors

In 1989, the first real network competition was introduced, as one alternative mobile license was awarded to the consortium of Mannesmann: Two additional licenses where awarded several years later. Opening up this market at first seemed very similar to the partial deregulation observed for terminal equipment and VAS services, since mobile operators still had to rely on Deutsche Telekom for their backbone network, and mobile services at that time were at best considered a marginal market compared to the large and lucrative fixed network services. However, with the rapid emergence of the mobile market and the further liberalisation of long-distance networks in 1996, developments in this market were important pointers for the competitive powers faced by the newly commercialised Deutsche Telekom before the whole network was to be opened to full competition in 1998. Against this background, it is therefore useful to consider the emergence of the future competitors as illustrated in Figure 9.2.

There were 10 consortia that applied for the first alternative mobile license, many comprising several firms that were grouped in different consortia. It is interesting to observe that many members of these groups later became significant players in the larger fixed network market, even though they were not successful in the actual license application. Some entered the market for mobile service provision and later became mobile virtual operators (MVO), and/or entered the market for fixed networks when it opened in 1996.

Looking at the different groups in Figure 9.2 and starting at the top, Foreign Service providers quickly became active competitors. At first they started to enter the consortia formed for mobile services, and in the market for VAS services. Some of the banks, which had operated their own VAS services, became interesting partners for new fixed network entrance, both from within Germany and abroad. There was little interest from the media side, or from equipment providers who tried to keep good relations with major network clients. Instead, it was the infrastructure providers in the form of utilities that became the other important group of entrants into network competition.

The Mannesmann consortium, which was awarded the first additional mobile licence, did not come from any of these groups just discussed, since at its core it was an engineering company that acquired telephony and mobile experience from foreign operators within the consortium. It quickly became a significant competitor and was the leader in this market, a great shock to Deutsche Telekom. This clearly showed that the operating experience in a protected monopoly had not prepared the incumbent for the competitive onslaught that followed liberalisation.

Deutsche Telekom had created a separate nucleus for its activities in competitive markets early on through its privately managed subsidiary Detecon, a consulting company majority-owned by Deutsche Bank, but run by Deutsche Telekom. In the past, this company had never had more than 800 employees selected on merit and paid market salaries. Now in the preparation for the competition in the mobile market it grew rapidly to more than double its former size, until later when the mobile subsidiary was moved back into the main company and set up separately as T-Mobil within Deutsche Telekom.

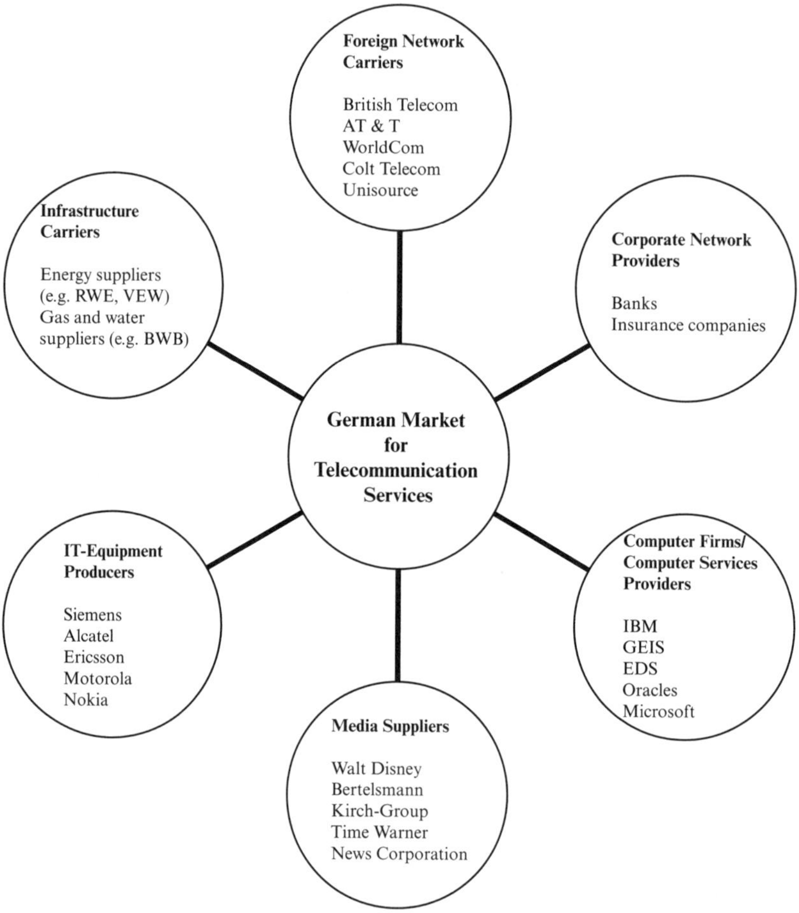

Figure 9.2 The origins of new and potential competitors of Deutsche Telekom

Source: according to Gerpott (1998: 254) (English translation by the authors).

Competition in Fixed Networks

The new regulatory framework provided not only for a new institution and a regulatory framework in line with the EU directives, but also provided the option of structural regulation. This related to restructuring before privatisation,[22] and to reducing barriers to entry. On the positive side, we note that the telephone network of the federal railroad was auctioned off to one of the network competitors, Arcor, thereby giving it a head start in the construction of new networks. On the negative side, however, the important CATV network was left with the privatised Deutsche Telekom, with an obligation to spin it off and privatise it at a later date. Thus, the company had control over an important strategic tool and was able to keep out potential competitors that could have made use of this large network.[23]

Who then were the important competitors in this regulatory environment? Compared to the entry strategy in the mobile sector, where competition was limited due to the number of licenses issued (options for resellers and virtual operators were offered in addition) the spectrum of entry strategies to be observed in the fixed network sector was much wider. If one analyses the entrants according to strategic groups, it can be seen that a number of companies entered as full service carriers, but also that several others concentrated on different segments of the value added chain. Around the year 2001, therefore, we find the following picture:

Analysis of Entrants According to Strategic Groups I

- *Incumbent*: Deutsche Telekom AG,
- *Other national full service carriers* (Mannesmann Arcor, Otelo und Viag Interkom, all from the electricity sector),
- *Switch-based Carriers* (MobilCom, Debitel, TelDaFax und Talkline, all from mobile resellers)
- *Resellers* – (for example, 01051 Telecom, Mox Telecom).
- *Carriers' Carrier* (Star Telecom as 'Carrier-Hotel').

Analysis of Entrants According to Strategic Groups II

Some concentrated on different product offerings:

- *Mobil Providers* (Mannesmann Mobilfunk (D2), Viag Interkom (E2), DeTeMobil (D1), E-Plus),
- *Internet Service Providers* (for example, Nikoma),
- *Metropolitan Area Networks (MAN)* (Colt, MFS, MCI WorldCom),

---

22 And handing out additional licenses in the mobile area.

23 Deutsche Telekom kept the CATV network until 2002, and the new owners began offering competitive telecommunications services only in 2005, thus enabling the use of this important competitive network only at a very late date. See Vogelsang, 2003: 332.

- *Communal City Carriers* (for example, Berlikomm, NetCologne, ISIS, a special „German' phenomenon),[24]
- *CATV Providers* (z.B. Primacom, tss, Telecolumbus).

However, there were significant differences in the individual markets as competition developed. Whereas Deutsche Telekom held 100 per cent of the market share for voice telephony before global entry deregulation, the market share of the competitors quickly increased from 10.3 per cent in 1998 to 34.7 per cent (share of national long distance calls, including regional calls traffic, volume in minutes) in 2001. The competitors' market share for international calls increased from 20 per cent in 1998 to 51 per cent in 2001 (Monopolkommission, 2001: 45).[25] By 2002, alternative carriers had gained a revenue share of 47.6 per cent, but 86.6 per cent of alternative carriers revenue came from mobile services, where Deutsche Telekom already faced three other competitors and several important resellers. In the market for fixed network and data services, just 13.4 per cent of the revenue went to competitors[26] (compared to 22.8 per cent of traffic minutes) whilst DTAG had a long-distance market share of 62 per cent (RegTP, 2002). Nevertheless, since entry became possible, the performance of the German long-distance telecommunications market improved strongly: we have already seen the emergence of a large number of service providers providing an increasing scope of services, the entry of several full service network carriers, and as a consequence strongly decreasing prices for long distance calls etc. (cf. Gabelmann and Groß, 2003: 107; Stumpf and Schwarz-Schilling, 1999).

During the competition process differences in the price-setting behaviour of the different types of firms could be observed. The intense price competition in the winter of 1998/99 not only reduced the overall level of prices, it also resulted in a convergence of prices. The internet and printed media were full of price information; agencies also provided information and the providers themselves advertised aggressively with price as the decisive variable in long distance telecommunications (Brunekreeft and Groß, 2000: 932).

The overall development can be summarised as follows (Brunekreeft and Groß, 2000: 932): Deutsche Telekom lowered its average price by 62 per cent, the alternative network operators by 66 per cent and the service providers by 52 per cent between February 1998 and April 1999. In April 1999 the service providers charged on average only 32 per cent of what consumers had had to pay to Deutsche Telekom for comparable services 16 months earlier. After the initial period of strong price decline during 1998/99 the price level began to stabilise. The price for foreign calls was 36.5 per cent lower in 2001, as compared to 2000, and

---

[24] There is a strong tradition of communal enterprises in Germany, which extended quickly to telecom services, once this market became open.

[25] At that time no pre-selection and call-by-call were available for local calls.

[26] And their local traffic share was only 1.6 per cent.

then became stable. In contrast, prices for local access and local calls remained relatively unchanged (Monopolkommission, 2001: 52).[27]

Integrating the East German Network

Just as network competition started to take off and mobile competitors were eating into Deutsche Telecom's market share, German reunification took place in October 1990. This brought additional challenges[28] for the new management, faced with the task to modernise and upgrade the East German network and to increase penetration rates to normal European levels. A large labour force with a very different corporate culture had to be integrated and retrained, and significant management resources had to be diverted from the urgent restructuring in West Germany to the even more pressing needs of the East.

In particular, the East German network was small and outdated with long waiting lists. As a consequence, new – and from the viewpoint of the traditional telecom management – revolutionary strategies had to be implemented. For the first time, network planning and implementation was outsourced to equipment suppliers, giving the management a taste of taking over turnkey projects instead of the traditional in-house procurement and installation. Technology choices also differed, favouring mobile networks and satellite receptions versus traditional cable TV networks. Concerning mobile services, competition and market developments were much more intense than in the West, at least for while, given the large backlog of orders for the fixed network and the much quicker time with which customers could be provided with mobile services. Satellite dishes could also be installed much more quickly than CATV networks could be laid, so that today penetration rates still differ significantly between the two parts of Germany. As the network was so outdated and so small in the East, upgrading the system also offered new technological possibilities, for example, large-scale experiments in providing fibre-optic services to the home could be carried out. In summary, this challenge to management led to many new and innovative solutions for customers and revealed some management talents that had lain dormant in the more quiet monopoly times.

---

27 See also Statistisches Bundesamt, Verbraucherpreisindex für Telekommunikationsdienstleistungen, Mitteilung Nr. 41 vom 31. January 2001.

28 One of the options considered by the East German Post and Telecom Administration just before unification was a separate privatisation of its telephone network, which would have been an interesting entry strategy for potential competitor. While this would have right away captured the East German customers, and thereby have made Deutsche Telekom an entrant in its new home market, this option never got beyond the planning stage. Instead, that telephone network of the Deutsche Post, the East German network provider, was integrated into DeutscheTelekom after unification.

The New Deutsche Telekom

Competition Led to a More Commercialised Deutsche Telekom AG

Given the new regulatory framework on network access and interconnection, local loop unbundling and third party billing, the move to a commercialised organisation in an increasingly competitive environment has been ongoing for over fifteen years. Table 9.1 gives an overview over the different stages of regulation and helps to understand the changed regulatory framework and its effects on the organisation.

Table 9.1 Stages of regulation

	Monopoly/ Duopoly	Transition	Normalisation
Retail price control	Controls on all services	Gradual relaxation of controls	No controls
Access pricing	Not relevant, or arbitrary pricing of small range of services	Services gradually decontrolled Unbundling Use of price caps	Platform competition Remaining monopolistic bottlenecks within local loops controlled
Universal service obligations	Borne by incumbent	Costed and shared (or ignored if not) material	As in 'transition', with possibility of competitive provision

The most important changes took first place in those markets, where competition was first most keenly felt, like in the market for terminal equipment, mobile services and VAS applications. As we have seen in the market for mobile services above, organisational forms were tried outside the traditional DBP organisation, thereby accelerating organisational learning and providing for extra flexibility.

Similar to other European countries, German telecommunications policy has been strongly influenced by asymmetric market power regulation with an intrinsic bias against incumbent carriers. As a consequence, excessive regulation due to an oversized regulatory basis occurred. The specification of the regulatory basis is not explicitly founded on the identification of network-specific market power. Instead, classification as a dominant firm as laid down in competition law is chosen as the central precondition to justify sector-specific regulation. For example, the provision of long-distance telecommunications infrastructure and voice telephony services by a carrier classified as dominant in those markets has been considered non-competitive, although active and potential competition in itself is sufficient to discipline market power. A necessary requirement for future regulatory reform is the application of a symmetrical regulatory approach, focussing on network-specific market power based on monopolistic bottlenecks with no intrinsic bias towards any firm or technology (Knieps, 1997: 326–8).

It is to be expected that for the near future the period of over-regulation will continue. Due to the unspecific regulatory obligations of the EU Directives[29] the European Commission would seem to have broad discretionary power in defining the regulatory basis, including the interaction between the European Commission and national regulators. This increasing complexity of EU regulation is resulting in a tangle of contradictory decisions and statements, involving also new markets such as interactive cable television, Internet etc. (Knieps, 2005: 80 f.).

Privatisation Changed the Organisation

Three types of influences are easily visible. The first concerns the organisational changes required by the telecommunications arm of the DBP on being transformed into a joint stock company (AG), even though initially all stocks were still held by the Federal Ministry of Finance.[30] This required a board of overseers (Aufsichtsrat) to be appointed, where in addition to the officials of the government, external experts were added to the board. This of course added a much more commercial outlook and orientation to its strategy. The second effect related to the auditing and disclosure process associate with actual privatisation, in which the traditional accounts of the DBP had to be brought in line with modern accountancy requirements. As a consequence, a much more commercially-oriented controlling system could be used to evaluate current and future projects. But the most important effect was to establish an entrepreneurial culture at DT and reorganising the business on functional lines, in order to meet the new competition. This also meant downsizing the workforce, from 230,000

---

29 See in particular: Directive 2002/21/EC of the European Parliament and of the Council of 7 March 2002 on a common regulatory framework for electronic communications networks and services (Framework Directive), OJ L108/33, 24 April 2002. Directive 2002/19/EC of the European Parliament and of the Council on access to, and interconnection of, electronic communications networks and associated facilities (Access Directive), OJ L108/7, 24 April 2002.

30 In November 1996, approximately 25 per cent of the company was sold, so that the DTAG initial public offering was only a partial privatisation; the government held on to 74 per cent, making it the dominant shareholder. Under the Stock Corporation Law of 1965, 23, a 50 per cent holder has the power to elect all the shareholder representatives of the supervisory board and controls the disposition of all other routine matters that come before the shareholders meeting, including ratification of the acts of the management board and the supervisory board. A 75 per cent holder has distinctive powers, including the right to recall a member of the supervisory board, and the right to amend the articles of incorporation (Gordon, 1999b).

at year-end, 1994, to a targeted 170,000 by 2000 (through traditional German means of attrition and early retirement rather than layoffs).[31]

Organisational Change since Privatisation

In the attempt to establish an entrepreneurial culture at DT and reorganising the business on functional lines, a large number of organisational improvement projects were initiated that completely changed the structure, culture and performance of Deutsche Telekom. Major objectives have been the improvement of sales and customer orientation, cost reduction and increased efficiency, improved and speedy processes and decision making, better innovation, faster growth and better shareholder value. Here four major phases can be distinguished:

1) Before 1996 until 1998 management attention was strongly focussed on privatisation and the processes of going public.
2) From 1998 until 2002 the introduction of competition, the regulatory battles and the internationalisation of the company were the main focus of management.
3) Phase 3 from 2002 until 2004 was centred on debt reduction and restructuring.
4) Recently the 'Excellence Programme 2005–2007' is aiming to become 'Europe's No. 1' and focuses management attention on growth and shareholder value.

There have been no less than 12 major re-organisation projects on the top-level of Deutsche Telekom, affecting more or less each organisational unit and employee. When Dr Ron Sommer replaced Mr Helmut Ricke as CEO in 1995, he took over a formally privatised, but still 100 per cent state-owned company. Dr. Sommer's prime objective was to make the 1996 'going public' process a success and to introduce private sector procedures and tools. In 1996 the project 'PERFORM' aimed at optimised processes, roles, and responsibilities in the newly privatised company with the objective of preparing Deutsche Telekom for full competition and the creation of a customer-oriented business culture.

In 1998, when the last monopoly rights fell, 'GK-, PK Direktionen' was a project that restructured the regional Directorates and created separate units for business and residential customers to better defend the market against competitors focussing in particular on the business segment. In 1999 the program 'HQ' was the first major efficiency improvement project creating a lean central headquarters in

[31] This was against the background that approximately 3.3 per cent of the initial public offering – nearly 1 per cent of the company's equity – was sold to employees under various preferential arrangements designed to 'increase employee identification' with the company, a particular challenge since nearly half the workforce were at the time tenured civil service employees whose salaries and benefits are set by government regulation.

Table 9.2 Organisational change since privatisation

Major Phases of Organisational Reform of Deutsche Telekom			
1996–1998 Privatisation and fit-for competition	1998–2002 Competition and internationalisation	2002–2004 Debt reduction and restructuring	2005–2007 Profitable growth
CEO: Dr Ron Sommer		CEO: Mr Kai-Uwe Ricke	
• 'Perform' re-organisation • Business – and Residential Directorates • HQ restructuring • ZNI – operational restructuring • SLIM – productivity improvement in operations • 4 pillar strategy • 'Prisma' – HR reform • 'Nice' – restructuring of production and service • 'ErGo' – cost reduction at common cost level		• 'E3' – improved efficiency and debt reduction • SMH – Strategic Management Holding • Excellence Program 2005–2007 – growth initiatives for SBUs, customer and brand, product innovation, operations, profitablity HR, company culture	

a new building in Bonn that strongly slimmed down and centralised the numerous overhead and management functions of the company. In the same year the program 'ZNI' started to lay the way for a future network infrastructure strongly reducing the number of switching centres. In all, 39 technical local areas were centralised into 13 new regional areas with the aim of improving the innovation climate and shortening decision-making processes. In 2000 the program 'SLIM', a major project for cost reduction and optimised processes in the operational units, and for gaining a significant productivity increase in the central functions, was launched.

With the subsequent '4-pillar-strategy' (with T-Mobile, T-Online, T-Systems and T-Com,) Dr. Ron Sommer aimed at aligning the company into 4 central growth areas along product family lines – mobile services, online services, system solutions and fixed network. The idea behind this reorganisation was born in the years of the booming IT and Telco stock markets and aimed to improve shareholder value by issuing four focused rather than one central share value on the stock markets. The four pillars therefore were prepared as independent legal entities led by a central holding each with its own IPO. However, only T-Online finally went public, T-Mobile withdrew the share issue when the 'IP-bubble' finally collapsed. Meanwhile the T-Online shares have been re-transferred to 'Deutsche Telekom' shares to cope with the growth potential of a strengthened combined marketing initiative, with large losses for those who bought shares at the initial IPO. Dr. Ron Sommer had to accept, that the strong expansion strategy went to the financial limits of Deutsche Telecom, in particular when the share prices dropped dramatically. Restructuring and cost reduction came into the focus again.

In 2001 three major projects were initiated: 'PRISMA' aimed at an optimisation of all HR functions of the company; 'Nice' started a comprehensive restructuring of the product portfolio, the network infrastructure as well as customer service; and 'ErGO' was a project that strongly reduced the common costs of the central services and aimed at an optimisation of common costs. This was followed in 2002 with 'SMH', a project to reorganise the HQ into a strategic management holding with new central steering and leadership principles. The number of staff allocated to HQ and shared services were reduced from 56,585 to 19,366.

In 2002 the debt of Deutsche Telekom rose dramatically. Major acquisitions in the year 2000, in particular 'Voicestream' in the US at a price of US $ 24 bn and the auctioning of UMTS licenses for Deutsche Telekom's frequency block at a price of €16.6 bn, endangered the financial health of the company. Dr. Ron Sommer resigned and Mr Kai Uwe Ricke, the son of the former CEO Helmut Ricke, took over as CEO. Kai Uwe Ricke's major priority in the first two years was consequently debt reduction. The 'E3' project of 2002 was therefore dealing with major sell-off activities and cost reduction programmes. Within one year net debt was reduced from €64.2 bn to less than €50 bn.

In 2004 the latest ambitious re-organisation project 'Excellence Program 2005-2007' was initiated by Mr. Ricke. The concept of the '4-pillar-strategy' based on product centric units was given-up in favour of three purely growth-oriented strategic business units – Broadband, Business Customers and Mobile. Broadband includes fixed network platforms and services, wholesale business (before T-Systems) and T-Online. Business Customers is the former T-Systems business including the LE and SME business customer part of T-Com, while Mobile is more or less the old T-Mobile business. The new strategic change is discussed further below.

Internationalisation Strategy in Fixed and Mobile Services

Efforts by the European Commission to open up the market for telecommunications services were not only aimed at reducing barriers to trade in services, but also to unlock the potential of European operators on a larger scale. Their potential growth had been hindered by geographic limitations and therefore resulted in a somewhat artificial 'national' industry structure. The new competitive environment changed this with new regulatory rules providing the framework for the international restructuring in the sector.

Deutsche Telekom management was convinced that market share losses in the German market could only be compensated by expansion into foreign growth markets. However, much management capacity was absorbed by the competitive battles in their home markets and the need to create new management system as they moved away from the status of a former state-owned enterprise. Creating a global management system therefore had to wait. Nevertheless a new board member 'International Affairs' started to look at opportunities for equity participation in privatised incumbents or mobile start-ups, particularly in Eastern Europe and Asia, the common sense high growth regions of the nineties. In the beginning such acquisitions were made by Deutsche Telekom Holding and did not distinguish between type of core business like fixed access, backbone, online, mobile, etc. In Eastern Europe, however, distorted tariff structures limited investments mainly on international gateway business (for example, in Ukraine and Kasakhstan, or mobile operations in Moscow, Ukraine, Hungary, Slovakia, and Poland etc.). In South-East Asia Deutsche Telekom was successful in Indonesia, Philippines, and Malaysia but had to learn that steering an Asian family company with a minority share and very few people is impossible, and very difficult even with majority shares.

Privatisation in the large European countries was mainly aimed at broadly distributed share holdings, so the chances to become a strategic share holder with the benefits of integrating the operation internationally were few. They actually happened only in the smaller countries emerging from transition, where the sellers wanted to bring in managerial expertise and industry experience, as well as easier access to financial and capital markets. DTAG was successful in Hungary and Croatia, but failed in Latvia. The attempt by DTAG to take over Telecom Italia as a white knight failed.[32] [33]

Before these options in the transition countries opened up, DTAG had made its first international expansion into the international market together with France Telecom by taking a minority stake in the US carrier Sprint and the creation of Global One. Clearly, size and economies of scale and scope were significant and Deutsche Telekom, like other national operators, was setting up or joining various alliances. In the case of Global One, the aim was to capture jointly the profitable international VAS market and to provide special services to large corporate customers. This strategy followed the creation of 'Concert', which included British Telecom and AT&T, World Partners, and Unisource,[34] all focusing on a small, but significant international market.

This type of strategy – joint ventures with other incumbents in the selected product markets still partly or totally under regulation – however, was soon overtaken by the new options of liberalised markets. In the year 2000, when Deutsche Telekom reorganised itself into the product-oriented strategic business units T-Mobile (mobile services), T-Online (ISP and content), T-Com (fixed network services) and T-Systems (complex IT and Telecom solutions for large business customers), each of the 'pillars' became responsible for some of the

---

[32] In April, 1999 Deutsche Telecom emerged as a possible 'white knight' for Telecom Italia against a hostile bid launched by Olivetti. Ultimately Olivetti was successful. Among the roadblocks to the DT offer was the post-privatisation ownership position of the German government. This raised hackles with the Italian government which held a 'golden share' in the post-privatisation Telecom Italia. See Curwen, 1999b.

[33] This adventure also put a stop to the close relation with France Telecom, which was initially characterised by spheres of influence agreements (Wind in Italy, Global One with US Sprint), until break down of relations over Telecom Italy takeover.

[34] Unisource, where the largest of the four constituent members was Telefonica of Spain, which in turn was linked to AT&T.

foreign investments along major product lines. Nevertheless, they also became free to follow their own individual internationalisation strategy.

T-Mobile was the most successful business unit in terms of further internationalisation. There was a clear strategy along the lines of: a) only majority shareholdings; b) single brand strategy for all subsidiaries; c) focus on Europe and North America with a tendency to integrate neighbouring networks; d) process- oriented integration of the international business. T-Mobile made further acquisitions in Europe, and a very large acquisition with Voicestream in the USA. Meanwhile most minority shares that could not be converted into majority holdings were sold (all Asian participations as well as UMC in Ukraine and MTS in Russia. T-Mobile US is likely to overtake Germany as the largest mobile market segment in the next three years. Among the roughly 87 million subscribers end of 2005 only one third are from T-Mobile Germany, two thirds are in the US, UK, Austria, CZ, NL, Hungary, Croatia, Macedonia, and Slowakia. T-Mobiles revenue share of Deutsche Telekom rose from 27 per cent in 2001 to more than 47 per cent in 2005.

T-Com now managed the earlier acquisitions in Hungary and Slovakia. Further internationalisation, for example, in Croatia were of minor revenue importance. Consequently T-Coms share of total Telekom revenues fell from 55 per cent in 2001 to only 34 per cent in 2005. The integration of T-Com with T-Online with its subsidiaries in Austria, Switzerland, France, Spain and Portugal may increase the revenue share and international focus slightly, but will have no significant quantitative effects. The possibility to take over fixed line business with high growth potential in emerging markets is also not in the current focus of T-Com, where management attention is mainly absorbed by technical transition to NGN, broadband service expansion and the erosion of national (PSTN) voice revenues and subscribers.

T-Systems have the largest number of international subsidiaries in more than 27 countries. Most of theses subsidiaries are re-structured former debis offices[35], 3 new ones in South America come from the integration of gedas, the former Volkswagen IT unit. These subsidiaries are employing local sales and delivery staff; in addition there are a large number of network-access points with some technical staff in other countries to serve the communication needs of the top 60 largest German multinational companies and their affiliates world-wide. However, the international revenues of these subsidiaries are only about 11 per cent of total TSI revenues, and T-Systems' share of total Deutsche Telekom revenues remained at a constant 15 per cent share from 2000 to 2005.

In 2005 the T-Systems management initiated a focused growth strategy, based on an-organic growth in 8 major European countries with the objective to become at least the fifth ranking player in relation to its largest competitors. Unprofitable

---

35 The 'debis Systemhaus' was a subsidiary of the Daimler Benz AG and with a turnover of about €3 bn the largest German IT service provider in 1999. In the year 2000 it was taken over by Deutsche Telekom and integrated into the newly created 'T-Systems'.

subsidiaries will be sold and a large number. of measures taken to realise global delivery around the clock for multinational customers.

Market Performance of Deutsche Telekom

In the last year before liberalisation (1997) the number of personnel of DTAG increased from 195,000 to 244,000 in 2004, although most of the additional people are employed in foreign subsidiaries. In Germany the number of personnel was reduced by 8.3 per cent in 1998 to 179,000; today the figure is approximately 170,000 and further reductions of about 30,000 employees have been announced. In addition, productivity per employee grew from €198,000 in 1998 to €234,000 in 2004 and is expected to accelerate further if staff reduction measures planned for 2005-2007 are implemented.

Revenues rose from €35 million in 1998 to €60 million in 2005, despite a dramatic price decrease in the German market and strong market share losses. For example, as seen earlier, prices for national long distance calls at daytime fell from 30.7 ct. in 1997 to 9.7 ct. in 1998 and have reached about 0.8 ct. in 2005. Deutsche Telekom did not follow this trend completely and is not among the cheapest German operators; however it was forced to stronger price reductions than comparable European incumbents so that when looking at the national residential price basket of 28 OECD countries in 2005, Deutsche Telekom (DT) is among the 5 cheapest operators, from a high price position in 1998. The same trend is true for typical international calls of residential customers as well as typical national and international traffic basket of business customers (see Figures 9.3 and 9.4).

According to the Regulator (BNetzA) market shares of competitive fixed network operators in Germany have reached 68 per cent in 2005 in international LD calls, 51 per cent in national LD calls and 37 per cent in local calls. In line with BT these are the heaviest market share losses in the retail business in the EU, significantly larger than in France or Italy. In Italy competitive operators have about 33 per cent market share in minutes of all three segments, in France competitors could only win more than 40 per cent share in national long distance minutes.

Despite these facts Deutsche Telekom could not only increase revenues but also Earnings before Interest and Taxes (EBIT). This can be explained by Germany's strong service competition market rather than infrastructure competition. The combination of call-by-call competition, relatively cheap interconnection and local loop unbundling prices as well as third party billing obligation of Deutsche Telekom, all whilst using the network facilities of Deutsche Telekom, made service competition for market entrants easy. In return large portions of the value added returned to Deutsche Telekom in the form of wholesale revenues and profit.

Relative performance of Deutsche Telekom compared to other European incumbent operators, however, shows different results. If one compares revenue

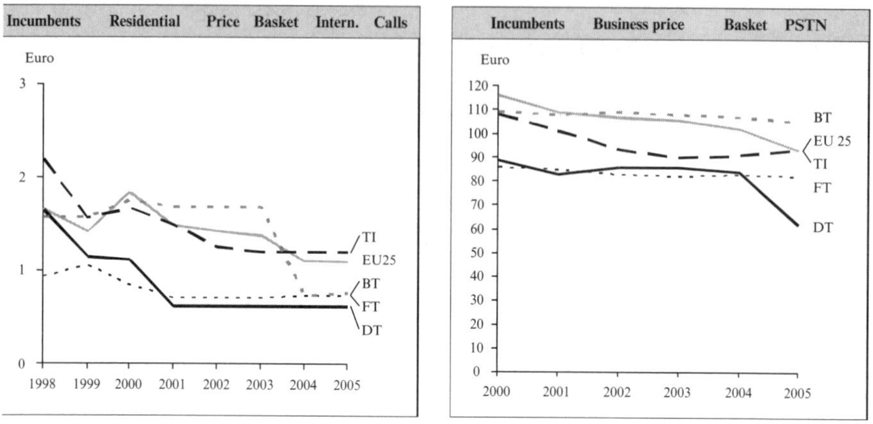

Figure 9.3 Price comparison between Deutsche Telekom and other operators

Source: *Teligen*, Telecoms Price Report 2005 for DG INFSO: 115 and 112

and EBIT growth over the last six years,[36] Deutsche Telekom managed to grow significantly in terms of revenue, only outperformed by France Télécom. BT and Telecom Italia´s revenue in contrast grew only marginally, mainly due to the lacking mobile business.

EBIT of DT also grew by 25 per cent over this period, also only outperformed by France Télécom. However, the operating margin (Revenue/EBIT) fell from 22 per cent in 1998 to only 13 per cent in 2005, the lowest of the four large European incumbent carriers.

In total privatisation and liberalisation had a positive impact on the productivity of Deutsche Telekom and the company is still operating a healthy business. This may support the thesis that major economic impacts of liberalisation measures in the ICT markets will result from productivity increase of the incumbents rather than the direct impact of new competitors.

Actual Strategic Objectives and Initiatives

According to Mr Ricke, the CEO of Deutsche Telekom, the ongoing 'Excellence Programme' has a clear strategic objective: In three years DT aims to become the strongest growing integrated Telco of the industry. To reach this goal a bundle of initiatives and projects has been initiated (three central growth programmes of the SBUs (re-invent, save for growth, focus on growth), five company-wide offensives (customer and brand, product and innovation, operations, profit, HR), and a change of company culture (T-Spirit)).

Among others the major levers for success are seen in

36 All figures from Reuters Knowledge, 2006.

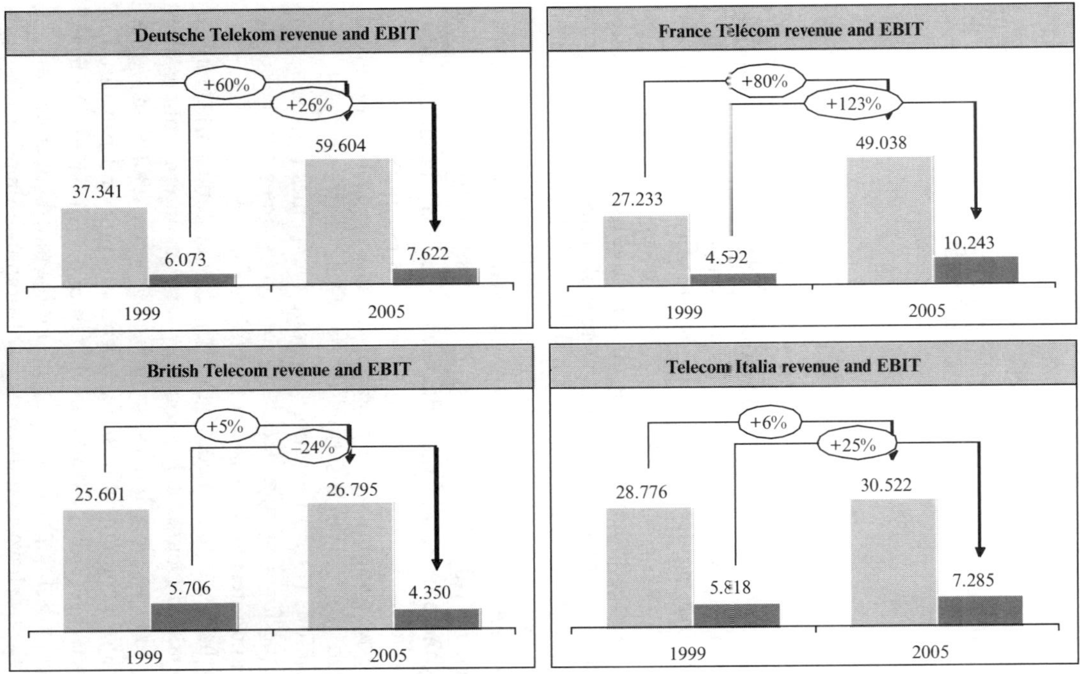

Figure 9.4 Revenue of Deutsche Telekom compared to other operators

- defending the core business fixed network and expand mobile;
- 'conquer the home' by broadband internet and triple play;
- expanding broadband seamless mobile services and create fixed-mobile services;
- strengthen the telecommunications business with business customers and grow with ICT solutions.

This means, in contrast to British Telecom, Deutsche Telekom is clearly focusing on the advantages of being an integrated fixed and mobile carrier for the foreseeable future.

Conclusion

In this chapter we have analysed the evolution of the German telecommunications industry structure and the emergence of Deutsche Telekom from a domestic monopoly provider to an internationally positioned company. We have seen that the institutional setting of the German deregulation and privatisation process and the subsequent regulatory structure have critically influenced this development, as have operational considerations of the incumbent and the *de novo* entrants. Aside from such external factors, company strategies of course mattered.

The current role of the state concerning infrastructure provision cannot be understood without looking at its past role during the time of state monopoly for telecom services and the strong political position of the labour unions and domestic equipment provider. The challenge in the mid 1980s by large users and external policy factors (such as the influence of the EU) and the imitation of liberalisation policies employed in other countries (such as the UK and the United States) was responsible for much of the change that we observed. This also influenced the 'corporatisation' of the German Ministry of Post and Telecommunications (DBP) into three separate companies (for post, giro and telephony) in the form of joint stock holding companies (AG) and the commercialisation and internationalisation that followed.

In particular, we have shown how competition in the domestic market has led to a more commercialised Deutsche Telekom with a strong internationalisation strategy in mobile and IT services, but less so in fixed services. Whilst it has often been stated that major economic effects from liberalisation and privatisation policy result from better services of new market entrants, we also find significant competitive achievements and productivity gains for the much larger incumbent DTAG. To achieve this we have seen the process of organisational learning and adoption of Deutsche Telekom to the new market structure, its organisational changes and strategies for growth and productivity increase.

The German economy, once burdened with expensive telecommunications services, has now access to one of the most advanced and cheapest ICT portfolios of all OECD countries. Unlike BT, Deutsche Telecom has opted for an integrated fixed, mobile and IT carrier now also targeting online media services. This has resulted in a healthy revenue growth. The major threat of the future will be to reverse the falling trend of operating margin, in particular by further cost reductions in the production platforms as well as in personnel.

Chapter 10

Fast Mover in a Reluctant Political Environment: The Case of Telenor

Stine Ludvigsen

As one of the last of the former telecommunication monopolists in Western Europe, the Norwegian incumbent Telenor was partially privatised in the Autumn of 2000. Thus, by contrast to most of its counterparts, Telenor continued to operate with full government ownership after the telecommunication sector had been opened for full competition in 1998. Although *privatisation* (that is, the transfer of ownership from public to private owners) has not been a dominant issue in the Norwegian telecommunication debate, the Norwegian state is yet to be characterised as an early mover with regard to important aspects of telecommunication *liberalisation* (that is, the opening up of competitive forces). Early liberalisation efforts included the establishment of an independent regulatory authority in 1987 – making Norway stand out as one of the first countries in the world to separate regulatory activities from the production part of telecommunication services. Moreover, when the Norwegian markets for telecommunication terminal equipment, in-house telephony, and cable networks for television were opened up for competition in the late 1980s, this implied that the Norwegian liberalisation process was ahead of EU developments. The pace of liberalisation slowed from the beginning of the 1990s, however, when the restructuring of the incumbent from an administrative enterprise into a joint-stock company owned by the state proved controversial (Skogerbø and Storsul 1999, 2003). In the 1990s, the Norwegian state thus went from being a policy-maker to become a policy-taker, committed to implement EU directives through its membership of the European Economic Area (EEA) Agreement (ibid.). Following the EU's schedule for the implementation of a single telecommunication market, full liberalisation was then achieved in 1998 with free competition for all services.

Within this political and regulatory context, Telenor has persistently pushed for increased latitude in order to position itself favourably in the new marketplace. Like several of the other Western European telecommunication incumbents, Telenor embarked on an expansive strategy to counter growing competition in their home market from the early 1990s. Being organised as a highly diversified and decentralised company and backed up by financial resources from the state, Telenor has engaged in a series of alliances, acquisitions and greenfield investments over the past decade. International expansion centred primarily on mobile and satellite communications, and the company was awarded mobile licences first in Central and Eastern Europe, then in South East Asia. By 2004, the company was ranked among the 12 largest mobile operators worldwide.[1] Moreover, and by contrast to most other incumbents, Telenor has been saved from dramatic divestitures as the state left the company with financial discretion, and sales options on mobile operations in Ireland and Germany brought in billions of extra cash in the early 2000s. As the time for privatisation drew closer, however, investors' preferences for 'pure plays' could no longer be ignored, making the company open the value chain and establish a clearer distinction between its core and non-core businesses (Ulset, 2002). Today, Telenor has opted for a strategy of control of or exit from its subsidiaries – seeking to cultivate the industrial profile of the company and thereby satisfy investors' demand for synergies and cost control.

In order to examine how the Norwegian incumbent manoeuvred throughout the transformation process from monopoly status to become a listed company, the first part of the chapter focuses on the political and regulatory environment of Telenor. Whereas some of these developments need to be seen as coercive forces from the incumbent's point of view, the progress of liberalisation, corporatisation and privatisation has also been highly influenced by the company itself. In the second part of the chapter, three phases are identified to describe how Telenor both adapted to and actively influenced external conditions: the period from 1988–1994, characterised by the company's effort to get prepared for competition and corporatisation; the period 1995–1999, in which Telenor expanded its businesses to international markets by use of alliances, acquisitions and greenfield investments; and the period 2000–2005, focusing on the effects of privatisation on the company's finances and strategy. The final part of the chapter provides a summary and conclusion of the key characteristics of the Norwegian case.[2]

---

1 Ranked by the GSM Association in terms of number of subscribers. Source: Telenor Information Department, 2004.

2 The empirical account in this chapter is based on several data sources, including interviews with former and current members of Telenor's top management team, official publications from the government and Parliament, and press releases and information available at the company's homepage (www.telenor.com). Moreover, previous research on the developments of Norwegian telecommunication policy and the role of the incumbent therein (mainly in Norwegian language) has provided a valuable source to inform several topics of this chapter, most notably the political and regulatory context of Telenor. Seeking to keep the text in a reader-friendly fashion, the main sources from which this chapter draws are referenced only once and include Sørlie (1997); Vatne (1998); Skogerbø (2001); Storsul (2002); Skogerbø and Storsul (1999, 2003); Elter (2004); and Thue (1995, 2005). Other, more issue-specific contributions are, however, referenced as the chapter proceeds.

The Norwegian State – an Early, but Reluctant Mover

The Norwegian Telecommunication Sector as a Policy Instrument

Ever since the establishment of the Norwegian Telegraph Administration in 1855 the political debate about telecommunications in Norway has been characterised by the dominant role of regional policy, welfare issues and employment.[3] During the post-war period, these concerns manifested themselves in several ways. First, Norway was among the leading states in the world in terms of telephone penetration, seeing it as a public responsibility to supply services to all parts of the country. Second, as the service was governed by the state administration, the Parliament could use its authority to control telephone tariffs in detail to ensure the provision of services in all parts of the country at equal prices.[4] Third, the role of the districts was formally strengthened in 1970 as Parliament decided on a three-tier structure for the telecommunication operator, consisting of a central administration, a district administration, and a local administration. Finally, the incumbent has been a vital source of employment across the country, and in several districts the single most important employer of female workers. The strong concern for regional unemployment became particularly apparent at the end of the 1970s, when a majority of the Parliament supported the Ministry's decision to postpone the automation of the telecommunication network in areas having major problems with unemployment. Moreover, the decision to purchase most of the incumbent's terminal equipment from domestic suppliers revealed politicians' concerns for unemployment rather than profitability.

Whereas the focus on regional, welfare, and employment issues provided political gains in these areas, the financial aspect of telecommunication services received less attention from politicians. Until the late 1970s, the incumbent was frequently in a struggle with Parliament to increase investments – most often without success. As a result, the degree of automation was among the weakest in Western Europe and long waiting lists for the installation of telephones remained throughout the 1970s and early 1980s. A major increase in telecommunication investments in the late 1970s helped to improve the situation as the automation of exchanges was speeded up and productivity enhanced. However, as political priority primarily centred on automation, and to a lesser extent on the waiting list problem, waiting lists were not abolished before the mid-1980s.

---

3 The Norwegian incumbent has had several names over the years. From 1969, the service shifted its name to Norwegian Telecommunications (Televerket) in connection with the advent of data transmission via the telecommunication network – a name that was not changed until 1 January 1995 when the firm became a joint-stock company.

4 Equal prices were ensured by means of state funding and cross-subsidisation within the enterprise through which profits from the cities were used to build networks and provide services in non-profitable areas. As to the role of the Parliament in deciding on telecommunication issues, this is due to the fact that Norway for much of the post-1945 years has been governed by minority governments.

Yet, the conflicts between the incumbent and politicians were not only a matter of financial priority and budgetary limits. On a more general level, disagreements reflected a continuous debate between the telecommunication operator and politicians of how to organise the provision of telecommunication services. As the incumbent was part of the state as a legal person and included in the government's budget, this meant that Parliament fixed the incumbent's net budget and total investment level. Moreover, income was partly bound through parliamentary decisions on prices, quality and coverage of the services to be provided. As these financial restrictions were perceived as severe limitations to the objective of being an efficient provider of telecommunication services the incumbent persistently argued for the necessity of being given greater autonomy and the freedom to run the enterprise according to normal business practices. However, as will be discussed in the next section, the decision to corporatise the public enterprise was probably the most controversial issue in the Norwegian telecommunication debate.

A Shifting Political Climate

Entering the 1980s, there was a widespread perception among politicians and the general public that Norwegian Telecommunications (NT) was trapped in a deep crisis, due to a mix of budgetary constraints, poor customer service, low productivity, and mismanagement. Apart from the decision to increase the investment level, the Labour government sought to handle these problems by establishing two committees in the early 1980s – one dealing with current challenges regarding the organisation of the Norwegian telecommunication market, the other with future challenges related to technological developments and the monopoly status of the incumbent.[5]

With regard to the role and structure of NT, the committee emphasised the inherent conflicts in the political demands put on NT to be both a political tool for solving unemployment, welfare, and regional issues and at the same time being run efficiently according to business principles. For NT to be able to provide efficient services it was suggested that competition should be introduced in certain business areas and that the administrative enterprise be restructured into a joint-stock company.[6] In the second report the boundaries between monopoly

---

[5] NOU 1982:2; NOU 1983: 32.

[6] The committee suggested that competition was introduced in an area in which NT lacked the capacity to meet the demand, that is, for the installation of telephony services. It should be noted, however, that the Norwegian telecommunication market was exposed to competition as early as in the 1960s. In fact, private operators originally dominated the areas of radio-based mobile telephony, data communications, and cable networks for television. Moreover, as competition was introduced for the telefax service in 1980, this indicated that the Parliament would be more open toward competition in areas that were brought about by technological innovations and did not interfere with the monopolist's traditional sphere of activities.

activities and competitive activities were discussed more thoroughly, and the committee unanimously suggested that NT should be allowed to compete in the sale of terminal equipment in the business market and that the competitive activities of NT be separated from the basic organisation. Moreover, a majority favoured extending competition to include all customer premise equipment, including installation. While the Parliament did not reach a decision regarding the proposals raised by the two reports, the board of NT decided to establish a project organisation – TBK (NT's Business Communications) – to handle the sale of terminal equipment in the business market. The future of this interim organisation was soon to be decided as the government in 1983 appointed a new committee to elucidate the future organisation of telecommunication activities in Norway, based on the insights and propositions of the previous reports.[7]

The 1984 committee suggested that NT be divided into three areas: administration, commercial activities, and a basic organisation. Following a 1985 white paper from the non-socialist government (the Willoch government), Parliament decided on the future organisation of NT in accordance with the recommendations from the committee.[8] The restructuring led to an administrative governmental body being established to be responsible for licences and type approval (which until then had been overseen by NT), that TBK was turned into a joint-stock company responsible for terminal equipment and network activities facing competition, and that NT became responsible for monopoly activities.[9] In this way, cross-subsidisation between the competitive activities and the monopoly activities should be avoided. The committee's proposal to establish the basic organisation as a joint-stock company was, however, not accepted. Thus, NT continued to be organised as an administrative enterprise.

Alongside these structural changes, the 1985 white paper called for the introduction of competition in certain service areas. Although initially being in opposition to these propositions, the Labour government (the Brundtland II government) followed up and implemented several liberalisation measures from 1986 to 1989. Specifically, competition was introduced for in-house telephony, terminal equipment, and for cable networks for television.[10] In a Western European context, Norway thus stood out as one of the early movers as the EU had not yet formalised a common framework for telecommunication policy.[11] In the following years, the liberalisation process continued: in 1989 competition was introduced for value-added services; in 1990, the government decided to issue

---

7 NOU 1984:29.

8 St.meld. nr. 48 (1984–85).

9 St.prp. nr. 98 (1985–86); St.prp. nr. 92 (1986–87).

10 Ot.prp. nr. 56 (1985–86); St.meld. nr. 32 (1986–87).

11 In should be noted, however, that neither of these areas had ever been under NT's monopoly. By contrast, they were originally dominated by private operators and represented new market opportunities that NT only more recently had started to take part in.

two licences for the GSM network for mobile telephony – one for NT and one for privately owned NetCom; and leased lines were liberalised for other purposes than telephony in 1992 and for satellite infrastructure and services in 1994.[12]

Whereas the 1980s marked a period of organisational transition, early liberalisation initiatives, and improvements in the incumbent's investment level, one major area of dispute between NT and the government as well as between the political parties in Parliament still remained – namely, the legal status of the enterprise. In the early 1990s, NT was among the few incumbents that were still organised as an administrative enterprise, closely tied to the government by legal and financial means. Although the board had proposed that NT should be restructured into a joint-stock company effective from 1992, the proposal did not gain acceptance either from the Parliament or from the government at that time. However, the Parliament accepted a partial corporatisation of the administrative enterprise as this was seen as necessary to ensure transparency and to increase the competitiveness and flexibility of the former monopolist. As a result, the competitive activities of the incumbent were reorganised in one separate company (including TBK and other business areas which operated in competitive markets), whereas monopoly activities were still kept in the base organisation.[13]

Perceiving this reorganisation to be the first step toward a structural devolution of the administrative enterprise as a whole, proponents used the same arguments to defend a transformation of the administrative enterprise into a joint-stock company a few years later: as the process of corporatisation was already started, a structural devolution of the incumbent would ensure the freedom and flexibility necessary to counter growing competition in the domestic market and to make politicians refrain from political interference. More importantly, this solution was also gradually accepted by opponents of the corporatisation process as restructuring was seen to be necessary to ensure a viable national telecommunication operator and continued political control of telecommunications in a liberalised market. However, in order to convince sceptical politicians, the Labour government (the Brundtland III government) needed to make some modifications to the organisational form of the joint-stock company. These modifications included the rights and protection of employees, the legal establishment of the state's share of ownership, and a statutory duty stating that all issues deemed to be of principal, political or social importance should be presented to the Minister who was to perform the owner function vis-à-vis the company. Moreover, every other year the company was instructed to submit a report to the Parliament dealing with strategic and financial long-term issues

12 St.meld. nr. 38 (1988–89); St.meld. nr. 49 (1989–90); St.meld. nr. 8 (1991–92).

13 As regards TBK, an important non-event was the Labour government's (the Brundtland III government) withdrawal in 1990 of the recently departed Conservative government's (the Syse government) proposal to partially privatise TBK. If accomplished, this proposal would have implied that NT was to be confronted with a privately owned Norwegian competitor.

for the company as a whole and for its subsidiaries. Over the years, however, the Parliament has only modestly exercised its potential for steering and controlling the company.

The telecommunication monopolist was restructured into a joint-stock company fully owned by the state at the end of 1994, and from January 1, 1995 the company changed its name from Norwegian Telecommunications to Telenor.[14] As the restructuring process was controversial, this meant that other telecommunication policy issues received less attention in this period. Consequently, Norway went from being an early mover in the liberalisation process in the late 1980s to being more receptive to EU influence as the Norwegian process was slowed in the mid-1990s. Another reason for EU developments having a more direct impact on the Norwegian liberalisation process was due to the Labour government's instructions to let all new directives be made in accordance with EU law as a means of preparing the application for Norwegian EU-membership in 1994. Although Norway did not became a member of the EU at this time, the harmonisation continued during the 1990s as Norway committed itself to implement major parts of the EU legal framework through the EEA Agreement. Following EU's timetable for liberalisation, a majority in the Parliament then decided to liberalise the remaining monopoly rights on networks and voice telephony from 1 January 1998.[15]

Though neither the restructuring of the incumbent nor the liberalisation of the Norwegian telecommunication market implied privatisation, a partial privatisation of the company was gradually launched as necessary to provide Telenor with financial stability and resources – thereby make the company fit for further positioning in the international market. As for the restructuring issue, there were strong disagreements about privatisation within the government, in Parliament, and also within several political parties. Yet again, a political compromise was struck, this time between the minority coalition government (the Bondevik I government) and the Conservative Party over the State Budget in the Autumn of 1999.[16] As a result, Telenor was floated on the stock exchanges of Oslo and New York (Nasdaq) in 2000 and a minority of shares in the company were sold to private owners. Compared to the early liberalisation initiatives of the Norwegian state a decade earlier, Norway was a late mover with regard to privatisation – an outcome most notably explained by the lack of need to increase the state's finances, the strong traditions of state industrial ownership, and the high level of conflict concerning privatisation in Norway. Despite this scepticism against privatisation of state-owned companies, the Parliament later endorsed the further selling of shares in a handful of companies, including Telenor. Additionally, the Parliament directed the government to focus its efforts on how to improve the

---

14 St.prp. nr. 43 (1993–94); Ot.prp. nr. 61 (1993–94).

15 St.prp. nr. 70 (1995–96).

16 St.prp. nr. 66 (1999–2000).

management of state-owned companies and how to stimulate profitable and sustainable industrial growth and development in Norway.[17]

In the early 2000s, the Norwegian telecommunication sector had thus been reversed compared to the situation 20 years earlier: the Norwegian telecommunication monopoly had become liberalised; the incumbent had gained increased freedom and flexibility through structural devolution and, later, a partial privatisation of the company; the long waiting lists of the early 1980s were replaced by a domestic market which was now among the top performers internationally; and Telenor had left its status as a domestic monopolist to become an international telecommunication operator with a presence in more than ten countries world-wide. How can these developments be explained?

First, as the state-owned telecommunication monopoly in the 1980s was a relatively new construction, this may have made the system less embedded in established ideas of how the sector should be organised and, consequently, more receptive for structural changes.[18] Second, the 1980s marked a period when neo-liberalist ideas started to dominate the Western world. In Norway, these ideas were pushed forward by the non-socialist government (the Willoch government), but very soon they also gained a strong foothold among central members in the Labour Party, which held the government position for long periods of the 1980s and 1990s.[19] Third, the political debate about liberalisation was characterised by a gradual shift throughout the 1990s in which several parties changed their argument from defending monopoly to promoting liberalisation. Traditionally, the basic argument against liberalisation was the concern for distributive justice and that a monopoly, especially on networks and voice telephony, was necessary in order to realise a national network with equal prices for all. A majority in Parliament had concurred with this statement until 1996, when a majority of the political parties agreed that universal service obligations could be taken care of by regulatory control. Fourth, through the EEA Agreement Norway was obliged to implement EU regulations on telecommunication policy. However, as early liberalisation efforts were triggered at the national level ahead of EU developments, the EU influence has been more important for the timing of liberalisation than for the direction this development has taken. Finally, the incumbent itself has been a vital force in the processes of liberalisation, corporatisation and privatisation. In particular, the managers of Telenor have been pushing for increased latitude in order to prepare for increasing competition

---

17 NOU 2004: 7.

18 The state had implemented its legal monopoly by buying up private exchanges, a process that was started already in 1898, but not finished before 1974. Additionally, private telecommunication operators were already in existence in certain areas.

19 However, their ideological concerns for pursuing such ideas differed markedly. Whereas the non-socialist parties emphasised the benefits of increasing competition, the Labour party stressed how market-reforms might be beneficial to deal with industrial challenges.

and take part in the internationalisation process. Greater autonomy from the political level was, however, counterbalanced by a more vital regulatory regime. The organisation and functioning of this new regulatory body is the topic of the next section.

Developments in the Regulatory Regime[20]

In order to advance liberalisation of telecommunications and ensure non-biased sector management, the regulatory functions were separated from the incumbent and placed in an independent administrative body called the Norwegian Telecommunication Authority (PT).[21] Being established as early as 1987 this regulatory reform stands in contrast to that of other countries in Western Europe, except for Britain, as reform there took place earlier and was unrelated to EU developments (Thatcher, 1999b). However, although PT was established as an independent body endowed with its own resources and with considerable discretion in the interpretation of national legislation, there were still close links between the regulator and the Ministry of Transport and Communications, from which responsibility was delegated.

First, the government appoints the director general of PT. The director is not a political appointee, however, and is not required to resign upon a change of government. Second, PT reports directly to the Ministry, which also sets the instructions for the regulator. Moreover, on its own initiative or upon request, the PT advises the Ministry on matters relating to postal and telecommunication services. Third, for matters that are of a political and principal telecommunication nature, appeals against PT's decisions are submitted to the Ministry. Because of the difficulties in deciding whether a particular decision is of a 'political and principal nature', the Ministry has in fact been the overall decision-making authority with power to overturn a decision taken by the regulatory body. Fourth, because the Ministry of Transport and Communications also managed the state's ownership interests in Telenor, the neutrality of government in its regulatory role has been questioned. The role conflict inherent to the Ministry's position as regulator and owner tried to be reduced by transferring the ownership of Telenor to the Ministry of Trade and Industry (effective September 2000), allegedly in response to pressure from the EFTA Surveillance Authority (OECD, 2003). Whereas the state is still the majority owner of Telenor, this means that it can no longer use its

[20] In addition to the sources already mentioned, this section draws on annual reports and publications from the Norwegian Post and Telecommunications Authority.

[21] The regulatory body changed its name to the Norwegian Post and Telecommunication Authority as postal market responsibility was added from 1 June 1997. Originally, the administrative body was responsible for licences and type approvals, which until then had been the overseen by the incumbent. Today, PT is responsible for a larger set of activities related to the objective of securing competition in the telecommunication market (see http://www.npt.no).

ownership role to influence telecommunication regulation.[22] Finally, the political influences on telecommunication policy were recently strengthened in the sense that challenges to case-specific decisions that were previously resolved by the PT Complaints and Advisory Board, have became the domain of the Ministry of Transport and Communications.

The telecommunication sector in Norway is regulated through both sector-specific and general laws and regulations – the latter including Norwegian and EU competition laws. In 1995 a new Telecommunications Act substituted the old Telegraph Act of 1899.[23] The objectives of the new Act were to implement the telecommunication directives enforced through the EEA Agreement and to prepare for a stronger competition in the Norwegian market. Whereas the Act did not liberalise new services, it established a new regulatory regime that enabled further liberalisation. The *ex ante* regulation of telecommunication operators with significant market power (SMP) is at the core of these sector-specific regulations – defined as an operator that attains more than 25 per cent of the market share for a given product. For example, Telenor is the only company that is deemed to have SMP in the fixed telephony market.

As the EU agreed upon a new regulatory framework in 2002, the Telecommunications Act of 1995 was replaced by the Norwegian Electronic Communications Act (ECA) of July 2003.[24] The ECA marked a shift toward sector-specific regulation of electronic communications networks and services based on competition law methodology. In accordance with the European Commission's Guidelines, the term 'significant market power' will therefore be close to the competition law term 'dominance'. Accordingly, only operators who posses and are expected to retain a dominant position (which usually requires a market share in excess of 40 per cent) on a relevant market, both as defined in competition law and jurisprudence, can be subject to regulation. Under the transition rules of the ECA, however, PT considers Telenor still to have SMP in nearly all markets (including voice telephony, transmission capacity and interconnection services). As a result, Telenor is subjected to specific obligations with respect to these services regarding universal services, non-discrimination and transparency, interconnection and access, pricing, accounting and reporting. In particular, Telenor is designated as an operator with universal service obligations through purchasing agreements between the government and the incumbent. This means that the company is required to offer a particular set of services to wholesales customers and end users at cost-oriented prices on non-discriminatory terms. Moreover, Telenor has to abide by certain principles of accounting in order to keep these services separate from the company's account for other business activities.

---

22 Regardless of organisation, however, the state's role as regulator and owner will come together either in the government or the Parliament (OECD 2003).

23 Ot.prp. nr. 36 (1994–95).

24 Ot.prp. nr. 58 (2002–2003).

Despite the aim of the asymmetric regulatory framework to make it possible for entrants to enter the Norwegian market profitably, it has provided the grounds for several legal proceedings brought against the incumbent by its competitors and customers. Most of these cases involve failure or delay in providing access to the incumbent's network on terms required by law, including failure to deliver cost-oriented prices and late implementation of carrier pre-selection. As the Ministry of Transport and Communications has until recently held the dual role of regulator and owner, entrants in the Norwegian telecommunication market have frequently accused the Ministry of favouring the incumbent. In fact, anecdotal evidence suggests that the ESA (European Surveillance Authority) and the European Commission seem to have been more willing to intervene against the Norwegian incumbent than Norwegian regulatory authorities.[25] More recently, the Nordic Competition Authorities (2004) have rejected the claims of favoritism by arguing that in Norway a high gross margin on local calls and the public switched telephone network offered on the basis of access to the local loop are among the highest in the Nordic region, which allows others to enter the Norwegian market profitably and to be able to undercut the incumbent's prices.

The Norwegian Incumbent – Fast Mover with Healthy Finances

The term 'fast mover with healthy finances' is used to illustrate how the incumbent manoeuvred throughout the transformation process from monopoly status to become a listed company in the period 1988–2005. Since this description represents a remarkable break with the incumbent's situation only one decade earlier, a useful first step is to look at the major challenges facing NT in the 1970s and early 1980s.

In the 1970s, NT was confronted with two interrelated problems. One was the number of customers applying for the installation of telephones, which continued to rise during the 1970s. The long waiting lists were caused partly by the lack of a competent workforce to install telephones and partly by delays in the delivery of automation equipments.[26] Even more important, however, were the financial problems experienced by NT. Although the state's budget proposals for the first part of the 1970s presumed major parts of telecommunication investments to be

---

25 For example, in 1995 an agreement was signed by the Ministry that gave Telenor the sole right to exploit excessive capacity in the Norwegian Rail's fibre network. Claiming that it favoured the incumbent at the expense of its competitors, ESA stopped this agreement.

26 Given the strong political concern for unemployment, the lack of a competent workforce to install the telephones might seem like a paradox. However, as the automation of the telecommunication network had already brought upon NT a major redundancy problem, the management refrained from hiring new groups of workers who would be likely to suffer from unemployment when the automation process was finished.

financed by the incumbent's own means, this required large rises in the tariffs for telephone calls. As a result, the Norwegian tariff level was among the highest in Western Europe. Seeking to avoid further increases in telephone call tariffs, in 1975 Parliament decided to reverse the decision of self-financing, presuming instead all investments to be financed by granting state-financed loans to the incumbent. Even though the investment level rose significantly in the period 1977–1980, the financial problems of NT were not solved as the amount granted was not sufficient to dispose of the long waiting lists.

At the start of the 1980s, the major claim of the enterprise was increased freedom to dispose its own finances. Soon, however, the board started to demand more radical changes and a structural devolution of the enterprise was put on the top of the board's agenda. While this new offensive might be explained by the incumbent's need to solve the waiting list problem and adapt to technological developments, the shift in management and board positions provided another impetus for change. In particular, the new managing director and two externally recruited board members were influential in the market orientation of the incumbent.[27] The major challenge identified by the board chairman was the severe productivity problem of the enterprise. The remedy to this problem was to improve the financial management system and bring the financial reporting in line with normal business principles. As a result, NT was able to repay its loan to the state and increase its level of self-financing, so that from 1987 NT covered its investments from own funds. Moreover, under the leadership of Kjell Holler the traditional bureaucratic culture of NT was put under pressure as one of his top priorities was to develop a more flexible and business oriented organisation capable of improving NT's relationship to its customers. Thus, by the late 1980s, the incumbent was to a large extent modernised and adapted to the upcoming market situation. Additionally, as NT in the 1970s had developed a high level expertise in the fields of satellite and mobile communications, the incumbent was well prepared to engage in these areas as soon they were opened up for competition.[28]

---

[27] By contrast to the previous managing directors who were promoted from within the enterprise, the new managing director, Kjell Holler, was externally recruited. Holler had broad political and business experience, as he previously had held the position as Minister of Industry, chairman of NT's board, and CEO in an insurance company. The two externally recruited board members were Egil Abrahamsen (board chairman) and Egil Bakke, both proponents of a more liberalised telecommunication market and stronger business orientation of NT.

[28] NT had opened satellite connections from the mainland to oil installations in the North Sea already in 1976. Moreover, in 1980 the Nordic automatic mobile telephony system NMT-450 was launched, covering the whole of Norway five years later.

Phase I: 1988–1994: Preparing for Corporatisation and Competition

From monopoly to competition – internal transformation of NT: 1 January 1988 marked the end of the Norwegian telecommunication market in its original format. NT was now allowed to compete in the market for terminal equipment through its wholly-owned subsidiary TBK. TBK failed, however, to succeed in the market and bankruptcy could only be avoided after major rationalisation of the company. The failure of TBK became an important experience for NT, so that the incumbent was much better prepared when new business areas were liberalised a few years later.

From the late 1980s, the management and the board perceived it as unlikely that the incumbent would be able to preserve its monopoly rights in new service areas, such as value-added services. Instead, NT opted for the opposite – increased liberalisation and greater organisational autonomy for the incumbent. The reasoning was simple: being allowed to enter the competitive arena as early as possible, the incumbent would gain the opportunity to position itself favourably in emerging markets and to develop the business competence necessary to maintain a dominant share of the existing telecommunication market. This argument was further strengthened as early liberalisation efforts in UK and US had showed that the incumbents maintained large market shares even after several years of competition.

Following this strategy, the new management team embarked on a major internal transformation process in the early 1990s. Two aspects of this transformation process were particularly instrumental in order to bring about increased market orientation of the old monopolist. First, the management attempted to construct an internal crisis by reducing the prices of telecommunication services. As the price reductions resulted in lower profitability for the enterprise, the management could more easily gain acceptance for the decisions to downsize and restructure the incumbent. Second, the restructuring meant that the whole organisation was stripped and then rebuilt according to the needs of a modern business company. In this process, more than 4,000 people were made redundant. In sum, therefore, it was the *threat* of future liberalisation and increased competition, rather than actual changes in the incumbent's market conditions, that initially triggered internal transformation.

The speed of transformation is most notably explained by the fact that key persons in the board and top management team were strongly enthusiastic about liberalisation and commercial freedom from the state. Notably, several of the new managers were recruited from the Electric Bureau (EB), a privately owned supplier of telephone equipment. The externally recruited managers, who were mostly economists or 'business engineers', brought with them a market-oriented culture that was perceived as superior to the old-fashioned 'network culture' of the old monopolist. In 1991, the appointment of Tormod Hermansen as new CEO reinforced this trend. A few years earlier, Hermansen had been the leader of an expert committee proposing modernisation and liberalisation of the state administration.[29] Moreover, as a member of the Labour Party and former Secretary General in the Ministry of Finance, Hermansen had strong personal relations with the Labour government, the trade unions and the state administration. Although in the committee's proposal Hermansen had suggested NT was to be kept as an administrative enterprise, entering the CEO position made him change his opinion on this issue. In fact, Hermansen soon became a strong proponent for a structural devolution of the incumbent and has been described as the single most important person behind the restructuring of NT from an administrative enterprise to a joint-stock company.

Employment policy: As one the largest employers in Norway, NT carried a high degree of social responsibility beyond the provision of telecommunication services. Economic and technical issues thus had to be continuously balanced against the issues of regional policy and employment. As previously noted, the automation of the telecommunication network represented an important political challenge, as this process negatively affected the female workforce living in the districts. A majority in the Parliament therefore supported the Ministry's decision to postpone the automation process by two years in areas that were particularly vulnerable to problems of unemployment. After the process of automation was finished in 1985, however, new challenges arose as the digitalisation of the telecommunication network necessitated further staff reductions. Once again, the prospect of downsizing was strongly opposed in the regional parts of the incumbent's organisation, with the result that the redundancy problem was not dealt with until several years later.

The major impetus for further downsizing of personnel came with the partial corporatisation of the administrative enterprise in 1992, when NT went from being a geographically oriented organisation structured around telecommunication districts to a functionally-oriented organisation structured around business activities. The process of building up the new organisation required the old organisation to be stripped and then re-staffed with people according to the needs of a business company. Consequently, a major redundancy requirement was identified. To solve this problem, NT decided in 1993 to establish a Resource Pool – inspired by a similar project in the Norwegian oil company Norsk Hydro. With a state funding of two billions NOK, an organisational unit was designed to absorb redundant staff by obtaining income-generating activity within or outside NT. Being transferred from the basic organisation to the Resource Pool, surplus staff members were given the opportunity to raise their level of competence, participate in job-seeking activities, and initiate business developments. On the other hand, the Resource Pool was also a source of dissatisfaction in terms of representing a concentration of employees who either did not perform well in the old organisation or lacked the skills necessary to keep their jobs in the new one. The Resource Pool was dismantled in its original form in February 1997.

29 NOU 1989: 5.

During the four years it had been in existence, the project had benefited from an absorbing labour market and cooperation with outside companies that helped to provide jobs that could be offered to the Resource Pool's employees. As a result, roughly 4,700 employees found new assignments within or outside Telenor.

Whereas the establishment of the Resource Pool was considered to be an effective tool for handling redundant staff, it was also a legitimating device to gain public and political acceptance for the downsizing. The legitimacy aspect of the Resource Pool became evident as it was initiated by the management – not by the employees who would be severely affected by downsizing efforts. The importance of creating a legitimate process for the downsizing was also the responsibility of the Ministry, which responded by establishing a localisation committee with the objective of reducing the political controversies following from downsizing. Lacking an actual mandate for its work, however, the committee was restricted to act merely as an advisor on regional and employment issues.

The restructuring of the incumbent from an administrative enterprise to a joint-stock company was another issue on which employees and the management disagreed. In this process, the labour movement experienced a line of conflict between the elite, who gradually accepted a structural devolution of the enterprise, and the members of the Telecommunication and IT Workers Union, who resisted this change. The most influential trade unions, however, sought cooperation rather than confrontation. Assuming that liberalisation of the telecommunication market was inevitable, their members realised it would be a better option for NT to act rapidly in the market so that revenues would increase, unemployment could be reduced, and more jobs could be created.

The remaining conflict revolved around the legal status of employees under the new organisational form. As an administrative enterprise NT was governed by the state administration, and the employees has had the status of civil servants. Since there are different laws in Norway regulating the conditions of employment for civil servants and employees in private or public firms, the legal status of employees became a major issue for the labour movement in accepting a restructuring of the enterprise. The labour movement in particular, as well as the Labour Party, considered state-owned companies being free to join the Confederation of Norwegian Business and Industry (NHO) to be a problem. As a solution, the government decided in 1993 to establish the Norwegian Employers' Association for Businesses Linked to the Public Sector (NAVO) – designed exclusively for the increasing number of administrative enterprises which were now about to be restructured into legal subjects in their own right.

Early internationalisation initiatives: When the EU regulatory framework in the late 1980s gradually opened up for competition across national boundaries, NT had already gained experience with international activities. In particular, the incumbent had been a member of the International Maritime Satellite Organisation (Inmarsat) for nearly 15 years. In the Inmarsat system, NT administered the Norwegian participation in the project on behalf of the government. However, as this system was more directed toward political issues rather than business concerns, NT faced a remarkable new situation as the telecommunication market became liberalised.

To counter the growing competition in the domestic market NT outlined a two-fold strategy: It planned to secure and increase its income by international expansion, and it endeavoured to keep as many of its Norwegian-based business customers as possible. The pursuit of international expansion was reasonable in the sense that the Norwegian market was highly developed (expected to reach a degree of digitalisation of 100 per cent during 1997) and to make proper use of excessive employment capacity. Thus, NT was forced to look beyond national boundaries in order to expand. Rather than being grounded in a need for a larger customer base for which the costs of product development could be shared, however, the internationalisation strategy was seen as a window of opportunity for the mobile part of the company. In particular, the prospect of a highly competitive telecommunication market pushed incumbents into a race to secure access to new markets (Grøgaard, 2005). Moreover, a strategy of internationalisation was perceived as necessary when anticipating a listing of the company and changes in ownership structure. The idea behind this strategy was simple: If the company were not capable of growing, it would be outperformed by its competitors or become a target for acquisition. Furthermore, the management realised it would be easier (but also more attractive) to counter growing competition by pursuing growth rather than following a strategy of cost-reduction, which was the alternative approach to maintain profit margins.

The very first initiative of internationalisation of NT took place in 1993, when a possibility arose to enter the Russian market. Following the initiative of key persons in NT and based on the argument that it would be possible to make use of excessive employment capacity in the incumbent's organisation in Northern Norway, NT joined an alliance with the Finnish incumbent Sonera and Swedish incumbent Telia to run a fixed network in the Murmansk region. In the following years, however, it was mainly in the field of mobile telephony that NT sought to expand its international activities. In general, the entry opportunity in most mobile markets was to win first-order licences. Greenfield investments were not just a question of money, however, as it was necessary to compose a consortium that benefited several stakeholders. In order to win such 'beauty contests', NT sought to form alliances with both local partners and other incumbents. From NT's point of view, the building of alliances also helped to eliminate some of the competition in the market. In cooperation with Telia and Sonera, NT made its first international mobile investment in 1993 through the establishment of Northwest GSM in St. Petersburg. In the same year, NT formed an alliance with the three Nordic incumbents and the Dutch incumbent PTT Telekom, which won the licence to deliver mobile telephony in Hungary through Pannon GSM.

The second part of NT's strategy to counter growing competition was to keep hold of its domestic business customer base. Thus, NT looked for ways to deliver telecommunication services in countries where these companies had invested.

The solution to this problem was offered in 1994, when NT joined a strategic alliance with the British incumbent BT, which meant that global services could be offered to Norwegian customers by drawing from BT's Concert portfolio of business customer solutions. The BT alliance was deemed to be of great strategic importance, since BT was expected to be the winner of the European telecommunication market.

Phase II: 1995–1999: Corporatisation, Expansion and Internationalisation

Corporatisation, decentralisation, and merger breakdown: On 1 January 1995, Norwegian Telecommunications changed its name to Telenor and became a joint-stock company wholly owned by the state. Telenor was thus given the opportunity to operate under the same overall conditions as competing telecommunication operators. Following this legal change the company emerged with a market-oriented organisation that included seven business areas ranging from telephony and leased lines, through IT applications and operations, to the Internet, multimedia and selected content services. This organisational structure was soon to be changed, however, as Telenor engaged in a continuous series of modest reorganisations over the following years, adapting to changing technologies, regulations and market conditions (Ulset, 2002).

One key characteristic of the corporatisation process was the high degree of authority delegated from the top management team to the different business units. As the managers were granted extensive decision-making authority, this made it possible for the business units to operate as almost autonomous actors.[30] The effects of this management philosophy were two-fold: on the one hand, autonomous units were clearly sources of innovation, which in turn were considered necessary to deal with increased competition. Moreover, a high degree of decentralisation made it possible for the company to pursue several business opportunities at the same time. One notable result of this strategy was the development of 'Internet in all channels', including mobile communication, value-added services and media. On the other hand, the high degree of decentralisation became a source of internal conflicts as the business units were competing for resources and attention from the top management.

One particular source of internal conflicts was found between the 'network' and 'market' branches of the company. The discussion centred primarily on whether network or services would bring added value to the company in the future. In the mid-1990s, this conflict became particularly evident as the CEO decided to separate mobile network activity from value-added services (data services, reporting and content services). Despite strong opposition to this decision from

[30] To some extent, the high degree of decentralisation was counterbalanced by the fact that the top management team was also expanded. However, as the new members of the top management team were largely the same people who were in charge of the business units, they were in practice free to pursue their own strategies.

the mobile group, the separation was announced publicly in the 1996 annual report. However, as the process created such a heated internal dispute and led the director of the mobile operations stepping down from his position, the proposal was withdrawn in 1997. This policy reversal might be explained by the strong position of the business units, but more importantly, perhaps, was the effect of the strong financial position of mobile communications in the Telenor system.

Expansion and internationalisation: As previously noted, Telenor opted for an expansive strategy to counter growing competition in its home market.[31] Choosing mobile communications to be its primary focus, Telenor concentrated on markets where strong growth was expected, such as in Central and Eastern Europe and in South East Asia. In general, however, there was limited strategic thinking regarding geographic spread and how to enter a market (Grøgaard, 2005). Rather, the internationalisation process was strongly opportunity-driven and the company's risk exposure was significant. As one manager described it, 'It was like the Vikings, we sailed out and planted our flags wherever we managed to get our hands on anything'. The investment profile of Telenor contrasts significantly with that of its international counterparts, most notably BT, as the speed of decision-making and the risk exposure was much higher in Telenor. The overarching internationalisation strategy was one of 'land grabbing' – to buy as much as possible and sort out the investments out afterwards.

Two factors stand out as particularly important with which to explain such an investment profile. First, as described above, Telenor functioned as an extremely decentralised organisation in which the business units were granted considerable freedom to pursue their own internationalisation strategies. As a consequence, the corporate strategy of Telenor equalled the sum of the strategies of the business units. Moreover, since each unit sought to generate profit for itself, the total risk exposure exceeded the preferred risk level for the company as a whole. A second explanation relates to the role of state ownership. The general argument is that a passive and amenable state ownership would allow incumbents to over-invest and over-diversify into new exciting growth businesses. In particular, grants from Parliament gave Telenor increased flexibility to pursue further investments abroad.

After the strategic alliances with the Swedish incumbent Telia in the early 1990s, Telenor and Telia chose to enter into competing alliances from 1995. Whereas Telia joined the Dutch, Swiss and Spanish incumbents to establish the Unisource alliance, Telenor entered into an alliance with BT and TeleDanmark called Telenordia with the aim of being the second largest operator in Sweden after Telia. Like the previous internationalisation investments, this joint-venture would hardly have been feasible for Telenor alone due to capital requirements. The alliance supported the overall strategy of Telenor from the second half of

---

[31] It should be noted, however, that although the domestic market was gradually opened for competition, Telenor continued to dominate the Norwegian market.

the 1990s, which was to perceive the Nordic region as its home market, to have a presence in Europe, and to exploit opportunities in the rest of the world.

In the following years, Telenor continued to expand its mobile operations in foreign markets, among them Russia (Kaliningrad and Stavropol), in which Telenor already held ownership positions. In 1995 Telenor won the contract to build the second GSM network in Ireland through the ESAT Digifone consortium, and in 1996 Telenor acquired the licenses to build GSM networks in Montenegro and Bangladesh. In 1997 Telenor entered into an alliance with BT and German VIAG to get a license for building and operating both a digital mobile network and a fixed network in Germany. In the same year, Telenor entered into a consortium to build mobile networks in Ukraine and was also awarded licences to build GSM networks in Austria and Greece. In 1998 Telenor acquired 25 per cent of the Russian mobile telephone company VimpelCom, and in 1999 Telenor entered the Malaysian mobile market through the acquisition of a 30 per cent share of Digi.Com. In sum, the international expansion of Telenor resulted in a total of 13 foreign mobile subsidiaries over the period 1993–1999 – mostly minority shareholdings in European countries.

Whereas major parts of Telenor's international activities were made in the field of mobile communications, the company also expanded its activities on an international basis in other business areas. For more than 20 years Telenor had supplied maritime satellite communication as a key operator of the Inmarsat system. As Telenor entered the broadcasting field in 1992, purchasing the communications satellite Thor I at the orbital position one-degree west, it also became the leading actor for distribution of TV channels to the Nordic market. This position was further strengthened in the late 1990s when two more communications satellites, Thor II and Thor III, were launched and put into operation at the same position, that is, covering all Europe. By these investments, Telenor reaffirmed its position as one of the three largest suppliers of satellite-based services within broadcasting, mobile and business communications. Moreover, in 1998 international expansion took another step forward with the establishment of Internet activities abroad. By 2000, therefore, Telenor was involved in major international operations, the dominant areas being mobile, satellite communications and the Internet.

Merger breakdown and privatisation initiative: A major event at the end of this period was the announcement, and the later breakdown, of the merger between Telenor and the Swedish incumbent Telia. Following a heated dispute about the location of the merged company's prestigious mobile unit, and the subsequent Swedish request that Tormod Hermansen (the new CEO of the merged company) be replaced, the break-down of the merger became a reality just one year after its announcement (Drexhage, 2000; Meyer, 2001; Thue, 2005). The process became increasingly difficult as concerns about national control were confused with business interests, but also because there were considerable differences between the two companies as regards their internationalisation strategy, organisational structure and 'management style' (Meyer, 2001; Thue, 2005).

Overall, it seems as if both parties had underestimated the national and cultural differences, in particular the strong national sentiments on the Norwegian side and the history of Sweden-Norway 'rivalry' (Fang et al., 2004). Whereas Norwegian politicians and company managers emphasised the principle of equality between the two firms, the Swedish representatives paid strict attention to business concerns (Thue, 2005). More specifically, there were considerable differences between the two firms with respect to their internationalisation strategy. Whilst Telenor opted for a high-risk investment profile in emerging markets, Telia followed a low-risk strategy seeking to capture nearby markets (that is, the Nordic and Baltic countries). Moreover, the organisational structure differed widely between Telenor and Telia in that they represented two different management philosophies. As previously noted, Telenor cultivated an organisational profile with great autonomy at the business unit level and the freedom to seize new business opportunities. By contrast, Telia was characterised by strong centralisation and engaged in a narrower set of business activities. Closely related to this point, the speed of decision-making was much faster in Telenor than in Telia, which made the latter disapprove of the Norwegian 'cowboy-culture'. Finally, the merger failure can be explained by a lack of personal trust between the two negotiating parties, where the initial personal chemistry and confidence between the two CEOs vanished with the resignation of Telia's CEO Lars Berg (Meyer, 2001; Fang et al., 2004).

Following the unsuccessful merger with Telia, Telenor's management could now concentrate on another issue, namely privatisation of the company. Although Telenor's CEO in the mid-1990s argued that a corporatisation of the incumbent did not imply privatisation, Hermansen increasingly became a strong proponent of a partial privatisation of the company. In particular, Hermansen expressed his concern for the state's dividend policy, which allowed politicians to adjust the dividends to budgetary needs and thereby adversely affect the company's ability to raise investment capital. Furthermore, the company's instruction to report strategic and financial long-term issues to the Parliament forced the company to reveal its strategy, thus creating a competitive disadvantage for the company. Finally, in order to gain legitimacy among possible alliance partners and capital market analysts it was perceived necessary to reduce the state's ownership.

2000–2005: Privatisation and Strategic Focus

State ownership and corporate governance: As one of the last of the former telecommunication monopolists, Telenor was partly privatised and listed on the Oslo Stock Exchange and the NASDAQ Stock Market in New York in December 2000. The Norwegian state retained an ownership stake of about 78 per cent after the initial public offerings, but Parliament were soon to endorse the selling of further shares in Telenor. Following the coalition government's (the Bondevik II government) goal of reduced state ownership, the state reduced its ownership stake from 100 per cent to about 54 per cent during the period 2000–2004. As a left-wing government (the Stoltenberg II government) was appointed in the Autumn of 2005, no further reductions of the state's ownership share are likely to be carried out in the coming years.[32]

As a shareholder of publicly listed companies, the coalition government sought to commit itself to the position that businesses in which the government has an ownership stake should operate under the same conditions as other commercially oriented businesses. Specifically, the Ministry's ownership report stated that, "The state seeks to exercise ownership in a way that is perceived as professional and straightforward, and which contributes to creating value and solid progress for the company" (Ministry of Trade and Industry, 2003: 14). To support such an ownership policy, a considerable amount of work was dedicated to identifying a set of corporate governance principles on which the state's management should be based. Most notably, a partial privatisation of the company implies (at least in principle) that the government can no longer use its ownership role to pursue its broader political interests. For example, whereas politicians can use the dividend from fully state-owned companies to balance the state budget, shareholders in partially privatised companies cannot approve a higher dividend than the board proposes or accepts. Thus, no special requirements should be put on the incumbent other than creating value for its owners.

After four years of privatisation, however, the CEO of Telenor, Jon Fredrik Baksaas, questioned whether private owners would generally be in a better position to meet the requirements for professional ownership and argued that the state's primary interests (that is, to secure national control of the company) could be realised even by negative state control, which would require the state to reduce its ownership stake to 34 per cent.[33] More recently, this concern about the government's ownership role has been accentuated as political representatives of the Stoltenberg II government have signalled that the government should use its voting power in Telenor (as well as in other state-owned companies) to influence governance decisions. For example, claims were made that the government should veto the sale of one non-core activity (Directory Enquiries 1881), since this might negatively affect employees in the districts. Moreover, the Telenor board has been strongly criticised by the government for granting managers new share options, as this would be interpreted as a sign that the government is pro-business and uncaring about income distribution. Thus, since the partial privatisation of Telenor in 2000, we have witnessed a shift from a passive state ownership regime based on the shareholder-value concept towards a more politically active ownership policy where the government seeks to use its voting rights to emphasise broader political concerns, such as employment and income distribution.

---

32 Although the partial privatisation of Telenor was in fact implemented by a Labour-party government (the Stoltenberg I government).

33 Source: Presentation by Jon Fredrik Baksaas, CEO of Telenor, at the 'Ownership Conference 2005', Ministry of Trade and Industry, 17 March 2005.

The impact of privatisation on corporate strategy and finances: In general, the privatisation of incumbents has forced them to withdraw activities and break up into more specialised firms. Unlike the situation for most of the other incumbents, however, Telenor's finances continued to be pretty strong even after international expansion and growth. 'Beauty contests' saved the company from using billions of NOK on UMTS auctions whereas the 2001 stock emission plus recent sales options on mobile operation in Ireland and Germany brought in billions of extra cash (Ulset, 2002). As a cash-rich incumbent preparing for a listing of the company, the challenge for Telenor was to set down an investment plan in which potential shareholders would have confidence. The management's decision was to acquire a 53,5 per cent share of the Danish mobile operator Sonofon to signal success in the Nordic market. By contrast, the least preferred alternative would have been to sell off the company's international activities and thus become a target for acquisition.

As to the effects of privatisation on Telenor's corporate strategy and finances, four major effects are identified. First, as the state could no longer use its ownership position to extract dividends from the company to balance the state budget, the company was provided with a more stable and predictable financial situation. Furthermore, privatisation ensured that the company would be provided with equity from private investors as long as the investment proposals were deemed profitable. Second, private investors have not constrained Telenor from making new investments – their main concern is rather to control whether the company actually realises its intended strategy. Third, as the time for privatisation drew closer, private investors' demands for external monitoring and preference for 'pure plays' could no longer be ignored. Consequently, Telenor established a clearer distinction between its core and non-core businesses as well as between the different core businesses. Today, the company distinguishes between four business areas: mobile, fixed, broadcast, and other activities. By contrast to other incumbents, however, the company's healthy finances have enabled Telenor to engage in only modest reorganisations, thereby keeping most of its operations.

Finally, privatisation seems to have significantly influenced a shift in the company's internationalisation strategy. After the major international expansion in the 1990s, the number of subsidiaries peaked in 2000 when Telenor had ownership in 16 mobile companies. However, as the company's investment portfolio was dominated by minority shareholdings, a shift in the company's internationalisation strategy was deemed necessary. The chosen strategy was one of global integration, meaning that Telenor sought to cultivate its industrial profile and create cross-border synergies through control of or exit from subsidiaries. Partly, this shift in strategy may be perceived as a reaction to competitors' strategy, as more and more operators tend to follow a strategy of global integration. Another driving force relates to the influence of external shareholders. Notably, Telenor had to convince its shareholders that the company's investment portfolio was financially sound and that each subsidiary created added value to the company as a whole – otherwise, shareholders could more efficiently diversify their own portfolios.

Whereas Telenor has achieved its aim of exiting from minority positions by selling its ownership stakes in seven subsidiaries by the end of 2004, the company has struggled to attain its strategic goal of global integration, mainly due to management unawareness of implementation needs and the existing management culture (Grøgaard, 2005). Furthermore, and in contrast to the company's strategic thinking, increased equity has not significantly increased the headquarters' control over its subsidiaries (ibid.).

Summary and Conclusions

Ever since the establishment of a national telephone administration 150 years ago, party politicians, board members, managers, trade unions and employees have argued about the proper mix of political control of and commercial freedom for the incumbent. For decades, strong concerns about regional, welfare, and unemployment issues made it difficult for the incumbent to solve its financial problems and satisfy customer demands. Although these problems were gradually resolved as investment levels increased in the 1970s and further improved in the 1980s, new challenges arose as the issues of liberalisation and corporatisation were put on the political agenda. Developments of these issues, however, went in different directions. As to regulatory change, Norway actually stood out as an early mover with regard to liberalisation of telecommunication services. Moreover, Norway was one of the first countries in the world to separate regulatory functions from the incumbent's production activities. By contrast, Norway was among the last of the Western European countries to accept a restructuring of the incumbent from an administrative enterprise to a joint-stock company. Although not so controversial, the decision to privatise the company some years later was also subject to strong political disagreement.

Whilst these developments might be explained by shifting political climates and EU regulatory developments, the management and the board of Telenor have themselves been pushing for increased latitude from political control. More specifically, three phases have been identified to describe how the Norwegian incumbent manoeuvred throughout the transformation process from monopoly status to become a listed company. In the period 1988–1994 it was shown that the incumbent embarked on a major internal transformation to prepare for the upcoming market situation and increasing competition. Most notably, this process involved a major downsizing that was to be resolved by designing an organisational unit to absorb redundant staff. While the transfer of redundant staff to the Resource Pool was clearly frustrating to the people involved, the unit helped to create nearly 5000 new jobs. In this way, it was also a legitimising device to gain political and public acceptance for the downsizing. Moreover, this period was characterised by early internationalisation initiatives in Russia and Hungary. Of particular strategic importance was the BT alliance, which beside signalling the acceptance of the Norwegian incumbent as an international partner also made it possible for the incumbent to hold on to its Norwegian-based business customers.

After being restructured into a joint-stock company from 1 January 1995, Telenor continued to expand its businesses to international markets in the period 1995–1999. In particular, the company concentrated on mobile operations in markets where strong growth was expected, which included countries in Central and Eastern Europe as well as South East Asia. Following an internationalisation strategy that was largely opportunity driven and highly exposed to risk, Telenor had investments in a total of 13 foreign mobile subsidiaries by the end of 1999. The incumbent was also strategically positioned in the field of satellite communications and took another step forward by establishing internet activities abroad. At the end of this period most managerial attention was directed to the merger attempt with the Swedish incumbent Telia. While the merger was formally dissolved due to a dispute over the location of the merged company's mobile unit, the merger process had for long been undermined by national, organisational and personal conflicts.

The third period, covering the years 2000–2005, is characterised by governance changes and the effects of privatisation and stock market listing on Telenor's finances and management strategy. In particular, it was noted that whilst Parliament has afforded Telenor the necessary grants to expand its operations into an international market, a partial privatisation had the benefit of providing the company with a more stable and predictable financial situation on business grounds. Moreover, privatisation forced the incumbent to prepare for its investments on a long-term basis and to cultivate its international operations. Choosing a strategy of global integration either through exit from or control of subsidiaries, during the early 2000s Telenor sold off several minority positions and increased its ownership positions in other subsidiaries, respectively.

Attempting to draw some conclusions from this chapter as regards factors instrumental in the internal transformation of Telenor and, in particular, in the corporatisation and international expansion of the company, three aspects are particularly notable:

1) The *recruitment of outsiders*, mostly economists and 'business engineers', to management and board positions in the 1980s. Arguing on the basis of prospective competition, these executives were eager to adapt the incumbent's organisation and operations to rapidly changing conditions. However, whereas the recruitment of outsiders was clearly instrumental in the internal transformation of the old monopolist, it was also a source of conflict between the traditional engineering culture, which had brought Telenor to the technological front in several business areas, and the market culture, which sought to revitalise the business from inside and expand into new areas.
2) The restructuring of the incumbent from an administrative enterprise to a joint-stock company would have been extremely difficult to achieve without the *personal relations* and *legitimate power* of Tormod Hermansen, the CEO

of Telenor. Also, the Labour government's ability to make some modifications to the organisational form of the joint-stock company made it possible to convince sceptical politicians and the trade unions.

3) During the corporatisation process, the company achieved a high degree of *diversification* and the business unit managers were granted considerable *decision-making authority*. Moreover, as the company was financially backed by the state, this resulted in an international expansion strategy that was largely *opportunity-driven* and *highly exposed to risk*. Whereas this strategy has been modified by the partial privatisation and listing of Telenor, the investment profile (that is, the speed of decision-making and the choice of markets) has differed significantly from that of other incumbents.

PART III
THE TRANSFORMATION OF STATE MONOPOLIES

Chapter 11

The Complexities of Business Orientation

Johan From and Lars C. Kolberg

Introduction

This volume has repeatedly stressed the need for and utility of analytically separating the processes of *privatisation*, as the transfer of ownership from that of *corporatisation*, the making of a business oriented company. Across Europe and across the public sector we can observe how traditional forms of integrated, hierarchically-controlled service provision are being taken towards the market. Deregulation of sectors and the opening up of monopolies juxtaposing the public producer with external private enterprises places new demands on the productivity and responsiveness on the incumbent producers.

Current theories see this development as a result of changes in ownership and regulation. Liberalisation of the market and the introduction of private owners are seen as necessary (and potentially sufficient) causes for the transformation of companies into well-functioning business firms. Effective regulation creating competitive pressure is an efficient selection mechanism forcing change to company structures and strategies. However, under a state ownership the required measures for change are not readily available to the companies. Hence, it is the combination of competition and private ownership that creates sufficient pressure.

This approach, although providing valuable insight into the effects of regulation and ownership does not facilitate a deeper understanding of changes to these companies regarding the transition from traditional public organisations to business firms. First, the organisations exposed to the pressures of change are often largely 'black-boxed'. The explanations offered are functional in the sense that they treat companies' responses to the changing environment as given. If effective competition results in efficient firms there have to be actors mediating pressure and implementing changes. This has to do with the level of analysis. Second, there is a bias in considering the most significant changes as happening after, and as a consequence of deregulation and privatisation. This has to do with the temporal dimension of change.

The country studies in this volume have presented and discussed the increased business-ness of the national incumbent telecommunications operators in five selected countries. An instant impression is that there were many things happening in these companies also in the long period before full liberalisation of the sector in 1998. For most of the companies this was a period where the state was the owner. This raises the question of what were the companies doing in this in-between period?

A process approach to social phenomena will argue that an explanation of a social phenomenon is not found in the relation between variables but rather in the story that connects them (Pentland, 1999). As shown by the country chapters, there is a chain of events flowing from the traditional companies of the 1980s to the privatised companies as of today. This process takes place within and is shaped by the various national institutional settings. We regard ownership and regulation as key elements in the institutional setting in the sense that they constitute a framework for the companies' change. The government qua principal of the companies has interests in how the transition towards a modern telecommunications industry is undertaken. Yet, authority does not rest merely with the government. The company-agents possess information unknown to the principal and their actions are not readily observable (cf. chapter 2). The issues the companies are dealing with demonstrate the institutional complexity of the relationship between principal and agent. Ownership and regulation can be understood as relational concepts, with the interaction between owner and company, between regulator and regulated, between principal and agent being central.

This chapter seeks to frame the stories of the telecommunications companies analytically so as to give some new insight into the processes of change. Primarily, the data material comes from the country chapters in this volume, but in the case of Telenor we also use additional written material (Thue, 2006) and extensive interview material This will shed light on what the challenges are and how such challenges might be dealt with when a public organisation starts out towards the market. The puzzle is how the construction of these market hybrids is undertaken. It is our modest view that this will further our understanding of change in the telecommunications sector.

Exploring the Process

The country studies in chapters 6–10 have told the stories of how the national operators in France, UK, Belgium, Germany and Norway have changed during the last 15 years. One striking feature is that across the different institutional settings the outcomes of the transformation processes have been broadly similar: The 1960s and 1970s saw a growing dissatisfaction with the telecommunications services. Some measures towards change were taken, but the fundamental transformation did not occur until the 1990s when the traditional organisations were transformed into business-oriented enterprises fundamentally reorganised and partly or wholly privatised. As of today, across the countries, the incumbents still possess a dominant market position. One major vehicle in these processes of change has been the creation of private law corporations with greater autonomy and flexibility. These new corporations face the possibilities but also the challenges of increased autonomy, the creation of new organisational structures, and new 'stakeholder management'. Striking the right balance between autonomy from the political system and being under the protection of a benevolent owner has been an issue at firm level as well as being a challenge for the owner. There is no agreement on the appropriate organisational structures for doing competitive business. Convergence on an 'Anglo-Saxon model' is one reported finding (Whittington and Mayer, 2000), while others stress distinct national systems (Whitley, 1992). The recruitment of new competence to deal with a changing environment combined with the often extensive dismissals is an issue that seems difficult to undertake within a traditional model of union influence on public policy.

On the basis of the country chapters four common dimensions that all the companies have dealt with can be condensed: First, the companies have been searching for a new identity; second, they have struggled with issues of autonomy; third, various groups of stakeholders had to be contended; and finally the organisations have gone through extensive restructurings.

Managing Identity

The question of identity concerns what kind of enterprise the telecommunications operators will be and ought to be. Initially, up until the 1970s, the companies were predominantly suppliers of nationwide voice telephony, generally referred to as Pots, 'the plain old telephone system'. Technological developments, such as digitalisation and satellite technology, and a general decreasing trend in the prices of transmission technology meant that new opportunities were opened up but they also represented new challenges for the traditional companies. Entering new markets was facilitated, but it also meant the possibility of competitors entering the domestic market. In addition, various content services were gradually emerging (for example, the Value Added Network Services (VANS), and mobile telephony). Consequently, the answer to what kind of company the incumbents were and could be became more ambiguous. Would it be sufficient to remain a national actor, or would internationalisation be a viable, not to say inevitable strategy for growth? Would infrastructure continue to be a core area or would it simply be a support discipline for value added network services?

To some degree the development of identity can be interpreted within a 'logic of consequences' (March and Olsen, 1989) whereby actors are seen as choosing among alternatives based on calculations of expected outcomes. With an emerging market and a dynamic technological situation, a new, efficient and more business orientated modus operandi is required. In the classical theory of the firm, under conditions of perfect competition, the firm is supposed to 'maximize net revenue in the face of given prices and a technologically determined production function' (Cyert and March, 1963: 5). If 'content is king', access to the infrastructure should be cheap. Hence we see how the traditional power base in the companies is altered. The engineers and the network departments gradually decline in importance. Further, the companies increasingly (but to a varying degree) come to see themselves as international business corporations delivering a broad range of services to the market. The size of the market is one factor that differs and that shapes the quest for identity. In small markets there are few customers to share the innovations costs, which can cause a pull in the direction of expanding into international markets.

However, this development is not unambiguous. Over a long period of time the companies exercised a hybrid identity – they were supposed to be a public monopoly and a business actor simultaneously. This is not simply a matter of organisational form and ownership. Even British Telecom, early privatised, struggled for a long time with the culture of the company. The bureaucratic culture was seen as an impediment to customer orientation for a long time after privatisation. What we see here can be the result of conflicting norms and expectations resulting in questions such as: 'what kind of a company are we, and what should a company like us do in a situation like this' This is the 'logic of appropriateness' (March and Olsen, 1989) where action is based on identities, obligations and conceptions of what constitutes appropriate actions. Whether the company acts from a strictly economic basis is not simply a matter of skill in forecasting the future and of calculus. Actions and identity will also be shaped by expectations in the environment and routines within the organisation.

The development of identity in Telenor is a story about how a new identity develops within the traditional organisation. During the 1990s the company was transformed into an international high-tech business so that in 2006 it was referring to itself as 'a leading provider of communications services and one of the largest mobile operators worldwide'. The adaptation of the company to what was perceived to be an emerging new reality started gradually from the 1980s. Management by Objectives was introduced and some authority was decentralised to geographical units, while at the same time the central administration was strengthened. In addition, the employees were trained in customer orientation. Still, the *raison d'être* of the company up until the 1990s was connected to the infrastructure. The engineers, the technocrats and fixed line telephone dominated the agenda. This had some had some important bearing upon how the company regarded itself and its mission. It was a logic of appropriateness more than a logic of consequences. The digitalisation of the network is one example. In 1997 the network had become fully digitalised as one of the first in Europe. Interestingly, the last subscribers to get a digital line lived in the central areas of the two largest cities in Norway. When digitalisation had started some 10 years earlier, it began in the ultimate periphery of Norway and only reached the central and densely populated areas gradually.

With the new CEO taking up position in 1991 'businessification' intensified. The perceptions of future competition pushed the managerial perception of what the company should be in the direction of a business firm. Competition was believed to be inevitable in the early 1990s and the viable strategy was regarded to be a development of the company into a competitive business firm. How was this change in identity brought about? For a large part the business identity grew out of the first competitive branch of the tele-adminstration, namely the TBK, which was responsible for terminal equipment in the liberalised market from 1987. As a subsidiary, the TBK was allowed to use pay-schemes comparable to private sector companies and hence many employees with private sector management experience could be recruited. The new generation of managers recruited held a different view of what the company would and should be.

The expansive internationalisation strategy contributed to the transformation of Telenor. With a small domestic market such as the Norwegian, there are few customers to bear the costs of innovations. Hence, expansion into foreign markets became a 'security valve' and meant that the company gradually became a global actor. Further, the mid 1990s saw large buy-ins into IT companies. This propelled the shift in what the company was doing and in what kind of a company it was: It was no longer a company just for voice telephony. Content services were generally seen as the future.

The establishment of Norwegian Telecom as a holding company for the subsidiaries in 1993 created a quasi-concern model. As still a part of the state administration being prohibited from establishing a genuine concern model, the tele-administration and Norwegian Telecom were formally two different units, but they had the same board and the same CEO. After corporatisation in late 1994, the two could merge. In fact, more accurately it was Norwegian Telecom that acquired the tele-administration than the other way around: The competitive branch grew under the tele-administration until it was able to virtually 'take over' the rest of the organisation.

However, the transformation towards a business identity was not without its limits. The attempts to separate content from infrastructure in the mid 1990s proved too controversial and had to be reversed. This separation could well be regarded as a sound development of the business. But evidently the network culture still held some influence in the company as it managed to stop the division

The general shift away from the network centred identity can be seen across all the cases. Technological development was a driver in the shift and to some extent the old identity was left behind with the old technology. However even though there is this similarity, the actual ways in which it was done and the degree of it varies.

Managing Autonomy

The question of autonomy concerns the degree to which the companies have freedom to act without intervention. The market situation obviously constrains what a firm will be able to do, but more significant in the period before full liberalisation this is a question of the relationship between the owner and the company, between principal and agent. This relationship will not be clearly defined once and for all, but rather it develops over time as it is influenced by shifting principal interests and the actions of the companies.

One major obstacle when public services are to be exposed to the market is the fact that with traditional integrated service production the public sector is, so to speak, at all sides of the table. Public officials are regulating the area; the production is arranged (purchased) by the authorities; and the producers are financed over public budgets. To approach a credible competitive situation, the various roles of government have to be made clear (Savas, 1987). The regulatory tasks must be kept separate from the state's interests as owner and the potential political interests in employment; district development etc. must not interfere with company strategies. Establishing a private law corporation with or without state shares removes the company from the hierarchical line of command and depending on the ministry responsible for the ownership it can hinder a twin-hatted minister being responsible for both the framework of the sector and a company operating in the sector. In Norway this has been a major discussion (for example, Statskonsult, 1998b).

For companies en route to business, the issue of autonomy is a question of balancing freedom to manage with potentially beneficial dependency on the state. This tension is mirrored in the literature on New Public Management where the slogans 'let the managers manage!' and 'make the managers manage!' exist side by side (Kettl, 2000). Is it the case that managers of public telecommunications companies know how to improve the sector but are hampered by rigid rules and structures such as public employment law and salaries, or must the government design systems forcing them to change? In the telecommunications sector both situations are found indicating that reform elements are not general as such but rather contingent on their context. For example, the Belgacom case indicates how little progress was made until the government decided to privatise the company in 1995, that is, the managers had to be 'made to manage'. The Telenor case however, shows something of the other approach. Here the management pushed for increased autonomy in order to be able to transform the company. The gradual increase in discretion is appreciated and converted into business development, indicating that letting the managers manage may have been a viable strategy.

Formally, different organisational forms define the firm – authority relation. In state-owned service delivery, the production unit can be organised more or less close to the political core. Increasing the distance to the polity typically implies increased discretion over budget, salaries, decisions, and strategy. Removing production units from the hierarchical line of command also necessitates new forms of control. Various configurations are possible concerning the state companies' link to the polity. Looking at the abstract model it is not entirely clear which configuration should be preferred by either party.

The government principal is many-sided and has multiple concerns to attend to. One concern for the government is to secure low prices and good quality in the services delivered to the citizens and a viable competition is a means to achieve this. Establishing a market implies attracting private companies who need to be assured of a level playing field, which in turn suggests the need for a strict separation between the state and the company. Yet, the state has interests in developing a strong nationally owned actor within the telecommunications. From the state's point of view this can pull the companies inwards: government has interests in the development of national industries. Sustained 'politisation' of the firm can help in addressing societal concerns.

Also from the firm's point of view both more and less autonomy can be good. For state companies the concept of autonomy is often equalled to the greatest possible distance from the polity. However, from the firm's point of view, autonomy can denote being able to do what is necessary to become competitive. Complete separation from the state is no guarantee for this in a process of transformation. State ownership can imply cheap access to capital, and it can effectively be a barrier to take-overs. Hence the degrees of freedom may well be greater under state ownership than under private ownership. The companies have interests in maintaining a favourable position versus its (future) competitors. This can bring about a game-like situation between principal and agent where the firm's degrees of freedom is a matter of negotiations.

In all the countries investigated, except the UK, the initial process of transforming the companies took place under a relatively tight connection to the respective political system. Generally, the parts and services exposed to competition (terminal equipment, VANS, mobile and subsequently voice) are gradually trimmed away and gain degrees of freedom as subsidiaries of the incumbent companies but the 'residual organisation' is kept under tight control. Regulatory authorities are established to take care of the market and to monitor the companies. Why does the process unfold like this? One obvious alternative it seems would have been to keep the network as a state bureau and hive off the services to the market.

In the traditional model, the hierarchical structure secures the principal's control in a relatively simple environment. The overriding issue is to secure telephone service to every citizen at an affordable cost. Additional services such as coastal radio and services for disabled can be demanded from the companies without compensation. The principal is not omniscient and thereby omnipotent, but the situation is less complex than what is to follow. The power structure changes as new services, new technologies, new regulations and new ownership structures are introduced. For instance, the national regulators often start out as a one-person office that is supposed to deal with and change the direction of century-old, large organisations. In addition, the ministries have to deal with demands from increasingly professionally managed companies for which the state ownership policy is not necessarily well adjusted. In the still assumed future, some of the previous clarity is re-established: Within a private sector framework the power structure is once again not straightforward but is at least formally well defined. Competition policy can probably deal with telecommunications as routinely as with other sectors, such as air transport.

The private owners of the company possess the highest formal competencies, and financial analysts provide feedback on companies' strategies. These three stages although slightly caricatured, point to the reason for our interest, not to say obsession, with the in-between period. This period of transition has a strong element of *uncertainty*, making it worthwhile investigating what the actors do and what they can achieve.

In the Norwegian case, up until 1994 the telecommunications company was organised a part of the state administration. The board expressed a need for increased autonomy at various time during the late 1980s and early 1990s, and under the short period of a conservative government from 1990–1991, plans existed to establish the company as a state owned corporation. However the subsequent labour government cancelled the plans and instead gave some increased autonomy within the existing model. Most important, the company was allowed to buy and form subsidiaries. In practice, in the 1990s before the corporatisation there were few limits to what could be achieved. For example in 1991, it was possible to acquire a satellite instead of the Swedish Telia that needed to get authorisation first. It was also possible in 1993 to form what in practice was a concern model with its own holding company. The formal association to the state defines the autonomy, but it is possible to exploit and expand what it is possible to do. Eventually it seems, the biggest impediment was the fact that the minister had to be consulted regularly.

The period as state owned corporation from 1994–2000 was evidently a comfortable one with healthy finances through capital enlargements. However it seems the money did not result in extensive slack in the company. Instead it financed large scale growth, somewhat analogue to Niskanen's (1971) budget maximising bureaucrat: it financed investments that would probably not have been possible under private ownership with financial analysts reviewing company strategy. This is an example of autonomy under state ownership. Still, it was the company that pushed further for privatisation. In order to merge with Swedish Telia, stock listing was a requirement. Although the merger failed, the process for privatisation continued. Even a benevolent state ownership may limit business orientation eventually.

Managing Stakeholders

In the process of change the companies face various groups of *stakeholders* that have to be dealt with. The concept of stakeholders stems from the management literature, with the basic idea that firms stand in interdependent relationships with groups (stakeholders) in the environment (Jones and Wicks, 1999). As opposed to *shareholders* there is no one dominant group of stakeholders. Thus, no single set of interests is assumed to dominate and all the legitimate stakeholders' interests are important in managerial decision-making. Generally, firms are dependent upon support from external stakeholders which according to resource dependence theory is the reason for stakeholders' leverage over the firms. An asymmetry in the exchange relation between the stakeholders and the firm shifts the power from one part to the other (Pfeffer and Salancik, 1978).

To achieve competitiveness in a dynamic environment, former public monopolists will normally be required to change the competence profile of the workforce. This is especially true in technology driven businesses such as telecommunications. During the period covered in this volume, mobile telephony, satellites and internet are among the new areas telecommunications companies start to explore. The competence to cope with these and other areas are not necessarily held within the companies. The need for motivated and competent employees can be a particularly challenging task when the restructuring uncovers an overstaffing of the companies. The central problem is the required shift in competence. In a situation with dynamics in the environment, recruitment freeze is problematic. New technologies require new competencies in the company, and thus, the reduction in existing staff must be larger if new recruitments are to be possible.

One key discussion area following public sector market orientation tends to be the resulting employee status. A within civil service status will expectedly represent higher job security and standardised salary schemes whilst the opposite may be true for private sector status. In the country studies we see how the issue of retaining a civil servant status for the employees has been an important and difficult subject matter. In the France Telecom case the status of the employees hindered reforms for a long period of time. Proposals to increase the company's autonomy were met with large scale strikes.

The *labour unions* are often regarded as a major impediment to public sector change unions in that they generally see the 'marketisation' of public services as a threat. The threat is related to supposedly inferior working conditions for employees as well as a reduction in union density and power. Given the unions' traditional strong standing in many European countries, how union relations are dealt with it is potentially of great significance. From the literature it is well known that 'voice' and 'loyalty' are connected (Hirschman, 1970), that is, that the 'management' of stakeholders and the stakeholders' choice of influence strategy are interdependent (Frooman, 1999). Trust-based approaches towards stakeholders may keep reduce union opposition but perhaps at the cost of watering down the changes. More radical approaches might prove more effective, at least in the short run. In the companies studied in this book, those that retained a state ownership in the transition period consulted the unions regularly. Strikes and negotiations have accompanied the processes. Yet, the fact that the corporatisation and privatisation processes have continued indicates that the companies and the owners have eventually managed to establish legitimate models. One of the fundamental questions in all of the processes has been that of redundancies. Managing the downscaling often of thousands of employees, it has been a challenging and costly task finding models that are effective and legitimate.

During the time under review *customers* became a new stakeholder group for the companies. Traditionally the tele-administrations dealt with *subscribers* with relatively simple and homogenous demands. Admittedly, there were private users and corporate users, but the products were relatively standardised. During the 1960s and 1970s there was an increase in discontent among users, as waiting lists, quality and service level were not satisfactory. In the 1980s the companies gradually realised that they had customers of different types and increasingly with new and diverse demands. The technological developments and liberalisation also resulted in potential 'exit' possibilities. This was particularly the case for large businesses who had the resources to create private infrastructure. Since the corporate customers have often been the most profitable for the telecommunications companies, concerns to accommodate their needs, for example, for cheap international calls can shift the balance between private and corporate customers.

The political system has been and continues to be an important stakeholder for the companies. Basically there are economic interests regarding the establishment of an effective market and interests concerning the societal consequences of the transformation processes: Examples of the latter are: how can nation-wide delivery be secured, what are the consequences for the disabled, what happens to employment in the districts, can equal pricing throughout the country be maintained? Regulatory authorities can be used to take care of both economic ad societal interests (Genoud and Varone, 2002). Economic regulation aims at providing stability and competition in the market. With the gradual liberalisation of the sector new firms enter and the incumbent companies are required to give access to their infrastructure on a non-discriminatory basis. The Open Network Provision made sure that new operators are given access to the existing infrastructure. The access pricing of the incumbents is monitored by the national regulatory authorities. An example of social regulation is a requirement on companies with a dominant market position that they have to deliver services universally.

Overall, it seems that the stakeholder dimension grows in complexity throughout the period. Existing actors obtain new interests and demands, and new actors emerge. When the environment within which the transforming companies manoeuvre is complex, decision-making gets a strong dimension of uncertainty. The decisions and choices undertaken at firm level cannot be strictly instrumental and rational but rather attempts at progressing within what seems sensible, possible and appropriate.

Managing Uncertainty

Service production not formerly exposed to market forces is assumed to be less efficient than services produced in the market. This is acknowledged to be less a consequence of the ownership being public than of the non-competitive nature of traditional public service production. A monopoly situation means that the environment is relatively stable and that pressures to change are largely absent. In addition, a stable technological environment can help a non-efficient producer to survive. Dealing with a standardised set of tasks means that challenges can be managed within the existing structure. This changes when the business changes. In the strategy literature from Chandler (1962) onwards, it is noted that the business strategies need to be coupled with appropriate business structures. In the 1990s European firms are reported to be more diversified (Whittington and Mayer, 2000). A 'M-form' structure where operations are decentralised whilst strategy is kept central is argued to be better suited to a diversified strategy than a traditional functional 'U-form' where tasks are organised according to functions (production, sales, marketing etc.). The fundamental reasoning behind M-form divisionalisation is the requirement of being able to give separate responses in separate markets (Stinchcombe, 1990).

In telecommunications decreasing prices of electronic equipment hid the inefficiency of the public monopoly providers for a long time (Eliassen and Sjøvaag, 1999). The emerging liberalisation and perceptions of a future market impacted on the companies' understanding of the environment. In order to become competitive, that is, delivering services at a price and quality at least at the same level as alternative providers, a transformation of the public sector incumbents was apparently required. There was an inherent uncertainty here with questions such as: what will the market be like, when will it come, what will be the company's role in it, and how should the company organise itself in order to meet market demands? Parallel to this, the technological changes from the 1980s produced a wide range of new business opportunities. Digitalisation of the infra-structure meant that network capacity increased. Further, satellite, mobile and eventually internet were among the areas largely unheard of when telecommunications were still a part of the postal and telegraph administrations.

We see that all the telecommunications companies undergo extensive structural reorganisation processes in the early to mid 1990s. Partly this has to do with an adjustment of structures to strategy. Going in to new areas puts strains on the traditional organisational structure and restructuring into business units and divisions can easily be seen as a consequence. This sits well with the functional explanation of divisionalisation. However, the reorganisations can also be interpreted more broadly as a response to the fundamental uncertainties found both in technological development and the (perceived) market situation. Initially, up until the 1980s, new demands were taken care of within the existing model. Employees were trained in customer orientation, some authority was decentralised, recruitments were frozen, and there was an acknowledged need to change the culture of the organisations. Large scale fundamental reorganisations were not an issue because the existing degree of uncertainty could perceivably be managed within the traditional structure. However, when the uncertainty increases, reorganisation in order to establish a new logic becomes somewhat inevitable. With the new CEO entering Telenor in Norway in 1991 it is rapidly established that pricing, manning and organisation issues must be dealt with synchronically and radically. Hence, the shift from a geographically-based structure to a divisionalised structure is coupled with downscaling and a new price regime. Also in the case of BT we see an analogue reorganisation happening at pretty much the same time, and in the case of France Telecom a matrix structure is established from 1993. In sum, the fundamental logic seems rather similar across the cases, but the actual implementation varies. Reorganisations have continued throughout the period. New divisions, new principles and new logics have been explored. A reasonable interpretation of this is that the initial answers to the challenges were relatively crude. Business logic was instituted but further refinement was required.

Discussion

As stressed above, a striking feature of the national telecommunications companies is the broadly comparable outcome of the transformation processes. As of today, in all West-European countries the old incumbent companies have been transformed to business-like companies. How can we account for and understand this? According to methodological canons differences in causes cannot account for similarities in outcomes. The explanation of complex events with actors at different levels (multiple categories of units of analysis) and causal links across levels and categories (intercategory causal mechanisms) (Abell, 2001) poses challenges for our methodology. Insight into the complex phenomenon of transforming telecommunications requires a well-suited methodology.

Observations indicate a variation in the processes at micro level. The UK stands out as the most noticeable anomaly, because of the en-bloc sale of British Telecom to private owners in 1984 and the subsequent ownership structure that sets it apart from the other companies. Also the regulator in the UK dealt initially with the BT company and not with the market. Yet the challenges have been similar with a persistent bureaucratic culture, struggles over identity, challenges with groups of stakeholders, and extensive restructuring processes. Also under private ownership the transition has been long. The Belgacom case demonstrates an approach where the questions were long approached from within the state, that is, from the top down. As late as 1994, the CEO was prohibited from appointing the management team, and the board was put together politically proportionally. It was not before 1995 that the government fully appreciated that liberalisation was an upcoming challenge and that fundamental changes to the company were required. Privatisation was regarded a viable strategy. The reluctant approach to changes in the company, the slow transition to a new identity, was accompanied (and perhaps facilitated) by a hesitant implementation of regulation for liberalisation.

Convergence in outcome does not necessarily mean that the various national institutions does not matter (as Serot, 2002, concludes). Rather it can be an indication that mechanisms are contingent – relating to the same dimensions in different ways gives similar outcomes. For example, a car can skid off the road in a curve because of too high a speed despite an alert driver, or the same outcome can result from sand on the road and alcohol consumption despite new tires and clear sight. These are examples of complex causation. Statistical control procedures have been developed to deal with complex forms of causation, but there are problems grasping the nature of a transformation process within a variable-based ontology. Alternatively, therefore, process approaches can trace the decision process by which various initial conditions are translated into outcomes (George and McKeown, 1985: 35). Below, these different approaches to social science explanations are discussed. These two approaches have different implications for how we come to regard the nature of change in telecommunications and the public sector more generally.

Variance Oriented Approaches

When examining public sector reforms, a frequent line of inquiry in the social sciences is to examine the associations between variables, and consequently this is a dominant method within the literature on new public management reforms: There are variables on the input side of the system, these variables impacts on the system, and an effect can be measured on variables on the output side. Indeed, there are numerous studies covering the input side of reforms: why do reforms (not) occur. The answers can be sought in theoretical underpinnings (Barzelay, 2002) or in the role of ideology and political will (Sørensen and Bay, 2002). Also the output side is extensively covered. Ownership and regulation / marked situation are prime candidates for having an effect on the output side. The effects of change on economy, quality, and democracy are frequently considered (Boyne, 1998). Finally the 'values' on the variable 'change' are assessed, such as the scope and type of change often related to different polity types (Pollitt and Bouckaert, 2000).

Causation in these type of studies is analogue to 'causal effect': that is, the change in the value of the dependent variable that would have occurred if the explanatory variable had assumed a different value (King, Verba and Keohane, 1994). The fact that rerunning the history in order to allow explanatory variables to assume another value is normally not feasible, is sometimes referred to as 'the fundamental problem of causation' (King, Verba and Keohane, 1994), that is, it is not possible to examine a case where owners are both private and not-private at the same time. Various techniques have been developed to deal with this. In short, the intention is to create 'closed systems', that is, systems with a definite and limited number of variables where it is possible to observe change whilst accounting for or avoiding interference from external variables. Empirical regularities are therefore regarded as necessary and sufficient for establishing causality. We can draw inferences of causes and effects from regular associations. If firm efficiency co-varies regularly with private ownership, we infer that they are casually related. This is the nature of inference in statistical analysis where large numbers of observations are used to estimate partial correlations between independent and dependent variables.

However, this fundamental variable-oriented epistemology is also shared by many 'small-N studies'. The comparative method is argued to be similar to statistics in all respects but one: the number of cases is too small to allow for control by means of partial correlation (Lijphart, 1971). The methodological basis of comparative case studies is the seminal work by J.S. Mill. The methods of agreement and difference set out to eliminate causes that differ across cases with a similar outcome or are similar across cases with different outcomes respectively. The rationale is that different causes can not be considered *necessary* for the similar outcomes found and similar causes cannot be *sufficient* for different outcomes (Mahoney, 2000). We see this in Historical Institutionalism studies, a tradition concerned with the impact of enduring national institutions on particular outcomes. The institutions mediate changes in exogenous background variables and the joint effect explains the particular national outcome (Lieberman, 2001). Again, a variance-based epistemology is invoked.

Applying this logic to our five country cases, however, we encounter problems. Within the logic of comparative methods, the outcome, the privatised, business-oriented companies, is broadly similar across all cases. Using the method of agreement implies comparing the cases' scores on independent variables. Causes that differ across the cases cannot be necessary causes for the outcome. We are forced therefore to remove institutional features such as ownership, national polity variation and various regulatory implementations as potential causes. Does this mean that these system features are irrelevant for the business orientation and transformation of the companies? This illustration can indicate why the 'input to change' and the 'output of change' is usually comprehensively covered whereas change itself although described in quantitative terms, is largely 'black boxed'. One reason can be that studies in the social sciences often rest in positivist logic where empirical regularities are the only source for causal inference. The argument is that two things are casually related if and only if they co-vary systematically. 'Change' can only be considered a variable that can assume different values. However, large variations across different reforms, contexts and services (for example, Hodge, 2000) suggest more thorough inquires into the local translation and implementation of reforms are required. The next section, therefore, will direct the attention towards the contingent nature of change processes.

A Process-oriented Alternative

A process approach to explanation argues that the dynamics of change must be acknowledged and variance-based approaches to change will not capture this. The approach takes the stance that provision of an adequate explanation of an event requires its cause to be identified and the casual relation between this cause and the event be demonstrated (Salmon, 1984). The event to be explained is fitted into a pattern of regularities, but the regularities as such have no explanatory power. What is required is knowledge of underlying mechanisms: What are the mechanisms linking initial explanatory variables (say competition) to outcome (say increased business orientation)? Such causal mechanisms will be contingent on the context. For example dynamite has the potential of exploding with a substantial causal effect, but its activation is dependent upon contextual factors (Tsoukas, 1989). The same mechanism can bring about different results and different mechanisms can generate the same result (Sayer, 1992), the concept being consistent therefore with situations when explanatory variables are not independent of one another (George and Bennett, 2005: 145). In these situations empirical regularities are neither necessary nor sufficient for establishing causality. The fact that ownership structure varies across our cases does not make ownership irrelevant as a factor in our explanation Variance-based approaches face problems when this basic axiom of positivism is challenged.

One research tradition worth highlighting is that of historical sociology. Here a small number of cases are selected for analysis and theory and history is used to identify the causes of a clearly identified outcome. Skocpol's (1979) account of revolutions is perhaps the most well known example. The explanatory frame offered by historical sociology has little to do with the 'pastness' of the phenomenon under investigation. *It is the nature of the data and the analysis that distinguish it*: it is the use of a 'narrative mode to examine and exploit the temporality of social action and historical events' (Griffin, 1992: 405). 'The dependent variable, the thing to be explained [is] something that comes about through a series of steps' (Becker, 1992:208). This is very much the case for our analysis: the business-orientation of the incumbent companies is a process spanning more than a decade. Various events, such as the establishment of a private-law company, structural reorganisations, and internationalisation strategies, contribute in increasing the 'business-ness' of the company, and narrative analyses can consider and highlight the temporal and historical nature of such change processes. Actions, events and processes are situated in their broader (temporal) contexts. Thus, *actors*, not variables, are established as the agents of change (Abbott, 1992), it is human agency that transforms states of the world (Abell, 2004). The owner has discretion in designing (or choosing) the agent to perform the task of modernising national telecommunications. The national regulator has discretion when implementing the EU regulatory directives and the management of the companies can pursue various strategies on behalf of the company. These actors all contribute to the process of transformation. It is uncontroversial to assume that these actors are not perfectly rational and that they do not possess complete information about the world. Their judgements and actions will be influenced by what makes sense and by what can be achieved in the given institutional setting. Examples of this are the climate for radical change under the Thatcher regime in the UK; the Belgium polity with strong elements of consensus policy making (Lijphart, 1984); and the strong notion of '*service public*' in France (Marino, 2005). Hence, when all the incumbents are eventually transformed into listed companies, and they all retain a dominant market position, they converge through different processes. This highlights how the mechanisms linking the stages in the processes are contingent: same mechanisms can have different effects, and different mechanisms can have the same effect depending on the framework.

Implications for Telecommunications

Taking the process-oriented stance and attempting to grasp the within-firm processes of change reveals a multitude of issues. The dimensions of identity, autonomy, stakeholders and uncertainty are dealt with not in a strictly instrumental sense. The fact that the outcomes bear resemblance to each other does not warrant the conclusion that the transition has been a smooth one, nor that the process has been a top-down process where the framework has been defined external to the firms. The firms and the management have been significant actors in defining the framework. The ambiguous state ownership in transition being neither professional nor traditional (cf. chapter 3) has made the boundaries of what is possible blurred. In addition, the establishment of a new regulatory framework in the sector has left some room for negotiations between company, regulator and owner.

The importance of the four dimensions discussed in the transformation of the companies points to the institutional complexity of the principal–agent relation set out in chapter 2. The owner's interests are evidently many and shifting. The power and impact of regulation can also be questioned. The central discussions along the dimensions of identity and autonomy take places in relation to the owner. The regulatory framework establishes some imperatives, but the companies' responses seem to be more a function of perceptions of an emerging future market than of regulation as such.

The firms as agents shape this relation between principal and agent. The insight to be derived is that regulation and ownership can be regarded as relational concepts. It is not only who owns, and who regulates that is of significance. An account of who *is* owned and who *is* regulated are necessary elements of an explanation of the change in the telecommunications sector. More generally applied this also has a bearing on our insight into public sector modernisation as such. The study of the impact of changes in ownership and regulation can only take us so far. In order to fully appreciate what is happening, the complexity of the principal side, the significance of the agent side, and the nature of the relation between them should be taken into account. The investigation of the chain of events in the change processes is a promising and relatively rarely undertaken venture to reach this end.

Chapter 12

Structures and Business Strategies

Catherine B. Arnesen

Economies need to respond flexibly to what global and regional economic forces are telling them if they are to maintain their competitive position. The increased application of information and communication technologies to all parts of the economy is symptomatic of such a response and is believed to deliver competitive 'flexible' enterprises into the new millennium (Turner, 1997). In turn, these developments increase the pressure for change on the incumbent telecom companies. EU telecommunications regulation was intended as a temporary measure, which would more or less fall away as competition developed. This initial regulation had effects on several economic, as well as institutional factors, but did not initially have a major effect on organisational structures. A typical first step towards liberalisation, and one that was a legally binding requirement from the EU for all EU member states (Directive 95/62/EC), was to separate regulatory from operational functions in the former telecommunications organisations. In addition to separating regulation and operation, EU legislation demanded that an independent regulator be established at national level. The independent regulator's tasks are to ensure fair and free competition and to implement a transparent decision-making process, especially with regard to interconnection agreements, which are at the heart of competition in telecommunications. Moreover, regulators are responsible for representing the country in international organisations, and for licensing requirements in areas involving limited resources, such as frequencies in the mobile sector (Eliassen and Sjovaag, 1999).

All these changes and developments happened during the 1990s up to full liberalisation in 1998 and had little effect on the organisational structure of the different incumbent telecom operators (ITOs). However, as it became clear that the telecommunications regulation and regulatory intervention would be around for some time, European telecom companies were forced to think differently. Going from a monopoly situation to one of an open market and competition obviously required new strategic goals and subsequent changes in business strategy for the firms.

Ownership Structure and Competition

Complete changes in the structuring of the telecommunications sector following the opening up of the market can be observed during the last decade. These changes have had a direct effect on changes in company strategies within the different telecom operators. Firstly, changes can be observed in ownership strategies of the different ITOs as a direct result of the opening up of the telecom market. The EU regulatory framework on telecommunications has had a visible impact on the incumbent operators with regard to ownership and legal structure, explained by the fact that all 15 EU incumbent operators[1] have been through the same phases of corporatisation and privatisation, although at different points in time and at a different tempo and intensity. Such transformations in ownership structures are clearly part of the liberalisation and re-regulation process.[2] This 'ownership structure level' can be characterised as the *politicians' strategy level.* By this it is supposed that the observed changes in ownership structure is a direct result of a political process, namely the politicians' decision to liberalise the telecommunications market. The changes in ownership can therefore be characterised as the initial direct reaction on the liberalisation process. Secondly, a significant number of the incumbent telecom operators in the EU have also found themselves changing their organisational strategies. Great transformations in the organisation's strategy occur, and such changes seem to be significantly varying between the different ITOs. With 1998 looming, many Member States realised that they would be unable to protect their ITOs from competition, and that the ITOs therefore had to be given greater management flexibility, freedom from bureaucratic constraints and access to private capital. As will be seen in the discussion part of this chapter, it is only the changes in *organisational strategy* that in reality help the ITOs confront a new competitive marketplace. This 'two-stage logic' can be summarised as in Figure 12.1.

However, these changes are not chronological phases representing the same pattern for all ITOs. It is evident that some ITOs started changing their organisational strategies before getting involved with changes in ownership strategies. The following parts of this section will discuss developments in ownership structure and competition, whilst an examination of new business strategies within the ITOs at organisational level is covered in the next section of this chapter.

There has been a worldwide move towards privatisation of government-owned ITOs, a process that has been part of the general trend of reducing the

---

1 The time-perspective of the analysis in this chapter is 1998–2001 when the EU included 15 Member States.

2 Corporatisation and privatisation has become a clear response among all the ITOs to the EU regulatory framework opening up the markets for European telecommunications. However, it is important to be aware of the fact that there was never any obligation in the telecommunications framework forcing the ITOs to neither corporatise nor privatise.

1st level: Ownership structure
The politicians' strategy

2nd level: Organisational strategy
The operators' own strategy

Figure 12.1 Level of ITOs' organisational developments

state's role in the economy and the rise of market-orientated policies (Blackman and Denmead, 1996). Governments' past arguments that it was necessary to retain control over national ITOs have become harder to justify in recent years and it has become increasingly apparent that the state is unwilling to fund the necessary investment in infrastructure. Firstly, telecommunications is no longer seen as a natural monopoly,[3] and secondly, new approaches to universal services indicate that government ownership is not the only solution (Armstrong, 1998; Newbery, 2001). Furthermore, some governments, led by the UK and the USA, have sought to reduce the role of the state in the economy and have pursued related political objectives, for example reducing government spending, limiting trade union power, and widening share ownership (Newbery, 2001). The most important motivation for privatisation of ITOs, however, has been the perceived failure of public ownership to deliver high-quality services efficiently and cheaply. Economists have recognised that incentives for management to tackle long-standing inefficiencies are maximised when a business is privatised *and* the market is made more competitive (for example, Vickers and Yarrow, 1988). Privatisation leads business to become accountable to the private capital market, and raising finance in the private capital market rather than through government, exposes the management to continuous monitoring by finance centres around the world (for example, the City in the UK and Wall Street in the USA).

The first major change in the incumbent telecommunications operators as a reaction to the liberalisation process was corporatisation. Most governments came to the conclusion that the ability to raise investment capital without being subject to government borrowing restrictions was necessary for network modernisation.

3 An activity can be described as a natural monopoly if it is most cost-effectively carried out by a single firm rather than by several. Typically, this is a case where there are very large fixed costs. Within telecoms, local fixed network operations have the most widespread natural monopoly cost conditions. This is largely because of economies of density, whereby it is cheaper per person to build a local network connecting 5,000 people in a give area than it is to connect 500 (Helm and Jenkinson 1998). Clearly, economies of density imply that it is more cost-effective to have a single local network in a given local area than to have several.

Corporatisation is one way of allowing ITOs greater budgetary and operational autonomy, whilst retaining state ownership. However, this was just the first step towards privatisation, as ITOs were otherwise unable to make long-term investment commitments. Whilst corporatisation allows budgetary autonomy, it does not necessarily address the major problem of state-owned enterprises, which is their ability to encourage managers to operate efficiently and in the interest of customers. Partial privatisation is seen as one way of changing the motivation of management towards profit making, while still retaining some measure of control over the ITO (Newbery, 2001).

Studying the 15 incumbent telecommunications operators (ITOs) within the EU from 1995 to 2002, we can see that there are great changes with regard to *ownership structures* within these companies.[4] Given that the case of complete government control has been weakened, there seem to be three options open to governments: corporatisation, partial privatisation, and full privatisation. The first two options may also form stages in an incremental process of privatisation.[5] For the most part, European telecommunications companies were run as government-owned monopolies as late as the 1990s. However, looking at the end of the 1990s/beginning of the new millennium all the incumbents (except Luxembourg P&T) were partly or fully privatised. The investigation of all 15 incumbents in the EU at that point in time reveals that EU regulation has had a direct influence on the ownership structure of the ITOs (Monsen, 2004). Facing impending liberalisation of the telecom market, the first reaction from the old telecom monopolies was to look for external capital in order to be competitive. As public administration organisations have no possible entries into capital markets corporatisation of the old- style public administration of telecoms was a first step in this direction. This was followed by partial or full privatisation with listing on the stock market. This is a natural act for a firm going from a monopoly situation to being introduced to competition and represents the preparations for full opening of the telecommunications market in 1998.

It is, however, only when changes in ownership (in this context corporatisation and privatisation) are coupled with increases in *market competition* that further efficiency incentives are introduced. In a competitive market the business must be managed efficiently if it is to survive. One way to illustrate the interplay between privatisation and competition is illustrated in Figure 12.2. Cell A in the figure is associated with public ownership and monopoly supply and is therefore where the least efficiency incentives exist. Investment and other managerial decisions are regulated through the political process and politicians can be expected to pursue non-commercial objectives (Mitchell, 1988 as cited in Parker, 1994). By contrast, the efficiency incentives are maximised in cell (D), where private ownership and competition combine. Here both capital market and product market incentives

4 Refer to Appendix I for figures.

5 For a closer description of the three options for changes in ownership strategies see for example Laffont and Tirole (2000) and Wellenius and Stern (1996).

to operate efficiently are maximised (Parker, 1994). In other words, competition is extensive and increasingly effective. The other two cells, (B) and (C), involve private ownership with monopoly, and public ownership with competition, respectively. They can be viewed as intermediate stages with some, but not full, efficiency incentives, as in the initial phases of liberalisation.

	PUBLIC OWNERSHIP	**PRIVATE OWNERSHIP**
MONOPOLY	(A) Low efficiency: little competition + state ownership	(B) Potential for monopoly use
COMPETITION	(C) Competition should lead to efficiency, but state interventions could lead to inefficiency	(D) High efficiency: full product and capital market incentives to be efficient

Figure 12.2 Ownership structure and competition

Source: based on Parker, 1994.

Although highly simplified, this ownership-competition framework can be usefully applied when studying the developments within European ITOs during the last decade or so. Such developments can broadly be divided into two patterns; the first including countries that decided to privatise before liberalisation (and competition) – like the UK, and the other, the countries that choose to privatise more as a result of liberalisation and increased competition, that is, most of the other countries in the former 15 EU member states.[6] The UK typically moved from cell (A) to cell (B), and then later towards 'the ideal' cell (D). When BT was privatised it was a monopoly in a non-liberalised market. At this point in time only one other national network provider had been licensed, Mercury Communications, a subsidiary of Cable and Wireless that started operating in May 1986. This was the result of an action from the British government with the

6 Telecom Austria, Belgacom, Tele Danmark, Sonera Corporation, France Telecom, Deutsche Telecom, OTE, Eircom, Telecom Italia, KPN, Portugal Telecom, Telefónica, and Telia. Luxembourg P&T were still (by 2002) 100 per cent state owned.

intention that competition should be encouraged so that over time there would be a major decline in BT's market share (Littlechild, 1983; Carsberg, 1989, 1991). In the meantime, a regulatory structure – Oftel – was created to prevent monopoly abuse. However, weak regulation and a long period of transition from monopoly to competition meant that BT was able to maintain its dominant status comfortably during the years until full liberalisation of the European telecommunications market. The important issue here is that the British case was not so much about liberalisation initially as about privatisation (Thatcher, 1999c). The BT example, which is often regarded as a prime example of liberalisation, was in reality, therefore, 'just' a change from a publicly to a privately owned monopoly. The now former regulator, Oftel,[7] became instrumental in introducing a competitive regulatory regime only after the initial public offering.

On the other hand, although at a different pace and to a different degree, almost all the EU member states except UK decided to privatise primarily as a reaction to liberalisation. In other words, these countries decided to liberalise their market and open up for competition before or in parallel with the privatisation of their incumbent telecom operator. The typical moves here, therefore, were from cell (A) to cell (C), and then later towards 'the ideal' cell (D). If we define 1988 and the Terminal Equipment Directive (EEC/88/301) as the first sign of a clear movement towards competition within the telecommunications sector, the argument that the UK started privatising long before liberalisation was initiated at an EU level and that the rest of the EU countries started privatising more as a result of liberalisation, seems to hold. If we take a look at the table in appendix I, we can see that in 1987 all PTOs with the exception of BT were completely public owned.

These examples have a twofold message: First, that there is not necessarily a chronological development in changes in ownership structure and liberalisation. As we have seen, some countries, such as the UK, privatised their ITO at an early stage, long before experiencing a fully liberalised market whilst some privatised their ITO more as a result of market liberalisation (for example, Spain, France, and Norway). Furthermore, others liberalised their telecoms market at an early stage, but privatised at a late stage (for example, Sweden). Second, it is important to note that it is *real* competition that makes the difference. None of the European ITOs reveals further changes in organisational strategies (beyond ownership structures) in order to adapt to a competitive environment until they are exposed to actual market competition. Once ITOs experience actual competition, however, the earlier monopolists are forced to 'think market and competition', so that business strategy and efficiency become decisive (Monsen, 2004).

---

[7] From 1 January 2003 the duties of Oftel was inherited by Ofcom, which today represents the independent regulator and competition authority for the UK communications industries, with responsibilities across television, radio, telecommunications and wireless communications services (www.Ofcom.org.uk).

To sum up, privatisation can be expected to lead to a new logic of management and to major changes in internal organisation as a firm moves from the public to the private sector. This is typically associated with a movement away from rule-bound and centralised management to more local management accountability, profit centres and consumer awareness – developments that compel new logics of business strategies.

Business Strategies

If we take a look at the earlier monopolists we see that any form of strategy is almost absent, at least the kind of strategy defined within the sphere of business management, where the main focus is on strategy process, content and context (de Wit and Meyer, 1998) in relation to high performance evaluated by economic efficiency, market shares, customer satisfaction etc. The ability to operate in a competitive marketplace requires ITOs to take on a company structure that permits them to raise capital in the marketplace. Going from a monopoly situation towards market and competition obviously require new strategic goals for the firms. A typical indication on a first step towards such changes can be found in the annual reports of the ITOs after the full liberalisation of the European telecom market in 1998. The strategy is now described to 'create value for shareholders', 'keep a relentless focus on improving customer satisfaction' and 'achieve competitive advantage through cost leadership'(Belgacom, 1999; British Telecom, 1999; Telefónica, 1999; Telia, 1999). These are just words, however, and it is of superior interest to learn how the different ITOs actually have adapted their strategies to the changing regulations and a new, competitive marketplace.

In the early 1990s most incumbent ITOs were still 100 per cent state owned and operated as monopolists (appendix I). The main goal at this time was to protect (high) employment rates and to secure universal service obligations (USO). Also, because of cross subsidising, there was little transparency that could reveal inefficiency within the different business units. Further, because of little or no competition in the marketplace the monopolists did not have to focus on business strategy and efficiency. However, after the liberalisation of the European telecommunications market the situation changes. In particular, the ability to operate in a competitive marketplace required ITOs to take on a company structure that would permit them to raise capital in the marketplace.

During the period 1998 to 2001 significant changes in organisational strategy within each and all EU incumbents can be observed. Typical changes besides the shifting ownership structures are buyouts, sell-outs, and diversification, etc. In other words, gone were the times when telephone companies were like other regulated utilities with predictable earnings and stable corporate structures: Liberalisation of the telecommunications sector (that is, real competition) forced the incumbents to adapt to new management practices and new *strategies* were needed to handle the new competitive marketplace.

An interesting question in this regard is whether a certain composition of strategic actions can identify a pattern reflecting certain types of strategic orientation within the European ITOs. One way to make such an evaluation is to take a closer look at the operator's *cost accounting systems, the separation of new business, and the operator's degree of internationalisation.* These are all highly important issues when describing an ITOs strategic adaptation to the EU regulatory framework and thus, preparation for a competitive market place. High scores on these classifications correspond to a modern, flexible organisation able to adapt to grand transformations within the marketplace – like new regulatory reforms. Four ITOs will be studied in particular; Belgacom, British Telecom, Telefónica, and Telia. The time-perspective is 1998–2002,[8] which is within the period studied in this book.

Cost Accounting Systems

Cost accounting requirements in the liberalisation and open network provision (ONP) directives are intended to fulfil a primary function of preventing dominant suppliers from foreclosing market entry in certain segments by cross subsidising prices from other, less competitive, segments (European Commission, 2001). In order to enforce the tariff principles set out in the regulatory framework, National Regulatory Agencies (NRAs) must ensure that the cost accounting systems adopted by the operators are implemented in a transparent way. In particular that they show the main categories under which costs are grouped together with the rules used for the allocation of costs, especially with regard to the fair attribution of joint and common costs. Accounting separation is imposed specifically under the Interconnection Directive to ensure transparency where operators have special and exclusive rights for the provision of services in other sectors, and where SMP operators[9] provide interconnection services to other organisations (European Commission, 1998a).

Competition is first and foremost introduced on price. Rebalancing prices and controlling tariffs are seen as essential components in the stimulation of a competitive market. In order to determine the correct level of rebalanced prices, one first step is to adopt adequate cost accounting systems that will include

---

[8] In order to investigate the operator's *cost accounting systems, the separation of new business, the operator's degree of internationalisation and technological innovation*, the 'Report on the implementation of cost accounting methodologies and accounting separation by telecommunication operators with significant market power' prepared for the European Commission DG Information Society (Andersen Business Consulting 2002) is used, in addition to the reports on the implementation of the telecommunications regulatory package (European Commission, 1987; 1998a, 1999, 2000, 2001), Interconnection Directives (European Commission, 1998b and 1998c, European Council, 1997), and other written material as the Yearbook of European Telecommunications (CIT, 2002 and 2003). For a closeer analysis than given in this chapter see Monsen (2004).

[9] SMP operators refers to operators that hold significant market power (SMP), which at the time studied is defined to be 25 per cent or more of the relevant market.

account separation to reveal the real costs of providing specific services (imposed by the EU). The objective is to ensure that competitors and regulators understand the costs, revenues and capital employed by the incumbent and are able to challenge them, where necessary. Accounting separation also forces the company to show that prices for interconnection are based on relevant costs; whether cross-subsidising or discrimination is taking place; that the incumbent is charging itself the same interconnection rates it charges others and is fully recovering those charges and any other relevant costs in the retail prices it sets (Andersen Business Consulting, 2002). If correctly implemented, accounting separation and cost accounting should give competitors and regulators the confidence that no anti-competitive discrimination or cross-subsidies are taking place.

Only one out of the four incumbent telecom operators studied in this chapter – BT – follows most of the European Commission Directives and recommendations on cost accounting and accounting separation, although the other three are working on achieving greater compliance. In Belgium the NRA acknowledged in 2001 that it had interpreted the obligation of cost-orientation with reference to the practice in other Member States. The Belgian NRA considers that cost-orientation must in any case be implemented gradually taking into account its effect on the market. Belgacom's retention rates for fixed-to-mobile calls remain significantly higher than its equivalent termination rates. At the end of 2001 the NRA was having discussions with Belgacom in order to review these retention rates.

In Spain, the principles, criteria and conditions for the development of the cost-accounting systems of SMP operators are laid down in law (July 1999), and in 2000 an obligation on SMP operators to present their cost accounts by 31 July each year was established, in accordance with both its 1999 and 2000 cost accounts based on historic and current costs. The regulator considered that Telefónica met the above-mentioned requirements and criteria to a reasonable extent, that is, not too well.

End 2001 there were still concerns in the Swedish market about the lack of transparency of accounting information required for verifying accounting separation, cost orientation of end-user tariffs, and non- discriminatory pricing. This made it difficult to assess the cost structure and the degree to which end-user tariffs had been re-balanced. At the same time, several other operators in the market were still calling for the incumbent to be required to provide and publish relevant accounting information – at the very least its cost allocation and cost allocation principles – to show that cross-subsidisation was not occurring.

By 2001 BT had already implemented accounting separation, and its cost accounting system was generally seen as complying with Community law. As such it was one of the few Member States to have in place a cost-accounting system for interconnection for SMP operators based on forward-looking cost. By the end of 2001 all BT's accounts were subject to an independent auditor's report and were published in accordance with accounting policies and procedures agreed with Oftel. However, tariffs on voice telephony services, interconnection and leased lines were set by BT itself, and Oftel was only involved with regard to local loop unbundling. Obviously, this is a very important issue regarding the level of real competition in the marketplace

Separation of New Business

As 1998 drew near and the liberalisation process became fact, a restructuring of the ITOs can be observed. This aspect includes changes in the corporate strategy of the firm, that is, the way the firm organises its different business units (Andrews, 1971). Starting in the early 2000s developments within the telecom sector suggest that the ITOs seem to outsource the business areas to be subjected to competition into separate business units. A typical example is the way in which most incumbents sourced out their mobile operations into separate business units, or have even de-merged this business, as British Telecom did by turning its domestic and international mobile arm, BT Wireless, into an independent company, mmO2, in 2001. Mobile telephony is the area within telecoms that has been most exposed to competition (both with regard to time perspective and degree of competition). As will be seen, separation of businesses has become 'the rule' within all ITOs, although this has happened at different points in time within the different European telecom operators.

The partial privatisation of Belgacom in March 1996 was regarded as an unprecedented step by the Belgian government and took many observers by surprise. A 49.9 per cent stake was sold to the ADSB consortium[10] with the purpose of it acting as a strategic investor. Since then, the Belgian telecoms have settled into a firmer and quicker pace, as the Institut Belge des services Postaux et de Telecommunications (BIPT) and the former state monopoly Belgacom both work towards further liberalisation of the market. Nevertheless, as centre of the EU, Belgium has had a less than exceptional reputation with regard to the implementation of European competition legislation and policies. The Belgian Government only just made the EU liberalisation deadline of 1 January 1998, by means of a final legislative push. Three years on from full liberalisation, Belgian telecoms was finally emerging from the EU-state shadow as a force of its own rather than an EU enigma (PNE, 2001). With Belgium's position, due to EU activity, as a base for multinationals, the country was placed in prime positions as a potential major international telecom hub. New entrants pour into Belgium for this very reason and as of mid-2000 the market according to the BIPT consisted of 36 public network operators holding individual licenses, 27 non-public network operators, and more than 500 registered declarations of services (PNE, 2001). Although Belgacom still controls a majority of the market share on local, long-distance and international calls, the increase in competition from new entrants is taken seriously.

In 1998 and 1999 Belgacom worked on streamlining its operations and networks, introducing several new services. In 1999 the launch of Belgacom

[10] The ADSB consortium consists of Ameritech (35 per cent), Tele Danmark (33 per cent), Singapore Telecom (27 per cent) and three Belgian banks.

European Solutions, a new telecoms package supported by a managed ATM/SDH regional network with points of presence in France, Germany, the Netherlands, the UK, and Luxembourg, was designed to improve Belgacom's 'adjacent country' strategy to develop its business in neighbouring markets. The initiative was an attempt to capitalise on the increasing financial and economic integration of the EU. In 2000, two new services were added to this network: Extended Leased Lines Services for secure point-to-point connections and the Extended BiLAN Frame Relay Service which meets local area network (LAN) interconnection needs in Europe.

Since 2001, the activities of the Belgacom Group have been organised around four business units: *Wireline* – handling all fixed- line communications services; *Mobile* – dealing with mobile telephony services offered by the Proximus network of Belgacom Mobile and the Ben network in the Netherlands; *Carrier and Wholesale* – providing network capacity to other telecom providers in Belgium, international operators and Internet providers; and *Internet* – encompassing all the Group's Internet activities and related services (Belgacom, 2002). In addition, Belagcom has put all the other activities and subsidiaries of the Group under the heading 'Others'. This includes the turnover of subsidiaries such as Belgacom Services (coordination centre), as well as that of the subsidiaries that previously belonged to the Internet business unit and have not been attached to Wireline such as the Skynet portal activity, Eduline and Citius.

The year 1998 was a key one for both the Spanish economy and Telefónica. In January, the country's second fixed-line telephone operator Retevisión began offering interprovincial and internal services in competition with Telefónica. Meanwhile, the group began reorganising its shareholdings, developing a structure that enabled it to provide each business area with its own legal identity, and with clear profiles as regards shareholders' equity and earnings. As the parent company Telefónica SA became the corporate nucleus of the main subsidiaries, and these subsidiaries in turn acted as the heads of each separate business line. Towards the end of 1998 the company unveiled its new corporate image. The objective of the change in identity was to offer a single brand in all its markets. 1 December 1998 marked the effective deregulation of basic telephony, allowing new operators to set up in Spain and apply for licenses to provide this type of service. From this point on, all telecommunications services in Spain, without exception, are provided under a competitive framework. As from January 1999, the parent company transferred its domestic telecommunications business to another company, which adopted the name of 'Telefónica de España'.

The group's internal reorganisation also moved ahead, with assets continuing to be allocated among the various global business lines. In this respect, in January 2000 Telefónica, SA approved the creation of two new global businesses: Telefónica Móviles, which comprises all the group's mobile operations; and Telefónica DataCorp for the data and corporate services business.

Telefónica has an organisational model that aims to combine the versatility of operational autonomy for its Business Lines with the horizontal policies and benefits of synergies offered by a Corporate Centre. The Corporate Centre is responsible for the definition of global strategies and global corporate strategies; for the organisation of common activities (shared services, purchasing, logistics, and property management); and for the creation of support policies in areas including human resources, information systems, communication, marketing, finances and legal issues. Telefónica de España manages the fixed-line telephone business in Spain, whilst Telefónica Latinoamérica is responsible for carrying out the same kind of operations in Latin America. The mobile communications business worldwide is controlled by Telefónica Móviles SA, (except for Chile) which includes both the Spanish and Latin American markets and, to a lesser extent, those of the Mediterranean Basin. Two of these business lines played an important role in 2000: Telefónica Móviles, which was floated on the stock market and began to offer the first mobile internet services, and Terra, which acquired the US company Lycos to form the new Terra Lycos.

Apart from these lines of activity, Telefónica has a series of subsidiary companies (CIT, 2002) that are separate from its business areas and which offer value-added services: Telefónica R&D, financial companies (Fonditel and Antares), insurance companies (Pléyade), Shared Services (t-gestiona) etc. In this business model, Telefónica SA is the parent company of the Group, with its business being mainly carried out through subsidiary companies that are in turn responsible for the operations of other companies involved in the same business area (Telefónica, 2002). By using this structure the aim of the Group is to seek reciprocal development of the company and to ensure synergy between the different Business Areas

Sweden has had a liberalised market since 1975, but opportunities to compete with Telia were limited until responsibility for regulation was removed from the telecom operator in 1993. Televerket (now Telia) de facto held a monopoly in almost all services. Whilst there were no restrictions theoretically, in practice potential operators had to agree interconnection terms with Televerket, which was also responsible for all regulatory functions. The entrance of Tele2 in 1993 showed that it was eventually possible to negotiate terms, but that there still were considerable difficulties in reaching agreement. These difficulties in negotiations forced the separation of operational and regulatory functions, and in 1993 the Swedish National Post and Telecommunications Agency, Post- och Telestyrelsen (PTS), was established to regulate the telecoms sector, issue operating licenses and address questions of interconnection and frequency allocation[11] (Blackman and Denmead, 1996).

---

[11] Nevertheless, even after the establishment of PTS, Telia and Tele2 were only able to reach agreement on network interconnection following arbitration by a Swedish court four months afterTele2's original agreement with Telia. The PTS was heavily criticised by the Swedish audit office for naivety in expecting interconnection to stay within the commercial market.

However, it was not until the full implementation of the telecom regulatory programme of the European Commission after 1998 that Telia could expect real competition within the marketplace. As with all the other European ITOs until this point in time, Telia had never been under greater pressure in the Swedish fixed-line sector. At the end of 1999 it had an 87 per cent share of the market for fixed-line telephony services, which represented a slip of three percentage points from its position in 1998 (Telia, 1999). Whilst this may not seem a great decline, the list of strong competitors moving into Swedish telecoms presented the greatest threat yet to the operator's position. With competitors such as Tele2, Bredbandsbolaget (B2), Telenordia and Tele1, Telia was now forced to accept losses in the fixed-line market and to recognise the new competitive situation. Telia, therefore, entered the new millennium on an uncertain footing. Following the collapse of the planned merger with Telenor of Norway in December 1999 (Meyer, 2001), the company was left to pick up the pieces of its shattered pan-Nordic strategy. It was only in 2001 that Telia re-organised its business in accordance to a competitive marketplace.

Even though a number of organisational changes were carried out in 1999, 2000 and 2001, with operations shifting between the business areas, it was not until 1 April 2001 that a new Group structure was introduced (Telia, 2000). This had the aim of strengthening Telia's orientation and promoting internationalisation whilst laying the ground for Telia to participate in the restructuring of the industry. Before this re-structuring, Telia's operations were organised into five business areas, each having total responsibility for its respective products in all markets. These business areas were; Mobile, Carrier and Networks, Enterprises, Business Solutions and People Solutions. However, as the telecom market experienced an increase in competition, both at home and internationally, at the end of the 1990s, a new organisational structure was needed in order to strengthen the orientation and to promote internationalisation. The new business areas consist of; Telia Mobile, Telia International Carrier, Telia Networks, Telia Internet Services and Telia Equity and each continue to be responsible for their respective products in all markets (Telia, 2000, 2001). In addition, a joint sales and customer unit for consumers and business customers was established for the Swedish market to serve the business areas, indicating that Telia was focusing on its customers as would any other private business.

The British Telecommunications Act of 1981 transferred the responsibility for telecommunications services from the Post Office thereby creating two separate corporations. At this time the first steps were taken to introduce competition into the UK telecommunications industry. On 19 July 1982, the government formally announced its intention to privatise British Telecom with the sale of up to 51 per cent of the company's shares to private investors. This intention was confirmed by the passing of the Telecommunications Act, 1984.[12] The 1984 Act, in addition

---

[12] For a further description of BT's history see: www.btplc.com/Thegroup/BTsHistory/index.htm.

to providing for the company's privatisation, abolished its exclusive privilege of running telecommunications systems and established a framework to safeguard the workings of competition. This meant that British Telecommunications finally lost its monopoly in running telecommunications systems, which it had technically retained under the 1981 Act despite the Secretary of State's licensing powers, and that it now required a licence in the same way as any other telecommunications operator. The principle licence granted to British Telecommunications laid down strict and extensive conditions affecting the range of its activities, including those of manufacture and supply of apparatus, and is still subject to close scrutiny and review by the Director General of Telecommunications who is also head of the Office of Telecommunications (Oftel).[13]

It was not until 1991, however, that British Telecommunications made a real move towards a more open market. On 5 March, the government's White Paper on 'Competition and Choice: Telecommunications Policy for the 1990s' was issued. In effect, this ended the duopoly that had been shared by British Telecommunications and Mercury Communications in the UK since November 1983 and the build up to privatisation. The new, more open and fairer policy, enabled customers to acquire telecommunications services from competing providers using a variety of technologies. Independent 'retail' companies were permitted to bulk-buy telecommunications capacity and to sell it in packages to business and domestic users.

In the first quarter of 1991, following 12 months of reorganisation, BT unveiled a new organisational structure. The objective was to set up a commercial framework best suited to face the telecommunications challenges of the 1990s and one that would reflect the company's commitment to meeting customers' needs. However, not much happened in the way of a well-planned market oriented structure until beginning of the year 2000. Following a radical re-organisation in April of that year BT announced plans to begin operating via six distinct businesses, four global and two UK-based operating divisions (British Telecom, 2000; CIT 2002). The four global businesses; *BT Wireless* – an international mobile business emphasising mobile data and next generation services, *BT Ignite* – a worldwide broadband and internet network operation, *BT Openworld* –handling the consumer market for Internet products, and *Yell* – an international directories and e-commerce business, began operations 1 July 2000. Meanwhile, UK operations were reorganised into *BT Retail*, serving UK fixed-line customers, and *BT Wholesale*, responsible for marketing and fixed line products.

However, in the year to March 2001 the global downturn of telecoms stocks, coupled with the financial burden of the acquisition and costs of third-generation licenses in Europe and the UK, hit BT hard. By that date the net debt had increased

[13] From 1 January 2004 the duties of Oftel was inherited by Ofcom. Ofcom is the independent regulator and competition authority for the UK communications industries, with responsibilities across television, radio, telecommunications and wireless communications services (www.ofcom.org.uk).

to GBP27.9 billion, prompting an immediate change of strategy (CIT, 2002). In May 2001, as part of a new restructuring and debt reduction programme, BT announced a three for 10 rights issue (the UK's largest ever) to raise £5.9 billion and the sale of Yell for £2.14 billion (www.btplc.com). In November that year, BT Wireless – BT's mobile business, re-branded as mmO2 – was de-merged from BT on a one-for-one share basis. 16 November 2001 was the last day of trading in BT shares and on 19 November mmO2 plc and the new BT Group plc shares commenced trading separately (CIT, 2002). The de-merger of BT Wireless served to change the structure of the company again, whereby under the new organisation BT Group plc provides a holding company for the separately managed businesses that make up the group. These are *BT Retail*, *BT Wholesale*, *BT Openworld* and *BT Global Services*, each of which has the freedom to focus on its own markets and customers. In addition to these four business units, two support divisions are established; *BTexact Technologies*, including engineering and technology research and development, and *BT Affinitis*, which operates management consultancy services (CIT, 2003). The aim of this new corporate and divisional structure is to provide enhanced financial and operational flexibility.

The aim of separating into divisions is a better understanding of customers' needs, and so that BT can move quickly to seize opportunities and meet challenges. BT Exact, BT's research and development organisation, supports these businesses. This structure is meant to combine the strength of the BT Group as a whole with speedy and responsive individual business units, each of which has specialised knowledge of the markets in which it operates and of the customers it serves. The BT Group has re-focused its core activities on voice and data customers primarily based in the UK and elsewhere in Europe.

Internationalisation

Internationalisation is the third category describing the ITOs changes in organisational strategy as a reaction towards the liberalised telecommunications sector. Aggressive investments in international subsidiaries indicate that the incumbent telecom operators are aware of the changes in the marketplace involving the introduction of competition in the home market, and the new possibilities in the international marketplace.[14]

Between 1999 and 2002 Belgacom concentrated on establishing an international presence in Europe through its wholly owned subsidiaries in France, the UK, Germany and the Netherlands, as well as its 40 per cent stake in the Dutch telecom operator Tritone Telecom and its 35.3 per cent holding in the Dutch mobile operator Ben Nederland (CIT, 2002). Through the joint venture Combellga, Belgacom also has a presence in Russia, and more recently has begun establishing a presence in Asia. In March 2001 it signed an agreement with

---

14 For a closer description of internationalisation strategies see chapter 13, and with particular focus on Telenor, see chapter 10 of this volume.

Singapore Telecom to explore possible joint ventures in Europe and Asia. The two operators will also make use of each other's international networks to bring end-to-end telecommunications services to their respective customers. In addition, Belgacom has been in discussion with a number of companies over possible mergers including the Dutch ITO; KPN, and the French operator Cegetel.

The end of the 1980s and the decade of the 1990s also saw Telefónica expand internationally, with the company's businesses and services being extended to other continents, in particular to Latin America. In 1990, Telefónica acquired stakes in certain telecommunications network operators in other countries (CTC and Entel in Chile, and Telefónica de Argentina). A year later, the consortium in which Telefónica Internacional was a member was awarded the Venezuelan operator CANTV when it was privatised. Also in 1991, the company took control of Telefónica Larga Distancia of Puerto Rico. Other important successes were the award of a mobile telephony licence in Rumania and a radio-paging licence in Portugal.

Throughout 2000, Telefónica continued to strengthen its position as one of the leading players in the world telecoms market. Despite the poor performance by equities markets during the year, the company moved up the operators' ranking in terms of market capitalisation. The group's internal reorganisation also moved ahead with assets continuing to be allocated among the various global business lines. In this respect, in January 2000 Telefónica, SA approved the creation of two new global businesses: Telefónica Móviles, which comprises all the group's mobile operations, and Telefónica DataCorp, which covered the data and corporate services business that were added to the other three units created the previous year: Terra, Telefónica Publicidad e Información (TPI) and Telefónica Media. Later in year 2000 others were added such as Atento, Business to Business, and Emergia. At the same time Telefónica Latinoamérica was consolidated as the business line responsible for fixed telephony assets in Latin America (Telefónica de España for fixed telephony in Spain).

Telia's immediate response to the break-up with Telenor in 1999 was to redefine its priorities. The company announced that it would focus on the Nordic region, the Baltic States, Poland, Russia, and the larger markets such as the UK, the US, Germany, France, and Italy. Telia at this point in time also announced that it would also divest stakes in more distant markets such as Namibia, Uganda, Sri Lanka, India, the Philippines and China. This tighter regional focus was accompanied by a long-awaited initial public offering (IPO). The Swedish Government's sale of 30 per cent of its share in Telia in June 2000 represented the largest ever IPO in the Nordic region, and the third largest in Europe (PNE, 2001).

The realignment of Telia's business is in keeping with its recent strategy of strengthening its pan-Nordic mobile presence and its carrier business in Europe and the US. In June 2000 it acquired a 51 per cent stake in the Norwegian mobile operator NetCom ASA and six months later bought the remaining 49 per cent from Tele Danmark. In November 2000 NetCom was awarded a Norwegian UMTS licence, which supplemented the third-generation concession in Finland that Telia had won in 1999.[15] As part of its focus on Nordic cellular markets, Telia also withdrew from a number of international activities. In February 2001 it sold the Slovenian operator SiMobil to Telecom Austria and two months later finalised the sale of Tess (Brazil) to Telecom Americas. In June 2001 Telia was also in negotiations to dispose of its 35 per cent stake in the Irish operator eircom to the Valentina consortium, but has maintained its cellular interests in India, Namibia and Uganda.

Although BT's performance in the high-growth areas of wireless and the Internet (at least in terms of its home market in the UK) was unspectacular at the beginning of the new millennium,[16] BT started out as a strong investor in international businesses. During 1999–2000 BT outshone its peers in the creation of a wider-ranging pan-European portfolio of fixed telephony and mobile assets. It also attempted to consolidate these through the buy-out of local partners to gain majority control of these operations. Hence, in January 2000, BT took over Esat Telecom in Ireland, and in April the same year took over the remaining 50 per cent of Telfort, the second carrier in the Netherlands (originally formed with the Dutch railway company, Nederlands Spoorwegen). Furthermore, in August 2000, it bought a 45 per cent stake in Viag Intercom of Germany held by Eon, the utility company formed by the merger of Viag and RWE. This took BT's share to 90 per cent, with the remainder held by Telenor of Norway. Also, in August 2000, BT and Telenor bought out Tele Danmark of Denmark from the Telenordia venture in Sweden. In addition, by the end of 2000, BT's holdings in other key European markets remained minor: Albacom in Italy (where BT held 23 per cent), the Airtel cellular operation in Spain (17 per cent), Cegetel in France (26 per cent) and Sunrise in Switzerland (34 per cent). BT also made investments in Asia. At this point in time, all of these companies appear to have other partners or shareholders who seem more determined to stay the course in the telecoms business, which could seem to be the development in the 2000s.

After radical restructuring in 2000, however, BT set itself the goal of reducing its debt burden by sell-offs and de-mergers. BT off-loaded its international directories business Yell in May 2001, and this move followed the sale of its 17.8 per cent holding in Spanish Airtel to Vodafone. BT's efforts to slim down also

---

15 However, Telia's 3G ambitions suffered a setback in December 2000 when the Swedish regulator decided against awarding it an UMTS licence. Although Telia appealed against the decision, it did not take long before it signed a joint venture with one of the winners, Tele2, giving it the right to offer UMTS services in its domestic market.

16 BT's Cellnet cellular arm, over which it assumed full control in 1999 after buying out its partner Securior, has long trailed market leader Vodafone and was to fall to number three behind its nearest challenger Orange. As an ISP, BT's narrowband access business did not achieve the same prominence as equivalent telco-led operations such as T-Online in Germany, Wannadoo in France, Terra Networks in Spain, Planet Internet in the Netherlands or tin.it in Italy (PNE, 2001a), all of which were at that time (2000) among the top five European ISPs. BT was criticised for being slow to grasp the Internet's full position.

affected its activities in Asia. In March 2001 it was seeking a buyer for its 18 per cent stake in Singapore cellco StarHub and two moths later BT signed an agreement with Vodafone to sell its combined stakes in Japan Telecom and its mobile subsidiary J-Phone. In November, BT sold its 33.3 per cent stake in the Malaysian mobile operator Maxis, and in the same month completed the sale of its 44 per cent stake in the Indian mobile venture Bharti Cellular. Apart from these sales, in 2001 BT signalled a wish to dispose of its stakes in Cegetel and the Italian mobile operator Blu.[17]

Summary and Conclusions

Evaluating the findings from the earlier comparative analysis, Belgacom and Telefónica represent organisations that have continually searched for market opportunities and that regularly experiment with potential responses to emerging environmental trends. Such organisations are often the creators of change and uncertainty to which their competitors must respond (Miles and Snow, 1978). However, because of their strong concern for product and market innovations, these organisations are not completely efficient. All ITOs are organisations that operate in two types of product-market domains, one relatively stable (that is, networks) and the other changing (that is, services such as mobile, Internet etc.). However, only Telia and BT seem to have truly adapted to these conditions. In their stable areas these organisations operate routinely and efficiently through the use of formalised structures and processes. In their more turbulent areas, however, top managers watch their competitors closely for new ideas and then rapidly adopt those that appear to be the most promising (Miles and Snow, 1978).

Belgacom, which possesses no cost accounting separation and just some separation of new business, can only be described as an operator with a small degree of internationalisation, and even here its position seems to be more defensive than aggressive (Miles and Snow, 1978). Typical for such a strategy is to maintain a narrow and stable domain, as well as having a tendency to ignore developments outside of its sphere. Compared to Telefónica and Telia, Belgacom holds a small number of stakes in international subsidiaries. Telefónica on the other has little cost accounting separation, some separation of new business, and several international subsidiaries. Telefónica represents the ITO with the highest degree of internationalisation of the four incumbents studied, with its presence being especially high in Latin America. With regard to this indicator Belgacom obtain more a kind of defender position

Moreover, both Belgacom and Telefónica score medium high on separation of new business, not because these ITOs do not include business separation in their strategies, but rather because any separation seems to be quite unplanned. Typical for these ITOs is that their organisational structure appears to be in a

[17] During 2002 both Cegetel and Blu were sold off (CIT, 2002).

constant state of flux. The main problem is how to facilitate and coordinate numerous and diverse operations. Both Belgacom and Telefónica have changed their strategies for separation of business units several times during the years 1994–2001. This is not to claim that Telia and BT have not been indecisive with regard to separation of new business during this period, more that it would appear these two operators have finally arrived at a more stable organisational structure. Although not implemented until 2001, it seems as if these two ITOs have been able to create a better solution to the administrative problem than Belgacom and Telefónica, which is to differentiate the organisation's structure and processes in order to accommodate both stable and dynamic areas of operation.

Telia scores high on separation of business and internationalisation. However, Telia does not have an approved cost accounting system. Furthermore, at the end of the period under investigation (1998–2001) British Telecom (BT) is weakly represented abroad. Up until the beginning of 2001 BT had subsidiaries in several countries, but many were sold off because of BT's high debts, partly due to the downturn in the global telecoms market. By March 2001 BT found itself saddled with debts of GBP28 billion, mostly because of expensive overseas acquisitions and the cost of third-generation mobile licenses. BT's overseas subsidiaries were the first to come under scrutiny, particularly in Asia where it began the process of selling off virtually its entire portfolio. Although BT had subsidiaries in more countries before 2001, compared to at least Telefónica and also Telia, BT has always lagged behind with regard to internationalisation. Two possible reasons both relating to the issue of ownership structure, can explain this situation. Firstly, BT has a long experience operating as a private company, as it was 50 per cent privatised in 1984 and was fully privatised in 1996. Based on the argument that even partly privatisation is regarded as one way of changing the motivation of management to operate more efficiently (Newbery, 2001), it could seem as if BT has a more professional group of managers, that is, strategic decision makers. Secondly, since the state does not have any shares in the British operator anymore, BT cannot ask the British government for financial support. Compared for instance to Telia, where in 2001 the state still owned a 70.6 per cent stake in the ITO (appendix I), government 'support' is a minor problem. The ITOs who are still fully or partly owned by the state could seem to be more interested in investing in (expensive) international subsidiaries as long as they have the possibility to ask the state for financial support. International investments make them believe that their value on the stock markets will increase. However, BT has experienced otherwise, and consequently, BT's international strategy of keeping subsidiaries in a small number of countries might not be so unwise.

To sum up, it may be that the strategy implemented by Telia and BT is the most appropriate with regard to developments within the telecommunications sector. Typical for ITOs that experience major changes in organisational strategy is that some parts of their business have moved into a kind of 'revolutionary phase' (Mintzberg, 1998) and experience new challenges characterised by more flexible strategies in order to manage a dynamic environment. Other parts of the business, however, are still in a more stable stage, following 'old recipes' for strategic planning. It is also usual for companies with such a proactive strategy to operate in two types of product/market domains – one relatively stable, the other changing. In their stable areas, these organisations operate routinely and efficiently through use of formalised structures and processes. In their more turbulent areas, top managers watch their competitors closely for new ideas and rapidly adopt those that appear to be the most promising. The idea that new businesses do best when separated from their corporate parents is argued as being quite evident (Christensen, 1997; Day et al., 2001). Separation is a used model of choice when the new and the old differ greatly – a typical situation for traditional industry trying to catch up with new business. The telecommunications business is a clear example of such a traditional industry, where it is imperative that the natural monopoly and competitive segments of the relevant industry be effectively separated (OECD, 2000).

Where the experiences of companies that have failed to take advantage of innovations are studied several authors argue that new business should be kept far away from already existing business (for example, Christensen, 1997). Others argue that companies seeking both performance and growth should give entrepreneurial activities plenty of space but also that they should have access to their parent company's resources, knowledge and goals (Day et al., 2002). However, achieving such balance of separation and integration calls for the full range of organisational and leadership interventions: structure as well as management processes, human-resource policies, and corporate culture (Day et al., 2001). Such thoughts on how to handle strategy and structure in a turbulent environment in which the company wants maintain high performance in existing businesses whilst also producing high growth in new businesses reveals many new challenges. Planning and resource allocation processes designed for established businesses can wither away the prospects of a new one, which is where Brown and Eisenhardt (1998) would introduce the model of *competing on the edge* as a possible solution. The underlying logic behind competing on the edge is that strategy is the result of a firm's organising for constant change and letting a semi-coherent strategic direction emerge from that organisation (Brown and Eisenhartd, 1998). This is a very loose form of configuration that maybe even better described as a 'conceptual platform' always ready to handle rapid and unpredictable change. However, such flexible configurations give full priority to new businesses and could result in ruining existing business. Furthermore, leaders of existing business know that new initiatives may eventually replace them, and that it is often cash from core operations that finances innovative challenges. Thus, managers may for instance acquire illiquid assets to make their units harder to sell or distort news about the newcomer's success (Day et al., 2001). For such reasons, it often makes sense to place new and old businesses in separate entities and to limit the interaction between them. A major challenge though, is that this will push the recognition and selection tasks involved in innovation and business building up to higher levels of management. Chief executives must recognise new ideas wherever they appear, combine them with other ideas and give them an appropriate organisational form, without actually showing allegiance to either the old or the new business. Top managers are thus faced with the well-known problem of growing information overload (Barnard, 1938; Andrews, 1971). This is, however, not to say that it is impossible to both separate and integrate at the same time. From the end of 2001, all the four ITOs investigated in the earlier case studies seem to try managing both. The truly innovative activities are apparently being separated from the operating business units and moved to new business units, such as focusing on Internet and mobile services. At the same time, however, the ITOs develop a range of mechanisms that closely link existing business groups with the new venture, like coordination centres and separate R&D divisions. However, only BT seems to have introduced a solid system with regard to managing both separation and integration at the same time. The British telecom operator was not earlier than the other operators in changing their organisational structure, but it seems that once implemented, BT's organisation of the different business units, both old and new, has been more coherent.

Nevertheless, these are very new developments within all the four ITOs studied, and it is difficult to make any concrete suggestions concerning the outcome of new organisational forms, including concurrent separation and integration. It could seem like there is a war in which all the ITOs try to come up with the best fit between strategy and structure, but (as yet) no one has reached anything like a best-practice model of business strategy.

Appendix I

Ownership and privatisation of ITOs 1984 – end 2001

Incumbent	State share-holdings 1984[1]	State share-holdings 1992[2]	State share-holdings 1996[3]	State share-holdings 1998[4]	State share-holdings 2001[5]	Year of privatisation[6]
Telecom Austria (Austria)	100%	100%	100%	100%[7]	47.8%	1998[8]
Belgacom (Belgium)	100%	100%	51%	51%	51%	1995
Tele Danmark (Denmark)	100%	89%	51%	0%	0%	1992
Sonera Corporation (Finland)	100%	100%	100%	78.8%	53.1%	1998
France Telecom (France)	100%	100%	100%	62%	62%	1997
Deutsche Telecom (Germany)	100%	100%	100%	61%	58%	1996
OTE (Greece)	100%	100%	100%	65%	36%	
Eircom (Ireland)	100%	100%	100%	80%	0.4%	1996–97
Telecom Italia Infostrada (Italy)	100%	50%	42%	5%	3.46%	1992
Luxembourg P&T (Luxembourg)	100%	100%	100%	100%	100%	–
Koninklijke KPN (The Netherlands)	100%	100%	45%	43.8%	34.7%	1994
Portugal Telecom (Portugal)	100%	100%	71.7%	25%	11%	1995
Telefonica (Spain)	100%	35%[9]	20%	0%[10]	0%[11]	1991
Telia (Sweden)	100%	100%	100%	100%	70.6%	2000
BT (United Kingdom)	50.2%	22%	0%	0%	0%	1984

Notes

1 Annual reports on each incumbent telecom operator.
2 OECD Economic Studies No. 32, 2001/I.
3 Figures from the Briefing Report Series '1998 – A New Era for EU Telecoms Regulation' (Blackman and Denmead, 1996).
4 OECD Economic Studies No. 32, 2001/I.
5 Figures from *The Yearbook of European Telecommunications 2002* (Hatton et al., January 2002), and European Commission (2002a).
6 All sources in the above footnotes.
7 The mobile service subsidiary of the PTO (Mobilkom Austria AG) was partially privatised in 1997–98.
8 The mobile service subsidiary of the PTO (Mobilkom Austria AG) was partially privatised in 1997–98.
9 1991.
10 The Spanish state holds a 'Golden share' in the operator, which enables it to intervene in any major changes in shareholder structure.
11 The Spanish state still holds a 'Golden share' in the operator end 2001.

Chapter 13

Internationalisation

Kjell A. Eliassen and Birgitte Grøgaard

The deregulation processes within the previous public monopoly services in Europe, such as telecommunications, gas, postal services, electricity, water, and airlines have triggered a large wave of international expansion activities from the former monopolies. The drive towards internationalisation has been most prominent in the deregulation front-runner telecommunications sector, but has also gradually developed in the other sectors as the deregulation process has unfolded domestically. With some exceptions (Bonardi and Quelin, 1998; Bonardi, 1999; Sarkar, Cavusgil and Aulakh, 1999; Bonardi, 2004; Monsen, 2004; Cohen and Héritier, 2005), the strategic behaviour of former monopolists regarding internationalisation after the industries have been deregulated has received limited attention. The development has, on the other hand, been extensively covered in newspaper articles and non-academic management journals.

In general, there are limited studies focusing on liberalisation, corporatisation and/or privatisation processes and their effects on international business behaviour. Existing studies have primarily looked at the transformation process, the role of different actors, or the effects on public services in the different countries, thus overlooking the strategic choices facing former incumbents. The empirical evidence regarding these issues are also scattered and mainly not collected for scientific purposes. The national case studies contained in this volume will serve as one source of more systematic information about the internationalisation of the incumbents within the countries covered.

With regard to the European incumbents in telecommunications, they have already been focused on expanding their businesses to other countries from the first phases of the corporatisation process of the former state agencies. Some of the companies had also been involved in international activity in the field of satellite and fixed line activities, often mainly oriented towards former colonies or the international activities of their own national business clients, prior to the deregulation process. The large wave of internationalisation of the European telecommunications companies, however, started in the mid 1990s with the introduction of new mobile licences in all European countries and most other countries in the world. (For a detailed overview of the internationalisation processes of the mobile business in major European telecommunication companies see Monsen, 2004: 225–8.) Accordingly, the most rapid expansion of the international presence of the European incumbents has been in the mobile markets, both in the other European states and all over the world. There are also several examples of foreign expansion in fixed line, cable, directory services and Internet services, although they are not as substantial as in the mobile telephone sector. One obvious reason for the emphasis on mobile activities is the brand new character of this technology with few important incumbents involved in this business prior to the introduction of GSM (Global System for Mobile Communication) licences. The only exception in Europe is perhaps the Nordic telecommunications companies who were leading players in NMT (Nordic Mobile Telecommunications) wireless services. Furthermore, compared to expansion of the fixed line network, a rapid expansion of the GSM service due to the technology involved more moderate costs.

In general, this chapter focuses on the relationship between industry deregulation and the internationalisation strategies of former monopolists with the main empirical focus being on the internationalisation strategies in the mobile sector, specifically of the incumbent telecommunications companies in Western Europe. The effects of liberalisation and market opening is not only limited to publicly owned monopolies as heavily regulated private service industries in Europe show the same tendencies. 'The pattern of emergent renewal and herd behaviour is not necessarily restricted to large firms in the European telecommunications industry. Other European industries that were confronted with similar forces, may display similar results, as previous research has already revealed for the European financial services industry' (Volberda et al., 2001). The internationalisation of many of these industries, such as airlines, road transport, and shipping, as well as financial services, was made possible in Europe by the Internal Market legislation from the beginning of the 1990s. Internationalisation in the rest of the world was dependent upon the different rules and regulations in the WTO services liberalisation regime established by the Uruguay Agreement.

One important perspective in this volume is the consequences of change in the character and functioning of the principal over time. Initially change was introduced both by transforming the role of the state from combining ownership and regulation to the situation of an independent regulator and a corporatised state company, and then again following the change of ownership from state limited company through part privatisation eventually to a full privatisation of the companies. What impact have these changes in the role and functioning of the principal had for the development and implementation of the internationalisation strategies in the agent, the former public monopolies? Do state owned agencies or state owned limited stock companies have a different strategy compared to a listed company, and how do changes in corporate structure and ownership influence the internationalisation process? One central question is the availability of funds for international acquisitions in the case of a state agency compared to a state owned company and when the company is partly or fully privatised. Another is the role of the board versus the top management in internationalisation processes in incumbents, state owned corporations, and partly and fully privatised companies. In many countries we see gradual attempts at the professionalisation of the role of the state as an owner and one assumption that can be drawn from this is that during this decennium differences in the governing principles and practices related to internationalisation decisions have become less marked. Other important aspects to be dealt with are the type of internationalisation the services focused upon, the geographical focus, and the willingness to take risks.

Within the mobile telephone sector most internationalisation efforts in the early 1990s were green-field operations[1] where the operators competed for the right to get stakes in new companies in other countries – often without any auction involved: This process was dominant both in Europe and in the rest of the world. Licences were rewarded on the basis of a 'beauty contest' with some elements of political considerations involved. The focus was mainly on second or third licenses, normally after the incumbent had acquired its first GSM licence. During the 1990s there was also a growing interest in portfolio reorganisation and an increased willingness to buy into existing mobile companies so that it was critical to get as many licences as possible. The next phase, which is still in effect today, consists of attempts to rearrange the ownership structure in the new markets and to acquire full ownership or at least a majority position. If neither is possible the present tendency is to sell the stakes in the company in question. Telenor is a good case for studying all these different phases in the development of the mobile internationalisation process within former incumbents as it has shifted its international strategy accordingly. Finally, there is substantial variation among the incumbents in the geographical orientation of their expansion from a narrow regional focus to nearly global ambitions.

In sum, this chapter sets out to provide a general analysis of the changing patterns of internationalisation in former incumbent companies with special emphasis on the telecommunications sector. In addition it seeks to answer the questions of what are the different strategies employed by the companies, how are they linked to the changing role of the principal, and what are the roles of the regulators in this process both at home and abroad?

The Drivers for Internationalisation in Deregulated Industries

The deregulated telecommunications (and other former monopolists) have a drive for internationalisation primarily because of the realisation that competition would be introduced in their domestic markets. Oligopolistic reaction theories suggest that we can expect firms competing in the same industry to invade each others home markets (Graham, 1978) or see a chain reaction of internationalisation if one competitor starts to internationalise (Knickerbocker, 1973). Such reactive internationalisation patterns would, however, only continue until a certain market concentration has been reached (Flowers, 1976). For fixed line telephony in Europe, former monopolists have generally managed to retain

1 That is, establishing a new company as opposed to acquiring an existing company.

around 50–70 per cent of the market share several years after competition was introduced. The general argument put forward by the incumbents regarding their internationalisation is directly related to their need to increase their customer base to compensate for the reduced share of the home market and secure future growth potential. A broader customer base would not only generate revenues but also enable the development of new technologically advanced products where the declining size of domestic customers was too small, particularly for Norway and other small countries. Previous research supports the argument of an internationalisation drive among the major actors, the former monopolies, to keep their dominant positions in the sectors of telecommunications, gas, postal services, electricity, water, airlines etc. The companies have accordingly acquired or established subsidiaries in several foreign countries and/or entered into different types of regional or global alliances. This development started in the telecommunications and airline industries, but is currently visible in several other sectors that are still in the early phases of deregulation in many countries. Electricity and postal services are prominent examples of this (Bonardi, 2004). Despite the willingness to expand rapidly in deregulated markets abroad they seem to be reluctant to open up their home market, for example, Electricity de France (*Financial Times*, 24 May 2001) or complain vigorously of the tough treatment by the new independent regulatory authorities in the partly or fully deregulated home markets, (interviews with Telenor managers). In this way the former monopolists tend to display asymmetric behaviours. They impede the entry of foreign competitors in their own home market by using defensive political strategies, whilst simultaneously exploiting maximum access to foreign markets through actively lobbying their political institutions.

In any case, up to the start of the new millennium we have witnessed a strong drive for internationalisation of the telecommunication companies. Whilst the initial period after the deregulation in the early and mid 1990s was characterised by intense pressures for market access, for example, 'land grabbing', without significant long-term strategic focus, the quest for growth quickly came to a halt in the late 1990s. The market also experienced a sharp fall in the value of ICT companies around the turn of the century. Consequently, the sector has recently focused more on consolidation and restructuring of the portfolio to realise expected values. Firms have focused on expanding their customer bases in existing markets and increasing ownership in already established subsidiaries.

The development of the internationalisation process of Telenor is a good illustration of this, as indicated in chapter 10. Telenor had a rapid expansion of its global mobile business in Europe, former Soviet countries, and South East Asia in the middle and last part of the 1990s. The focus was primarily on speed of accessing new markets rather than on strategic long-term positioning in selected markets. Even though Telenor was only moderately hit during the collapse of the ICT sector, in the early 2000s the company refocused its strategy towards industrialisation of the strategically most important mobile assets rather than on further geographic expansion. The primary strategic objective has thus become to extract synergies and realise values from existing investments. One of the key instruments to achieve this has been a targeted effort to increase ownership in selected subsidiaries in order to gain control and influence, or to exit markets where this is not a feasible or an interesting option. To secure the influence and control that is central for Telenor's current strategic direction, the most recent expansion into Pakistan has been entered into as a wholly owned venture. Similar developments can be seen in other European incumbents such as France Telecom and British Telecom as shown in other chapters in this volume[2].

For many incumbents the success and failures of the investments in large foreign mobile companies have implications of financial magnitude that are more important than the traditional running of their business at home, as for example in the sale by Telenor of its minor sakes in a German and Irish mobile operator with a two digit billon NOK profit. In many countries it was easier to get funding for a rapid international mobile expansion as a fully state owned company than as a privatised company. The state generally held a consistently long-term perspective, allowing for substantial strategic flexibility. Private shareholders, on the other hand, have so far been much more short-term oriented, pressuring the firms to deliver visible results in order to secure their own investments. This has put significant pressure on the firms to focus on efficiency, synergies and consolidation rather than continued expansion.

Before entering into a more detailed study of the process of internationalisation of the European telecommunications incumbents in the 1990s, it is necessary to review the theories behind firm internationalisation in general. The interface of economics, organisational science and strategy can guide us into a more comprehensive understanding of the logics behind this development.

Internationalisation Theories

We have extensive literature focusing on why and how firms internationalise, particularly emphasising decisions about entry into new markets and whether to internalise or contract activities. What can we then learn from this literature and these theories regarding the internationalisation process of former public monopolies in a deregulated business environment?

The majority of studies of internationalisation processes have grown out of an economic tradition (Buckly, Burton and Mirza, 1998) focusing on how firms can exploit ownership and location advantages. Dunning (1988; Dunning, 1977) incorporated these perspectives into a framework, the eclectic paradigm, which suggests that firms' internationalisation patterns depend on the combination of their potential ownership, localisation and internalisation advantages. Ownership advantages reflect particular assets or resources within the firm that are owned and

2 The development occurred at an earlier stage in BT as the company privatised and professionalised its management.

controlled by the firm, and all firms require some type of ownership advantage in order to remain competitive in the long run. Examples of ownership advantages include competencies, technology, information, brand names and capabilities. The advantage of these resources must outweigh the potential 'cost of foreignness'[3] and enable the firm to compete on a par with local firms (Benito and Tomassen, 2003).

For firms with ownership advantages, the decision of where to locate activities is central when internationalisation is considered. Location advantages reflect benefits of locating operations in certain geographical areas, such as access to raw materials, competence, lower labour costs, good infrastructure and distribution channels. The type of advantage largely depends on the firm's motive to internationalise. In other words, whether it is market-, resource-, efficiency- or strategic asset-seeking (Benito and Tomassen, 2003). Despite the existence of ownership and location advantages, however, it is not certain that the firm will benefit from internalising its activities. Transaction cost theory suggests that firms should primarily use the market (that is, contract with other actors that specialise in a given area) unless there are specific advantages of internalising the activities (Williamson, 1975). Advantages of internalising activities are highly related to control needs and risk willingness. For activities with high degrees of uncertainty and asset specificity[4] or low transaction frequency, firms may benefit from internalising the activities to maintain the necessary control and reduce potential transaction costs (Williamson and Ouchi, 1981).

When we use the eclectic paradigm to understand the internationalisation process in the mobile telephone industry better, we see that the former monopolies had managed to develop strong ownership advantages such as competence, technology, and experience with successful distribution channels. Furthermore, several former monopolies found location advantages primarily in terms of developing strong customer relationships and local distribution channels. The location advantages were highly influenced by market seeking motives. The degree of internalisation varies, however, partly due to industry characteristics (for example, the pressure for consortiums to win the 'beauty contests' for new licenses) and partly due to the firm's individual focus on control and risk. It is interesting to note that all incumbents actively used joint ventures to enter new markets (reducing their degree of control through internalisation) regardless of whether the firm was more risk willing, such as Telenor, or had a stronger focus on risk and returns such as BT (see chapter 7). This suggests strong industry pressures for joint ventures to access available partners. These joint ventures not

---

3 The term 'cost of foreignness' is here used to include any additional cost related to operating in a foreign country such as lack of local knowledge, experience or customer recognition, transportation costs, tariffs, etc.

4 Such as site specificity, physical asset specificity, human asset specificity, dedicated assets, brand name capital or temporal specificity (Williamson, 1981).

only secured a combination of top international expertise but also often required a strong presence of local partners.

In the economic tradition, internationalisation decisions are often seen as discrete and independent. A number of studies have increasingly focused on behavioural factors where internationalisation is treated more as an ongoing process. The internationalisation patterns are thus influenced by the firms' accumulated experience and knowledge (Johanson and Wiedersheim-Paul, 1975; Johanson and Vahlne, 1977) and characteristics of their internal decision making processes (Aharoni, 1966; Björkman, 1990). In general, the internationalisation process perspective argues that firms initially tend to internationalise to geographically and culturally close markets and to expand gradually into more distant markets (Johanson and Vahlne, 1977). Firms in highly regulated industries, however, are more influenced by external factors that determine which markets are available. We would thus not expect the same internationalisation patterns in these industries, which the analysis of Telenor and the mobile telephone industry confirms. As the previous case analyses suggest, most incumbents engaged in 'shopping frenzies' to access licenses, regardless of geography. Belgacom represents an exception to this as the company primarily internationalised in close markets (Vanhoucke, 2006) shows in his chapter in this volume. This seems to be a result of more precautious and modest bidding, however, than of a strategic focus on culturally close markets.

Closely linked to a more general investigation into the role of ownership is an analysis of the impact of ownership on the ability to fund the internationalisation process. Here it is important to consider how willing the states as owners are to invest in a rapid international expansion of the company compared to a situation where there are some or only private owners. Indeed there seems to be a tendency that public owners are more willing to put up capital for foreign investment than private owners in a listed company. At least several of the European incumbents reduced their foreign investments substantially with the introduction of private owners in the companies; again Telenor is a good example.

The Internationalisation Strategies

What type of strategies do the telecommunications companies pursue in their internationalisation efforts? How do they do it? Once the firm has decided to internationalise, there are a number of different internationalisation strategies that greatly affect how the firm operates across national borders. In this chapter we discuss international strategy as 'the way in which the organisation positions itself with regard to the global business environment and creates and sustains competitive advantages across national boundaries' (Harzing, 2002: 212). The integration-responsiveness framework is by now commonly accepted for examining firms' international strategies (Prahalad, 1976; Prahalad and Doz, 1987). Accordingly, firms must choose whether to integrate activities globally or respond to local needs. Bartlett and Ghoshal (1989) further introduced transnational and simple international strategies where MNCs attempt to compete successfully by combining high global integration with high degrees of local responsiveness (transnational) or without significant strategic focus on either global integration or local responsiveness (simple international). Consequently, four commonly accepted and empirically tested strategies can be identified from the integration-responsiveness framework: global, multidomestic, transnational and simple international firms (Porter, 1986a; Martinez and Jarillo, 1991; Segal-Horn and Faulkner, 1999), as shown in Figure 13.1.

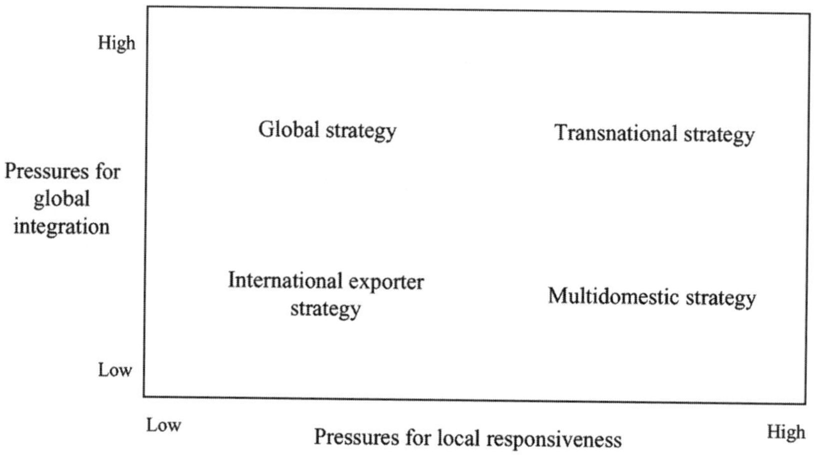

Figure 13.1 International strategies

Sources: Prahalad and Doz, 1987; Bartlett and Ghoshal, 1989.

Organisations pursuing a global strategy typically strive for strong internal cohesion across national borders. This often requires higher levels of headquarter control and coordination over ongoing activities (Bartlett and Ghoshal, 1989; Hall and Taylor, 1996), and emphasis on integrating value activities (Yip, 1989) standardisation, and efficiency (Levitt, 1983; Harzing, 2002). Creating cross-border synergies often necessitates a more centralised key decision-making in order to integrate value activities effectively across borders (Fairbrother, 1998). Multidomestic strategies, on the other hand, treat national markets as detached from each other and induce firms to adapt products, services and policies to local market needs (Fairbrother, 1998). MNCs with multidomestic strategies typically function as decentralised federations with autonomous subsidiaries (Hill, Hwang and Kim, 1990; Harzing, 2002). This in turn may lead to some replication within the MNC as units in each local market operate independently of other internal units.

Transnational strategies incorporate both global and local dimensions by approaching the organisation as an integrated network, thereby placing less emphasis on dyadic headquarter-subsidiary relationships. Transnational strategies, assume a high degree of strategic coordination and extensive communication flows to benefit from the global integration of certain processes whilst simultaneously allowing sufficient local adaptation (Bartlett and Ghoshal, 1989). Power and influence thus results from the individual units' competence, experience and strategic importance within the MNC rather than from its geographic or organisational position. Finally, firms with international strategies often also localise activities in foreign countries but the activities are typically motivated by following existing clients abroad or as a response to international customers approaching them (Segal-Horn and Faulkner, 1999).

When using the international strategy framework to identify the corporate level strategy of the former incumbents under investigation, the internationalisation strategies of the former telecommunications incumbents can in most cases be described as a multidomestic strategy. This multidomestic focus seems to result from the industry characteristics of license awards where firms entered into consortia of multiple firms, often with a significant local partner, to signal local commitment to the regulatory authorities. As the case studies in previous chapters illustrate, the former incumbents have repeatedly entered into joint ventures for their international expansions. The individual firm's degree of direct control in the local company was thus often reduced to a minimum. In some cases, such as Telenor, firms have later tried to adapt a transnational strategy, but with rather limited success. Although there seems to be an increasing global focus among competitors, such as British Telecom and Deutsche Telecomm, there are few if any companies with a truly global strategy (where some mobile companies like Vodafone are mentioned as exceptions). There are several reasons for this. First of all, implementing a true global strategy is very costly, particularly when the initial investments have led to highly autonomous local subsidiaries. In addition, the ability and willingness of MNCs to carry out a strict integrative or 'industrial' strategy[5] in the different subsidiaries varies all over the world. Furthermore, Bonardi (2004) argues that the asymmetric behaviour found in former monopolies of protecting their home market whilst simultaneously internationalising in foreign markets primarily results from lacking cooperation between governments. This external barrier can also lead to firms experiencing difficulties in pursuing global strategies successfully as implementing common management and control processes across national boundaries. Interviews with managers in Telenor also revealed variations in the degree of buy-in to actually implementing global efficiencies and synergies through more stringent control and coordination mechanisms. In general, firms often overlook the feasibility and costs of implementing strategic change (Jemison and Sitkin, 1986).

---

5 The global integration strategy was referred to as an 'industrial strategy' by several interviewees indicating an effort to achieve synergies across activities and locations.

In general, firms choose operating modes that are aligned with their strategic focus (Hill, Hwang and Kim, 1990) or to minimise uncertainty and thus potential transaction costs (Williamson, 1975, 1979; Anderson and Reeb, 2003; Hill, Hwang and Kim, 1990). Firms pursuing global strategies thus generally seek high levels of control, often exercised through greater ownership (for example, wholly owned foreign units). On the other hand, firms pursuing multidomestic strategies generally choose operating modes with lower control (for example, alliances with local partners). Hence, we can expect the internationalisation patterns to reflect the risk willingness of the owners (principals). With a change from public to private ownership structures, however, we can expect internationalisation patterns to shift as private investors generally tend to pursue more short-term financial goals that could pressure firms into geographic locations and operating modes that minimise risk. The early privatisation of BT, where the private owners pursued a more 'professional management' by placing greater emphasis on the degree of risk and expected returns, supports this argument.

The Internationalisation Process in Telecommunications Companies

Most former European incumbents, like Telenor, started their internationalisation processes in the mobile sector just after the introduction of GSM services at home. For Telenor the internationalisation process started in 1994, even before the corporatisation of the company in 1995. It had, however, a previous history of internationalisation dating back to the 1980s with both satellite and global alliances. The new drive for mobile internationalisation at the beginning of the 1990s was followed by the internationalisation of both directory and Internet services. In both cases, however, the company has now divested itself of these business areas because they have chosen to focus the company on mobile services – at least outside Scandinavia – and indeed mobile remains by far the most important internationalisation activity, together with satellite and a limited amount of fixed line ownership in Scandinavia and Russia.

In order to determine how general this pattern was throughout Europe we need to ask some basic questions about the internationalisation strategy linked to the different theories and assumptions in the literature. First of all: which business areas were internationalised? Was it only the mobile telephone sector or was it other business areas as well? Why do we, in most cases, find this strong emphasis on mobile internationalisation? Secondly: which foreign markets were entered? Is there any particular logic behind the selection of the geographical dimension of the expansion of especially the mobile telephone business? How did they do it and what was the mode of entry in the different markets for mobile telephone communications? After addressing these issues we turn to the question of the more detailed links between internationalisation patterns of mobile telephone companies and the regulatory regimes in the different countries of the world.

What Businesses Firms Internationalise

For all the former incumbents in Europe mobile services are the most important part of the internationalisation process after GSM was introduced in 1992. In 1994, wireless communications accounted for only 9 per cent of revenue in the sector (Stienstra et al., 2004) whereas today it accounts for more than 50 per cent and the number of mobile users recently surpassed the number of fixed line users in the world. Thus, the expected growth in this sector made it a logical choice for global expansion for the West European telecommunications operators that had world-class competence within this technology and had already been involved in a rapid development of this technology in their respective home markets. Other public services like postal services, railways etc. did not possess such unique technological advantages for leading a rapid international expansion in their fields. Even so these industries have followed an internationalisation track similar to that of the telecommunications companies, albeit more modestly.

Internationalisation of the mobile business was partly driven by economies of scale. Even for the big incumbents in the larger European countries, the home market was no longer sufficient to offer cost effective mobile services while deregulation also lead to an increasing number of new entrants. Hence, internationalisation became a necessity for most firms merely to maintain the same revenue levels as before deregulation. Growth to increase size and scale of operations was also seen as helpful for remaining independent in this dynamic industry (Marino, 2005). New entrants were typically large actors, such as Vodafone and Orange, the foreign subsidiaries of other incumbents, such as Singapore Telecom, and many small players. The two large companies, Vodafone and Orange, entered the European national home markets quickly in order to destroy the strongholds of incumbent operators in leadership positions (Stienstra et.al. 2004).

National regulators often supported the new entrants in order to gain a more competitive edge in the telecommunications sector as soon as possible (Information Society, 1997). This subsequently increased the pressure on the incumbents for both new advanced products at home and to increase the number of customers abroad to create a larger customer base to share the development costs.

Where Do They Go?

The Western European markets represented the most well known arena for the incumbents, and became the first choice for both green-field operations and acquisitions for several incumbents, as shown in this volume. The European Economic Area (EEA) including both the EU and the EFTA countries had the general advantage of establishing a pan-European telecommunications regulatory framework (Eliassen and Sjovaag 1999). At the same time the EEA represented markets with a high degree of competition and very advanced and demanding users. These countries were the prime targets for the incumbents' strategies for internationalisation, although emerging markets and very underdeveloped markets such as South East Asia and Latin America were alternative arenas for expansion, representing somewhat less competition from other European players due to higher risks and uncertainty. Nevertheless, several of the European incumbents tried to enter one or several of these markets in the late 1990s. Telenor was one of the most active companies in South-East Asia. Asian countries represented a substantial growth potential long after the penetration rate would have passed 100 per cent in Western Europe. Central and Eastern Europe also fell into this category, but had the additional advantage of being closer to home and with most of these countries rapidly trying to adapt to the common EU regulatory telecommunications framework. This was an important element in their attempt to prepare for later EU membership. Some countries, like Russia and the Ukraine, were not expected to become members of the EU, but were still big, emerging markets close to home which made them interesting. Other emerging markets represented the advantage of being former colonies with historically strong links to the European power in question, like France. Some also had a long history of fixed line telecommunication cooperation or as main partners for developing aid such as some African countries where Telia was involved. These explanatory elements are also found in the internationalisation drive from other former monopoly sectors like electricity.

How Do They Do It?

Historically, the only international cooperation among European telecommunications incumbents was cooperation on standards, international connections, and regulation of the cross border tariffs and payment systems. The same holds true for other heavily regulated service industries like railways, airlines, and electricity. From the end of the 1980s, new levels and types of cooperation developed first and foremost in telecommunications and airline industries. The new trend was global strategic alliances. This was to a large extent a first reaction from the dominant players, mainly in the US and Europe, to try to continue to dominate their particular sector even in a more deregulated environment whilst still serving their multinational clients – now on a global level. In the airline industry this has been very successful and has today developed into a situation where there are basically only three international airline alliances, Sky Team (with Delta, Northwest and Air France as the most prominent members), One World (with American and British Airways) and Star Alliance (with United, Lufthansa and Scandinavian Airlines amongst others). These totally dominate the industry and nearly all the major international players in the industry are members. Within the telecommunications industry these kinds of alliances were previously very popular, like MCI and BT forming Concert in 1994; and France Telecom and Deutsche Telecom with Sprint forming Global One. Indeed, such developments seemed a necessity to win licenses and gain access new markets, as previously discussed in terms of strategies to enter new markets. Today these alliances are either dissolved or of minor importance. The main reason behind this difference seems to be the various stages of global and regional/national deregulation in these two industries. The airline industry is still regulated, especially at the global level, and is not able to develop a fully competitive market with a natural reorganisation of the company structure. Only inside the EEA we have seen some tendencies towards a restructuring of the industry with some bankruptcies (Swissair and Sabena) and some mergers and acquisitions (Air France and KLM). In telecommunications the WTO rules and the further liberalisation in different regions and countries have facilitated rather substantial company reorganisations – even if most of the former European incumbents still exist as independent companies. With privatisation, firms are increasingly seeking efficiencies and more calculated risk and returns, leading to consolidation of activities and sales and acquisitions of ownership shares in existing licenses. The need for the alliances of the 80s and early 90s is no longer there. In some sectors, such as mobile, more product-oriented alliances, for example, cross-boarder service of business clients, has been developed in Europe to meet the pan European competition from Vodafone and Orange. Entering into such long-term international alliances has not, however, been a typical pattern in any segment of telecommunication internationalisation. The strategy has rather been investment-oriented by establishing, buying, or merging portfolio reorganisations etc.

Regulation, Competition and Internationalisation

The next question addressed in this chapter is the link between the regulatory framework and changes in the role of the principal in relation to the internationalisation strategies pursued by the former incumbents, first and foremost the changes from state ownership to partly or full liberalisation. It seems like the willingness to risk an unclear political, legal and regulatory environment was much higher in a situation with the state as an owner than with private owner in the company either in a majority or even in minority. The listing of the companies made the predictability and rationality of internationalisation decisions much more in demand.

It could be argued that internationalisation in emerging marked for telecommunication companies is mainly a question of regulation not products, marketing and organisation. Outside EU and a few handful of Western countries telecommunication companies faces substantial and persistent regulatory problems. The focus on regulation and the wider regulatory framework is a continuous challenge for the former incumbents expanding into these rapidly growing markets. They often arrive with an extensive experience from dealing with regulatory issues in their own countries, but these experiences often prove to be rather useless in an Asian or African framework with its mix of law and politics, lack of solid legislative basis, corruption and a very slow and not incremental development in these issues. Local companies with long experience of dealing with this political and legal framework are better suited and situated to cope with all these problems and hurdles. On the other hand it seems as if having local partners is not always a remedy for reducing these problems. In any case these problems often create a persistent unclear market situation with a legal framework at the best fragmented and unclear and with no efficient regulatory authority to intervene in the market situation.

This situation could be foreseen when entering into these markets, but on the other hand a thorough legal scrutiny would most likely only lead to missed market opportunities. For example, Telenor was able with little or limited legislative scrutiny undertaken to enter into markets which even 10 years later are characterised by a high level of legal uncertainty and limited power of regulatory agencies, but nevertheless developed a very successful business case in these countries. Another example is BT who undertook a very comprehensive legal scrutiny when faced with the same business opportunities as Telenor, but due to perceived legal complexity and uncertainty did not exploit the business opportunities in some of the emerging markets in the same way.

The Internationalisation Strategies

This chapter has addressed questions related to the importance of changes in the role and position of the principal in pursuing internationalisation strategies in the incumbent public utilities in Europe, focusing mainly on telecommunications companies. The main questions examined were why, how, and with what kind of ownership involvement the newly corporatised or partly or fully privatised company embarked upon an internationalisation journey.

Our analysis confirmed the very close link between the regulatory environment at home and abroad, the ownership structure and the strategies pursued by the incumbents in a gradually liberalised foreign and domestic environment. The drivers for the internationalisation process were the opening up of the home market and the need for compensating reductions in market shares at home by acquiring new customers abroad. In this respect, the companies in question were to a large extent dependent upon a symmetric reduction in the regulatory restrictions in other countries. The European Commission was very much aware of this, and when Telefonica tried to acquire shares in telecommunications companies in other countries, the European Commission forced the Spanish government to open up the Spanish market for free competition.

Regarding the question of why the former monopolies started an internationalisation process, this chapter has provided indications for three main reasons: 1) the basic logic of compensating for reduced market share at home by expanding into new markets; 2) a special case of number 1 where the incumbents to try to create a large enough market globally to have an economic base for the cost of rapid technological development and the development of new products. This reason was particularly relevant for incumbents with small home markets; 3) to be able to continue to dominate these sectors even after they have lost their monopoly position at home and thus being even better able to serve the big multinational clients. The latter was also the reason behind the first wave of telecommunications internationalisation in the 1980s. We then witnessed internationalisation both in the development of satellite communications and in the development of global telecommunications company alliances. In the next phase, the idea behind internationalisation, especially in the state agency and corporatised state owned limited company period, was simply to continue purchasing what was available – without a detailed analysis behind where and how to get involved. The internationalisation patterns show a primary focus on 'land grabbing' as new opportunities emerged rather than developing a clear internationalisation strategy. This approach to internationalisation has later proved to limit the firms' strategic flexibility as the foreign subsidiaries have initially developed a high degree of autonomy that is both difficult and time consuming to reverse.

The rapid expansion of the internationalisation process of Telenor was very closely linked to the IPO and the need to dress the bride as beautifully as possible. The generous funding willingness of the Norwegian state as an owner made this possible. The funding available and the willingness to continue a rapid international expansion were substantially reduced after the company was partly privatised in 2001. There seems to be a tendency that the state as an owner is more willing to take risks in pursuing foreign investments than private owners, both in a partly and fully privatised company. It is argued that private ownership also introduces a greater degree of 'professional management' in terms of focusing on analysis of risk and returns (Marino, 2005). The expectations of both private owners and investment advisors of return on capital, low risk, and predictability thus tend to result in a more conservative international expansion strategy.

Chapter 14

Conclusion: Incumbent Company Transformation – How Far and Why

Kjell A. Eliassen and Johan From

Introduction

In this chapter we will try to outline some of the basic findings from this volume. The main topic of the book has been to unveil how the transformation of Western European telecommunications companies from state agencies to listed companies took place, what were the main stages and dimensions of change and what were the driving forces behind this development? The transformation of the incumbents in this book is studied primarily over a period of 15 years from the mid- to late 1980s until the turn of the millennium. The transformation process continues, however, and there are clear signs of an intensified internal dynamism in the business development pattern of these companies. The trend in the last two years towards more private owners, public listing and even the complete takeover of former incumbents by investment funds is also briefly commented upon even if the focus is on the previous 15 years.

Summing up

The analyses in this volume start, however, with a situation where we can identify three basic drivers for the tremendous company transformation taking place over a rather short period of time. The first is the total change in the regulatory regime in Europe from state monopolies to more or less fully liberalised and deregulated telecommunications markets, second there is the corresponding introduction of EU competition rules and regulations in this area, and finally there is the change of ownership from state ownership to different degrees of private ownership of the former incumbents. As we have shown in this volume, these developments are interrelated, but not totally dependent on each other whereby one does not necessarily imply either of the others. In addition no theoretical logic or legal argument existed, for example, in the EU rules and regulations did not say that liberalising the market requires the privatisation of the former monopolists. Most European governments assumed that they could retain the state ownership of the national telecommunications companies even if they liberalised the telecommunications markets. The strategy to achieve this was through the corporatisation of the former monopolists into stock companies to make them better able to compete in the market place. The government would then own all the shares in the newly established limited companies. It turned out, however, as discussed in chapter 12, that within less than 10 years nearly all of the former incumbents in Europe had been either fully or in most cases partly privatised. It would seem that the exposure to market forces and the need to compete with professional private companies in the market place also increased the pressure to introduce private ownership and listing on the stock exchanges for the new fully state owned limited companies. In addition budget problems in some of the EU member states provided an impetuous to sell off part or all of the very valuable state companies.

The deregulation and then the necessary process of a substantial reregulation of the telecommunications sector in Europe was, as we have seen in conflict with the idea of creating a truly liberalised market in Europe that would be only governed by EU competition rules. To have only basic competition rules as the governing principle for the telecommunications and ICT sector in general was definitely in contrast to the vision of many of the EU competition officials, and as this book has shown, the situation today is as far away from the ideal situation as it was when the liberalisation process first started. The ICT sector will require special sector regulation for the foreseeable future due to the special characteristics of this sector and the need for both regulation of an imperfect market, social concerns and interoperability and quality. Furthermore, a complicating matter in relation to the framework of company transformation is that the framework itself changes over time as government ownership is established, professionalised and eventually diluted, old regulation is replaced with new regulation and the significance of competition policy is increasing.

The essence of this volume has been to discuss these three characteristics of the transformation process, ownership (chapter 3), regulation (chapter 4) and competition (chapter 5) and to use these aspects to frame and to try to explain some of the company transformations and systematic variations in the transformation process identified in the empirical case-studies of France (chapter 6), Britain (chapter 7), Belgium (chapter 8), Germany (chapter 9) and Norway (chapter 10).

When first approaching the transformation process in telecommunications, the process can easily be regarded as a 'black box' in which the traditional telecommunications operators enter and eventually exit fundamentally transformed. In order to start to approach the mechanisms and change processes taking place and to identify fundamental questions and problems, a principal–agent framework proved helpful. The theory stressing divergent interests and asymmetrical access to information between the actor with a task to assign and the actor allotted to the task, has enabled us to identify central factors in the transformation process: The shifting and often ambiguous interests of the government attempting to balance societal concerns with business development;

the developing companies with self-interests that can collide with those of the government; and the relation between the parties where it is not always clear which is the dominant actor. These aspects were intended to direct attention towards the central question of the book: How was the transformation of European telecommunications companies brought about?

Chapter 3 sets out to establish the significance of ownership for the transformation processes and shows that much research has demonstrated the significance of different forms of ownership for company output. These are obviously valid and important findings. However, the fact that the important parts of the transformation processes in the telecommunications sector in many countries have happened under state ownership spurred the interest of investigating the conditions for developing a firm under state ownership. The BT case with private owners from the outset on serves as an interesting contrast to this and chapter 7 points to the need to refine our view on state ownership. Just as there are different types of private owners with various characteristics and interests, the state as an owner can differ over time and between countries. A traditional state owner can be compared to a dominant private owner, except that political interests enter the decision making processes. In the transformation process, the state as an owner aims at becoming a professional owner and economic and social regulation is gradually established in order to create a market and secure societal concerns. Yet, many of the issues that arise during this process are infused with political values: downscaling of the workforce, equal access and pricing throughout the country, and the company's mission and role in the national industry continue to attract politicians' interests. Interestingly enough, we see much of the same pattern in the British case under private ownership: Political issues continue to be vital. The main lessons to be learned are that the investigation of how ownership is carried out can be more enlightening than the study of ownership characteristics. This can be witnessed in the transformation process in that similar (state) ownership can nevertheless constitute a different framework, and different (state vs. private) owner ship can be comparable.

In the next two chapters the basic characteristics of the deregulation and reregulation process in the total ICT sector are outlined and the attempts of the DG Competition to employ competition policy in this sector are examined. The main conclusion, as stated in chapter 4, is that although the ultimate goal is to roll back sector specific regulation and revert to generic competition law, the very concept of SMP implies a permanent re-evaluation of markets and a subsequent adjustment of regulatory measures to changed conditions. Therefore, it is doubtful whether telecommunications regulation will ever be truly 'simplified'. Moreover, even though many tasks have been 'devolved' to the NRAs, the Commission (as Principal) retains a firm grip on the decision of its agents, and this is likely to continue for the foreseeable future. Within this sector regulation the main development now is linked to the implementation and future application of the new common directive for the ICT sector. This new regulatory framework, which was put into operation in July 2003, was designed to strengthen competition in the electronic communications markets in the EU for the benefit of consumers and the European economy. The central aim of the new framework was to speed up the liberalisation of the telecommunications markets by adapting regulation to the requirements of the Information Society and the digital revolution, which implies that a service can be delivered across a range of platforms and received via different terminals, borrowing technologies from previously separate sectors such as audiovisual media and the internet. As stated in chapter 4, therefore, reforms were geared towards providing the best conditions for a dynamic and competitive industry across the ICT sector, that is, for all electronic communication services. The reasoning was that in a rapidly changing technological environment where, at least supposedly, only fierce and fair competition will yield lower prices, better quality and innovative services.

The five case-studies serve as a basis for empirical evidence for the discussions in the remaining chapters of the common characteristics and patterns of national variations in the liberalisation, reregulation and corporatisation and privatisation processes in these countries. In 1980 all of them had a common point of departure in the existence of a state monopolist in this sector covering everything from regulation, though networks to service provision. They were all old fashioned and inefficient – but with some variation in the level of technical sophistication - and the path taken was contingent on the system within which the changes took place. All in all, there are national idiosyncrasies as well as sector generalities.

The three concluding chapters, The complexities of business orientation (chapter 11); structure and business strategies (chapter 12); and internationalisation (chapter 13) try to put the empirical evidence provided by the five country chapters (and by other countries) into a common framework along three important aspects of company development, namely the processes of corporatisation, 'businessfication' and internationalisation. The first two have some kind of link to each other in that they both deal with some of the stages and processes in the path towards becoming more businesslike both in strategy, operation and structure. Chapter 13 is more of an in-depth study one aspect of businessfication, i.e., the drive to internationalise company activities. Thus, the topic of internationalisation has been touched upon in several places both in the corporatisation, and in the strategy and structure chapters of this volume. What are then the main dimensions of change taking place in the telecommunications incumbents in Western Europe in the 1990s?

The Main Dimensions of Change

The different theoretical and empirical chapters in this volume have examined several important aspects of organisational transformation in European telecommunications companies that are relevant for an understanding of what happened and where they are now in terms of strategy and structure. In this concluding chapter we will try to combine them into some of the dimensions discussed in the three previous chapters.

- First how *much change has actually taken place and what is the end result in each of the five countries?*
- Second, one recurring discussion in several chapters has been *how did the companies manage the change process*?
- Third we will focus on certain aspects of the business strategies of the different companies at different phases in the businessfication process of the organisations. One important aspect is the separation of business both in accounting, and in operational terms.
- Finally, internationalisation has been a core element of the strategy of all five companies, although to different degree, at different points in time and with variable degrees of success. It is, however, very closely linked to the shift from a national monopolist to a company competing in a competitive national environment. The questions presented in chapter 13 and in earlier chapters are, therefore, *why do companies internationalise and how did they do it?*

How Much Transformation with What Results?

In general, results of the transformation processes in the different incumbent companies studied in this volume have been rather similar. There has been a shift during a period of 10–15 years from state monopolies to listed public companies operating in a competitive ICT environment and with rather business-oriented structures and operational strategies. In addition all the incumbents still posses a dominant market share both in the former monopoly sector of, for example, voice telephony, as well as in the newly liberalised and competitive emerging sectors, for example, in mobile communications. However, in each of the countries under investigation, this came about in slightly different manner and at a different pace.

Chapter 11 revisits the case studies undertaken in chapters 6–10 and attempts to extract the central dimensions in the transformation process across the countries studied. One interesting feature is that the outcome is broadly similar across all cases. How can this be accounted for? The methodological stance basically determines what we can draw from this observation. From a traditional variable-oriented stance, similarity in outcome implies that factors which differ across cases are not significant, if the outcome is similar the variables must be removed as potential causes for the outcome. However, a thorough investigation shows that in all countries similar issues have been dealt with in the transformation process, but in a slightly different manner when it comes to implementation, sequence and tempo. This indicates that a process approach to the phenomenon of transformation can be valuable. Accounts of the key actors, what they do and how the institutional framework restricts or facilitates their actions give additional insight. Hence, the fact that ownership, regulatory implementation and national culture varies across the cases does not in our view imply that these factors are insignificant when it comes to understanding and explaining the transformation process. Rather, it is argued that these factors must be understood as an institutional framework under which actors with bounded rationality act and interact.

The success or failure of the liberalisation of the telecommunications sector is regularly judged from a market/customer point of view: Have the services become cheaper and better, or, is the market efficient etc? Obviously these are valid and important aspects with a direct impact on us as consumers. However, taking the transformation process from a political science angle seriously, there are additional aspects that need consideration. How should we judge the process and the outcome of the process as institutional change - as a paradigmatic change in the way public services are produced and delivered? What can be the criteria of success from the point of view of the owner and the company?

The mixed and ambiguous interests of government have been pointed to in chapters 2, 3 and 11. Evidence would seem to suggest that success in the transformation of the telecommunications sector is multifaceted. In economic theory dividend is the central aspect and the motive for owners to control the company. This approach has limited value in our setting. We observe owners that balance various aims. For instance there are concerns to secure the infrastructure, to maintain the public values of the services, to maintain and develop national industry, whilst at the same time gradually realising that it is inevitable to support development towards a more business-like organisation. Such balancing acts of the government are at the core of politics. In the development of the telecommunications sector the governments of the countries in question over time, have had to establish equilibrium between such concerns. With government being accountable to society this equilibrium must be legitimate and sustainable. This stands out as a demanding task.

From a company's point of view, a central aspect of success is simply survival. In the process of change within a rapidly changing environment this necessitates freedom to do what is necessary to survive. This freedom does not imply maximum freedom, i.e., a total separation from the state in all phases. Further, the success of the company is not only related to 'who owns' but also to 'who governs' and to how it is governed (cf. chapter 3). Evidently, an owner who is willing and capable to yield what is necessary in various phases can be crucial for the development of the companies. The managing of autonomy, manoeuvres in order to exploit and develop autonomy, can be crucial in the survival strategy of the company.

Separating Businesses as a Business Strategy

In chapter 12 it is argued that 'The idea that new businesses are doing best when separated from their corporate parents is argued to be quite evident'. This seems also to be a core strategy for the telecommunications companies, both when forced upon them and when chosen voluntarily. First of all, the EU required that the regulatory authority be separated from the incumbent to form an independent entity, but not necessarily that the regulatory authority be given to a more or less independent regulatory authority as all countries. Secondly, EU regulation forced companies to separate the accounting of monopoly business from the accounts of the competing parts of the incumbent companies. In addition, most incumbents at some stage in the early relaxation of the bureaucratic structures needed to create new entities to meet tough market competition in a flexible and businesslike manner. The establishment in all five countries of mobile operations outside of the old organisational structure, and, the provision of more business-oriented or internet services in several of the countries is an example of this. However, the idea of separation raises question of how to coordinate and utilise the parent company's resources and skills. Whilst Telenor is an example of coordination through deliberate inside competition between independent units, and France Telecom an example of the creation of coordinating organisational structures, as given in chapter 12, only British Telecom seems able (albeit at later stage) to implement a coherent organisation of the different business units. The continuous development of the transformation of the incumbents to fully competitive private firms is not primarily linked to regulation or ownership changes, but can be seen as more related to their increased exposure to market forces and real competition in the different ICT markets. The more competition there is the more radical and thorough are the changes taking place in the structure and operation of these firms (Monsen, 2004). The corporatisation, part-privatisation and even public listing are important steps in the transformation process, but the heat of competition is perhaps the most relevant factor for the creating dramatic change in the way the former incumbents are structured and operate.

Internationalisation: Why Did They Do It?

In chapter 13 we first addressed the question of why all of the deregulated incumbents had such a drive for internationalisation. The first reason is that we can expect firms competing in the same industry to invade each other's home markets or to see a chain reaction of internationalisation if one competitor starts to internationalise. The incumbents argue that they need to increase their customer base to compensate for the reduced share of the home market not only to generating revenue, but also to enable the development of new technologically advanced products. Thus, most of the former monopolists have established subsidiaries in other counties, often far from their home market, and entered into regional or global alliances. Chapter 13 argues that the former monopolists tend to display asymmetric behaviours; they impede the entry of foreign competitors in their own home market using defensive political strategies, whilst simultaneously exploiting maximum access to foreign markets through the active lobbying of their political institutions. The period immediately following deregulation in the early and mid 1990s was characterised by intense pressures for market access, for example, 'land grabbing', without significant long-term strategic focus; the quest for growth quickly came to a halt in the late 1990s. After the turn of the century the sector focused on consolidation and restructuring of the ICT companies portfolio to realise expected values. Firms have focused increasingly on expanding their customer bases in existing markets and increasing ownership in already established subsidiaries. For many incumbents the success and failures of investments in large foreign mobile companies have implications of financial magnitude that are more important than the traditional running of their business at home. Chapter 13 also argues that in many countries it was easier to get funding for a rapid international mobile expansion as a state-owned company than as a privatised company. The state generally had a long-term perspective, thereby allowing for substantial strategic flexibility compared to private shareholders pressuring firms to deliver visible results in order to secure their own investments.

Internationalisation: How Did They Do It?

The previous chapter argues that when the incumbents decided to internationalise, there were a number of different internationalisation strategies that greatly affect how the firm were going to operate across national borders. Four commonly accepted and empirically tested strategies can be identified: global, multidomestic, transnational and simple international. This framework is used in this book to identify the corporate level strategy of the former incumbents, which in most cases can be described as a multidomestic. This multidomestic focus seems to result from the industry characteristics of license awards where firms entered into consortia of multiple firms, often with a significant local partner, to signal local commitment to the regulatory authorities. In many cases, however, they have tried to adapt a transnational strategy, but often with rather limited success. Although there seems to be an increasing global focus among competitors, such as British Telecom and Deutsche Telekom, there are few, if any companies with a truly global strategy (where some mobile companies like Vodafone are mentioned as exceptions). The chapter argues that there are several reasons for this, implementing a truly global strategy is very costly, the ability and willingness of the MNCs to carry out a strict integrative or 'industrial' strategy in the different subsidiaries all over the world varies and the asymmetric behaviour found in former monopolistic of protecting their home market while simultaneously internationalising in foreign markets primarily results from lacking cooperation between governments. With the shift from public to private ownership structures, we can expect internationalisation patterns to shift, however, as private investors generally tend to pursue more short-term financial goals that could pressure firms into geographic locations and operating modes that minimise risk.

What is then the basic lesson from all this for the telecommunications sector as such? First we see substantial effects of the liberalisation drive in all European countries on the market situation of the old incumbents, in how they were organised, and in the way they operated in the market place. The revolution was largely willed by governments because they believed that an efficient telecommunications sector could serve as an engine for more rapid economic growth due to the potential of the digital revolution. We also see that for a long time 'non-business concerns' accompanying the transformation towards business logic.

Lessons from the Telecommunications Sector

The developments addressed in this book have taken place both in the more narrowly defined former telecommunication incumbents in Western Europe and in other (formerly) public owned companies in the ICT sector, such as public broadcasters, newspapers etc. The development of the company structures in these former state or public owned institutions in the ICT sector is closely related to both the general technological and political development of telecommunications and media in Europe. The process of digitalisation created an integrated ICT sector in the middle of the general liberalisation process in the EU and as shown in chapter 4 the result was a rewriting of the EU's total legislative framework of the ICT sector in 2003 creating a common legislative framework for this sector. The effect of this on company transformation and in particular on business strategy was to create more competition through the establishment of a more equal playing field for different type of ICT actors. This issue will be addressed in more detail later in this chapter. In addition the transformation of telecommunications companies resembles developments in several other public sectors like post, water, electricity, rail etc. where a general European liberalisation process and the introduction of competition policy and private owner ship initiated a substantial transformation of the former incumbents. Here one can speculate to what extent and by what means the approaches and experiences presented in this volume could increase the understanding of similar developments within other public sectors and with other public companies.

The willingness to accept radical incumbent transformations were much more pronounced within the telecommunications sector than within other public sectors and for other public utilities. The argument for this was linked to the belief that the telecommunications and particularly the converged ICT sector would become the basis for increasing economic growth in the member states. The same argument was not at hand for driving the logic of liberalisation in other sectors. At the same time the independent effect of the technological dimension of digitalisation created a brand new and much more potent framework for more capacity, higher speed, and a lot of new services in ICT than in other sectors. In fact, as this volume has tried to show,, the uniqueness and potentiality of the technology has been the driving force behind the liberalisation processes in the telecommunications sector. As shown in chapter 4, this was why the DG Competition was able to exercise its legislative power in this area much more than in other service public sectors.

The role of technology and of politics in the willingness of politicians to accept liberalisation processes and the transformation and privatisation of former incumbents in different sectors constitutes a fascinating topic for future research. The more general perspectives of comparative studies of company change within former incumbents in the telecommunications sector and within other public sectors have only been addressed in the literature to a limited extent. And in case where studies have been undertaken, the focus tends to be more on regulatory developments and the more superficial organisational changes taking place. There are also obviously challenges both in comparing across time and across countries. For example, the political period of the 1980ies in Britain in relation to telecommunications privatisation is very different to that of the Latin countries in the middle to this decennium and their attempts to liberalise and privatise gas and electricity services.

When it comes to the basic conclusions of the book is also seems that real market exposure and fully privatised companies are the best determinants for a complete transformation of the incumbents not only into listed companies but into truly market-oriented and consumer-focused entities with a corresponding organisational structure and strategies. The tendency in most of the countries covered in this volume is also in the direction of more privatisation in these terms: TeleDanmark is first old incumbent have been taken over by a hedge fund, in others the average remaining share of the state in the listed companies are reduced, and the industrialisation of the functioning of the multinational companies like Telenor takes the form of a normal operational modus of a private company.

This book has basically addressed three questions: what were the consequences of the transformation of telecommunications incumbents within the five countries under study during the 1990s? What were the effects of the drivers for change outside of the narrow focus of the book compared to the role of the elements of transformation studied in this volume (ownership, regulation and competition)? Finally to what extent can we generalise to other countries and time periods and to incumbents from other public sectors in terms of a more general understanding of the incumbent transformation process? First of all, even if the strategies and patterns of change and most notably the speed are somewhat different in the five countries, the end result of the process of company transformation in the telecommunications sector is very similar. Secondly, within the generally rather similar regulatory framework, the two most important factors to explain differences in tempo and temporary differences in company structure and business strategy are ownership and degree of competitiveness in the market more than country variations in regulatory regime. Finally, it seems as if telecommunications and the media sector have a unique driving force for change in the digitalisation processes that created a willingness of the owners to liberalise, corporatise and privatise at the same time as the digital revolution stimulated increased the competitive pressure in the ICT industry. These factors were not relevant to the same degree in the other public sectors on the bumpy road to a more liberalised regime. The ability and willingness of the EU Commission to use its legislative powers to kick start the liberalisation process was also much more limited in the other sectors mainly due to the belief of both the Commission and the member states of the telecommunications industry's key importance for increased economic growth. On the other hand it seems that the owners' willingness and possibility to create a true competitive environment over time can be true also for other sectors.

Overly Simplified Models for Public Sector Transformation?

In this final section we will attempt to derive some general insight from our in-depth inquiry into the telecommunications sector over the last decades and to determine what it can tell us about public sector organisational change.

For this volume a bottom-up approach to the changes in the field has been utilised. This is not to say that changes are initiated and happening only at the micro level, but rather that our prime interest has been how the incumbent companies have developed as business enterprises within the framework constituted by institutions in a broad sense. Institutions can be seen as constituting 'the rules of the game' whereas the organisations with their actors can be seen as the ones playing the game (North, 1990). Developments in ownership, regulation and competition policy were covered extensively in chapters 3–5. These institutions constituted the main polity framework for the developing companies. Developments in the technological environment were explicitly and intentionally left out. Typical accounts of change in the telecommunications sector (and in the public sector as such) see organisational changes as driven by markets and regulation, through technological change, and as resulting from formal structural change in, for example, ownership structure. The basic logic is that changes in the organisations' environment must be necessarily followed by some sort of institutional reform in the framework. When globalisation, new technologies and new user demands require a liberalisation of the telecommunications sector, a corporatisation and eventual privatisation of the companies stands out as a rational model. These institutional changes are expected to subsequently trigger a degree of change in an organisation's output. The main assumption is that institutional change is an independent variable that has a causal effect on organisational performance in given situations. The effect and relative importance of the independent variables can and will vary.

Our approach deviates somewhat from this. Questioning whether it is ownership or competition that matters for company performance can be seen as a 'wrong-problem problem' (Fredrickson, 1996). However, although we do not want to rule out factors such as regulation or ownership structure from the analysis, for our purposes the important question is not whether competition has an effect, or what effect public or private ownership may have on organisational output, rather it is why when say, competition is introduced, do some companies end up doing well while others fail.

What we have found is that in our case the institutional changes at polity level have a certain course and direction so that when viewed from a macro perspective and in retrospect the movement towards liberalisation and privatisation is instantly recognizable. This development reduces the degrees of freedom for the companies: Everything is not possible to accomplish. In this respect the institutions remove some uncertainty and facilitate strategic action (Beckert, 1999). However at the organisational level changes in the institutional framework are not unambiguous and clear-cut. Here there is still room for local mediation and micro choice. Neither does the government principal have a clear and unambiguous goal: Development of markets and competitive pricing clash with genuine public values and means-ends associations are riddled with uncertainty. The company agents also act under uncertainty. In a process of public sector transformation such as the one we have studied in the telecommunications sector, strategic actors at micro level need two distinct sets of competencies: First the ability to read, understand, and act upon the changing institutional framework, and second, and subsequently, the ability to run a normal business. The transition period, be that under private ownership as in the case of British Telecom or under state ownership in the other cases studied, accentuates this tension between being an expert in working with changing institutional frameworks and running a normal business. In the telecommunications incumbent companies this tension is not fully solved even today several years after privatisation.

Bibliography

Abbamonte, G.B. and Rabassa, V. (2001). Foreclosure and Vertical Mergers – The Commission's Review of Vertical Effects in the Last Wave of Media and Internet Mergers: AOL/Time Warner, Vivendi/Seagram, MCI Worldcom/Sprint. *European Competition Law Review*, 6, 214–26.

Abbott, A. (1992). From Causes to Events – Notes on Narrative Positivism. *Sociological Methods and Research*, 20(4), 428–55.

Abell, P. (2001). Causality and Low-frequency Complex Events – The Role of Comparative Narratives. *Sociological Methods and Research,* 30(1), 57–80.

Abell, P. (2004). Narrative Explanation: An Alternative to Variable-centered Explanation? *Annual Review of Sociology*, 30, 287–310.

Aberbach, J. and Christensen, T. (2003). Translating Theoretical Ideas into Modern State Reform. Economics-inspired Reforms and Competing Models of Governance. *Administration and Society*, 35(5), 491–509.

Aharoni, Y. (1966). The Foreign Investment Decision Process. In Buckley, P.J. and Ghauri, P.N. (eds). *The Internationalization of the Firm*. 2nd edn. London: International Thomson Business Press.

Ahlborn, C., Evans, D. and Padilla, A.J. (2001). Competition Policy in the New Economy: Is European Competition Law Up to the Challenge? *European Competition Law Review*, 5, 156–67.

Amesse, F., Latour, R., Rebolledo, C. and Séguin-Dulude, L. (2004). The Telecommunications Equipment Industry in the 1990s: From Alliances to Mergers and Acquisitions. *Technovation*, 24(11), 885–97.

Amintas, A. and de Swarte, T. (1997). France Telecom, un regard partagé sur la performance organisationnelle. *Communications and Stratégies*, 27(3), 49–74.

Andersen Business Consulting. (2002). Study on the Implementation of Cost Accounting Methodologies and Account Separation by Telecommunication Operators with Significant Market Power. Brussels. Prepared for the European Commission, DG Information Society: 3 July 2002.

Andersen, L.B. and Blegvad, M. (2006). Does Ownership Matter for the Delivery of Professionalized Public Services? Cost-efficiency and Effectiveness in Private and Public Dental Care for Children in Denmark. *Public Administration*, 84(1), 147–64.

Anderson, E. and Gatignon, H. (1986). Modes of Foreign Entry: A Transaction Cost Analysis and Propositions. *Journal of International Business Studies*, 17(3), 1–25.

Andresen, K., and Sjøvaag, M. (1997). Interconnection – An Issue on the European Regulatory Agenda. *Working Paper SEAS*:T:03.97, Norwegian School of Management.

Andrews, K.R. (1971). *The Concept of Corporate Strategy*. Homewood, IL: Irwin.

Antonelli, C. (1997). A Regulatory Regime for Innovation in the Communications Industries. *Telecommunications Policy*, 21(1), 35–45.

Apostolos, V. (2006). *European Competition Policy in the Telecommunications Sector – New Technologies, New Challenges*. Institute for European Studies, Brussels.

Armstrong, M. (1998). Network Interconnection in Telecommunications. *Economic Journal*, 108, 545–64.

Autin, J. (1995). L'Usage de la régulation en droit public. In Miaille, M. (ed.), *La régulation entre droit et politique*. Paris: L'Harmattan.

Bangemann, M. (1994). *Europe and the Global Information Society: Recommendations to the European Council.* Report, Brussels.

Barnard, C.I. (1938). *The Functions of the Executive*. Cambridge, MA: Harvard University Press.

Bartle, I. (1999). Transnational Interests in the European Union: Globalisation and the Changing Organisation in Telecommunications and Electricity. *Journal of Common Market Studies*, 37(3), 363–383.

Bartlett, C.A. and Ghoshal, S. (1989). *Managing Across Borders: The Transnational Solution*. Boston: Harvard Business School Press.

Barzelay, M. (2002). Origins of the New Public Management: An International View from Public Administration/Political Science. In McLaughlin, K., Osborne, S.P. and Ferlie, E. (eds), *New Public Management: Current Trends and Future Prospects*. London: Routledge.

Bauer, J.M. (2005). Regulation and State Ownership: Conflicts and Complementarities in EU Telecommunications. In *Annals of Public and Cooperative Economics*, 76(2), 151–77.

Bavasso, A. (2002). Essential Facilities in EC Law: The Rise of an 'Epithet' and the Consolidation of a Doctrine in the Communications Sector. *Yearbook of European Law*, 21, 63–106.

Becker, H.S. (1992). Cases, Causes, Conjunctures, Stories and Imagery. In Ragin, C.C. and Becker, H.S. (eds), *What is a Case: Exploring the Foundations of Social Inquiry*. Cambridge: Cambridge University Press.

Beckert, J. (1999). Agency, Entrepreneurs, and Institutional Change. The Role of Strategic Choice and Institutionalized Practices in Organizations. *Organization Studies*, 20(5), 777–99.

Belgacom (1999). *Annual Report 1999*. Belgium: Belgacom SA.

Belgacom annual results 1996, 1998, 1999, 2001, 2003, 2004, 2005, http://www.belgacom.be/investor/en/ jsp/static/reports.jsp.

Belgacom (1999). Press release, 22 January, Communications Department, Belgacom.

Belgacom (2002). *Annual Report 2002*. Brussels: Belgacom SA.

Belgacom (2003) Press release 27 February, Communications Department, Belgacom.

Belgacom (2005) Press release 1 February, Communications Department, Belgacom.

Belgacom (2006a). http://www.belgacom.be/web/com/staticsite/en/about/overview/history.htm.

Belgacom (2006b). http://cgi.belgacom.be/nl/about/operations/activities.htm.

Benito, G.R.G. and Tomassen, S. (2003). The Micro-mechanics of Foreign Operations' Performance: An Analysis Based on the Oli Framework. In Narula, R. and Cantwell, J. (eds), *International Business and the Eclectic Paradigm*. London: Routledge.

Bessant, J. (2005). Enabling Continuous and Discontinuous Innovation: Learning from the Private Sector. *Public Money and Management*, 25(1), 35–42.

Beunderman, M. (2006). *Fresh EU Presidency Attacks European Court of Justice*. EUobserver, 01/01/2006. http://euobserver.com/?aid=20621andrk=1.

Bjorkman, I. (1990). Foreign Direct Investments: An Organizational Learning Perspective. *The Finnish Journal of Business Economics*, 39(4), 271–94.

Blackman, C.R. (1998). Convergence between Telecommunications and Other Media. How Should Regulation Adapt? *Telecommunications Policy*, 22(3), 163–70.

Blackman, C. and Denmead, M. (1996). *1998, a New Era for Telecoms Regulation*. Cambridge: Analysis Publications Ltd, 101.

Blankart, C.B. and Knieps, G. (1989). What Can We Learn From Comparative Institutional Analysis? The Case of Telecommunications. *Kyklos*, 42, 579–98.

Blyaert, L. (2002). VNUNET, Belgacomdochter Tritone zet klanten op straat, http://www.nl.vnunet.be/ news/network_and_telecom/20020626002.

Boiteau, C. (1996). 'L'entreprise nationale France Telecom (Commentaire de la loi no 96–660 du 26 juillet 1996). *La Semaine Juridique*, 41, 379–84.

Bourniquel (1949). Sur l'emploi des organisateurs – Conseils Privés et sur l'organisation administrative. *Archive F90bis 2829*.

Boyne, G.A. (1998). Competitive Tendering in Local Government: A review of Theory and Evidence. *Public Administration*, 76 (Winter 1998), 695–712.

British Telecom (2000). 2000 Annual Report on Form 20F. London: British Telecommunications plc.

British Telecom. (1999). 1999 Annual Report on Form 20F. London: British Telecommunications plc.

Brown, S.L. and Eisenhardt, K.M. (1998). *Competing on the Edge: Strategy as Structured Chaos*. Boston: Harvard Business School Press.

Brunekreeft, G. and Groß, W. (2000). Prices for Long-Distance Voice Telephony in Germany. *Telecommunications Policy*, 24, 929–45.

Burns, T. and Stalker, G.M. (1966). *The Management of Innovation*. London: Tavistock.

Byrkjeland, M. and Langeland, O. (2000). *Statlig eierskap i Norge* (Fafo-notat No. 2000:22). Oslo: Fafo.

Bøhren, Ø. and Ødegaard, B. A. (2001). *Corporate Governance and Economic Performance in Norwegian Listed Firms* (Research Report No. 11/2001). Sandvika: Norwegian School of Management, Department of Financial Economics.

Börsch, A. (2004). What Happens after Privatization? Globalization, Corporate Governance and Adjustment at British Telecom and Deutsche Telekom. *Journal of European Public Policy*, 11(4), 593–612.

BT website: http://www.bt.com/.

BT (2006a). http://www.btplc.com/Thegroup/BTsHistory/1984-1990.htm#1984.

BT (2006b). http://www.btplc.com/Thegroup/BTsHistory/1991-1993.htm#1992a.

BT (2006c). www.btglobalservices.com/business/global/en/about_us/our_network/index.html.

BT (2006d). http://www.btplc.com/News/Articles/Showarticle.cfm?ArticleID=f76cc454-06ba-43e2-a97c-51da38f378c5).

Cainelli, G., Evangelista, R. and Savona, M. (2006). Innovation and Economic Performance in Services: A Firm-level Analysis. *Cambridge Journal of Economics*, 30(3), 435–58.

Carsberg, B. (1991). Office of Telecommunications: Competition and the Duopoly Review. In Velanjovski, C. (ed.) *Regulators and the Market: An Assessment of the Growth of Regulation in the UK*. London: Institute of Economic Affairs.

Carsberg, B. (1989). Injecting Competition into British Telecom. In Velanjovski, C. (ed.) *Privatisation and Competition: A Market Prospectus*. London: Hobart Paperback 28, Institute of Economic Affairs.

Carsberg, B. (1987). Regulation of British Telecom. *Telecommuications Policy*, 11(3), 237–42.

Catelin, C. and Chatelin, C. (2001). Privatisation, gouvernement d'entreprise et processus décisionnel: Une interprétation de la dynamique organisationnelle à travers le cas France Télécom. *Revue Finance Contrôle Stratégie*, 4(2), 63–90.

Cave, M. (1997). Cost Analysis and Cost Modelling for Regulatory Purposes: UK Experience. In Melody, W (ed.), *Telecom Reform: Principles, Policies and Regulatory Practices*. Den Private Ingeniørfond, Technical University of Denmark, Lyngby. http://lirne.net/2003/resources/tr/chapter19.pdf.

Cave, M. (2002). Is LoopCo the answer? *Info*, 4(4), 25–31.

Cave, M.E., Sumit, K., Majumdar, K. and Vogelsang, I. (eds) (2002). *Handbook of Telecommunications Economics*: Vol. 1: *Structure, Regulation and Competition*. Amsterdam: Elsevier.

Cave, M. and Crowther, P. (2004). Co-ordinating Regulation and Competition Law – Ex Ante and Ex Post. *The Pros and Cons of Antitrust in Deregulated*

Markets. Konkurrensverket: Swedish Competition Authority (http://www.kkv.se).

Cave and Larouche (2001). *European Communications at the Crossroads*. Report of a CEPS Working Party, Centre for European Policy Studies, Brussels October 2001.

CEC (2003). 9th Report on the Implementation of the Telecommunications Regulatory Package. Commission of the European Communities, Brussels [SEC (2003) 1342].

Cecchini, P. (1988). *Alles op alles voor Europa. De uitdaging 1992. Een verslag van het onderzoeksproject betreffende de kosten van een niet verenigd Europa*. Amsterdam/Brussel: Börsen International Publications.

Chaganti, R. and Damanpour, F. (1991). Institutional Ownership, Capital Structure and Firm Performance. *Strategic Management Journal*, 12(7), 479–91.

Chandler, A.D. (1962). *Strategy and Structure: Chapters in the History of the Industrial Enterprise*. Cambridge, MA: The MIT press.

Charkham, J.P. (1994). *Keeping Good Company: A Study of Corporate Governance in Five Countries*. Oxford: Clarendon Press.

Chevallier, J. (1989). Les enjeux juridiques: l'adaptation du service public des télécommunications. *Revue Française d'Administration Publique*, 52, 601–15.

Chevallier, J. (1996). La nouvelle réforme des telecommunications: ruptures et continuités. *Revue Française de Droit Administratif*, 12(5), 909–51.

Chin, P.O., Brown, G.A. and Hu, Q. (2004). The Impact of Mergers and Acquisitions on IT Governance Structures: A Case Study. *Journal of Global Information Management*, 12(4), 50–74.

Christensen, C.M. (1997). *The Innovator's Dilemma: When New Technologies Cause Great Firms to Fail*. Boston, MA: Harvard Business School Press.

Christensen, J.G. and Pallesen, T. (2001). The Political Benefits of Corporatisation and Privatization. *Journal of Public Policy*, 21(3), 283–309.

Cincera, P. (1999). *The European Union Content Regulation in the converged communication environment*. In Eliassen, K.A. and Sjøvaag, M. (eds) (1999), *European Telecommunications Liberalisation*. London: Routledge.

Cini, M. and McGowan, L. (1998). *Competition Policy in the European Union*. Basingstoke: Macmillan Press.

CIT (2003). *The Yearbook of European Telecommunications 2003*. Exeter: CIT Publications Limited.

CIT (2002). *The Yearbook of European Telecommunications 2002*. Exeter: CIT Publications Limited.

Clements, B. (1998). The Impact of Convergence on Regulatory Policy in Europe. *Telecommunications Policy*, 22(3), 197–205.

Coen, D. and Héritier, A. (2000). Business Perspectives on German and British Regulation: Telecoms, Energy and Rail. *Business Strategy Review*, 11(4), 29–37.

Collins, R. and Murroni, C. (1997). Future Direction in Telecom Regulation: The Case of the United Kingdom. In Melody, W (ed.), *Telecom Reform: Principles, Policies and Regulatory Practices*. Den Private Ingeniørfond, Technical University of Denmark, Lyngby. http://lirne.net/2003/resources/tr/chapter19.pdf.

Commission of the European Communities (COM) (1984). *Television Without Frontiers: Green Paper on the Establishment of the Common Market for Broadcasting, Especially By Satellite and Cable*. Brussels, Official Journal, COM (84)300.

Commission of the European Communities (COM) (1986). *Witboek ter voltooiing van de interne markt*. Brussels, Bulletin EG, suppl. 5. (Consulted version: Dutch).

Commission of the European Communities (COM) (1987). *Towards a Dynamic European Economy, Green Paper on the Development of the Common Market for Telecommunications Services and Equipment*. Brussels, Official Journal, COM (87)290.

Commission of the European Communities (COM) (1990). *Towards a Dynamic European Economy, Green Paper on the Development of the Common Market for Telecommunications Services and Equipment*. Brussels, Official Journal, COM(90)490.

Commission of the European Communities (COM) (1993). *Witboek over groei, concurrentievermogen en werkgelegenheid*. Brussels, Bulletin EG, suppl. 6. (Consulted version: Dutch).

Commission of the European Communities (COM) (2005). *i2010 – A European Information Society for Growth and Employment*. Brussels, Official Journal, COM (2005) 229.

Curwen, P. (1997). *Restructuring Telecommunications. A Study of Europe in a Global Context*. London: Macmillan.

Curwen, P. (1999a). Survival of the Fittest: Formation and Development of International Alliances in Telecommunications. *Info*, 1(2), 141–58.

Curwen, P. (1999b). Has Telecom Italia Broken the Mould of European Capitalism? *Info*, August.

Cyert, R.M. and March, J.G. (1963). *A Behavioural Theory of the Firm*. Englewoods Cliffs NJ: Prentice-Hall.

Daily, C.M., Dalton, D.R. and Cannella Jr, A.A. (2003). Corporate Governance: Decades of Dialogue and Data. *Academy of Management Review*, 28(3), 371–82.

Dandelot, M. (1993). Le secteur des Télécommunications en France. *Rapport au Ministre de l'Industrie, des Postes et Télécommunications et du Commerce Extérieur, Paris*.

Datanews (2003). Didier Bellens herschikt Belgacom top. 26 March.

David C. and Héritier, A. (eds) (2005). *Refining Regulatory Regimes: Utilities in Europe*. Cheltenham: Edward Elgar.

Davies, A. (1994). *Telecommunications and Politics: The Decentralised Alternative.* London: Pinter.

Day, J.D., Mang, P.Y., Richter, A. and Roberts, J. (2001). The Innovative Organization: Why New Ventures Need More than a Room of their Own. *The McKinsey Quarterly*, May 2002.

Day, J.D., Mang, P.Y., Richter, A. and Roberts, J. (2002). Has Pay for Performance Had its Day? *The McKinsey Quarterly*, 4, 46–55.

Delion, A.G. and Durupty, M. (1995). Chronique des enterprises publiques. *Revue française d'administration publique*, 73, 177–86.

Demsetz, H. (1968). Why Regulate Utilities? *The Journal of Law and Economics*, 11, 55–65.

Department of Trade and Industry. (1991). *Competition and Choice. Telecommunications Policy for the 1990s*. Cm 1461. London: HMSO.

Dethmers, F. (2005). Collective Dominance Under EC Merger Control – After Airtours and the Introduction of Unilateral Effects is There Still a Future for Collective Dominance? *European Competition Law Review*, 11, 638–49.

De Tijd (1997). Belgacom bereid controle Paratel over te nemen. 23 October.

De Tijd (1998a). Belgacom wordt ooit een Harvard case. 13 August.

De Tijd (1998b). Belgacom is tevreden over PTS-programma. 5 March.

De Tijd (1998c). Belgacom wil architect zijn van multimedialandschap. 18 July.

De Tijd (2000). Belgacom spekt kas van BMV met 1 miljard frank. 7 December 2000.

De Tijd (2001). Belgacom slorpt risicokapitaaldochter BMV op, 21 December 2001.

Devillechabrolle, V. and Monnot, C. (1993). Il n'y a plus d'obstacle juridique à la réforme de France Telecom. *Le Monde*, 20 November.

De Wit, B. and Meyer. R. (1998). *Strategy: Process, Content, Context*. London: Thomson Business Press.

Direction Générale des Postes et Télécommunications (DGPT). (1995). De Nouvelles règles du jeu pour les telecommunications en France. Consultation document, October.

Doern, G.B. and Wilks, S. (eds) (1996). *Comparative Competition Policy: National Institutions in a Global Market*. Oxford: Clarendon Press.

Doherty, B. (2001). Just What are Essential Facilities?, *Common Market Law Review*, 38, 397–436.

Doolin, B. (2003). Narratives of Change: Discourse, Technology, and Organization. *Organization*, 10(4), 751–70.

Douroux, P. (1993). Longuet le libéral réhabilite la politique industrielle. *Libération*, 13 October.

Douste-Blazy, P. (2003). Rapport fait au nom de la commission d'enquête sur la gestion des enterprises publiques afin d'améliorer le système de prise de décision. Assemblée Nationale 2002–2003, 1004.

Drexhage, G. (2000). Telaris: The Merger that Never Was. *Corporate Finance*, 183, 22–6.

Dunleavy, P. (1991). *Democracy, Bureaucracy and Public Choice: Economic Explanations in Political Science*. New York: Harvester Wheatsheaf.

Dunleavy, P. and O'Leary, B. (1987). *Theories of the State: Politics of Liberal Democracy*. London: Macmillan.

Dunning, J.H. (1988). The Eclectic Paradigm of International Production: A Restatement and Some Possible Extensions. *Journal of International Business Studies*, 19(1), 1–31.

Durand, R. and Vargas, V. (2003). Ownership, Organization and Private Firms' Efficient Use of Resources. *Strategic Management Journal*, 24, 667–75.

Durant, R.F., Legge Jr, J.S. and Moussios, A. (1998). People, Profits, and Service Delivery: Lessons from the Privatization of British Telecom. *American Journal of Political Science*, 42(1), 117–40.

Dyson, K. and Humphreys, P. (1986). The Politics of the Communications Revolution in Western Europe. *West European Politics*, 10.

Ehrlich, I., Gallais-Hamonno, G., Lin, Z. and Lutter, R. (1994). Productivity Growth and Firm Ownership: An Empirical Investigation. *Journal of Political Economy*, 102, 1006–38.

Eliassen, K.A., Monsen, C.B. and Sitter, N. (2003). The Governance of Telecommunications in the European Union. In Campanella, M.L. and Eijffinger, S.C.W. (eds), *EU Economic Governance and Globalization*. Cheltenham: Edward Elgar.

Eliassen, K.A. and Sjøvaag, M. (eds) (1999). *European Telecommunications Liberalisation*. London: Routledge.

Eliassen, K., Mason, T. and Sjøvaag, M. (1999). European Telecommunications Policies – Deregulation, Re-regulation or Real Liberalisation? In Eliassen, K.A. and Sjøvaag, M. (1999). *European Telecommunications Liberalisation*. London: Routledge.

Elter, F. (2004). *Strategizing in Complex Contexts.* Series of dissertations No. 7. Norwegian School of Management BI.

Emery (1966). Rapport sur les problèmes de personnel au ministère des Postes et Télécommunications. Paris: National Archive F90bis 2829.

Ergas, H. (1996). Telecommunications Across the Tasman: A comparison of Regulatory Approaches and Economic Outcomes in Australia and New Zealand. Discussion Paper, International Institute of Communications, The University of Auckland, New Zealand.

ESIS (1999) Regulatory developments. http://www.eu-esis.org/Regulation/BEregQ8.htm.

Etter, B. (2000). The Assessment of Mergers in the EC under the Concept of Collective Dominance. *Journal of World Competition*, 23(3), 103–39.

European Commission (2004). Report N567/2003, Brussels, 21 January.

European Commission (2003). *Thirteenth Report on Competition Policy*. Luxemburg: Office for Official Publications of the European Communities.

European Commission (2001). *Seventh Report on the Implementation of the Telecommunications Regulatory Package*. Brussels, Commission of the European Communities: 26.11.2001. COM (2001) 706.

European Commission (2000). *Sixth Report on the Implementation of the Telecommunications Regulatory Package*. Brussels, Commission of the European Communities: COM (2000) 814.

European Commission (1999). *Fifth Report on the Implementation of the Telecommunications Regulatory Package*. Brussels, Commission of the European Communities: COM (1999) 537.

European Commission (1998a). *Fourth Report on the Implementation of the Telecommunications Regulatory Package*. Brussels, Commission of the European Communities: COM (1998) 80.

European Commission (1998b). *Commission Recommendation of 8 January 1998 on Interconnection in a Liberalised Telecommunications Market (Part 1 – Interconnection Pricing)*. Brussels, European Commission: 98/322/EC.

European Commission (1998c). *Commission Recommendation of April 8 1998 in Interconnection in a Liberalised Telecommunictaions Market (Part 2 – Accounting separation and cost accounting)*. Brussels, European Commission: 98/195/EC.

European Commission (1987). *Towards a Dynamic European Economy – Green Paper on the Development of the Common Market for Telecommunications Services and Equipment*. Brussels, European Commission: COM (87) 290, 30 June.

European Council (1997). *Directive 97/33/EC of the European Parliament and of the Council of 30 June 1997 on Interconnection in Telecommunications with Regard to Ensuring Universal Service and Interoperability through Application of the Principles of Open Network Provision (ONP)*. Brussels, The European Parliament and the Council of the European Union, Interconnection Directives and Recommendations: Official Journal L 199.

Eyre, S. and Sitter, N. (1999). Towards a New Regulatory Regime? In Eliassen, K.A. and Sjøvaag, M. (1999). *European Telecommunications Liberalisation*. London: Routledge, 55–73.

Fabre, T. (1993). France Telecom investit un milliard dans l'UAP et les AGF. Les Échos 1 February.

Fang, T., Friedh, C. and Schultzberg, S. (2004). Why Did the Telia–Telenor Merger Fail? *International Business Review*, 13(5), 573–94.

Fershtman, C. (1990). The Interdependence between Ownership Status and Market Structure: The Case of Privatization. *Economica*, 57(227), 319–28.

Florio, M. (2001). On Cross-country Comparability of Government Statistics: Public Expenditure Trends in OECD National Accounts. *International Review of Applied Economics*, 15(2), 181–98.

Florio, M. (2003). Does Privatisation Matter? The Long-Term Performance of British Telecom over 40 Years. *Fiscal studies*, 24(2), 197–234.

Flowers, E.B. (1976). Oligopolistic Reactions in European and Canadian Direct Investment in the United States. *Journal of International Business Studies*, 7(2), 43–56.

Foreman-Peck, J. and Müller, J. (eds). (1988). *European Telecommunication Organisations*. Baden-Baden: Nomos.

Franza, R.M. and Grant, K.P. (2006). Improving Federal to Private Sector Technology Transfer. *Research Technology Management*, 49(3), 36–40.

Fredrickson, H.G. (1996). Comparing the Reinventing Government Movement with the New Public Administration. *Public Administration Review*, 56(3), 263–70.

Friedman, M. (1962). *Capitalism and Freedom*. Chicago: University of Chicago Press.

Frooman, J. (1999). Stakeholder Influence Strategies. *Academy of Management Review*, 24(2), 191–205.

Frydman, R., Gray, C.W., Hessel, M. and Rapaczynski, A. (1999). When Does Privatization Work? The Impact of Private Ownership on Corporate Performance in Transition Economies. *Journal of Economics Quarterly*.

Gabelmann, A. and Groß, W. (2003). Telekommunikation: Wettbewerb in einem dynamischen Markt. In Knieps, G. and Brunekreeft, G. (eds), *Zwischen Regulierung und Wettbewerb – Netzsektoren in Deutschland*. Heidelberg: Physika-Verlag, 2. Aufl., 85–130.

Galbraith, J.K. (1975). *Markten, machten, mensen. Economie en algemeen welzijn*. Amsterdam: De Bussy.

Garnaut, R., Song, L., Tenev, S., and Yang Yao, Y. (2005). *China's Ownership Transformation: Process, Outcomes, Prospects*. Washington, DC: International Finance Corporation.

Gedajlovic, E.R. and Saphiro, D.M. (1998). Management and Ownership Effects: Evidence from Five Countries. *Strategic Management Journal*, 19(6), 533–53.

Genoud, C. and Varone, F. (2002). Does Privatization Matter? Liberalization and Regulation: The Case of European Electricity. *Public Management Review*, 4(2), 231–56.

Gensollen, M. (1991). Les réformes institutionelles et réglementaires des télécommunications en 1990: le service public face à l'extension de la concurrence. *Communications et Stratégies*, 3, 17–34.

George, A.L. and Bennett, A. (2005). *Case Studies and Theory Development in the Social Sciences*. Cambridge, MA: MIT press.

George, A.L. and McKeown, T.J. (1985). Case Studies and Theories of Organizational Decision Making. In Coulam, R.F. and Smith, R.A. (eds), *Advances in Information Processing in Organizations*, Vol. 2. Greenwich, CT: Jai Press.

Gerber, D. (1998). *Law and Competition in the Twentieth Century: Protecting Prometheus*. Oxford: Oxford University Press.

Gerpott, T. (1998). Wettbewerbsstrategien im Telekommunikationsmarkt. Stuttgart: Schäffer-Poeschel.

Gillan, S.L. and Starks, L.T. (2002). *Institutional Investors, Corporate Ownership and Corporate Governance – Global Perspectives* (Wider Discussion Paper No. 2002/09). Helsinki: United Nations University: United Nations University, World Institute for Development Economics Research.

Goldstein, A.E. (2000). Corporate Governance and Regulation in Privatized Utilities: Telecommunications in Four European Countries. *Business and Politics*, 2(2), 189–223.

Gordon, J.N. (1999a). Deutsche Telekom, German Corporate Governance, and the Transition Costs of Capitalism. Working Paper No. 140, Columbia Law School, Center for Law and Economic Studies.

Gordon, J.N. (1999b). Pathways to Corporate Convergence? Two Steps on the Road to Shareholder Capitalism in Germany: Deutsche Telekom and Daimler Chrysler. *Columbia Journal of European Law*, 5 (Spring), 219.

Gore, A. (1993). *From Red Tape to Results: Creating a Government that Works Better and Costs Less*. Washington, DC: Government Printing Office.

Graham, E.M. (1978). Transatlantic Investment by Multinational Firms: A Rivalistic Phenomenon? *Journal of Post-Keynesian Economics*, 1(1), 82–99.

Gregory, R.J. (1999). Social Capital Theory and Administrative Reform: Maintaining Ethical Probity in Public Service. *Public Administration Review*, 59(1), 63–75.

Griffin, L.J. (1992). Temporality, Events, and Explanation in Historical Sociology – an Introduction. *Sociological Methods and Research*, 20(4), 403–27.

Gripaios, P. and Munday, M. (1998). Unforeseen Policy Impacts: The Case of UK Utility Privatisation. *Policy Studies*, 19(2), 127–39.

Gruber, H. (2005). *The Economics of Mobile Telecommunication*. Cambridge: Cambridge University Press.

Grundy, T. and Wensley, R. (1999). Strategic Behaviour: The Driving Force of Strategic Management. *European Management Journal*, 17(3), 326–34.

Grupp, H. and Schnöring, T. (1992). Research and Develpoment in Telecommunications. *Telecommunications Policy*, 16(1), 46–66.

Grøgaard, B. (2005). International Strategy Implementation: A Headquarter – Subsidiary Perspective. In Grøgaard, B., *Strategy, Structure and the Environment. Essays on International Strategies and Subsidiary Roles.* Series of dissertations No. 3 – 2006. Norwegian School of Management BI.

Hansmann, H. (1996). *The Ownership of Enterprise*. Cambridge, MA: Belknap Press of Harvard University Press.

Harper, J. (1997). *Monopoly and Competition in British Telecommunications. The Past, the Present and the Future*. London: Pinter Publishers.

Harzing, A. (2002). Acquisitions versus Greenfield Investments: International Strategy and Management of Entry Modes. *Strategic Management Journal*, 23(3), 211–27.

Haupt, H. (2002). Collective Dominance Under Article 82 E.C. and E.C. Merger Control in the Light of the Airtours Judgment. *European Competition Law Review*, 9, 434–44.

Helm, D. and Jenkinson, T. (eds). (1998). *Competition in Regulated Industries*. Oxford" Oxford University Press.

Héritier, A. (1999). *Policy-Making and Diversity in Europe: Escape from Deadlock*. Cambridge: Cambridge University Press.

Héritier, A. (2001). Market Integration and Social Cohesion: The Politics of Public Services in European Integration. *Journal of European Public Policy*, 8(5), 825–82.

Héritier, A. (2002). Public-interest Services Revisited. *Journal of European Public Policy*, 9(6), 995–1019.

Hill, C.W.L., Hwang, P. and Kim, W.C. (1990). An Eclectic Theory of the Choice of International Entry Mode. *Strategic Management Journal*, 11(2), 117–28.

Hills, J. (1986). *Deregulating Telecoms: Competition and Control in the United States, Japan and Britain*. London: Pinter.

Hirschman, A.O. (1970). *Exit, Voice and Loyalty – Responses to Decline in Firms, Organizations and States*. Cambridge MA: Harvard University Press.

Hodge, G.A. (2000). *Privatization: An International Review of Performance*. Boulder, CO: Westview Press.

Holcombe, A.N. (1911). *Public Ownership of Telephones on the Continent of Europe*. Boston: Houghton Mifflin Company.

Homet, R.S. (1979). *Politics, Cultures and Communication*. New York, Aspen Institute for Humanistic Studies.

Hood, C. (1991). A Public Management for All Seasons. *Public Administration*, 69(1), 3–19.

HRUpdate, (2002). Jaargang 1, No. 66, 13 November.

Hulsink, W. (1999). *Privatisation and Liberalisation in European Telecommunications: Comparing Britain, the Netherlands and France*. London: Routledge.

Huret, E. (1994). Restructuring Telecommunications: The French Experience. In Wellenius, B and Stern, P.A. (eds), *Implementing Reforms in the Telecommunications Sector. Lessons from Experience*, World Bank, 293–302.

Iazykoff, W. (1991). Le management participatif à France-Telecom. *Revue Politiques et management public*, 9(1), 121–32.

Ikenberry, J.G. (1990). The International Spread of Privatization Policies: Inducements, Learning, and 'Policy Bandwagoning'. In Suleiman, E. and Waterbury, J. (eds), *The Political Economy of Public Sector Reform and Privatization*. Boulder, CO: Westview Press, 88–110.

Ikenberry, J. (1997). Patterns and Theories of the Globalization Paradigm. Paper for the concurrent session on the 17th World Congress of IPSA, 18–19 August.

Jakubyszyn, C. (2000). France Telecom rachète l'opérateur international Equant. *Le Monde*, 21 November.

James, W. (2006). A Processual View of Institutional Change of the Budget Process within an Australian Government-owned Electricity Corporation. In *International Journal of Public Sector Management*, 19 (10), 5–39.

Jemison, D.B. and Sitkin, S.B. (1986). Corporate Acquisitions: A Process Perspective. *Academy of Management Review*, 11(1), 145–63.

Jenkinson, T. and Mayer, C. (1992). The Assessment: Corporate Governance and Corporate Control. *Oxford Review of Economic Policy*, 8(3), 1–10.

Jenny, F. (2000). Competition Law and Policy – Achievements and Failures from an Economic Perspective. In Hope, E. (ed.), *Competition Policy Analysis*. London: Routledge.

Jensen, M. and Meckling, W. (1976). Theory of the Firm: Managerial Behavior, Agency Costs, and Ownership Structure. *Journal of Financial Economics*, 4, 305–60.

Johanson, J. and Vahlne, J.E. (1977). Internationalization Process of Firm – Model of Knowledge Development and Increasing Foreign Market Commitments. *Journal of International Business Studies*, 8(1), 23–32.

Johanson, J. and Wiedersheim-Paul, F. (1975). The Internationalization of the Firm: Four Swedish Cases. In Buckley, P.J. and Ghauri, P.N. (eds). *The Internationalization of the Firm*. 2nd edn. London: International Thomson Business Press.

Jones, T.M. and Wicks, A.C. (1999). Convergent Stakeholder Theory. *Academy of Management Review*, 24(2), 206–21.

Kamall, S. (1996). Telecommunications Policy. European Union Policy Briefings. London: Cartermill.

Kettl, D.F. (2000). *The Global Public Management Revolution*. Washington DC: Brookings Institution Press.

Kiessling, T. and Blondeel, Y. (1999). Effective Competition in European Telecommunications: An Analysis of Recent Regulatory Developments. *Info*, 1(5), 419–39.

Kiessling, T. and Johnson, G. (1998). Strategic Alliances in Telecommunications and Media: An Economic Analysis of Recent European Commission Decisions. In MacDonald, S. and Madden, G. (ed.), *Telecommunications and Socio-economic Development*. The Netherlands: North-Holland Publishers.

King, G., Verba, S., and Keohane, R.O. (1994). *Designing Social Inquiry: Scientific Inference in Qualitative Research*. Princeton, NJ: Princeton University Press.

Knickerbocker, F.T. (1973). *Oligopolistic Reaction and Multinational Enterprise*. Boston: Harvard Business School.

Knieps, G. (1997). Phasing Out Sector-Specific Regulation in Competitive Telecommunications. *Kyklos*, 50, 325–39.

Knieps, G. (2005). Telecommunications Markets in the Stranglehold of EU Regulation: On the Need for a Disaggregated Regulatory Contract. *Journal of Network Industries*, 6, 75–93.

Knieps, G., Müller, J. and von Weizsäcker, C.C. (1982). Telecommunications Policy in West Germany and Challenges from Technical and Market Development. *Zeitschrift für Nationalökonomie/Journal of Economics*, Suppl. 2, 205–22.

Kole, S.R. and Mulherin, J.H. (1997). The Government as a Shareholder: A Case from the United States. *Journal of Law and Economics*, 40(1), 1–22.

Kramer, R.A. (1992). Divisions in European Telecommunications: EC Authority and the Illusion of Competition. *Communications and Strategies*, 7.

Krouse, C. and Krouse, E. (2005). Pricing Network Interconnection: Advantages Held by Integrated Telecom Carriers. *Review of Industrial Organization*, 27(1), 35–46.

La Tribune Desfossés (1993a). France Telecom: vers une privatisation du radiotéléphone. 30 April.

La Tribune Desfossés (1993b). Les plans de Longuet braquent. 13 May.

Laffont, J.-J. and and Tirole, J. (2000). *Competition in Telecommunications*. London: MIT Press.

Lane, J. (1997). Public Sector Reform: Only Deregulation, Privatization and Marketization? In Lane, J.-E. (ed.), *Public Sector Reform: Rationale, Trends and Problems*. London: Sage.

Lane, J. (ed.) (1997). *Public sector reform: Rationale, Trends and Problems*. London: Sage.

Lane, J. (2001). From Long-Term to Short-Term Contracting. *Public Administration*, 79(1), 29–47.

Lane-Martin, M. (1997). Belgium: The Privatisation of Belgacom. http://www.cwu.org/uploads/documents /research/rd95_203_3.html.

Larouche, P. (2000). *Competition Law and Regulation in European Telecommunications*. Hart Publishing.

Lave, C.A. and March, J.G. (1975). *An Introduction to Models in the Social Sciences*. New York: Harper and Row.

Lawrence, P.R. and Lorsch, J.W. (1967). *Organisations and Environment: Managing Differentiation and Integration*. Boston: Harvard University Press.

Le Coeur, P. (1993). Deutsche Telekom et France Telecom se branchent sur la même ligne. *Les Échos*, 8 December.

Le Coeur, P. (1994). Roulet s'engage à boucler la réforme de France Telecom pour le 1er semester 95. *Les Échos*, 13 September.

Le Coeur, P. (1995a). France Telecom: l'État maintient ses prélèvements. *La Tribune Desfossés*, 18 January.

Le Coeur, P. (1995b). France Telecom: le contrat de Plan est bouclé. *La Tribune Desfossés*, 29 March.

Le Figaro (1993a). France Telecom, bras séculier de l'État. 2 February.

Le Figaro (1993b). France Telecom entre dans les AGF et l'UAP. 30 January.

Le Gales, Y. (1993). France Telecom: Longuet joue la concertation. *Le Figaro*, 20 July.

Le Gales, Y. and de Saint-Victor, J. (1995). France Telecom: Matignon temporise. *Le Figaro*, 13 July.

Lehrer, M. and Darbishire, O. (2000). Comparative Managerial Learning in Germany and Britain. In Morgan, G., Quack, S. and Whitley, R. (eds), *National Capitalisms, Global Competition and Economic Performance*. Amsterdam: John Benjamins.

Le Monde (1993). France Telecom, vache à lait. 31 January–1 February.

Lensen, A. (1991) *Concentration in the media industry. The European community and mass media regulation.* Northwestern University, The Annenberg Washington program in Communications Policy Studies.

Les Echos (1995). France Telecom: le contrat de plan dans la dernière ligne droite. 30 March.

Levi-Faur, D. (1992). The Governance of Competition: The Interplay of Technology, Economics and Politics in European Union Electricity and Telecom Regimes. *Journal of Public Policy*, 19 (2) 175–208.

Levitt, T. (1983). The Globalization of Markets. *Harvard Business Review*, 61(3), 92–102.

Li, J. (1994). Ownership Structure and Board Composition: A Multi-country Test of Agency Theory Predictions. *Managerial and Business Economics*, 15, 359–68.

Libois, L. (1983). *Genèse et croissance des telecommunications*. Paris: Masson.

Libois, L. (1996). De la modulation d'impulsions aux réseaux de telecommunications numériques. Genèse et cheminement d'un grand programme de recherches. In Atten, M. (ed.), *Histoire, recherche, télécommunications. Des recherches au CNET 1940–1965*. Paris: CNET Reseaux, 163–81.

Lieberman, E.S. (2001). Causal Inference in Historical Institutional Analysis – A Specification of Periodization Strategies. *Comparative Political Studies*, 34(9), 1011–35.

Lijphart, A. (1971). Comparative Politics and the Comparative Method. *The American Political Science Review*, 65, 682–93.

Lijphart, A. (1984). *Democracies: Patterns of Majoritarian and Consensus Government in Twenty-one Countries*. New Haven, CT: Yale University Press.

Littlechild, S. (1983). *Regulation of British Telecommunications Profitability*. London: HMSO.

Loi relative à l'organisation du service public de la poste et des télécommunications [Law on the organisation of posts and telecommunications] du 2 Juillet 1990. *Journal Officiel*, 8 July 1990, 8069–8075.

Loi sur la réglementation des telecommunications [Law on the regulation of telecommunications, LRT], no 90–1170 du 29 Decembre 1990. *Journal Officiel* 30 December 1990, 16439–16447.

Loube, R. (2003). Universal Service: How Much Is Enough? *Journal of Economic Issues*, 37(2), 433–42.

Ludvigsen, S. (2006). *Four Empirical Essays on the Relationship between State Ownership and Corporate Governance*, unpublished Working Paper. Oslo: Norwegian School of Management.

Lyroudi, K., Glaveli, N., Koulakiotis, A., and Angelidis, D. (2006). The Productive Performance of Public Hospital Clinics in Greece: A Case Study. *Health Services Management Research*, 19(2), 67–72.

Mahoney, J. (2000). Strategies of Causal Inference in Small-N Analysis. *Sociological Methods and Research*, 28(4), 387–424.

Majone, G. (1990). *Deregulation or Re-regulation? Regulatory Reform in Europe and the United States.* London: Pinter Publishers.

Majundar, S.K. (1996). Assessing Comparative Efficiency of the State-owned, Mixed and Private Sectors in Indian Industry. *Public Choice*, 96, 1–24.

Manimala, M.J., Jose, P.D. and Thomas, K.R. (2006). Organizational Constraints on Innovation and Entrepreneurship: Insights from Public Sector. *Vikalpa: The Journal for Decision Makers*, 31(1), 49–60.

Mansell, R.E. (1993). *The New Telecommunications. A Political Economy of Network Evolution.* London: Sage Publications.

Mansell, R. and Steinmueller, W.E. (2000). *Mobilizing the Information Society: Strategies for Growth and Opportunity*. New York: Oxford University Press.

Mansell, R. and Tang, P. (1996). *Technological and Regulatory Changes Affecting Multinational Enterprises in Telecommunications: Aspects of the Impact on the Workforce*. Geneva: International Labour Office.

March, J.G. and Olsen, J.P. (1979). Attention and the Ambiguity of Self-interest. In March, J.G. and Olsen, J.P. (eds), *Ambiguity and Choice in Organizations*. Bergen: Universitetsforlaget.

March, J.G. and Olsen, J.P. (1989). *Rediscovering Institutions: The Organizational Basis of Politics*. New York: Free Press.

Marino, M.S. (2005). 'State Traditions in Institutional Reform: A Case Study of French and German Telephone Policy Debates from 1876 until 1997'. PhD. London School of Economics and Political Science.

Martin, S. and Parker, D. (1997). *The Impact of Privatisation*. London: Routledge.

Martinez, J.I. and Jarillo, J.C. (1991). Coordination Demands of International Strategies. *Journal of International Business Studies*, 22(3), 429–44.

McGowan, L. and Wilks, S. (1995). The First Supranational Policy in the European Union: Competition Policy. *European Journal of Political Research*, 28, 141–69.

Megginson, W.L. and Netter, J.M. (2001). From State to Market: A Survey of Empirical Studies on Privatization. *Journal on Economic Literature*, 39 (June 2001), 321–89.

Melody, W.H. (1997). *Telecom Reform. Principles, Policies, and Regulatory Practices*. Lyngby: Den private Ingeniørfond.

Mendes Pereira, M. (2002). EU Competition Law, Convergence, and the Media Industry. Paper presented at the Law Society of England and Wales, London, 23 April 2002, European Commission, DG Competition – Media and Music Publishing Unit. http://europa.eu.int/comm/competition/ speeches.

Meyer, C.B. (2001). Fusjonen mellom Telia og Telenor: Fra nyfiken forelskelse til bitter skilsmisse. In Ulset, S. (ed.), *Fra summetone til* informasjonsportal. SNF årbok 2001.

Miles, R.E. and Snow, C.C. (1978). *Organizational Strategy, Structure, and Process*. New York: McGraw-Hill Book Company.

Miller, G.J. (2005). The Political Evolution of Principal–Agent Models. *Annual Review of Political Science*, 8, 203–225.

Mintzberg, H. (1983). *Power In and Around Organizations*. Englewood Cliffs, NJ: Prentice Hall.

Mitchell, W.C. (1988). *Government As It Is*. Hobart Paper 109, Institute of Economic Affairs, London.

Monnot, C. (1993a). Priorité à l'alliance allemande? *Le Monde*, 21 July.

Monnot, C. (1993b). France Telecom va pouvoir ouvrir son capital. *Le Monde*, 21 July.

Monnot, C. (1993c). Les Allemands demandent la privatisation de France Telecom. *Le Monde*, 1 December.

Monnot, C. (1993d). Un entretien avec le président de France Telecom. *Le Monde*, 6 July.

Monnot, C. (1995). Le changement de statut de France Telecom n'est plus une priorité pour le gouvernement. *Le Monde*, 12 July.

Monopolkommission (2001). *Wettbewerbsentwicklung bei Telekommunikation und Post 2001: Unsicherheit und Stillstand*. Bonn: Sondergutachten.

Monsen, C.B. (2004). *Regulation, Ownership and Company Strategies – The Case of European Incumbent Telecommunications Operators*. Series of Dissertations 9/2004, Norwegian School of Management BI.

Monti, G. (2004). Article 82 EC and New Economy Markets. In Cosmo, G. and Smith, F. (eds), *Competition Regulation and the New Economy*. Oxford: Hart Publishing.

Moon, J., Richardson, J.J. and Smart, P. (1986). The Privatization of British Telecom: A Case Study of the Extended Process of legislation. *European Journal of Political Research*, 14, 339–55.

Moore, M.H. (2005). Continuous Improvement: Two Different Models of Innovative Processes in the Public Sector. *Public Money and Management*, 25(1), 43–50.

Nemec, J., Merickova, B. and Vitek, L. (2005). Contracting-out at Local Government Level. *Public Management Review*, 7(4), 637–47.

Newbery, D.M. (2001). *Privatization, Restructuring, and Regulation of Network Utilities*. Cambrigde, MA: The MIT Press.

Nexon, M. (1993a). France Telecom: dure bataille pour une réforme. *La Tribune Desfossés*, 27 October.

Nexon, M. (1993b). La réforme de France Telecom largement contestée. *La Tribune Desfossés*, 13 October.

Niels, G. (2001). Collective Dominance: More than Just Oligopolistic Interdependence. *European Competition Law Review*, 5, 168–72.

Nikolinakos, N.T. (2001). The New European Regulatory Regime for Electronic Communications Networks and Associated Services: The Proposed Framework and Access/Interconnection Directives. *European Competition Law Review (ECLR)*, 22(3), March 2001.

Niskanen, W. (1971). *Bureaucracy and Representative Government*. Chicago: Aldine/Atherton.

Noam, E. (1996). Media Concentration in the United States: Industry Trends and Regulatory Responses. *Communications et Stratégies*, 24, 11–23.

Noam, E. and Kramer, R. (1994). Telecommunications Strategies in the Developed World: A Hundred Flowers Blooming or Old Wine in New Bottles. In Steinfield, C., Bauer, J.M. and Caby, L. (eds), *Telecommunications in Transition. Policies, Services and Technologies in the European Community*. London: Sage Publications.

Nora, S. and Minc, A. (1978). L'Informatisation de la société. Rapport à M. le Président de la République. Paris: La Documentation Française.

Nordic Competition Authorities (2004). *Telecompetition. Towards a Single Nordic Market for Telecommunication Services?* Report No. 1/2004.

North, D.C. (1990). *Institutions, Institutional Change and Economic Performance*. Cambridge: Cambridge University Press.

Nugent, N. (1991). *The Government and Politics of the European Community*. 2nd edn. London: Macmillan.

OECD (1997). *Issues and Developments in Public Management: Survey 1996–1997*. Paris: OECD.

OECD (1997). *OECD Report on Regulatory Reform*. Paris: OECD.

OECD (2000). *Privatisation, Competition and Regulation*. Paris: OECD.

OECD (2003). *Regulatory Reform in Norway. Marketisation of Government Services – State-Owned Enterprises*. Paris: OECD.

OECD (2005). *Corporate Governance of State-owned Enterprises*. Paris: OECD.

Oswald, S.L. and Jahera Jr, J.S. (1991). The Influence of Ownership on Performance: An Empirical Study. *Strategic Management Journal*, 12(4), 321–26.

Parker, D. (1994). A Decade of Privatisation: The Effect of Ownership Change and Competition on British Telecom. Birmingham, Research Centre for Industrial Strategy at The University of Birmingham.

Pauwels, C. (1995). *Grenzen en mogelijkheden van een kwalitatief cultuur- en communicatiebeleid in een economisch geïntegreerd Europa*. Brussel: VUB.

Pauwels, C. and Burgelman, J.C. (2003). Policy Challenges Resulting from the Creation of a European Information Society: A Critical Analysis. In Servaes, J. (ed.), *The European Information Society: A Reality Check*. USA: Intellect.

Pedersen, T. and Thomsen, S. (1997). European Patterns of Corporate Ownership: A Twelve Country Study. *Journal of International Business Studies*, 28(4), 759–78.

Pedersen, T. and Thomsen, S. (2003). Ownership Structure and Value of the Largest European Firms: The Importance of Owner Identity. *Journal of Management and Governance*, 7, 27–55.

Pehrsson, A. (1996). *International Strategies in Telecommunications. Model and Applications*. London: Routledge.

Peitz, M. (2005). Asymmetric Access Price Regulation in Telecommunications Markets. *European Economic Review*, 49(2), 341–58.

Pentland, B.T. (1999). Building Process Theory with Narrative: From Description to Explanation. *Academy of Management Review*, 24(4), 711–24.

Persaud, A. (2005). Enhancing Synergistic Innovative Capability in Multinational Corporations: An Empirical Investigation. *Journal of Product Innovation Management*, 22(5), 412–29.

Petersen, T. (1995). The Principal–Agent Relationship in Organizations. In Foss, P. (ed.), *Economic Approaches to Organizations and Institutions: An Introduction*. Aldershot: Dartmouth.

Petit, V. (1993). France Telecom: Bonn exige une privatisation substantielle. *La Tribune Desfossés*, 30 November.

Pfeffer, J. and Salancik, G.R. (1978). *The External Control of Organizations*. New York: Harper and Row.

PNE (2001). *Public Network Europe 2001 Yearbook – A Comprehensive Guide to European Telecomms Markets, Regulation and Policy*. London: The Economist Group, Public Network Europe (PNE).

Pollitt, C. and Bouckaert, G. (2000). *Public Management Reform: A Comparative Analysis*. Oxford: Oxford University Press.

Porter, M.E. (1986a). Changing Patterns of International Competition. *California Management Review*, 28(2), 9–41.

Posner, R.A. (1992). *Economic Analysis of Law*. Boston: Little, Brown and Co.

Pospischil, R. (1993). Reorganization of European Telecommunications. *Telecommunications Policy*, 20, 603–21.

Prahalad, C.K. (1976). Strategic Choices in Diversified MNCs. *Harvard Business Review*, 54(4), 67–78.

Prahalad, C.K. and Doz, Y. (1987). *The Multinational Mission: Balancing Local Demands and Global Vision*. New York: Free Press.

Press release of the Flemish Christian Democratic Party (2005). *Belgacom 10 jaar later: 2 sociale plannen rijker, 10000 werknemers armer*, 24 November.

Prévot, H. (1989). Rapport de synthèse a l'issue du débat public sur l'avenir du service public de la Poste et des Télécommunications. *Le Débat Public*, Paris: Ministère des Postes, Télécommunications et de l'Espace.

Prieger, J.E. (2002). A Model for Regulated Product Innovation and Introduction with Application to Telecommunications. *Applied Economics Letters*, 9, 625–9.

Puxty, A.G. (1997). Accounting Choice and a Theory of Crisis: The Cases of Post-privatization British Telecom and British Gas. *Accounting, Organizations and Society*, 22(7), 713–35.

Quotidien de Paris (1993). France Telecom: la tentation allemande. 22 July.

Regulierungsbehörde für Telekommunikation und Post – RegTP (2002), Jahresbericht.

Renault, E. (2000). France Telecom renforce son dispositif international en rachetant Global One. *Le Monde*, 28 January.

Richardson, R. and Gordon, C. (2001). Collective Dominance: The Third Way? *European Competition Law Review*, 10, 416–23.

Roe, M.J. (1994). *Strong Managers, Weak Owners – The Political Roots of American Corporate Finance*. Princeton, NJ: Princeton University Press.

Ros, A.J. and Banerjee, A. (2000). Telecommunications Privatization and Tariff Rebalancing: Evidence from Latin America. *Telecommunications Policy*, 24(3), 233–42.

Rosanvallon, P. (1986). *La Crise de L'Etat-Providence*. Paris: Seuil.

Roulet, M. (1988). Comment: France Telecom. Preparing for More Competition. *Telecommunications Policy*, 20, 109–113.

Salmon, W.C. (1984). *Scientific Explanation and the Causal Structure of the World*. Princeton, NJ: Princeton University Press.

Sandbach, J. (2001). Levering Open the Local Loop: Shaping BT for Broadband Competition. *Info*, 3(3), 195–202.

Sandholtz, W. (1992). Institutions and Collective Action. The New Telecommunications in Western Europe. *World Politics*, 44, 242–70.

Savas, E.S. (1987). *Privatization: the key to better government*. Chatham, NJ: Chatham House Publishers.

Sayer, R.A. (1992). *Method in Social Science: A Realist Approach*. 2nd edn. London: Routledge.

Scherer, J. (1995). *Telecommunications Law in Europe*. The Hague: Kluwer Law International.

Schleifer, A. and Vishny, R.W. (1997). A Survey of Corporate Governance. *The Journal of Finance*, 52(2), 737–83.

Schmidt, S.K. (1998). Commission Activism: Subsuming Telecommunications and Electricity under European Competition Law. *Journal of European Public Policy*, 5 (1) 169–84.

Schmidt, S.K. (1991). Taking the Long Road to Liberalization. *Telecommunications Policy*, 15(3), 209–22.

Schmidt, V. (2001). Policy, Discourse, and Institutional Reform. The Impact of Europeanization on National Governance Practices, Ideas, and Discourse. Paper prepared for ECPR workshop, April.

Schmidt, V. (2002). Does Discourse Matter in the Politics of Welfare State Adjustment? *Comparative Political Studies*, 35(2), 168–93.

Schneider, V. and Werle, R. (1990). International Regime or Corporate Actor? The European Community in telecommunications policy. In Dyson, K. and Humphreys, P. (eds), *The Political Economy of Communications: International and European Dimensions.* London: Routledge.

Scott, A. (2002). An Immovable Feast? Tacit Collusion and Collective Dominance in Merger Control after *Airtours*. Working Paper CCR 02–6, University of East Anglia, Norwich, 1–21. http://www.ccp.uea.ac.uk/public_files/workingpapers/ccr02-6.pdf.

Segal-Horn, S. and Faulkner, D. (1999). *The Dynamics of International Strategy*. London: International Thomson Business Press.

Selznick, P. (1966 [1949]). *TVA and the Grass Root*. New York: Harper and Row.

Senker, J. (2006). Reflections on the Transformation of European Public-sector Research. *Innovation: The European Journal of Social Sciences*, 19(1), 67–77.

Serot, A. (2002). When National Institutions Do Not Matter. The Importance of International Factors: Pricing Policies in Telecoms. *Journal of European Public Policy*, 9(6), 973–94.

Shapiro, C. (2000). Competition Policy in the Information Economy. In Hope, E. (ed.), *Competition Policy Analysis*. London, Routledge.

Shearer, B. (2004). Who Will Survive the Telecom Shakeout? *Mergers and Acquisitions*, 39(5).

Shierley, M.M. and Walsh, P. (2000). *Public vs. Private Ownership: The Current State of the Debate*. Policy Research Working Paper No. 2420. Washington DC: World Bank.

Shleifer, A. (1998). State versus Private Ownership. *Journal of Economic Perspectives*, 12(4), 133–50.

Simon, H. (1958). *Administrative Behaviour*. New York: Wiley.

Skocpol, T. (1979). *States and Social Revolutions: A Comparative Analysis of France, Russia, and China*. Cambridge: Cambridge University Press.

Skogerbø, E. (2001). Fra Televerket til Telenor. In Tranøy, B.S. and Østerud, Ø. (eds), *Den fragmenterte staten. Reformer, makt og styring*. Oslo: Gyldendal Norsk Forlag.

Skogerbø, E. and Storsul, T. (1999). Telepolitikk – fra trendsetting til tilpasning. In Claes, D.H. and Tranøy, B.S. (eds), *Utenfor, annerledes og suveren? Norge under EØS-avtalen*. Bergen: Fagbokforlaget.

Skogerbø, E. and Storsul, T. (2003). *Telesektoren i endring. Mål, midler og marked*. Oslo: Unipub forlag.

Späth, M. (1999). Fusionen, Allianzen und Übernahmen als Wettbewerbs-instrument im Telekom-Markt 2000. In *Telekommunikation and Netze 2000*, Congress I, Online GmbH Kongresse und Messen für Technische Kommunikation (Hrsg.), Velbert, Kapitel C117, 1–36.

Statskonsult (1998). *I godt selskap? Statlig eierstyring i teori og praksis [Good Company? State Ownership in Theory and Practice]*. Rapport No. 1998:21. Oslo: Statskonsult.

Stigler, G. (1975). *Citizens and the State: Essays on Regulation*. Chicago: Unversity of Chicago Press.

Stiglitz, J. (1998). The Private Uses of Public Interests Incentives and Institutions. *Journal of Economic Perspectives*, 12, 3–22.

Stinchcombe, A.L. (1990). *Information and organizations*. Berkeley: University of California Press.

Stoffaës, C. (1995). *L'Europe de l'utilité publique*. Rapport au Ministre de l'économie, Paris: ASPEeurope Collection Rapports officiels.

Stoker, G. (1995). Introduction. In Marsh, D. and Stoker, G. (eds), *Theory and Method in the Social Science*. Basingstoke: Macmillan Press Ltd.

Stone, M. (2002). Can Public Service Efficiency Measurement be a Useful Tool of Government? The Lesson of the Spottiswoode Report. *Public Money and Management*, 22(3), 33–40.

Storsul, T. (2002). *Transforming Telecommunications: Democratising Potential, Distributive Challenges and Political Change*. Doctoral dissertation: Faculty of Arts, University of Oslo. Oslo: Unipub.

Stumpf, U. and Schwarz-Schilling, C. (1999). *Wettbewerb auf Telekommunikationsmärkten*. WIK Diskussionsbeiträge, No. 197, Bad Honnef, November.

Suleiman, E. and Courty, G. (1997). *Age d'or de l'Etat: une metamorphose annoncée*. Paris: Seuil.

Sørensen, R. and Bay, A. (2002). Competitive Tendering in the Welfare State: Perceptions and Preferences among Local Politicians. *Scandinavian Political Studies*, 25(4), 357–84.

Sørlie, J. (1997). *Tjenestemannsorganisasjoner og endring av tilknytningsform*. LOS-rapport 9704.

Telefónica (1999). Annual Report 1999. Madrid, Telefónica, SA.

Telefónica (2002). Annual Report 2002. Madrid, Telefónica, SA.

Telia (1999). 1999 Annual Report. Stockholm, Telia AB.

Telia (2000). 2000 Annual Report. Stockholm, Telia AB.

Telia (2001). 2001 Annual Report. Stockholm, Telia AB.

Test-Aankoop (2005). Edition 485, Test-studies-enquetes, Vaste telefonie: tevreden over uw operator? http://www.testaankoop.be/map/src/337391.htm.

Texte officiel (1993) *Décret relatif à l'organisation de l'administration centrale du ministère de l'industrie, des postes et telecommunications et du commerce extérieur*, No. 93 – 1272, 1 December.

Thatcher, M. (1999a). *The Politics of Telecommunications. National Institutions, Convergence, and Change*. Oxford: Oxford University Press.

Thatcher, M. (1999b). Liberalisation in Britain: From Monopoly to Regulation of Competition. In Eliassen, K.A. and Sjøvaag, M. (eds) (1999) *European Telecommunications Liberalisation*, London: Routledge.

Thatcher, M. (1999c). *The Europeanisation of Regulation: The Case of Telecommunications*. Working Paper RSC 99/12, European University Institute.

Thatcher, M. (2004a). Winners and Losers in Europeanisation: Reforming the National Regulation of Telecommunication. *West European Politics*, 27(2), 284–309.

Thatcher, M. (2004b). Varieties of Capitalism in an Internationalized World: Domestic Institutional Change in European Telecommunications. *Comparative Political Studies*, 37(7), 751–80.

The Economist (1998a). Surviving the Telecoms Jungle. 2 April.

The Economist (1998b). A Map of the Future. 2 April.

The Economist (1999). The Telecoms End-game. 30 September.

The Economist (2000a). Cocky Snook. 1 June.

The Economist (2000b). Better Broken. 9 September.

The Economist (2002a). Telecoms Troubles. 23 September.

The Economist 2002b). Le capitalisme sauvage. 3 October.

The Economist (2002). The Verwaayen Ahead. 11 April.

The Economist (2004). Will BT do the Splits? 29 April.

The Economist (2005). A Tale of Two BTs. 8 December.

Thomsen, S. and Pedersen, T. (2000). Ownership Structure and Economic Performance in the Largest European Companies. *Strategic Management Journal*, 21, 689–705.

Thomsen, S., Pedersen, T. and Strandskov, J. (2002). *Ejerskab og indflydelse i dansk erhvervsliv* (Magtudredningens skriftserie). Århus: Magtudredningen.

Thue, L. (1995). *Gode forbindelser. Televerket 1980 – Telenor 1995*. Oslo: Gyldendal Norsk Forlag.

Thue, L. (2005). *Nye forbindelser: 1970–2005. Norsk telekommunikasjonshistorie, bind 3*. Oslo: Gyldendal Fakta.

Tossavainen, P.J. (2005). *Transformation of Organizational Structures in a Multinational Enterprise: The Case of an Enterprise Resource Planning System Utilization*. Helsinki: Helsinki School of Economics.

Tsoukas, H. (1989). The Validity of Idiographic Research Explanations. *Academy of Management Review*, 14(4), 551–61.

Turner, C. (1997). *Trans-European Telecommunication Networks. The Challenges for Industrial Policy*. London: Routledge.

Ulset, S. (2002). *Restructuring Diversified Telecom Operators*. SNF-report 57/2002.

Valletti, T. M. (2003). The Theory of Access Pricing and its Linkage with Investment Incentives. *Telecommunications Policy*, 27(10/11), 659–75.

Vanhoucke, J. (2006). Belgacom. In Eliassen, K.A. and From, J. (eds), *The Privatisation of Telecommunications Companies*. Aldershot: Ashgate.

Vatne, T. (1998). *Fra forvaltning til forretning: mot opprettelsen av Telenor AS 1968–1994*. LOS-senter rapport 9805.

Vedel, T. (1991). Les filiales de l'Être dans le domaine des telecommunications depuis 1945: des colonies à la déreglementation. In Bertho-Lavenir, C. (ed.), *L'Etat et les telecommunications en France et à l'étranger*. Geneva: Droz.

Verhoest, P., Vercruysse J.-P. and Punie Y. (1991) *Telecommunicatie en beleid in België 1830–1991: een reconstructie van de politieke besluitvorming vanaf de optische telegraaf tot de oprichting van Belgacom*. Amsterdam: Cramwinckel: 175–87.

Verhoest, P. (2000). *Openbare telecommunicatie (1798–1998): twee eeuwen politieke economie van het netwerkbeheer in België*. Brussels: VUB Press, 158–164.

Vickers, J. and Wright, V. (1989). *The Politics of Privatisation in Western Europe*. London: Frank Cass.

Vickers, J. and Yarrow, G. (1988). *Privatization: An Economic Analysis*. Cambridge: MIT Press.

Vickers, J. and Yarrow, G. (1991). Economic Perspectives on Privatization. *Journal of Economic Perspectives*, 5 (2), 111–32.

Vogelsang, I. (2003). The German Telecommunications Reform – Where Did It Come From, Where Is It, and Where Is It Going? *Perspektiven der Wirtschaftspolitik*, 4(3), 313–40.

Walsh, K. (1995). *Public Services and Market Mechanisms: Competition, Contracting, and the New Public Management*. Basingstoke: Macmillan.

Wellenius, B. and Stern, P.A. (eds) (1996). *Implementing Reforms in the Telecommunications Sector: Lessons From Experience*. Aldershot, Avebury.

Wenders, J.T. (1987). *Economics of Telecommunications: Theory and Policy*. Cambridge, MA: Ballinger.

Werle, R. (1990). *Telekommunikation in der Bundesrepublik*. Frankfurt/Main: Campus.

Whish, R. (2003). *Competition Law*. 5th edn. London: LexisNexis, Butterworths.

Whitley, R. (1992). *European Business Systems: Firms and Markets in their National Contexts*. London: Sage.

Whittington, R. and Mayer, M. (2000). *The European Corporation: Strategy, Structure, and Social Science*. Oxford: Oxford University Press.

Williamson, O.E. (1975). *Markets and Hierarchies: Analysis and Antitrust Implications*. New York: Macmillan.

Williamson, O.E. (1979). Transaction Cost Economics: The Governance of Contractual Relations. *Journal of Law and Economics*, 22, 233–61.

Williamson, O.E., and Ouchi, W.G. (1981). The Markets and Hierarchies and Visible Hand Perspectives. In Van de Ven, A. and Joyce, W. (eds) *Perspectives on Organization Design and Behavior*. New York: John Wiley and Sons, 347–70.

Witte, E. (1988a). *Restructuring of the Telecommunications System*. Heidelberg: R.v.Decker's Verlag.

Witte, E. (1988b). Reports: Restructuring the Telecommunications System in West Germany. *Telecommunications Policy*, 12(6).

Witte, E. (1992). A History of recent German Telecommunications Policy. In Sapolsky, H.M., Crane, R.J., Neuman, W.R. and Noam, E.M. (eds), *The Telecommunications Revolution. Past, Present, and Future*. London and New York: Routledge.

Worthington, A.C. and Dollery, B.E. (2000). Measuring Efficiency in Local Governments' Planning and Regulatory Function. *Public Performance and Management Review*, 23(4), 469–85.

Yarrow, G. (1986). Privatization in Theory and Practice. *Economic Policy*, 1(2), 323–77.

Index